Don't Mention The Wars

Don't *MENTION* the WARS

A Journey Through European Stereotypes
New Edition

Tony Connelly

NEW ISLAND

DON'T MENTION THE WARS
First published 2009, this edition 2014
by New Island Books
16 Priory Hall Office Park
Stillorgan
County Dublin

www.newisland.ie

PRINT ISBN: 978-1-84840-352-9
EPUB ISBN: 978-1-84840-353-6
MOBI ISBN: 978-1-84840-354-3

British Library Cataloguing Data. A CIP catalogue record for this book is available from the British Library

Typeset by JVR Creative India
Cover design by Mariel Deegan
Printed by ScandBook AB, Sweden

10 9 8 7 6 5 4 3 2 1

Contents

Foreword

The first edition of this book appeared when it looked as if Europe had survived the worst of the global financial meltdown triggered by the collapse of Lehman Bros. Indeed, by November 2009 some European leaders were congratulating themselves that the EU's social model and its system of financial regulation had shielded citizens from the worst excesses of Anglo-American capitalism.

Had that been the case then national stereotyping might have remained what it was in the early 21st century: an ever-diminishing side-effect of what happens when a multiplicity of national groups share a crowded continent with an unhappy history. It was five years since the EU had taken in 10 new members, everyone was getting to know and, roughly speaking, like each other. The single market was facilitating the growing mobility of people, goods and services. Low-cost airlines were shifting tens of millions of passengers in and out of cities that belonged to other cultures. A single currency gave Europeans a tangible sense of belonging to something bigger than the nation state.

Stereotyping did, of course, still occur, but it was safely tucked away in the realm of humour and good-natured rivalry. It was certainly not the done thing, in the politically correct, enlarged Europe, for citizens of one country – never mind the leaders of that country – to publicly denigrate the citizens of another.

Then something happened.

A letter sent by the Greek finance ministry on 21 October to Eurostat in Luxembourg ruefully admitted that Greece's budget deficit for 2009 would not be 3.7 per cent of GDP as signalled just a few weeks previously, but 12.7 per cent. In the economic crisis that followed, one in which the very survival of the euro and the EU itself were threatened, Europeans re-discovered the knack of insulting one another.

This updated edition, while sticking to the time-honoured stereotypes of our fellow Europeans that we hold dear, also examines the anatomy of euro-related bad blood. There's a new chapter on the Greeks, who have been at the very epicentre of the disaster and whose national character has, in the minds of some (not all of them populist politicians or tabloid journalists), been responsible for ruining it for everyone.

While serious policy-makers have to weigh up the best for their voters, and to a lesser extent for Europe as a whole, they're not *only* operating on the basis of stereotypes. But they *are* operating within earshot of the feelings (and resentments) of their voters. Since the euro – to an extent that no one anticipated – would mean that the behaviour of one group of ethnic Europeans could have devasting implications for another group, the single currency has recalibrated – or perhaps even reversed – the general course of European integration and oneness.

In short, the euro crisis has taken the *fun* out of stereotypes.

Tony Connelly, Brussels, April 2014.

Introduction

Pictures in our Heads

Growing up in Derry in the 1970s, I loved foreigners. Loved them, that is, even though I never met any. There *were* British soldiers, but they weren't regarded as foreigners on either side of the sectarian fence. To nationalists they didn't really feel like foreigners (not the way Spaniards did), while to unionists the whole point of the Troubles was that they *weren't* foreigners: they were British, just like them.

So rare was foreign plumage that the only place to find them was on television. Outside the living room, Derry was grey and bomb-scarred, but on television you could watch foreigners in their hot countries and and in their colourful clothes. The men were handsome and the women were beautiful. They ate exotic food, lived in sunshine and had pre-marital sex.

I actually did meet some foreigners once. It was a Friday afternoon in 1977. Our chemistry teacher Mrs Quinn was off having a baby, so instead of double chemistry, we were granted two full classes worth of football. The deal was that we reported to 'Bootsie' Hughes, the cold-eyed head of discipline, at the toll of the final bell, to stop us mitching off into town.

Suddenly in the middle of our scuffing football game, a troop of foreigners appeared, moving up the tree-lined walkway from Bishop Street (they may have even *glided* up the tarmac). We all stopped in our tracks. They were clearly foreigners – they wore *cowboy* boots. Before we knew it, they had joined our game, whooping with hilarious laughter at their inability to kick the ball the correct way (that was when we realised they were Americans).

No one knew where they came from or what they were doing in a relative war zone. They were much cooler – and older – than we were. One girl, who left an aching imprint of unattainable beauty on my preteen consciousness, managed to land a cowboy-booted toe on the leather ball and, in a burst of golden dust, it headed off in the *right* direction. She laughed with delerious joy and something inside me melted. My infatuation with foreigners had begun.

The game ended and the foreigners – without ever giving an explanation – headed back down the tree-lined walkway, disappearing forever.

The trouble was, we were three minutes late for 'Bootsie' Hughes (the final bell had tolled). With a ruthlessness I'll never forget, the entire class was strapped the following Monday morning. The red welts lingered on the palm for a few days, but the whole injustice rendered the foreigners as alluring, sweet and unattainable as ever.

* * *

With the troubling cross-fire of media influence, colonial brain-washing and our own peripheral geography, I'm working on the premise that we as Irish people are confused about how much we should think about our European neighbours. Joining the EEC in 1973 allowed us to arch elegantly over Britain towards the continent, enjoying the new money and the elevated sense of importance. But our view of Europeans over the ages was probably shaped by the British influence (notwithstanding Catholic Ireland's hapless links with Catholic Europe). In the 20th century, anyone exposed to British television (and only those on the western seabord weren't) couldn't avoid ingesting foreign stereotypes pre-cooked by our former colonisers.

Especially in the 1970s. It was the golden age of British sitcom, which dominated the thought patterns of a Northern Irish youngster. Sitcom taught us that we were supposed to *laugh* at foreigners, or at least see them only as caricatures. In *Mind Your Language*, there was Ali the Pakistani 'hopping to be unrolled' in the English class. There was Maximilio Andrea Archimedes Papandreou, the Greek (no kidding?) who works with 'sheeps' (sheeps? 'No, *sheeeeps*'), and Juan Cervantes, the moustachioed Spaniard whose response to every question is '*Por Favor?*' ('are you really as stupid as you look?' asks the uptight Miss Courtney), or Giovanni Capello, the corkscrew-haired Latin lover who wants to take Max the Greek outside to have a 'punch down' over Daniele, the French *femme fatale*, who is too busy smouldering around Mr Brown, the teacher, to notice.

The loudest laughs were when foreigners were made to look silly, even if their linguistic pratfalls were kind of good-natured. Scriptwriters had it both ways. They could mock delusional little Englanders who clung to a disappearing empire (Alf Garnet, the cockney bigot in *Till Death Us Do Part*), or at the grotesqueries of the class system. But we all had a good laugh at foreigners, even if they occasionally outsmarted their hosts. *Fawlty Towers*' legendary Spanish waiter Manuel wasn't really – in his hapless, put-upon confusion – mocked for his *Spanish*ness, but that generalised *foreign*ness which rendered him dim, gullible, emotional and unreliable. The treatment of O'Reilly, the lazy, incompetent Irish builder, was less nuanced: he had no redeeming features, and when Cybil accused him of being a thick Irish joke, you realised she wasn't joking. We were supposed to laugh at Basil's toe-curling snobbery, but were meant to take Cybil seriously – just as Basil did.

By the 1980s, making fun of foreigners was a genre which the new generation of politically correct comedians left behind. As Thatcherism took hold, the new comics reserved their most eviscerating wit for the polarising effects of Thatcherite policies. When foreigners *were* stereotyped, as In *'Allo, 'Allo*, the French Resistence spoof, the caraicatures were so over-the-top that they mocked themselves into harmlessness.

In his book *The English*, Jeremy Paxman traces the attitude to 'funny foreigners' back to the very water surrounding Blighty. 'This insularity,' writes Paxman, 'gave the English a great self-confidence, but it did nothing for their sophistication. It is hard to escape the conclusion that, deep down, the English don't really care for foreigners.' Far from it being a source of insularity, Winston Churchill saw the surrouding waters as a straightforward political preference, especially when it came to declining the invitation to European unity: 'Each time we must choose between Europe and the open sea, we shall always choose the open sea.' More prosaicly, the deputy prime minister in the subsequent Labour government Herbert Morrison objected to the Common Market because 'the Durham miners wouldn't wear it'.

So from the lager lout to the sneering sophisticate, Brits have, through the ages, followed a mental pathway forged by their island status. When Henry VIII broke with Rome in the 1530s, national attitudes towards funny foreigners were spiked with religious hatred (indeed, British aversion to signing up to the European idea was partly driven by fear that it was somehow an unsavoury *Catholic* conspiracy). Once Britain had begun to rule the waves, the culture quickly attached rudimentary character traits to all and sundry: stereotyping took root. The treacherous Frenchman, the pious Spaniard, the drunken Dutchman were all born.

For those Englishmen who travelled to the Continent, there were guides on how to conduct oneself. In his *Instructions for Forreine Travel* (1642), James Howell advised travellers to France, Spain, Italy and Holland against stereotyping but had a whale of a time doing it himself. 'It is a kind of a sicknesse for a Frenchman to keep a secret long, and all the drugs of Egypt cannot get it out of a Spaniard,' he wrote. Not everyone got negative treatment: the Italians may have been wanton, hypocritical profiteers, but the Dutch had a 'democraticall' government, while the French had 'horsemanship and gallantnesse'. As the Dutch critic J.P. Vander Motten points out in *Beyond Pug's Tour*, England by the 18th century regarded herself as a chosen people: phlegmatic and rational, they set their Anglican face (and faith) against a superstitious, Popish continent.

Travel, though, wasn't necessarily the liberating concept we understand today. Discovering new cultures was all very well as long as you avoided dubious political or religious ideas. Travel was supposed to preserve the status quo at home, and above all remind the traveller that there was no place like England. The intellectual nourishment of travel did, however, have its – somewhat vain – appeal. In the 17th century a Catholic priest, Richard Lassels, invented the Grand Tour, a rite of passage for English gentlemen who toured the Europe of the Renaissance, enriching themselves on her ancient civilisations. 'According to the law of custom,' wrote the historian Edward Gibbon, 'and perhaps of reason, foreign travel completes the education of an English gentleman.' The gentleman thus returned blessed with knowledge of the classics, but also laden down with artistic treasures and oil portraits of himself at Pompeii.

English aristocrats erred in their attitudes almost before they left the shore. Insulated from the local culture by their retinue of staff, they wasted no time in complaining about food and smells, and making up their minds about the foreigners they encountered. For the 17th-century writer Jean Gailhard, in his *Compleat Gentleman* (1678), the take-home message was straightforward: 'French courteous. Spanish lordly. Italian amorous. German clownish.'

It wasn't just the English who were pigeonholing entire cultures. The Age of Enlightenment convinced the French that cultures could be scientifically assessed. The new French *Encyclopédie* (1772), declared that each nation had its character: the French were *léger*, (light-hearted and not taking themselves too seriously), the Italians were jealous, the Scots proud, the Germans drunks, the Irish lazy and the Greeks dishonest.

Thanks to Napoleon's new roads and railways, these ideas were spread and adopted by a new generation of travellers throughout the 19th century. In 1815, the Italian newspaper magnate Giovanni Galignani set up guided tours through Italy and France. In the 1830s, John Murray published a *Handbook for Travellers* to the Low Countries, Germany, Austria and Hungary. He later inspired the German publisher Karl Baedeker to launch his own guides for those travellers who couldn't bring an entourage of servants. Baedeker wanted to 'render [the traveller] independent, and to place him in a position from which he may receive his own impressions with clear eyes and lively heart'. Gone were the overblown descriptions of earlier writers, and instead there were just the bare bones of information for the traveller to make up his own mind.

Of course, early guidebooks relied on stereotypes for their readability, and that's largely what the traveller wanted. Take the mid-19th-century parson's wife from Shropshire, Mrs Favell Mortimer. She wrote a series of travel books, beginning with *The Countries of Europe Described.* In the first, she sneered at Italians and their Catholicism, but in subsequent works unleashed her odium on any foreigners she could think of. The Chinese were 'selfish and unfeeling', the Russians were 'untrustworthy', the Turks were 'dreadful', the Egyptians were 'hypocrites', the Kurds the 'fiercest' people in Europe and the Armenians 'lived in holes' (to avoid the Kurds). Victorian Britain bought tens of thousands of her books. The problem was that Mrs Mortimer had only travelled from her Shropshire writing desk *twice*: once to go to Edinburgh, and once to visit Brussels and Paris.

Stereotypes could be fixed in childhood. In 1824, *Pug's Tour through Europe* was a tale for children in verse form about a monkey called Pug who flies around Europe. He meets shoulder-shrugging Frenchmen and describes Italy as a 'land of apes'. The Turks are 'A swagg'ring blust'ring race', the Germans 'drink till they can hold no more' and the Dutch 'count their cash with glee'. Finally, the exhausted Pug returns to England, declaring that 'Whilst I have breath, From England I'll ne'er roam.'

For the majority of the British working class, their first taste of foreign travel was in the trenches of the First World War. Not surpisingly, that traumatic experience didn't enamour them to foreigners, even those on whose side they were fighting. 'The sole result,' wrote George Orwell, 'was that they brought back a hatred of all Europeans, except the Germans, whose courage they admired. In four years on French soil they did not even acquire a liking for wine.'

One world war later, it was hardly surprising that European stereotypes were as solid as ever. Orwell was highly critical of the boys' magazines like *Gem* and *Magnet* for perpetuating these stereotypes, whereby the Frenchman 'wears beard, gesticulates wildly', the Spaniard is 'sinister, treacherous', the Italian is 'excitable' and the Dane 'kind-hearted, stupid'.

* * *

These stereotypes are, therefore, as old as the hills, wrought by ancient historical prejudices and anachronistic rivalries. So why do we still fall for them? What exactly is going on in our heads when we stereotype? Walter Lippmann, the Pulitzer Prize-winning journalist who coined the term 'Cold War', argued in the 1920s that mass society could never make sense of the complexity of the world. 'For the real environment is altogether too big, too complex, and too fleeting for direct acquaintance,' he wrote in *Public Opinion* (1922). 'We are not equipped to deal with so much subtlety, so much variety, so many permutations and combinations. And although we have to act in that environment, we have to reconstruct it on a simpler model before we can manage it.'

Stereotypes, Lippmann suggested, are pictures in our heads that allow us to manage this new environment – 'the great blooming, buzzing confusion of the outer world' – and simplify it. The problem was it encouraged swift judgement of those with whom we shared the world, leading to conflict and tension. 'For the most part we do not first see, and then define; we *define* and then see.'

Social psychologists have explored every facet of stereotyping since Lippmann's seminal work, from the cultural contexts that shape the meaning of stereotypes, even to the neurological structures that drive the mental impulse. In the 1930s, a study of 100 American university students found their responses to be spectacularly consistent: Germans were industrious, intelligent, methodical; the English were sportsmanlike, fair minded and tradition loving; blacks were superstitious, lazy and musical. Since these ideas couldn't be based on *personal* experience, the authors concluded, then it was rather depressing evidence of a breakdown in social bonds.

Social psychologist Henri Tajfel went further. He warned that while stereotypes helped us make sense of a complex world, they also led to scapegoating and the justification of agression. Stereotypes could be modified to suit events: Americans had positive stereotypes of the Japanese before World War II, but they changed dramatically after Pearl Harbor. Tajfel believed that the groups we belong to – be they Italians, French, Arsenal supporters, etc. – are actually an extension of the self. So if we need to feel *good* about ourselves, then we automatically feel *good* about the group we're in (even Arsenal supporters). In turn we exaggerate the similiarities that might exist *within* that group, but we also exaggerate the differences between our group and its competitor.

Some observers argue there is nothing inherently evil about stereotyping: it's simply the normal activity of the human mind. By the 1990s, they saw stereotyping as a way to preserve our limited cognitive resources. Boxing off the Italians as a chaotic race of ice-cream-eating, gesticulating, Latin lovers may not be very complimentary, but it saved your brain for other, more pressing tasks.

More recent explorations have found that stereotyping foreigners – and even stereotyping ourselves – is a more subtle reflex than we might think. According to Marco Cinnirella, of the University of London, stereotypes can lie dormant, springing to the surface when people – even those who fancy themselves as tolerant and well travelled – are mentally stretched by stress, tiredness or doing too many things at the same time. How many times have we blurted out 'Bloody French!' when under stress, even though we think of ourselves as rather fond of the French?

Stereotyping may not just be something we learn from the media or *Carry On* films. In 1983, a study showed that the brain stores information in discrete mental structures called nodes. Each node corresponds to a single concept – a name, a place, a personality trait. The nodes are interlinked, and these links map out meaningful associations between the concepts. The linkages in turn build a mental image (e.g. French = arrogant). Some links are stronger than others, so the stronger the link, the stronger the mental image. The study suggested that knowledge and experience are captured and organised by these interlinked nodes. Some links can weaken and new ones can develop according to new associations, but the *biochemical* process of stereotyping happens when these strong, structured mental images flit from one node to another, flowing across the network at speed, with one node exciting and stimulating the other. So, on encountering a Frenchman, the poor brain lights up like a pinball machine.

How quickly do we categorise people? According to Don Operario and Susan T. Fiske in the *Blackwell Handbook of Social Psychology*, research using computer-aided timing techniques shows that perceivers categorise people immediately – within *milliseconds* of the first encounter.

* * *

When I was posted to Brussels in 2001 as RTÉ's Europe Reporter, the Slovak Embassy to the EU had just launched a competition inviting the public to suggest what was stereotypical about the Slovaks. As *what* as a Slovak? Who knew? Certainly not me, and probably not most other people living in Brussels either. The competition was dropped. It was true that the French and Germans provide us with a rich stew of stereotypes, but where should we start for the new countries?

In 1938, when Neville Chamberlain gave Hitler the green light to to annexe the Sudetenland, he described Czechoslovakia as 'a faraway place', a people 'of which we know nothing'. It was one of many veils to be drawn by the West over Central and Eastern Europe, because Central and Eastern Europe were basically bad news. The region was filled with cantakerous, restive peoples who had for centuries caused the big empires all sorts of trouble. They were fiercely independent, yet internally fractious. Already an incident in the Balkans had triggered the First World War, so it suited the West to wash its hands of the place in 1938, and again when the Iron Curtain came down in 1946. As such, during the Cold War we progressively blended a diverse collection of peoples into a single, monochrome image of drabness, smoke stacks, bread queues and Trabants.

With the collapse of Communism, we had to get to know them in a hurry. We started with weekend breaks in Prague and stag parties in Riga. We bought apartments in Budapest and Bulgaria (often without even setting foot in the countries). But these were fleeting, unreliable, not necessarily informative encounters. After 2004, when Ireland opened her labour market, *they* came to us. They brought strange accents and work ethics to building sites, meat-processing plants and mushroom greenhouses. We largely welcomed them, congratulating ourselves on what a progressive society we were to absorb so many immigrants. But could we say what was stereotypically Estonian, or Hungarian, or Romanian? Perhaps, but probably not. More likely, most were subsumed into a general 'hard workers' sub-stereotype, with mutterings about fighting and bad driving.

In France, fears about globalisation contorted attitudes into a new stereotype: the Polish plumber. Worried that low-paid Polish plumbers would undercut their French counterparts, the Poles were reduced to the caricature of a man who fixes your cistern. The fact that the number of Polish plumbers actually arriving in France was negligible, and that the country was *short* some 6,000 plumbers anyway, never got in the way of the stereotype.

But what are the more accurate stereotypes of the Poles, the Czechs, the Slovenes, the Hungarians?

In researching these, I found myself going back to the Austro-Hungarian Empire, the 19th-century power occupying most of Central Europe. Even then, it appeared that in the cluttered realms of Mitteleuropa, ethnic rivalry – the lifeblood of stereotyping – went back even further.

Where to start? The Romans, of course.

The Roman Empire left a footprint that roughly represented Christendom and beyond that footprint there were simply barbarians. As the Roman Empire receded, the footprint became the Holy Roman Empire, a shifting, sprawling mass of territory in Central Europe ruled for the first centuries by German speakers. The first Holy Roman Emperor, Charlemagne, was crowned in ad 800, and he was succeeded by a long line of Ottos, Henrys, Frederiks, Louis's and Leopolds. It wasn't finally dissolved until the Napoleonic Wars at the beginning of the 19th century.

Within this empire, tribes had coalesced into peoples who had grown up into principalities and kingdoms, dukedoms and feudal areas, all largely competing with each other for land, patronage, grazing rights, wealth, water and food. The Middle Ages turned into the Renaissance, before Europe was convulsed by the bloody religious wars – the Reformation and Counter-Reformation – of the 16th and 17th centuries. Meanwhile there was the conquest of the seas and the New World. Throughout, the fierce historical pressures encouraged disparate groups to create negative images of each others' opponents and positive images of their friends.

And while they could stick for centuries, stereotypes could also be short lived or migratory. We think of frogs when we think of the French, a sneering conflation of something they eat and something they are. Yet to the English mind the Dutch were the original frogs, living as they did on waterlogged terrain. In John Arbuthnot's *The History of John Bull* (1712), the Dutchman Nic Frog is described as 'a cunning sly Whoreson, quite the reverse of John in many particulars; Covetous, Frugal; minded domestick affairs; would pine his belly to save his Pocket, never lost a Farthing to careless servants, or bad debtors.' This diatribe was driven by a maritime rivalry which flared into a series of wars, with English satirists railing against Dutch ingratitude (Elizabeth I had helped the Dutch against Spain at the end of the 16th century and they now had the gall to attack the English).

It wasn't until the 18th century that the Frenchman took over as England's villain of choice. He was foppish, affected and arrogant, sometimes portrayed as a baboon since he could only *imitate* an Englishman's virtues. By the early 19th century, the frog motif had shifted completely from the Dutch to the French. It was possible that the consumption of frogs' legs was a French culinary vice that was too much for the rougher English palate, but in any event the French king Charles X was portrayed on his coronation day in an English print as a puffed-up frog with a sceptre and cross. The stereotype hasn't budged since. 'That this change should have taken effect so completely,' notes David Bindman, the History of Art Professor at University College London (*Apollo Magazine*, 2003), 'and then have been so completely forgotten, is a fascinating and in many ways chilling comment on the way such absurd and historically contingent stereotypes can work their way into the national consciousness.'

The Enlightenment, meanwhile, which the Frogs (French) claimed as their own, was soon to turn Europe upside down. It told citizens that they had certain inalienable rights rights under God, and Napoleon's armies were supposed to transmit these rights as they trudged across the Continent. When Europe's monarchs unleashed their backlash against liberal and democratic ideas with absolutism, the emerging middle classes, who had money to spend and wanted some representation, found in nationalism a lever to pull them ahead of rival ethnic groups. The nation state was a new idea. It presupposed some kind of collective national memory going back through the ages, which joined people together through folk culture, music and language and attached them to a notional territory – even if others had shared that territory. The arrival of the nation state fuelled competitive stereotyping even further. The revolutions that swept Europe in 1848, as well as the great migration of peoples off the lands and into the cities, the factories and the mills, further pitted rival groups against each other. The Hungarians loved the Poles because they shared more of their history and helped each other out in conflict, but the Poles didn't like the Czechs because they didn't rise up against their oppressors like the Poles had done. The Italians in Trieste, towards the end of the Austro-Hungarian Empire, lorded it over the Slavic Slovenes who had their own national ambitions. The Germans were liked by the English because they had the same Saxon roots, stood for hard work and (partly) Protestantism, and because they didn't like the French or the Spanish. Gentlemen travellers, meanwhile, who day-dreamed their way down from England and Germany, loved Italy, with its Renaissance treasures, but weren't so sure about the Italians. The French didn't like the

Spaniards and vice versa – an emnity deepened by Napoleon's invasion – yet Catalans often felt closer to the French than to their Castilian masters in Madrid.

The rise in literacy and the boom in political cartooning and pamphleteering elevated stereotyping to a serious art form. National caricatures could be easily shaped and solidified by a single powerful cartoon image (for the Irish, it was often-times an ape).

Yet royal marriages, and the promiscuous mobility of European monarchs, meant liking or not liking countries could change within a generation. As history headed for the 20th century, the Germans fretted that everyone was encircling them, while nearly everyone else feared the Germans were going to invade *them*.

Wars turned stereotyping into naked propaganda, and propaganda fed back into new stereotyping. The Germans, who had been adored by the English middle classes in the mid-19th century for their high culture and classical music, were converted, with the gathering clouds of war, into savage, Asiatic hordes emerging from the dripping forests to slaughter babies. In the Second World War, the dehumanising of the Russians (or the Slavs in general) by Hitler led to the official sanctioning of the most appalling excesses of mass murder and cruelty during the invasion of Russia in 1941. When the tide turned, the Red Army had a ready-made justification (and images in their heads of bestial Aryan Germans) to inflict enormous suffering on the German population as they fought their way towards Berlin.

* * *

Stereotypes are also the staple ingredient of jokes, adding potentially harmless spice to sporting fixtures. Reversing stereotypes through sport can actually go a long way in reducing prejudice altogether. As *The Economist* pointed out in May 2003, 'Football has probably made Britons think more amicably about their fellow Europeans than anything else.' We may have assumed that all Italians cheat and roll around to earn penalties, that the French are effete and lazy, that the Germans arrogantly control the midfield. But then Gianfranco Zola, the Italian at Chelsea, was adored not just because of his skill, but also because of his sportsmanship.

Arsenal were captained by Patrick Vieira, a Frenchman who was one of the toughest in the Premiership, while Jürgen Klinsmann brought a very un-German sense of humour to Tottenham Hotspur. Yet for every player who subverted the stereotype, another would come along to confirm it and fans and sportswriters loved them all the more for it (think of Eric Cantona, the Manchester United legend whose gnomic utterances about seagulls following trawlers to catch sardines were the very pinnacle of Gallic inscrutability).

Televised sport is one big comfort zone, sublimating, perhaps, warfare through tournaments. In some ways stereotyping has become part of that stable comfort zone. Football fans happily dress themselves up in their own stereotypes – leprechaun hats, Viking helmets, French berets. Yet, when confronted with an England v. Germany football game, tabloid newspaperes simply can't help themselves in turning nasty because they know what their readers expect of them. And, however much they try, the broadsheets can't resist disguised stereotyping either. So it's no wonder Germans have taken on the English at their own game. 'Dear me, she is chubby!' was how the German tabloid *Bild-Zeitung* welcomed David Beckham's sister Joanne to the World Cup in 2006. 'Arms, bust, bum, all very British. Joanne is the sort of girl who drinks sangria on the beach in Majorca. And then dances on a table with her top off.'

People will still turn to stereotypes as a source of fun and if everyone else is at it, then no one can take offence. Yanko Tsvetkov, a Bulgarian graphic designer, has made a cottage industry from the crude-but-topical stereotyping of national and ethnic groups. Having casually drawn a tongue-in-cheek map reflecting the gas crisis between Russia and Ukraine in 2009 (Russia was renamed Paranoid Oil Empire while Ukraine became Gas Stealers), Yanko suddenly discovered more than the normal number of hits on his website. Friends asked him to do more, and he did. Within a few months he had produced seven maps according to the stereotypes held by others of the inhabitants of each country. So, the map of Europe, according to the USA, had 'Mexico' for Spain, 'Commies' for Russia, 'Bombs' for the Balkans, 'Mummy' for Britain, and 'Thanksgiving Meal' for Turkey. Once the French, the Russians and even Silvio Berlusconi got their own maps, it had become a viral sensation (no prizes for guessing how the former Italian prime minister differentiated between the nations of Europe). With billions of hits on his website, seven maps became forty. By 2012 the project had been converted into the coffee-table book *Atlas of Prejudice* (it was translated into English and Russian, and became a bestseller in Germany). What made this such a sizzling prospect was the clever blend of old stereotypes with contemporary references that, in the internet age, everyone would understand: a 'Europe' according to the future (2022) map had Germany, France and most of central Europe as 'Merkelreich' (Neuberlin was the capital of the French region), Scotland was now the 'Kilt Republic', Ireland 'Taiwan', while Eastern Europe had became 'European Union', and the North Sea the 'Norwegian Windfarm Sea'.

* * *

Of course, when it comes to stereotyping, few do it better than foreign correspondents. News stories become stories because they either confirm or subvert a stereotype. How could the *Daily Telegraph* in January 2013 have resisted a story headlined 'Smelly French Family Ordered to Leave Museum'? Little did it matter that the museum in question was actually *in* France. The case of Anders Behring Breivik, the anti-Muslim fanatic who murdered 77 people – mostly teenagers – in a gun and bomb attack in August 2011 was so disorienting precisely because of how violently it overturned the hallowed notion of peace-loving, liberal Norwegians. When a European leader appears to single-handedly embody his nation's most lurid stereotypes (Silvio Berlusconi), not just headline coverage is guaranteed, but hand-wringing explorations of a nation's values. And then there are those occasions when a national figure simply invites himself onto the front pages of the world's media as if for no other reason than to personally, *radiantly*, demonstrate living proof that a national stereotype is 100 per cent true (take a bow, Monsieur Dominique Strauss-Kahn).

* * *

In October 2009 the newly elected Greek government quietly admitted that the budget figures the outgoing administration had been sending to the EU's statistic agency Eurostat were somewhat inaccurate. What followed was the greatest financial disaster to befall Europe since the 1930s. The façade of *politesse* crumbled: stereotyping moved out of the pub and language class and into politics, economics and voter anxiety. In short, the euro crisis weaponised the stereotype.

With breathtaking speed Greeks were suddenly lazy, cheating tax-evaders who should be slung out of the euro. Germans were austerity-obsessed, self-righteous autocrats whose fixation with fiscal discipline betrayed (once again) their time-honoured instinct to dominate Europe. Sentiment was not confined to tabloid newspapers: respected politicians and academics were happy to cast aside taboos and attack the national character of fellow Europeans.

As mutual hostility rose, some leaders fretted about the return of ghosts that were supposed to have been buried by the European project, and buried for good by the creation of the euro. Jean-Claude Juncker, the Luxembourg prime minister, warned on German TV: 'What was history, and what we thought we had definitely buried, it resurges fast,' he said. 'European integration remains a highly fragile undertaking. One has to deal carefully with European sentiments and not think history is history. No, no – history is present and we have to treat each other carefully.'

Stereotyping was not restricted to national borders: southern European countries were grouped into a pejorative club where lazy, sun-loving, siesta-worshiping individuals retired early and evaded their taxes (the acronym PIGS for Portugal, Italy, Greece and Spain was deliberately offensive). Northern countries were caricatured as obsessed with fiscal discipline, Triple-A credit ratings, cold-hearted indifference, and a penchant for making PIGS suffer. Somewhere in the middle was France.

In April 2013, the European Commission president José Manuel Barroso fretted about 'political extremes and populism tearing apart the political support and the social fabric that we need to deal with the crisis; disunion emerging between the centre and the periphery of Europe; a renewed demarcation line being drawn between the north and the south of Europe; prejudices re-emerging and again dividing our citizens, sometimes national prejudices that are simply unacceptable.'

Vague but nonetheless incendiary theories of religion entered the debate. With the northern creditor countries tending to be Protestant (Germany was, admittedly, half and half), and the southern debtor countries Catholic (with few apologies to the Greeks for being Orthodox or the Irish for not being southern), some wondered at a connection. The fact that Angela Merkel, the high priestess of austerity, was the daughter of a Protestant pastor added grit to the argument. Max Weber, the German sociologist, who famously argued at the turn of the 20th century that capitalism owed its success to a Protestant work ethic, was suddenly back in vogue. Such industrious virtues were, he had argued, a result of Martin Luther's rejection of salvation through servility to the Catholic Church. Since sinners had to find other signs that they were 'saved', they needed to look no further than their vocation, which should be pursued with as much 'zeal' as possible. Accumulating wealth in the process was a virtuous spin-off, so long as it wasn't squandered on luxury but instead begat further wealth. Protestants were therefore more suited to the capitalist work ethic (in 2007, academics Sascha O. Becker and Ludger Woessmann debunked Weber's theory by exhaustively revisiting the records of late 19th-century Prussia and found that Protestants were economically more prosperous because they had better access to education).

Indeed, the euro crisis was increasingly framed in moral terms. Countries which ran up huge debts were sinners; those who were fiscally responsible were saints (it was irresistably the case that the German word for debt, '*schulden*' was the same word as that for *guilt* or *sin*). Ex-communication from the euro could be avoided through an EU-IMF bailout which, naturally, came with the purgatory of austerity. Paul Krugman, the Nobel Prize-winning economist observed in the *New York Times*: 'Many people have a visceral sense that we sinned and must seek redemption through suffering.'

In a headlong analysis in May 2012, Stephan Richter, the publisher of *The Globalist* website, suggested that Protestant countries were entitled to be in the euro while Catholic countries weren't, and that if Martin Luther had been present in 1992 at the Maastricht summit, where the rules were drawn up, then he would have flatly refused entry to Catholic countries. Catholics were too used to having their transgressions waved away by confession – or by slipping indulgences to the clergy – to be trusted with a common set of fiscal rules. 'When viewed from that perspective,' he wrote, 'massive tax evasion and widespread bribery (witness Italy and Greece) can be viewed as stemming from a cultural tradition of offering money to have one's transgressions overlooked. In other words, sinning is OK, even if it is mostly fiscal these days.'

Responding in *Corriere della Sera*, the Italian columnist Massimo Franco warned against reopening notions of ethical purity which had no place in a Europe whose course had been set on *reconciliation*, not *redemption*. 'If debt is also a sin to be atoned for, a sin whose absolution can rightly no longer be bought, excommunications...threaten to reawaken demons that may well set Europe back – not a few years, but decades: to the darkest decades of the past century.'

No one needed reminding of those 'dark decades'. The euro was supposed to copperfasten European reconciliation. That it appeared to be doing the exact opposite left people scratching their heads. By 2012, when Greece was facing a second bailout, and with Spain and Italy on the brink of needing financial rescues that Europe couldn't afford, there was no shortage of parallels with the 1930s: mass unemployment, simmering resentments, crippling austerity, a recession bordering on a depression. In his book, *The Euro: the Battle for the New Global Currency*, David Marsh warned: 'An exercise in suprantional economic management that was supposed to mark a comprehensive break with the past seems in some ways to have brought it back to life.'

But how exactly was the single currency supposed to dispense with the past? When reunification loomed in 1990, France was adamant that Germany would have to commit itself more deeply to European integration by giving up its beloved Deutschmark and entering a single currency. For his part, a reluctant Chancellor Helmut Kohl agreed to join monetary union only on the condition that Germany's sombre, deeply-embedded culture of economic stability, central bank independence, fiscal discipline and low inflation would govern the new currency.

But there were other compelling reasons for the euro beyond keeping Germany in check. Differences in exchange rates between European countries had been problematic for centuries. From 1944 exchange rates had been managed by the Bretton Woods system, but when it collapsed in 1971 there were serious currency fluctuations in Europe, which led to inflation and high unemployment. In response, European governments created the currency 'snake', an attempt at limiting fluctuations to 2.5

per cent, later replacing it in 1979 with the European Monetary System (EMS) and the Exchange Rate Mechanism (ERM).

Dominating the currency order was, of course, the German Deutschmark. Its strength, and the low inflation policies of the Bundesbank, meant difficult adjustments for neighbouring currencies. Strong currencies had to become stronger, while weaker ones had to devalue every five to ten years. Although the notion of a single currency was first explored in 1961, pressure grew during the 1970s and 1980s, and, when a single European market was agreed, an accompanying single currency for consumers to spend *in* that market made sense. The political dilemma of German reunification propelled it to a fait accompli.

But the notion that it would bind Europeans closer, however admirable, was fanciful if not delusional. People cherished their currencies as a badge of national pride. For post-war Germany it was, in fact, their *only* permitted source of pride. 'The Deutschmark is our flag,' Chancellor Helmut Kohl reasoned. 'It is the fundament of our post-war reconstruction. It is the essential part of our national pride; we don't have much else.' Italians were perhaps the exception: they were quite happy to throw their old, oft-devalued, lire into the Trevi Fountain on the eve of the euro's introduction, but they subsequently turned against it when unscrupulous retailers rounded up 1,000 lire to one euro, when it should have been 51 cent. When currencies clashed, the instinct was reach for the war paint.

But the suspicions over some member states' willingness to play by the rules – and the elitist tendencies of others – were already hard-wired into the process. There had long been a 'hard' currency bloc, made up of Germany, the Netherlands, Austria, Luxembourg and Belgium, and a 'soft' currency bloc of Portugal, Italy, Greece and Spain. At Germany's insistence the Club Med countries (a somewhat less insulting nickname than the later PIGS acronym) would be bound by strict rules on deficits and borrowing (Italy suspected these rules were deliberately there to keep them *out* of the single currency).

In the fanfare of the euro's introduction on 1 January 2002 the elite dreamed it would break down what borders remained in a prosperous new Europe. Wim Duisenberg, the first ECB president, described it as 'the first currency that has not only severed its link to gold, but also its link to the nation state'. Realists, on the other hand, could see the seeds of future discord, fought partly in the arena of 'national character'. Because the euro demanded mutual responsibility between eurozone citizens, behaviour was everything and behaviour *mattered.* It mattered to people living in Düsseldorf how people in Thessaloniki – several thousand kilometres away – lived, when they retired, how they regarded tax compliance. 'I overheard two cleaners at Tegel Airport in Berlin,' Jorgo Chatzimarkakis, a German MEP of Greek origin, told me. 'One said to the other: "Have you heard? We won't get a salary increase because of the Greeks!"'

When it hurt in their pockets, politeness was tossed to one side. Before the euro we were neighbours, about whom you might grumble in private: now we were family – siblings capable of mutual anger and reproach.

In such an atmosphere, stereotyping, thought suppressed by the blandishments of integration, resurfaced. 'Stereotyping is useful in the blame game,' says Aristos Doxiadis, an academic and private equity professional in Athens who has written extensively about the negative stereotyping between Greeks and Germans. 'In the first stage politicians and national elites find it's convenient to blame outsiders. Then they try to explain their positions using stereotypes.'

No matter how far we had travelled since World War II, and no matter how much money German taxpayers were prepared to lend to Greece, no demonstration in Athens was complete without deptictions of Angela Merkel as a Nazi wearing a Hitler moustache. Yet this was not just a case of reawakening *old* stereotypes. 'Greek stereotypes of Germans are actually recent ones,' says Doxiadis. 'They're not rooted in historical memory. Germany was the occupying force during the war, they killed a lot of people and so on, but that was 60 years ago. Negative sentiment subsided: we became partners in Europe. In the '50s and '60s thousands of Greeks went to Germany to work, and money was flowing back to Greece. There was no deep-rooted animosity until very recently. We didn't start talking about German mentality until three years ago. We always had a deeper animosity towards the Turks.'

What Greeks did on the streets, Germans did through the press. From very early on a caricature of the lazy Greek took root. *Bild-Zeitung* became obsessed with the idea of Greece selling its islands to pay off its debts. In Italy, Silvio Berlusconi's family-owned newspaper *Il Giornale* ran a headline declaring that Europe was now under Germany's Fourth Reich, with a picture of Angela Merkel raising her hand as if in a Nazi salute. Given the exhaustive reconciliation process, the French were clearly uncomfortable – preferring to exhume Bismarck rather than drag out the Hilter effigy.

As Europe slid into internecine name-calling, the rest of the world gazed on in horror – and then followed suit. *Pravda* described Greece as 'a sort of kingdom of lazy people', adding helpfully by way of explanation: 'In this Mediterranean country where the daily temperatures in summer in Athens each year vary between 28 and 35 degrees Celsius, people are hardly likely to work as efficiently as in, say, Sweden.' Michael Lewis, the bestselling author of *The Big Short*, and regarded as the most ascerbic writer on the global financial meltdown of 2008, published his take on the euro crisis in *Boomerang*, a *you'll-never-believe-this-but* exposé of the character failings that led the Icelanders, the Greeks, the Irish and even the Germans, into self-inflicted disaster. 'An Irish person,' he concludes, 'with a personal problem takes it into a hole with him, like a squirrel with a nut before winter.'

* * *

It seemed, therefore, that the great strides in European harmony, the fond farewell to the nation state, the great leveller of globalisation – all these achievements were in the end powerless to blunt the primal instinct to insult the tribe on the other side of the mountain. Animosity only grew once we realised just how deeply interwoven our fates were. Everyone was beholden to everyone else. A bad decision in Madrid could send bond yields soaring in Dublin. A joke on Irish budget day suggested the delay in issuing the final text was due to it being translated into *German.* Reckless lenders in Paris and Berlin were just as blameworthy as reckless borrowers in Greece or Ireland. Bailout countries tried to distance themselves from each other. 'Ireland is not Greece' became a constant refrain of the Irish government: finance minister Michael Noonan's ill-advised quip, that the only thing Greeks exported to Ireland was feta cheese, was a particularly low point that did not go unnoticed in Greece. 'We are not

Irish,' screamed thousands of Greek demonstrators, meanwhile, in front of the parliament building on Syntagma Square in the Greek capital. 'We do not bow our heads before wealthy bankers!'

Politicians could parrot populist refrains about Greeks or Germans since voters in target countries didn't matter. At the same time, offensive stereotyping was often more about domestic politics than what was happening in Athens or Madrid. In Triple-A rated Holland the right-wing demagogue Geert Wilders switched his odium from Muslims to Greeks when his anti-Islam rantings began to lose him votes. 'In the last election,' explains Professor Paul Nieuwenburg from Leiden University, 'Geert Wilders sensed that Islam was a card that couldn't be played. The debate on integration had been submerged by the financial crisis, so during the election campaign they redirected their energies. They tried to replace an unfavourable image of Muslims with Greeks, who were lazy, corrupt, didn't work for their money and so on.'

When it came to insulting caricatures, Germans were quite capable of differentiating between the bailout countries. Neither Ireland, Spain nor Portugal attracted anything close to the vitriol directed at Greece. Germans seemed to view Ireland's horrific bank debts and subsequent bailout with a kind of pained sympathy at best, and at worst the kind of disappointment shown towards a favoured pupil who uncharacteristically lets the side down. There were certainly voices who wanted Ireland to be penalised for its low corporate tax rate, but they were never in the ascendant. One senior EU figure, closely involved in the long-running negotiations over ways to make Ireland's bailout terms less onerous, revealed that the official German view of the Irish was that they had 'over-succeeded' in their economic boom.

So why did Germany's view of Greeks plumb such depths? Certainly, there were plenty of political reasons why German tax-payers were horrified at being on the hook for the debts of a country whose attitudes to hard work and abiding by the rules seemed so inimical to their own (as we shall see later, these notions were ripe for challenge). One keen observer believes that the relationship soured so badly precisely because it had once been so close (German classicists were besotted with Ancient Greece and played a significant role in the creation of the modern republic in the 1820s). Michalis Pantelouris, a journalist and author, is the German-born son of a Greek diplomat. His grandfather had actually been a Greek resistance fighter against the German occupation, yet, despite his capture and torture at the hands of the Nazis, sent his son to the German school in Athens. 'He never said it was the Germans who tortured him,' Michalis recalls, 'it was the Nazis. It was quite a miracle that he sent my father to a German school and a sign that forgiveness and reconciliation are possible.'

Michalis grew up a German citizen, learning Greek from his summer holidays in his father's island of Evia. A qualified lawyer, his loyalty to Germany was shaken by the tide of anti-Greek sentiment unleashed by the debt crisis. He began a blog challenging what he felt were unfair myths and half-truths about Greeks. Newspaper articles and talk-show appearances followed. 'There has been so much stereotyping about lazy, free-loading, shifty southern Europeans,' he says. 'Even in the mainstream media, Greece has eaten up so much coverage. Greeks were threatened, they had hate mail, aggression. Every village has a Greek restaurant. Many restaurant owners felt unsafe and families felt in danger in case some drunk skinhead might get the wrong idea some night and burn down the restaurant.'

For Michalis, it was the very close relationship between Greeks and Germans itself, fostered by the arrival of tens of thousands of Greek workers after the war, and the hundreds of thousands of Germans heading in the opposite direction to beach resorts, that has, through some psychological twist, rendered the animosity all the more bitter. 'Greeks have always been the most popular visitors in Germany. Germans loved the Greeks and the Greeks loved the Germans. They would have a favourite Greek restaurant where they would go once a week. Greeks were always laughing, dancing, having a good time. There would be Ouzo on the house…'

Germans, perhaps, saw something in Greeks that deep down they sensed was missing in their own psyche. 'Germans think their relationship with life,' says Michalis, 'is what you have with your wife. Greeks see the relationship with life as what you have with your *mistress…'*

For Xenia Kounalaki, a correspondent with *Kathemerini* newspaper and a lone journalist who tried to understand the German point of view (she was born in Hamburg), it was something less subtle: 'The stereotyping never stopped. Greece was always a holiday destination for Germans, so to many of them it was never meant to be a *serious* European state. That sense was aggravated by the crisis – Germans even stopped coming on holidays to Greece.'

Stereotyping can, of course, provide cover for tricky policies. Many Greeks felt that Chancellor Angela Merkel was hiding behind the inflamed stereotype of the lazy Greek in her refusal to support a European rescue in February 2010 (she provoked fury when, in May 2011, she remarked that Greeks should take fewer holidays and retire later). Stereotypes could, of course, be toned down or turned off altogether. This is what appears to have happened in Germany. Some time after the Greek elections in June 2012, Chancellor Merkel was advised that a Greek exit from the euro would cause much more damage than it was worth. Suddenly, the official line changed: Greece would have to be saved, and Germans should start appreciating the suffering the Greeks had endured and the progress they were making. On cue, sentiment in the German press, both tabloid and mainstream, changed almost overnight.

Angelos Athanasopoulos, European affairs correspondent of the Greek daily *To Vima*, was one of a handful of Greek journalists invited on two trips to Berlin by the German embassy in Athens as part of an effort to reduce tensions. There were meetings with officials in the chancellery and in the foreign ministry, and also with editorial staff in newspapers, including *Bild-Zeitung*. During the first trip in 2010, the meetings were tense, even heated. On their return in 2012, the mood had changed dramatically. 'Our hosts were much more moderate,' recalls Angelos. 'They were also more willing to understand Greece and its problems, the idea that there are people in Greece who are trying to do their best, having to share a heavy burden of wage cuts, job losses and tax increases. After the Greek elections I believe there was a directive to the media: don't inflame passions any more, let us work out solutions.'

* * *

Europeans have become frightened, cynical and untrusting. Support for the EU has nose-dived, although most countries want to keep the euro. The relative prosperity of the currency's early years, when low interest rates fuelled a consumption boom, gave some countries perhaps the belief that they had left behind their historical poverty and backwardness. If wealth and modernity reassured citizens that those old slurs were simply myths, when the façade of wealth came crashing down, did they end up wondering if the stereotypes might be true? 'We had several years when there was a new idea of Spain as a competitive, modern country,' says Professor Gildos Seisdedos, Madrid Global Chair in International Urban Strategies. 'We thought that was here to stay. But we're getting back to this old tradition of instability, of corruption. It seems the old phantoms are back.'

With the release of the Anglo-Irish Bank tapes, which laid bare the crass villainy of a group of Irish bankers, did Irish people wonder in the night if, despite all our Celtic Tiger sophistication, we were underneath it all a race of cowboys worthy of a 19th-century pamphlet?

There's no doubt the crisis reinforced negative stereotyping just at a time when European integration had been promising to cast it into history. The EU had created a space in which millions of people, goods and services, enjoyed mostly unfettered mobility. In 2012, the Erasmus university exchange programme celebrated 25 years of students from 33 countries winning scholarships – some 230,000 each year – to study in other European cities. Ryanair has brought hundreds of millions of passengers from one city to another (from January to September 2013 alone, the airline shifted 80.4 million people). Altogether it has been an unprecedented familiarisation process which, one would have thought, would blunt chauvinism.

Yet surveys suggested Europeans were relying on reflex assumptions more than ever. In May 2012, the Pew Research Center found that every single country regarded the Germans as the hardest working (except, of course, the Greeks, who regarded *themselves* as the hardest working; their position was, indeed, backed up by the OECD). Despite the Eurostar, Arsène Wenger, and the ever-deepening love affair between the Brits and the French countryside, the British still regarded the French as the least trustworthy and the most arrogant nation in Europe. Italians were distrusted by the Germans and Spaniards (and by themselves). Everyone found the Germans the most trustworthy (except the Greeks), while all of the bailout countries regarded the Germans as the least compassionate.

Pew's director of economic attitudes Bruce Stokes argues that stereotypes remain strongly rooted in the European subconscious, more so than in the United States, where he has noticed a decline in regional stereotyping. 'The crisis has re-accentuated this stuff,' he says. 'I'd imagine many northern Europeans saw Greeks as lazy before the crisis. What eventually came out after the crisis didn't exactly shock. It's implausible that people came up with these stereotypes overnight. They were much more deeply rooted, and the crisis simply dug them up and polished them clean.'

Indeed, Stokes believes that, despite all the efforts to diminish cultural misunderstandings, stereotypes are the little stones that are tricky to get out of one's shoe. 'We thought that some people might be offended, or regard these questions as not serious, but every time I do a presentation people break out laughing. It somehow touches a nerve. It reflects exactly what they think. I've presented this stuff to the most serious of audiences, the IMF, the Bank of England, the US Treasury – people who are serious beyond belief – and, as much as my rational self would say these findings have limited value, we all carry these things around in our heads.'

He concludes: 'In Europe national identities are much more embedded than the visionaries of the European Union might have hoped. This is potentially much more human than we appreciate, that the sense of identity with one's group is not simply rolled over by reducing tariffs or making travel easier.'

Of course, those visionaries had hoped that integration would eventually create a *Demos*, a post-national agglomeration of citizens who would share an affinity with each other as *Europeans*, perhaps not as viscerally as they felt Irish or British or Polish, but in such a way as to further a sense of common identity forged through the single market, border-free travel, a single currency, and a set of values about human rights and democracy that could be projected throughout the world.

Some argue that the crisis *has* – paradoxically – forced a closeness, albeit an unhappy one, a kind of negative intimacy. Europeans have spent nearly five years learning about, commenting upon and fretting over what happens in other European countries. The crisis has dominated Europe's cultural space. Sometimes there is grim good humour ('Angela Merkel thinks we're at work!' read the Irish football-fan banner at the Euro Championships in 2012); other times newspaper columnists, bloggers and social media platforms appear hell-bent on perpetuating negative stereotyping. In many cases empathy has developed among even the most ardent eurosceptics for the sufferings of Greeks, Spaniards and Portuguese. 'This crisis has not just torn Europe apart,' writes Ulrich Beck in *German Europe*. 'It has also brought Europeans closer to one another… Will the prospect of the demise of the European Union end up promoting a European consciousness, a consciousness that takes issue with both the abstract Brussels-dominated Europe and with nation-state orthodoxy?'

At the time of writing, the euro hasn't collapsed, there's been no Greek exit, and German taxpayers are still willing to extend their earnings to Greeks. There's even been an outbreak of love between two arch-rivals in the contest for national chauvinism: with Britain forcing a re-examination of its relationship with the rest of Europe, *Bild-Zeitung*, has begged the UK not to leave the EU. Waxing about the royal family, the Sex Pistols, the Loch Ness Monster and Mr Bean, *Bild* declared, 'You taunt us as Krauts… and your favourite word is blitzkrieg, but dear Britons, we need you!'

Not to be outdone, the *Sun* newspaper listed 'not *nein*…but ten reasons to love Germany!' including Claudia Schiffer, German cars, footballer Rudi Völler's moustache, the *Oktoberfest* beer festival and the supermarket chains Lidl and Aldi.

In a remarkable act of dexterity, Ireland managed to be both the poster-child of economic growth and – when the bubble burst – of austerity Indeed, the crucible of the crash and the bailout involved a complete re-wiring of the national self-image: the Irish were now determined, stoical, productive, reform-minded and diligent in meeting the bailout targets – about as far from the 19th century buffonery stereotype as one could go. Observers in Brussels wondered, in the weeks after Ireland quit the bailout in December 2013, if Ireland would now align itself with the rules-obsessed northern creditor countries, or at the very least, promote itself – with its enviable record in attracting hi-tech foreign direct investment – as the model of a post-crisis economy.

In this book I've tried to explore how the stereotypes we hold about other Europeans have originated and evolved; if and how they are still relevant, and what they tell us about modern Europeans. Because I'm using a particular vantage point – and set of attitudes – it didn't make sense to write about stereotypes of the British or Irish: that's the job of a funny foreigner. Are the Finns all taciturn alcoholics, and if so why? How come the French are the louche lovers of Europe and not the Czechs? And are all Spaniards fiery, siesta-loving, bullfight aficionados? Why are the Germans order-obsessed and humourless? Are all Italian men obsessed by their mammas, and if so, why? When exploring these stereotypes, I have inevitably strayed into the treacherous waters of 'national character', a notoriously tricky thing to define and understand. I've canvassed numerous expats living in the 11 countries about their preconceived notions before arriving in, and what they thought having spent some time living in, their adoptive country. I asked what annoyed or maddened them, what they found just downright bizarre or what they loved about their hosts. As such, these are random perspectives and in no way scientific, and will be open to dispute.

Of course many stereotypes are clearly not that wide of the mark. What matters is how much they shackle us, to a detrimental degree, to a one-dimensional perspective. Research indicates that the higher you go within your own social group, the more likely you are to hold onto stereotypes, even to an oppressive degree (that might explain the laughter that Bruce Stokes encountered as he flicked through his slides in the US Treasury boardroom). According to Don Operario and Susan T. Fiske in the *Blackwell Handbook of Social Psychology*, people at the top are too busy to avoid lazy assumptions about ethnic minorities, tending to ignore new information which might correct their prejudices. On the other hand, if we're sufficiently bothered to pay attention, we can see people as individuals and not members of a category, acknowledging things that contradict the stereotype.

Stereotypes *can* be set aside over time. A major study by Princeton University in America in 2001 showed that, over a 60-year period, stereotypes held by 10 ethnic groups about each other *did* gradually change and become more positive, because people simply mixed more, and because there were new laws against discrimination. The ethnic Irish stereotype of the 1990s in America was much more favourable than that of the 1930s and 1960s. The same applied to blacks, Jews and Italians. 'Increased contact may have given people the opportunity to revise the content of their stereotypes, thus contributing to stereotype change,' the study concluded.

Writing in the 1920s the American journalist Walter Lippmann perhaps anticipated this research:

> What matters is the character of the stereotypes, and the gullibility with which we employ them. If our philosophy tells us that each man is only a small part of the world, that his intelligence catches at best only phases and aspects in a coarse net of ideas, then, when we use our stereotypes, we tend to know that they are only sterotypes, to hold them lightly, and to modify them gladly.

Let's not modify them just yet, though. We shall begin our journey through European stereotypes with *zee Germans*. After all, they started it.

Chapter 1

Germany

The Germans have no taste for peace; renown is more easily won among perils.
Tacitus, ad 98

Do not discuss German history, no matter how fascinated you may be by the subject.
'Business Practices in Germany', Enterprise Ireland advice to Irish companies exporting to Germany

The reclining sun breathes an amber softness over the parkland of Baden-Württemberg. I'm driving through small villages with their red-brick and onion-domed churches, enjoying the gentle pull of the asphalt and the light reflecting off the meadows. This south-western German state is one of the most industrial and prosperous corners of Europe, but I'm deep in mellow countryside.

I arrive at a car showroom on Max Planck Strasse in Heimerdingen. Klaus Kienle, every inch the comfortable middle-aged German male – bright suede jacket, blue shirt under a dark sweater – welcomes me at the door. He wears a trademark moustache at the centre of a modest but determined face.

Meet Swabian man.

Klaus's spacious workshop is incredibly clean. The red-tiled floor is spotless, not a finger smudge or oily footprint in sight. However, that's not what draws your immediate attention. Instead, I am suddenly transported into an ethereal paradise of 1950s glamour and verve. All around, immaculately restored supermodels of the golden age of European motoring abound, the heart-stopping blend of post-war German engineering and Hollywood fantasy (at any moment, Sophia Loren, in gingham suit, white headscarf and Cat Eye sunglasses, might emerge, stilettos first, from behind the wheel of one of Klaus's machines).

Everywhere are vintage Mercedes-Benz coupés, roadsters and SE600s, all shimmering in primary colours and all comprehensively restored. In motoring terms these 50-year-old models have been brought back from the dead. They speak old money, oil money, new money, Hollywood money. Some once belonged to Tinseltown icons, others still belong to desert sheikhs. Here is the King of Morocco's stretch black Mercedes 600, and over there is the Emir of Bahrain's 600 with the biggest engine Mercedes ever produced – seven whole litres.

With a nod, Swabian Man leads me down a staircase to a broad garage. In the middle sits a long white seven-seater Mercedes 600 Pullman. It hasn't undergone the full restoration of the snow leopards panting upstairs. In fact, there are stretches of masking tape here and there and bits of wood wedged in to keep the windows from slipping down. But amid the dust and gathering darkness there is an unmistakeable radiance.

The car I'm now leaning against, and whose tyres I'm trying not to kick, has had four previous, though not necessarily careful, owners. The first was a Mr John Lennon. 'Oh, yes, and then he sold it to George Harrison, and then that black American soul singer, what was her name?' John Lennon not only owned this car, he sat in it, drove it, listened to and possibly even recorded music in it. Through the windows are visible an eight-track recording deck and a Mignon MK-60 record player. 'He requested it specially,' announces Klaus.

I'm frankly star-struck. But then Lennon sold it to *George Harrison.* Eric Clapton may even have taken it for a drunken spin at George's Friar Park mansion before it was sold on to Mary Wilson of The Supremes. I'm trying to imagine the things, the sights, the smells, the *stuff* this Mercedes accommodated during the greatest era of rock music. Klaus, though, is fixated on the detail. Mercedes-Benz built the car to Lennon's personal specifications from an eight-track recorder to the reading lamps to the clunky telephone. When he bought it in 1965, Lennon wanted a white phone. In an airy response, Mercedes replied, 'We regret to inform you that, contrary to your wishes, it is not possible to obtain a white receiver, so that we have no alternative but to fit the black one delivered.'

Today Klaus Kienle is the custodian par excellence of the cars Mercedes-Benz produced when they made the most sophisticated cars in the world. He joined Mercedes-Benz in the 1970s, first as an apprentice, finally becoming a master mechanic. In 1984 he quit, setting up in his garage with one mission: to save from rusting obscurity the roadsters, 300SL coupés, 600s, 300Sc Cabriolets and 190SLs that were ageing as gracelessly as some of their starlet owners. 'Mercedes weren't bothered with old customers and old cars,' he explains.

Every car Mercedes produced required an archive inventory for each spare part. Since Klaus had access to the archive, he would scour the world to ensure as many of the original parts as possible were retrieved, repaired, buffed up and restored to the body of the original car. So when the golden generation of vehicles was heading to the car crusher (or the sea-bed in one or two cases), Klaus was the only man on the planet with the interest, the know-how and the archive to intervene.

A typical example was the Daimler-Benz 600 series, considered the best car in the world and the luxury liner of the pop-star-dictator set. 'They all had one and they've all come here,' he tells me. 'Mao Tse-tung, Nicolae Ceauşescu, Tito, the North Korean guy – what was his name? – he actually ordered 60 Mercedes 600s.' So while his people were starving, the Dear Leader of North Korea, Kim Jong-il, kept a fleet of 60 Mercs.

I'm now looking at a 1954 300SL coupé, a sleek, cream-coloured beauty with gull-wing doors, Rudge wheels, side-cooling vents, H4 headlights and cool avocado leather upholstery inside (complete with matching leather suitcases). It's been excruciatingly restored, at a cost to Klaus of €250,000, to its 1955 condition. The Croatian millionaire client will pay €600,000 when he gets delivery. 'He wants a couple more,' says Klaus.

Altogether Klaus has restored cars that once belonged to the Shah of Persia, Glen Ford, Gary Cooper, Gina Lollobrigida, Pablo Picasso, Yul Brynner, Zsa Zsa Gabor, the Aga Khan and other assorted sheiks, emirs, kings and acting legends. 'I went to Iran after the revolution to fix up the Shah's 600,' recalls Klaus, shaking his head sadly. 'But the government wasn't interested. There is a sense in the Middle East that if it's worn out, get rid of it. Just throw it away.'

Apart from the archive and his years of experience at Mercedes, there's one essential element in Klaus's success. He is *Swabian.*

For those not in the know, the Swabians were a tough Germanic tribe who migrated south from the Baltic 2,000 years ago, mostly settling around modern-day Switzerland and south-western Germany. When they pushed the Romans back over the Alps, so confident were the Romans of their return that they buried pots of gold and silver in the Swabian hills, never to retrieve them. Swabians claim that if Germany is the land of *Vorsprung Durch Technik* (Advancement through Technology), then the obsession with precision engineering starts here. Some even say it can be traced back to 1648 and the end of the Thirty Years War, when the Swiss infantry developed a lance with a hook that could pull down an armoured horseman.

Swabians had inventive minds, but not the mineral resources enjoyed by the Ruhr Valley. They were frugal and excelled at science. The King of Württemburg, himself fascinated by science, decided to exploit those virtues, funding science and engineering faculties in Stuttgart, Karlsruhe, Freiberg and Mannheim. The first generation to graduate from these schools included Graf Zeppelin, Rudolph Diesel, Robert Bosch, Karl Friedrich Benz, Gottlieb Daimler and Wilhelm Maybach, the latter two going on to design the first Zeppelin engines. Mercedes was the name given to an engine designed for Daimler in 1900 by Wilhelm Maybach, after an Austrian consul ordered 15 sports cars on the condition that the engine be called after his daughter. It became the biggest car company in the world. Swabians are proud of its roots.

'This was one big specialised engineering region,' says Klaus. One company led to another.' Today he can call upon dozens of small engineering companies when he needs a spare part. To him, the Swabian faculty for precision is as real a tribal stereotype as can be imagined. 'There's something about the people that makes them fascinated about precision, about design, how things work, about improving life through technology. You're either a Mercedes man or a Porsche man or a Bosch man. It's the Baden-Württemburg spirit of perfection, wanting things to work properly. I see it in my apprentices.'

While Swabians are staring at moving parts, other Germans regard them as overly serious prudes, hardworking, even obsessive-compulsive, communally agreeing, for example, which day of the week each apartment must clean their share of the stairwell. Above all they're seen as tight. 'Just today I had lunch with a colleague who went for the vegetarian dish in the canteen,' sighs an Irish woman working in a major car manufacturer. 'I asked him if he was vegetarian, and he said, no, it was just that he wasn't going to spend €3 on a piece of meat. And this was a man who would be on a pretty good salary.'

Their reputation for stinginess may relate to poverty: at the outbreak of the Franco-Prussian War in 1870, some 70 per cent of the Swabian population lived in poverty, working in farming or forestry, and not in heavy industry. Throughout the financial crisis Angela Merkel has argued that governments needed to be as 'prudent as a Swabian housewife'. In *The Seven Swabians* (*Die Sieben Schwaben*) by the Brothers Grimm, they're portrayed as simpletons. Despite the fact that many of the engineering ventures were funded by Jewish bankers, Hitler so admired Swabians that when he claimed sovereignty over part of the Antarctic, he renamed it Neuschwabenland.

'Swabians are canny in the extreme,' says Dr James McCabe, an Irish linguist and business commentator living in Germany. ' "*Schlau*", meaning "sly",, is a compliment. They're the first to have a seat booked. I went to a coffee machine last week and as I was approaching a guy jumped in front of me and laughed, "I tricked you!" There was no sense of embarrassment about it.'

Swabian claims of engineering supremacy are disputed by other Germans. 'Swabians overemphasise their engineering exploits,' says Professor Hermann Bausinger from the Ludwig Uhland Institute in Tübingen. 'The Badenians were more impressive. It was only later in the century that Swabians began to make a difference through private pioneers.'

* * *

We leave Klaus and his furrowed-browed apprentices, staring at a six-cylinder inline engine, to continue our journey into German stereotypes. There are good reasons for starting with the Swabians, though. The terrible burden of German history broods over most stereotypes: think

German, and within a micro-second you're thinking precision, order, jackboots, Nazis, Hitler. Or you might think sun loungers, no sense of humour and David Hasselhoff. We'll get to all these things later.

With the Swabians, at least, the *Vorsprung* idea is relatively benign: in the 1970s, the serious, dark excellence of BMW exposed the mediocrity of the British car industry. But in general Europeans have been fretting about *German-ness* for 150 years. Are they by nature hell bent on world domination, given half the chance?

When the Berlin Wall fell, and the prospect of an economically powerful united Germany was openly discussed, Margaret Thatcher invited a number of historians to Chequers to advise her. They included the Oxford professor Timothy Garton Ash and Fritz Stern, a German-born American scholar of German history. Despite the reassurances she received to the contrary, Thatcher insisted the Germans would dominate Europe once again through the European Union. 'The Germans had all sorts of virtues, she said, such as discipline and hard work, but they were dangerous by tradition and character,' recalls Stern in his memoir, *Five Germanys I Have Known.*

These were not simply private ruminations. One of Thatcher's cabinet ministers, Nicholas Ridley, expressed in public what many believed in private. The EU was 'a German racket designed to take over the whole of Europe ...,' he told the *Spectator*. 'I'm not against giving up sovereignty in principle, but not to this lot. You might as well give it to Adolf Hitler, frankly...'

The view that Germany was innately wicked was nothing new. It was inculcated when British-German rivalry began in the 19th century, and continued through two world wars. One generation of British historians after another reinforced it, seeing its origins in the mists of time. 'The history of the Germans is a history of extremes,' wrote A.J.P. Taylor, one of the 20th century's most respected historians. 'It contains everything except moderation, and, in the course of 1,000 years, the Germans have experienced everything except normality. They have dominated Europe, and they have been the hopeless victims of the domination of others.'

Even Tacitus was employed retroactively. In *Germania* (ad 98), the Roman historian depicted the tribes of Germany (including the

Swabians) as being terrifying in battle, with their 'fierce-looking blue eyes, reddish hair, and big frames.' In his introduction to the 1948 translation, the British classical scholar Harold Mattingly sombrely intoned: 'The German people in the time of Tacitus was already a force to be reckoned with in Europe. We know to our cost that it has not ceased to be so today.' What he failed to mention was that Tacitus also depicted a society marked by order, communal decision-making, and an array of deities, evincing a spiritual kinship with the forest.

It's no wonder Nicholas Ridley conflated the EU with a resurgent German tyranny – such fantasies were already in the realm of British pseudo-history. In *Fatherland*, the what-if novel by Robert Harris, not only is Hitler victorious, but the Third Reich survives and Germany becomes the 'leader' of the European Community, with the swastika dominating the flags at the European Parliament and the Reichsmark becoming the common currency (in an interview, Harris declared that Hitler's war aims had been achieved: 'National interest rates are effectively determined by the Germans.').

The irony is that up until the mid-19th century there was an important affinity between Brit and Kraut. The original Anglo-Saxon colonists were Germanic and their linguistic and cultural influences last to this day. Through the ages, when it came to asserting true Britishness, in fact, German roots rather than Norman (French) ones were the critical definers: concepts of free men, parliamentary democracy and, later on, naval power, were regarded as Saxon attributes. The Norman influence just meant tyranny and enslavement.

The bonds between England and the Germans grew during the religious wars of the 16th century, and were strengthened by the alliance of England, Holland and Germany against Catholic France and Spain. In 1714 Prince George of Hanover – German born and bred – succeeded to the English throne, afterwards spending as much time back in Hanover as protocol would allow. '[He] was able to eat roast beef as a King, while enjoying electoral sauerkraut when on vacation,' writes the historian John Ramsden in his recent study of relations between the two countries. The Hanoverian succession ran through three generations of the English monarchy.

Stereotypes of lower-born Germans appeared once the English began to travel. Germans were unclean, voracious eaters, greedy, poor, smoked and drank too much, an image strengthened by the fact that, since Germany wasn't generally geared for tourism, visitors were limited to rough-and-ready inns. By the time Thomas Cook organised his first package tours to the Rhineland, the imagery was more balanced: the Germans may have liked to eat to the point of over-indulgence (the English visitors, of course, didn't mind joining in themselves), but it was also a country of Alpine wonders, ruined castles, and medieval towns. Historians such as Thomas Carlyle actually liked Germans, whom he saw as romantic, dreamy, and hardworking. There was popular infatuation with the German arts following the publication of six different anthologies of *Grimms' Fairy Tales*. The tales reinforced 'those stereotypes of Germans as innocents from the woods and forests which were closer to Anglo-Saxon roots', Ramsden writes. British intellectuals were falling for Goethe and Schiller, the philosophy of Kant and Hegel, and the music of Wagner and Mendelssohn. German governesses were dandling the children of well-to-do English families on their knees, and Thomas Carlyle's *Frederick the Great* sold out in both Britain and Germany (Goebbels would later read extracts to a morose Hitler in the bunker as Berlin was falling).

But in an early hint of the stereotype that would predominate later, the 18th-century novelist William Thackeray noted that Germany was a land of order and regimentation: trees, even cattle, stood in straight lines. Later travelogues informed English readers that Germans even taught flowers to behave themselves and preferred China dogs to real ones because they were more orderly.

These soon chimed with growing worries about the Prussians. Under Frederick the Great, Prussia had become the dominant of the 300 German states, a power with a formidable army and bureaucracy. It was not yet a threat to England: in fact the Prussians were allies in the defeat of Napoleon at Waterloo (their field marshal Gebhar von Blücher was so admired by the British public that a locomotive was named after him). But Prussia's overwhelming victory over France in 1871 changed attitudes. Prussian militarism was now being analysed according to the fashionable racial theories of the time: the London Anthropological Institute heard 'evidence' that the victory could only be explained by the racially 'effete' and 'nervous' French crumbling before the 'bone and muscle' of the Prussian racial constitution. The notions of iron-willed military superiority, hard work and the physical strength of the Prussians were, in time, all vaguely blended into one rather frightening stereotype for the Germans as a whole. It suited both the Nazis in their later mythologising of German physical superiority, as well as the British who, as early as the 1880s, needed a reason for the Germans to be stopped.

Initially, Britain admired German economic growth in the 19th century. It was now seen as a modern country, no longer a backwater of fat, smoking drunks, and when the German Prince Albert married Queen Victoria in 1840, Anglo-German affinity seemed assured for the future. Victoria and Albert spoke German together at home, and their eldest daughter, Vicky, married Crown Prince Frederick of Prussia, the latter event adding the lines 'God bless our Prince and Bride!/God keep their lands Allied' to the British national anthem (how many Engerland football fans realise that one?). By 1873, there had been *seven* Anglo-German royal weddings.

But the Prussian menace loomed. In 1871, under Prussian Prince Otto von Bismarck, Germany was forged into a new empire. British public opinion now began blowing hot and cold on all things German. As with most stereotyping, economic rivalry was never far behind. In the 1860s, German manufacturing took off just as Britain's was peaking and trade disputes were growing tetchy. When the bellicose Kaiser Wilhelm II entered the stage in 1889, the fact that he was Queen Victoria's grandson, and brought up an Anglophile, failed to mollify the growing British angst about German ambition, especially its rapid naval expansion. When Britain preferred an entente cordiale with France to an alliance with Germany in 1904, war became inevitable.

When it broke out in 1914, anti-German hatred boiled over. Rudyard Kipling was one of its most zealous scribes: 'The Hun has been educated by the State since birth to look upon assassination and robbery, embellished with every treachery and abomination that the mind of man can laboriously think out, as a perfectly legitimate means to the national ends of his country.' As the war progressed, German measles was renamed the Belgian flush, and Boots had to reassure its customers that its eau de Cologne was not *actually* from Cologne.

Wilhelm II ('Kaiser Bill') had only himself to blame for this state of affairs. The term 'Hun' came from one of his own speeches; for him, it was a badge of honour, while for the British, it denoted a primitive, fighting aggression. In fact, World War I triggered a hatred of Germans among all levels of British society that was more visceral than that of the subsequent war. Germans were diabolical, bloodthirsty and void of any moral scruples, at once the masters of horrific modern weaponry and savage pre-Asiatic hordes emerging from dark forests. Mendelssohn was quietly and quickly forgotten.

* * *

After the war, the Treaty of Versailles heaped humiliation and economic ruin on a defeated Germany. For some sections of the British elite (even Churchill himself), the nectar of victory soured into something akin to guilt that the Allies had gone too far in punishing Germany. Some British intellectuals embraced Weimar Germany and were dazzled by the artistic flowering and sexual thrill of 1920s Berlin.

By the time the Nazis came to power, British opinion was nuanced. There were Germans, and then there were *Nazis*, a formulation helped by the flood of anti-Nazi *German* refugees. Even during the Second World War, some argued that Hitler, and not ordinary Germans, was to blame: while the previous war was about fighting a *people*, this one was about fighting a *system*.

The Holocaust, however, changed all that. After the war, Gallup polls found that 90 per cent of Britons blamed Germans, not Nazis. Noel Coward felt no admiration for 'a race, however cultured, sensitive and civilised, that willingly allows itself time and again to be stampeded into the same state of neurotic bestiality'. Yet when Russia became a threat, this attitude was recalibrated. Churchill announced, when he saw the ruination of Berlin in July 1945, that his hatred 'died with their surrender'. Later quoting Edmund Burke, he said, 'I cannot frame an indictment against an entire people.'

* * *

In the Kookaburra Club an American stand-up comedian is attempting to act out, using oddball charades-style prompts from the audience, the concept of swimming in beans with John Lennon (his rival from the red team has just tackled toe-sniffing with Ghandi). It's a wet Saturday night in December on Schönhauser Allee in Berlin. I am putting myself through this surreal endurance test to find out if the Germans have a sense of humour. This is my first port of call, although neither the comedians nor the audience are exclusively German.

'They're really different the way they express ideas,' says Rey, a 28-year-old Honduran comedian. 'They like to explain why things are funny, to explain the punch line. They try too hard. I heard this joke at a German club: what is red and green and goes around? A frog in a blender. What is green and not red and still goes around? A cucumber in a blender. I mean, what is that?'

Alan Glen, a Canadian who's been in Berlin for three years, says, 'It's not that they don't have a sense of humour – they get their style from watching British comedy on TV. But they dub everything into German so they lose that gateway.'

'Sometimes they can be so quiet,' says Ve Magni, a smart Californian and the best comic to have come off the stage. 'I'm wondering, do they understand the show? Yet at the end they applaud wildly and they come up and say, "That was awesome!"'

Fingal Pollack, a 26-year-old actress from New Zealand, joins in the discussion. 'They don't get sarcasm; they never understand it. The language is so structured, you can't play with words. Every sentence is a mathematical equation. There are no puns. They prefer belly laughs – all their jokes are about taking things that belong in one place and putting them in another place.'

These are hit-and-miss snapshots. A more considered response comes from Brian Kapell, a Madison, Wisconsin comic who has run comedy theatres all over Germany. 'Risk is something they don't take in their lives,' he says. 'We have to really keep things simple, keep things very dry, with no hidden innuendos.'

He goes on: 'But you know, they went through hell. This city was carved up and raped. Their sense of humour was based on a realism that can't be touched. They are a wounded people who weren't allowed to be proud of who they were. You've gotta keep that in mind: they were really fucked over. The older generation were humiliated, the younger generation have grown up not knowing what the Berlin Wall really was. To celebrate life has a very different weight to it here. It's difficult to know what's taboo, what's not taboo. You can't do Jewish jokes. Can I be proud of who I am? You'll see Jewish monuments everywhere, but there is only one monument to the German war dead. That's the only place you can go and say, that's the place my grandfather died and I have nowhere to go and be sad about that.'

Why are we convinced the Germans have no sense of humour? The notion has been bred into generations of non-Germans. Without a doubt, when the stereotype of the aggressive, order-obsessed, militarily muscle-bound German evolved in the 19th century, it was hard to fit humour into the portrait. The 20th-century horrors of the Nazis left even less room for laughter. In the meantime, the remote control search for light entertainment on any hotel TV only ever seemed to throw up televised cheese: variety shows with jugglers or Bavarian lederhosen and accordion music (and who hasn't been reminded that *Baywatch* star David Hasselhoff is 'big in Germany'?).

The next night I leave the Brandenburg Gate and walk along by the gable of the Reichstag towards the Tiergarten. On the right a thousand electric bulbs lead me into the Tipi, a big tent venue right across from the German Chancellor's official residence. Inside the split-level auditorium, footfalls and voices are hushed by the red velvet thickly covering the floors and walls. Jaunty, trumpet-led easy listening – lots of Beatles, but also Deep Purple's 'Smoke on the Water' – add to a sense of rather safe and cosy fun. The crowd is largely middle aged, with a generous smattering of tweed sports jackets.

Gayle Tufts, a 49-year-old Bostonian, sweeps onto the stage flanked by two singer/dancers: Stephen, gay and blond from Tuscaloosa, Alabama, and Daniella, a brunette from Swansea. For the next three hours, this unlikely trio bump and grind their way through a brassy, unapologetic tribute to Gayle's favourite thing in the whole world: rock music. Gayle's rapid-fire repartee is a mix of English and German (*Denglish*, she calls it). The tweed jackets and their wives and mothers love it, clapping along, or tapping their knees.

Ms Tufts has worked the highs and lows of the performing arts world: off-Broadway musicals, theatre, workshops, acting troupes, dance shows.

Sometimes singing, sometimes acting, she is always big, bold and brash. 'I'm trying to be the German Bette Midler,' she tells me afterwards over a generous glass of Chardonnay. 'Someone you can bring your mother to see. My audiences are mostly families, gay men, single mothers and the very occasional, very brave, single heterosexual male.'

She first visited Germany in 1985 and, having married a German, came back to stay in 1991, building her reputation on the cabaret circuit as the sassy American dame, playing every role from the comic gargoyle in the *Hunchback of Notre-Dame* to a part in the German premier of Eve Ensler's *Vagina Monologues*. Along the way she has worked as a songwriter, singer, stand-up comedian, columnist and writer. Does she think Germans have a sense of humour?

'There had been a Jewish sense of humour in Germany,' she says. 'They were the writers and performers and they either emigrated or were killed. After the war, it was not the funniest of times. You had to be a Brecht to deal with what was happening in Germany – really serious stuff. The Germans are serious people. We still think of the Germans as a weeny bit scary. There's the whole Romantic soul, this deep German thing. Other than that, there's a huge silliness. They can be incredibly silly – they love Mr Bean.' (They also love *Monty Python*, *Little Britain* and *Black Adder* – all big sellers on the DVD shelves.)

'There's not so much of the outsider humour,' continues Gayle, 'the way a black comedian, or a gay, or a woman can play on the outsider thing and challenge the audience with it. The comedians here are white and they're saying, I am one of you. I might be a stereotype of you, your backward cousin from the East, the old guy who delivers the mail, but I'm still one of you. I could see the market was wide open for a real woman who was funny, not a man dressed up as a woman, or a woman in a funny costume, but a real woman.'

So now we're getting somewhere. The tragic intensity of the 20th century, the rigidity of the German language, the loss of the Jewish contribution, the aversion to risk, the impact of disparate regional responses to humour: perhaps these all start to explain something.

What was left within the cultural space for humour? Not much. Popular culture was dominated by *Kabarett*, a hard-hitting form of political satire. But, argues Eric T. Hansen, an American writer living in Berlin for nearly 30 years, this wasn't necessarily *funny*. 'In America, you have satirical shows like *The Daily Show*. They're going for laughs even if it's political, but in Germany they don't go for laughs. They are really only interested in showing people how they're more intelligent than the politicians, or more right. They jab at authority and it's not very funny. Their goal is to show they'd be better politicians, not to make people *laugh*. In other words, authority and analysis are more important than humour. There's a word for it: *Besserwisser* – a better knower.'

But what of German comedians themselves? They seem to be catching up. Stand-up comedy only really took off in the mid-1990s; Germany's greatest exponent of the genre (in so far as he is also appreciated outside his home country) is Michael Mittermeier, a comedian from Bavaria. He began his career in, if I may say so, a very *German* way, writing a degree paper on stand-up comedy. But he put in the hard yards, touring his home country as well as Austria and Switzerland for 10 years before his breakthrough into German television and beyond. He has now performed stand-up in London and New York in English and was master of ceremonies at Germany's Live 8 concert.

'I guess I just had funny bones in me,' he tells me. 'It wasn't a career decision. I just liked being on stage. I'd done theatre work and sketches since I was a boy. I watched a lot of stand-up shows from America. I loved Lenny Bruce. Not many people knew him at all, but for me he was a hero. He was a maniac – I have a lot of similarities with him.'

Mittermeier is coy about describing his style, or what he thinks makes Germans laugh. 'I don't want to define it. It's hard to define, and definitions end up being too narrow.' But he adds, 'I do a mixture of slapstick, politics, sketches, storytelling. I tell stories that really happened, not just something you noticed in the taxi on the way to the club. I tell stories about things I encountered doing 21 years of stand-up. They're all true – of course you lie a bit and exaggerate some things.'

Germany's relentless exposure to the West, including the Americanisation of the post-war period, has seeped into new generations. In the 1990s, the supremacy of *Kabarett* satire was gradually challenged. RTL Television began an offshoot of the American series *Saturday Night Live*. Then, in 1992, the Quatsch Comedy Club was established in Hamburg before moving to Berlin, with a live TV version. Today, stand-up is improving and there are a growing number of comedians, but audiences are comparatively small.

'We killed our entertainment industry in the 1930s,' says Michael. 'In the '50s, '60s and '70s in America, the best comedians and writers were Jewish. But we killed them all – they weren't only Jews, they were Germans as well. After the war, if you provided entertainment it had to be feel-good movies, and not trying to experiment with humour. You couldn't be too funny: you needed to make routines about politics. Perhaps with the fall of the Wall, Germany was somehow complete, and comedy could start to grow.'

* * *

For a different perspective, I've travelled not to Berlin, but to London.

I'm taking the 18:26 Liverpool Street to Shenfield train, which tootles along through the Friday evening Essex heartland: Ilford, Romford, Gidea Park. We pass greyhound stadiums, King Harold pubs, light engineering works and storage depots, family homes with their extensions, dormer windows, back gardens and sheds.

It's the stomping ground of Essex Man, football hooligans and tattoos, warm beer and Sunday roasts. My destination is Brentwood, a town to the south of Epping Forest. It's the last place you would expect to meet a German (there are 26 Tory councillors to three Labour ones in Brentwood Borough Council). Not only a German, but a German *comedian.* He has come to make the people of the Essex Arms laugh. More to the point, he will make them laugh at themselves and their attitudes to the Germans.

Henning Wehn, a 34-year-old with a boxer's face, chestnut hair and a disconcerting accent (mostly English by now, but twisted by German notes), meets me off the train and we go for a curry. Henning cuts a curious figure on the cultural landscape. He plays on stereotypes (opening gag: 'People say Germans have no sense of humour. I don't find that funny.') and yet confronts the audience with how tiresome their own stereotypes of Germans are. It's a brave thing, challenging the reflex, inveterate dislike of Germans.

He grew up in Hagen on the eastern edge of the Ruhr Valley ('it was flattened during the war'), where the steel industry has suffered through outsourcing to China and where the last coal mine closed in the 1980s. It's the birthplace of Nena, the pop singer who, in 1983, told the world about 99 red balloons. Henning Wehn (pronounced *vain*) came to Britain to work as a marketing manager for lower-league football clubs. He stumbled upon stand-up comedy in a pub in Greenwich and tried his hand. 'My English was so poor that I didn't understand a word of all the heckling.'

An encounter with a comedy writer encouraged him to develop some stand-up ideas and to leave Wycombe Wanderers. 'The first night I did it in all innocence, I hadn't written any routines, just reading out pub jokes. Germans are supposed to be very methodical, so that kind of fitted. I dressed up in a silly German hat and had a folder just reading out the jokes [Henning's other standing prompt is a stopwatch]. There were 20 people there and a barking dog. It was free entry. There was a lot of heckling and shouting, but at least I got people to listen to me.'

That was May 2003. Since then, he's moved up the ladder with an act that anticipates a kind of comedy headbutt between comic and audience. 'I was in Billericay, not far from here,' he recalls, laughing into his chicken korma, 'playing in front of 200 people. My slot was after the break, and when I came out, the entire audience had spent the break cutting up little squares of black tape and sticking them on their upper lip. I said, "Well thank you, but I hope you haven't forgotten the shoe polish. There's a black man on after me." It's now a standard put-down. I don't even need to prepare it. It actually takes the pressure off, because once you know you've lost your audience before you begin, you've nothing to lose, so you go out and enjoy yourself.'

One night it got ugly. He was performing in the Royal Court Theatre in Liverpool when a fight broke out between rival gangs. 'The police had to be called, there was brawling. When I came on there was just constant booing. I ended up singing the German national anthem and reminding them all that they'd be hearing lots of it next summer [this was 2005, the year before the World Cup in Germany]. They were shouting, "Foreigners out!" What do you make of that? You have to laugh, don't ya?'

Henning has come to Brentwood to hone new material for the Edinburgh Comedy Festival. He's due in another pub later in Leytonstone, but he'd rather be playing the West End. In the Essex Arms the crowd is small, and difficult. There are 40 people, locals who seem to know each other, and heckling the warm-ups comes easy. One comedian spins a largely unsuccessful thread about how his father couldn't be a role model because he wasn't like Gregory Peck in the *Guns of Navarone.* Another decides the hecklers have ganged up on him, so he proceeds to call them twats. How on earth will Henning the German go down here?

But as I join him in the lobby during the break, there is an unpleasant atmosphere. It begins with confusion over who is to headline the event. Then it emerges that the second gig at Leytonstone has been cancelled due to poor sales. When the promoter realises the financial implications he tells Henning he will pay him less for performing only at the Essex Arms.

Henning is furious, and in a moment of very uncomic petulance, calls the promoter a cunt to his face. The promoter explodes. Suddenly, national hatreds are laid bare and the entire context of the evening – humour and laughter – vanish like mist off the fens. 'Don't call me a cunt, you German bastard!' screams the promoter. The two men, promoter and comedian, are eyeball to eyeball.

Before punches are thrown, Henning spins on his heels. 'Right, we're out of here!'

He strides off towards Brentwood Station with me in tow. 'He's shot himself in the foot, the promoter,' hisses Henning. 'If they start getting a reputation like that, then people won't work for them.'

The promoter, I realised through the hurled insults, was not English.

'He's Greek,' barks Henning. 'A shifty lot, the Greeks…'

On the train back to Liverpool Street Station, when he has calmed down, Henning promises to post his DVD, *Four World Cups and One World Pope!* (the fourth was the Women's World Cup in 2003). He professes to love England, yet the perpetually sneering attitude towards Germans rankles. It's not just that his national pride is piqued, but he sees a ubiquitous mediocrity that disappoints him. 'There are three free newspapers a day on the train, and every one of them is just filled with pictures of blonde slappers in a skirt. You can't be surprised if that's what people aspire to become. It's this big British disease: you don't need to have any quality to get anywhere. The idea, spread by reality TV, that nobody has to lose… it's a nonsense. Yes, people technically *lose* in reality TV, but they really win because they're instantly famous. Self-deprecation is so highly regarded here. I struggle with that.'

It's different in Germany, he says, and that's why people enjoy variety shows. 'You'll have musicians, dancers, jugglers, magicians. These are skills that people have excelled at, and that's what Germans like to enjoy, something where there's a kind of excellence. There are a few stand-up clubs starting out, but these evenings last two hours, and you can't really have a comedian banging out pub jokes for two hours.'

Henning is like a culture cop, policing both nasty and harmless stereotypes. Like David Hasselhoff. 'They always say, oh, David Hasselhoff is huge in Germany. He had *one* hit. It's like the Crazy Frog [the obnoxious free-floating computer-generated amphibian who does speeded-up motorcycle sounds]. The Crazy Frog had a hit in the UK. Does that mean everyone in Germany laughs and says, oh, the Crazy Frog is huge in Britain?'

He gets it from audience, colleagues and friends alike. 'When I worked in an office, we used to go to a Polish restaurant nearby, but usually one of my colleagues would say, oh, we can't go there, Henning will never leave. It's funny the first thousand times, then it's tedious,' he says glumly.

* * *

The fact that Henning Wehn has won acceptance from comedy audiences is a sign that change *is* possible. But given the extent to which anti-German stereotypes have clogged the national mindset (and spilled over into ours), change will be slow. A flood of books and films enjoyed by post-war generations portrayed Germans within the narrow confines of Nazi villains. They tended to be sadistic, humourless, servile, disciplined or bungling. Even Cold War thrillers by Len Deighton and John le Carré had their fair share of ex-Gestapo Germans, even though they were supposed to be about the Russians.

There have been notable exceptions: *The One That Got Away* was a film about a German soldier's bid for freedom from his British captors. 'I became more and more irritated by the depiction of the Germans as homosexual Prussians, Gestapo torturers or beer-swilling Bavarians,' wrote director Roy Ward Baker, 'all presented in ridiculous hammy performances.' Baker bucked the trend by casting a German, Hardy Krüger, in the lead role. Krüger's career took off, but his pigeonholing by audiences left him exasperated. 'In only five of my 60 films have I played a Nazi,' he told an interviewer in 1984, 'but I am sure people think I have a uniform at home to strut around in.'

In football, cliché-ridden hostility has flourished for generations. Even in June 2008, when Germany was being beaten in the European Championships, the BBC's John Motson crowed, 'They're not singing "Deutschland über alles" now!' Not only has the German anthem never been called that, but since the war, only the innocuous third stanza has been officially sung, and all references to 'Germany above all' dropped.

Individual Germans did occasionally earn the respect of the terraces. Bert Trautmann was a German POW (actually a paratrooper and committed Nazi), who sparked a hail of controversy when he signed as goalkeeper for Manchester City in 1949. While most fans abhorred his signing, there was occasional support. 'I don't give a fuck what you are and where you come from,' wrote one fan, 'as long as you can put some life into this fucking City team.'

In a tale worthy of *Roy of the Rovers*, he won the admiration of fans (the fact that during his non-league days he saved 60 per cent of all penalties may have helped). Later, due to his cup-final heroics in 1956, he won the affection of the wider public (he actually broke his neck in a collision with another player, but kept playing till the end of the match). When he saw images of Belsen he publicly apologised for the Holocaust.

Yet whatever about the 1966 World Cup Final (references to the war then were actually fewer than you might think), the English media have found wartime stereotypes compulsive whenever England and Germany meet. 'ACHTUNG! SURRENDER!' splashed the *Daily Mirror* across the front page for Euro 1996, while *Mirror* reporters 'invaded' the German team hotel to place Union Jack towels on their sun loungers. The paper also planned to send a Spitfire to 'bomb' the German training ground before thousands of protest letters forced a grudging apology. When England beat the Germans 5-1 in Munich in 2001, Fleet Street slipped into a frenzy. The *Sun* devoted 23 pages as a pull-out souvenir edition, crammed with as many war puns as their sub-editors could muster.

In comics and school books, in advertising, board games and computer games, in popular history and Biggles books, Germans were relentlessly targeted. When casual demonisation wasn't related to the war, then the apparent German penchant for grabbing sun loungers first (it's actually a Bavarian trait, northern Germans have barely heard of it) was taken up with the same bile and vigour. In 1987, the *Sun* responded to reports of sun-lounger competition on Spanish beaches with every wartime cliché imaginable, effortlessly assuming on behalf of their readers that people who got out of bed earlier must therefore be Nazis. A Carling Black Label advert, meanwhile, showed a bunch of geriatric Germans springing out of bed at dawn and charging towards the sun beds, only to be thwarted by a chisel-jawed Englishman who, from his balcony, hurls a rolled-up Union Jack towel, which bounces, Dambuster-like, across the swimming pool, before landing and neatly unfurling itself on a sun lounger ahead of the German posse.

When German ambassadors complained that there was little or no attempt to explore any positive aspect of German life, a torrent of tabloid opprobrium would follow. It's hard to see if things have really changed. In 2005 the *Daily Telegraph* concluded that Britain was as obsessed with the Second World War as ever. Even today, any German news story that features Nazis, German nudists or the German sense of humour is fast-tracked into British newspapers and onto websites, quality or tabloid. 'In some ways there's nothing malicious about it,' says Henning Wehn, 'but in other ways it's depressing. It's a kind of respectable racism. I was asked to do a thing called Comedy for Kids at a school in Maidenhead – you know the kind, pretentious parents, spoiled kids. I asked the class, what do you know about Germany? A few put their arms up. They bombed Yeovil, said one. Naughty Hitler, said another. These were *eight*-year-olds.'

* * *

In the 19th century Germans largely saw themselves as poets and thinkers – *Dichter und Denker* – angst-ridden and dreamy. Poet Heinrich Heine wrote:

> The Frenchmen and Russians possess the land,
> The British possess the sea,

But we have over the airy realm of dreams
Command indisputably.

After the Napoleonic Wars and the revolutions of 1848, Germany drifted away from Christianity to embrace a kind of provincial, bourgeois secularism. Religion was further relegated when the Protestant Otto Von Bismarck grabbed education from the Catholic Church in the so-called *Kulturkampf* (culture struggle). Then, in the mid- to late-19th century, came sudden and rapid industrialisation. In the 25 years leading to the First World War, Germany's GDP doubled, cities boiled up, steel production soared and colonies were conquered. A modern, prosperous empire, with its own social welfare system and new army and navy, were forged almost overnight. Joachim Fest, one of Germany's first critical biographers of Hitler, saw in those brutally unnerving processes the seeds that would flourish angrily into National Socialism. 'The process of technical and economic modernisation had been late in coming to Germany,' wrote Joachim Fest, 'but for that very reason struck with unusual speed and force.'

The effect, he concluded, was a turning inward. Fear of modernity's ghastly machines, the perceived destruction of an ancient, pastoral German *volk* and their simple pieties prompted great anxiety. Those who actually believed in science and learning were also worried that Germany was being encircled by powerful enemies trying to throttle its economic growth.

With confusion over the clashing forces of capitalism and socialism, many turned against the West and democracy, the poets and thinkers turned away from politics, the bourgeoisie turned away from God, the landed aristocracy and the conservative military caste turned towards nationalism, everyone, it seems, was turning against the Jews, many of whom had become professionals, bankers and financiers.

The upheaval and sense of encirclement fuelled the hysterical support for a German victory in the First World War. 'Germany was at the centre of Europe, with more neighbours at its borders than any other country,' writes the German-born American scholar Fritz Stern in his book *Five Germanys I Have Known*. 'For a long time German lands had been Europe's anvil; the new Germany was its hammer.'

When the war was lost, the shock was compounded by the Versailles Treaty, with its crushing demands on Germany; the forces deepened rather than dissipated. Amid the confusion there was a yearning for a national rebirth, a new community, a new leader. 'The ideas of liberalism,' writes Joachim Fest, 'had scarcely any advocates but many potential adversaries; *they* needed only an impetus, the stirring slogans of a leader.'

Remember, too, that Germany had invited in secularism during the previous century: with the retreat of religious imagery, the Nazis produced pseudo-religious and melodramatic symbols of their own to fill the vacuum. With the country in such a psychological state, the reason for the unhindered rise of the Nazis can perhaps be better understood, though never excused.

'Hitler, the man of violence,' writes Stern, 'rhetorically dissolved this political complexity into a Wagnerian battle between the pure and the impure, between German heroes and Jewish-Marxist traitors.'

In 1996, Daniel Goldhagen wrote *Hitler's Willing Executioners: Ordinary Germans and the Holocaust.* It was taken as a riposte to the preceding viewpoint that specific social and historical forces had violently collided to foment Germany's destructive impulses. Goldhagen, by contrast, argued that it was something in the Germans themselves, what he called an 'eliminationist' mindset, which had to be expressed in action. Ordinary Germans had bestial tendencies that must have come to the fore for the Holocaust to happen. Critics said it was an indictment of a whole people and contained sweeping generalities, but it was bought by lots of people, and clearly chimed with Margaret Thatcher's views.

* * *

So how do expats reconcile those cast-iron German stereotypes with the real life they experience there?

Let's start with German order: *ordnung.* It may cause a shiver among some, but *Ordnung* is a source of pride among Germans. 'Typical German expressions such as "*Alles klar*" (that's OK, or literally, everything clear) and "*Alles in ordnung*" (again meaning that's OK, but literally, everything in order) reveal a cultural preference for clarity and organisation,' says Dr James McCabe, our German-based Irish linguist. 'There is nothing, repeat *nothing*, in this culture which is not planned. The English expression "according to plan" itself is a direct borrowing from the German "*planmäßig*" and dates back to the trenches of World War I. Everything – from separating your trash to taking school holidays to handling German grammar – is minutely organised.'

Take Lego, for example. It had huge success in the German market, primarily because of the quality of the instructions – they were precise, colourful and refreshingly clear. 'They made construction with Lego blocks not only simple, but in some ways magical,' writes Clotaire Rapaille, the international marketing expert, cultural anthropologist and author of *Culture Codes*. 'If one followed the path through the instructions, tiny plastic pieces methodically turned into something grander.' Studies commissioned by Lego showed how German children would open the box, read the instructions carefully, then sort the pieces by colour, building an exact replica, step by step, according to the instructions. Mother would clap approvingly and put the model on the shelf, so, happily for Lego, another product needed to be bought. In America, the kids tore into the box, ignored the instructions, built whatever came into their heads and broke the model apart when they finished.

One Irish executive, Angela Byrne, lived in Germany for 14 years. 'There are so many rules: you can't have noise at certain times of day,' she says. 'If you live in an apartment block you aren't allowed to play music between 12 and 2 p.m. or between 10 p.m. and 6 a.m. It's *ruhezeit*, literally quiet time. It's strictly observed. If you want to have a party, then you need a contingency plan to have everybody out by 10 p.m. It feels restrictive and controlling at the start, but the funny thing is, the longer you're here, the more you like it.'

And yes, that devotion to *Ordnung* extends to jaywalking. 'People are very quick to pick up on things,' says Angela. 'If I was to cross the road, the German would say I was setting a bad example, and if there were children present he would read me the riot act. After it's happened a couple of times you look at a child and you decide, they've got a point, and you conform. In Ireland they'd just look at you as if you were mad. The trouble is, now I find myself standing in Kilkenny at a red light all the time!'

Ordnung, therefore, has its uses. Its objective – efficiency – is a cherished German virtue, to which the economic miracle (*Wirtschaftswunder*) is often attributed. It saw a devastated country become the motor of Europe. Are Germans as hardworking and efficient today? Yes and no. Yes, they work hard during office hours, but in the big corporations there's often little flexibility when it comes to going the extra mile if a project demands it.

'They take holidays very seriously,' says an Irish professional working for one of Germany's big car makers. 'I get 10 weeks a year and I'm expected to take them. The work ethic is not what it's cracked up to be. I'm the first in the office at 8 a.m., but on the other hand when they're there they're working and they *are* productive. You won't get fired for failing, but you'll be left in the corner. Promotion is on merit, but you have to work hard for it.'

'In Germany, the working day is the working day and that's it,' says Dr James McCabe. 'On a Friday they're out the door like a V2 rocket at 5 p.m. If a shop closes at 5 p.m., that means it closes when the staff leave, not when the customers leave. The customer is not a king, he has to play his part in the role organised for him.

'I met a woman working for a translation company in Aachen. She would take the lift in the morning to go to the fifth floor, but in the evening she would take the stairs. I asked her why. She said, what if the lift breaks down? In other words, if the lift breaks down in the morning, it's company time, but in the evening, it's *your* time.'

Germans, therefore, love systems which achieve maximum efficiency, but that can be frustrated by lack of flexibility. Some suggest that's why the merger between the German (Swabian, actually) Daimler and the American Chrysler didn't really work out. One executive who lived through the merger told me: "It's difficult enough to see a German company working with an American one, never mind a Swabian one working with an American one. It's the absolute and utter attention to detail. They would be the first to say something in the American side hasn't been well done. There's a deep concern too for doing things for a good price, since Swabians are so tight. There *is* respect for good design, but they won't tolerate spending money foolishly, even though sometimes it takes money to get good design.'

Germans in companies, large, small and medium, believe they have fine-tuned these rule-based systems so that they deliver, and that allegiance is passed down from management. The system isn't necessarily overly autocratic: there is room for dissent, and consensus is prized. But most employees tend to like to know where they stand and to know what their instructions are. In the UK, the big companies are in advertising, communications and financial services, areas that require a lot of abstract thought. In Germany, they are chemical, engineering and automotive – industries which require nuts and bolts.

Foreign companies that want to export to Germany therefore have to sign up to *Ordnung*. Take this advice from Enterprise Ireland to Irish firms targeting the German market:

> You must make an appointment for everything and you must stick to the agreed time. Meetings are generally set several weeks in advance, so don't expect a company to be able to see you within a week's time. Don't be late and don't change the appointment. If, for any reason, you are going to be late (even five minutes), then call the company and advise them of your new arrival time. When arriving, apologise for being late.

It doesn't stop there. The layers of *Ordnung* require the most meticulous respect. Irish businessmen are warned to 'shake hands with them *every* time you meet them, and again when you leave. Do not initiate using their first name, no matter how difficult their last name is. If your contact has a title like Dr, always address them with this title. When they are ready, they will let you know when you can move on to a first-name basis.' In meetings, mobile phones must never be answered, laptop presentations must never stall through lack of batteries and one should always allow a short period before the meeting to break the ice. The message is clear: steady confidence building, no alarms, no risk.

Risk is, in fact, a frightening concept for Germans. 'This is the most risk-averse culture in the universe,' is the advice Dr James McCabe gives Irish companies. 'A land of insurance and reinsurance where many are wary of credit cards, let alone internet commerce... Only when your contact feels instinctively that he is taking no risk whatsoever will he take out his wallet. German speakers love the so-called win-win scenario. This does not necessarily mean that both parties profit. What they really mean by this is that there is no way they personally can lose.'

Indeed, cash remains king in Germany. Only 33 per cent of Germans carry a credit card, and they have to ask their banks for one (rather than the other way around) and pay an annual fee. According to a June 2013 study by the Research Centre for Financial Services at Steinbeis University in Berlin in 2000 the average number of card payments as a ratio to GDP in Germany was around 5.3 per cent while the EU average, excluding Germany, was 8.6 per cent. Throughout the 2000s, the average EU credit-card penetration climbed to a total of 14.5 per cent by 2010, whereas in Germany credit-card expansion crawled, reaching just 6.8 per cent.

But there is also something in the Germans' fondness for *Ordnung* and being *gründlich* (precise, down to the last detail), which also governs the rigid subdivision of culture as well as business. In the 19th century, the German middle class developed implacable ideas about culture. *Bildung* (culture and education) was elevated to the highest social importance: everyone felt the need to have read Goethe, Schiller, Shakespeare. Great culture, the classics, poetry, shaped one's behaviour and values. The children of the bourgeoisie were expected to read the classics at home, while adolescents were supposed to *live* the great novels and dramas on their dreamy walks through the Alps.

The effect remains to this day. Anything seen as popular (or vulgar) culture is relegated to the other side of the fence. Critics say this has retarded German comedy since it straightjackets people into 'high' or 'low' culture.

'There's no room for comedy in that,' says Eric T. Hansen, the American writer in Berlin. 'Goethe was not a funny guy. Being able to look and talk and act intelligently – that's the important thing. Germans don't see the working class as having the right to intelligent humour. Ard and ZDF – extremely boring and serious. The other commercial channels are very low brow and unimaginative. The upper classes, the opera-goers, will go to see a circus, but they'll never go to see stand-up.'

Michael Mittermeier, the German comedian, agrees. 'People said, you have to do just humour or political satire, you can't do both. I didn't care what people thought.' That mindset, he argues, hinders the full potential of the German imagination, especially in the way German television develops its comedy. 'Sometimes they just cast people from soap operas for comedy shows – they're not even actors, never mind comedians. They should go to the clubs for the people who've been doing the circuit for years in front of audiences, people who know what they're doing.'

These are not just abstract ideas; cultural apartheid is written in stone. 'There's a huge gap between what they call *ernsthaft* (serious) and *unterhaltung* (entertainment),' says Gayle Tufts, the American singer. 'When I write a song, I have to fill out a form and declare whether I'm *ernsthaft* or *unterhaltung*. You have to be one or the other! In America, that would be ridiculous – think of Woody Allen!'

* * *

It shouldn't be forgotten that vices and virtues often have a regional provenance. *Ordnung*, regimentation, obedience to authority, discipline and frugality are seen as Prussian values. 'As a stereotype it's overemphasised, but there is some truth in it,' says Professor Hermann Bausinger of the Ludwig Uhland Institute. 'The Prussian way of order and organisation ran right across the whole of the Third Reich – at universities there were customs that were very military in their essence, the way students greeted each other, the way there was total obedience to their masters.'

Humour is regional too. Bavarians are hearty, in-your-face and slapstick-loving, with a sense of humour rich in regional dialect wordplay. Rhinelanders, especially those from Cologne, shut down to drink heavily for a week during *Karneval*. Berliners go for big-city sarcasm and irreverent putdowns of anyone declaiming too much *Bildung*. Hamburgers are also more inclined to cool, northern irony and understatement. Comedy clubs have been quicker to appear in Hamburg and Berlin.

But having a good comedy infrastructure does not necessarily mean, of course, that a people has a sense of humour. 'They *do* have a sense of humour, which the British and Irish don't see because they're often not in a social context with them,' says Dr James McCabe. 'But their humour is black, blacker than Irish humour, which is blacker than English humour. They call it *galgenhumor*, gallows humour. But they won't tell a joke if it's not connected with the context. They don't mix humour and business.

The time isn't right. Irony, self-deprecation, don't exist. "Is the Pope a Catholic?" often gets the response, "Yes".'

Are Germans learning to enjoy themselves? Their hosting of the World Cup in 2006 was seen as a watershed: not only could they wave the German flag without censure for the first time, but they were no longer angst ridden and uptight: they were party goers! But it wasn't easy. 'When the World Cup came around,' recalls Eric T. Hansen, 'the educated classes were actually very critical. Football was not intellectual, people were drinking too much, the worst part was all this flag-waving nationalism. Rock 'n' roll stars were even offended to be associated with it. It's not who we want to be, these outbursts of stupidity and nationalism. Then for two weeks a lot of people stood up and said, I love it! Then some groups actually apologised on stage for their earlier dismissiveness. Suddenly it was possible for Germans to be normal!'

* * *

But within three years of the World Cup, German normality was being tested to its limits.

When the Greek debt crisis erupted, the world looked to Germany for leadership and, frankly, money. What they got in return was austerity, moral superiority and a policy of delaying action until the last minute, making matters, in the view of many, much worse. When money *was* handed over the strictest of conditions were attached.

What *Germans* got in return was a torrent of criticism. They lacked leadership, they were forcing a culture of austerity down everyone else's throat, they were taking the benefits of the single currency but none of the responsibility, and they were turning inward. Finally – in a wearily inevitable charge – Germans were back to their old tricks. Given the inflamed mood in bailout countries, it was not surprising that Chancellor Angela Merkel was depicted as a Nazi, but respected media and academic circles were also exhuming the 'ugly German' stereotype. 'Nobody should be surprised that Germany has become the greatest threat to Europe,' warned economist Anatole Kaletsky. 'After all, this has happened twice before since 1914.' Emmanuel Todd, the French political scientist, suggested that Germany could not escape its history and that it wanted to 'exterminate' the industries of fellow eurozone members.

In June 2010 I travelled to Berlin just after Greece had been given its first €110-billion bailout. The debate that would soon paralyse Europe was taking shape: France was urging Germany to boost consumer spending so that Germans would buy the exports of other European countries. Germany was lecturing everyone else to become competitive, cut spending and tackle debt. To get a sense of the quinessential German approach to some of these ideas, I visited a pub in West Berlin, not to seek out their drinking habits but their *saving* habits. Every week some 16 regulars would slot coins into a custom-designed deposit box attached to the wall. Such savings clubs abound throughout the Bundesrepublik: in our West Berlin pub, members would squeeze €15 a month into the box for Christmas shopping or a weekend city-break. What did these über-savers think about bailing out Greece? 'I don't think it's right that those other countries end up living beyond their means,' one blond middle-aged saver said, 'because we are the ones who end up paying for it. People say, well, the Germans can afford it, but I don't think that's right.'

The next day I visited Berliner Seilfabrik, a company in Charlottenburg which first began in 1865 making ropes for the nascent elevator industry but which, by 2010, was making children's playground climbing frames, exporting 75 per cent of its output. 'A German product very often delivers more than others,' said floor manager Jens Zumblick. 'And the good thing about that – the beauty, indeed – is that we can demand a premium.' A short time later at the Reichstag, the ruling Christian Democrat party's budget spokesman Norbert Barthle told me: 'Countries that fuel consumption through high debt aren't successful in the long run. After two or three years they're in as much debt as before. With our policies, Germany will have sustainable growth. We want to set a benchmark for other European countries.'

As it turned out, these encounters provided a neat snapshot of how Germans viewed the crisis around them: don't rely on credit, don't live beyond your means, export good, reliable products like we do, don't spend your way into debt, let *us* show you how it's done. But the more Germany's self-righteous tone grated, the more German *character* was psycho-analysed. Not since reunification had Germany been under such scrutiny, and the supposed neuroses of her citizens under such attack. From Galway to the Peloponnese, German politicians and central bankers became household names. Angela Merkel was depicted as a Nazi, a latter-day Margaret Thatcher, or a stern schoolmistress. Germans wanted to dominate Europe by bond spreads not tanks; Germans were obsessed with inflation; Germany was an ageing society; concepts of debt and sinning invoked Martin Luther and the Reformation. But because no other country had the resources to tackle the crisis, Germany's opinion could not be ignored. Virtually every other country was sliding into recession, but German exports were surging ahead. Germany felt perfectly entitled to dominate not through power, but through example.

The sociologist Ulrich Beck has in his book *German Europe* (2013) criticised what he describes as 'German Universalism', the end-point of 70 years of post-war redemption. This is the notion that Germany alone is in possession of the reason-based criteria to decide questions of good and evil at home and abroad. 'Our own social experience and political values are turned into absolutes,' he writes. 'We boldly assert that what's good for the German economy is right for the European economy as a whole.' In other words, Europeans should become more like Germans, and less like Greeks.

Germany's writ has therefore run right through the eurozone, starting with its construction, to bailout conditions, to the Fiscal Compact, to a European banking union, to a future political union. The problem, Beck argues, is that Germany has arrived at this lofty pinnacle through a dialogue, not with others, but with *itself*.

* * *

The proposal that Germany's fixation with austerity is somehow related to its extreme Nazi past and a tendency to dominate is far-fetched to say the least. Germany's fundamental economic philosophy has been rooted in a determination to actually *avoid* any return to National Socialism. Pioneered in the 1930s by the dissident economist Walter Eucken, along with Franz Böhm, Leonhard Miksch and Hans Großmann-Doerth, the approach that would guide post-war Germany towards its economic miracle was known as *ordoliberalism* – essentially 'ordered liberalism'.

This approach has dominated German thinking ever since. It was designed to prevent both the state and big companies from repeating the worst excesses of the Nazis, who intervened massively in the economy through public-works programmes and the diversion of resources from consumption to the war effort. Ordoliberalism dictated that the state provide a strict legal framework for economic activity, one which prohibited undue government invervention, and demanded the avoidance of monopolies through rigid competition rules (the memory of the huge conglomerate, IG Farben, is the key reminder: it developed a cosy relationship with the Nazis and produced the patent for Zyklon B, the nerve agent used to gas millions of Jews). At its heart ordoliberalism meant vigilance against state intervention because concentrating power in one area could lead to power being abused, as it was in the 1930s. Despite the hallmarks of neo-liberal thinking, it did not, however, probihit a strong commitment to social welfare (indeed in its 1947 manifesto the conservative CDU party championed a 'socialist economic order' prioritising social spending and workers' rights).

In the new West Germany, ordoliberalism commanded the support the five main political parties. There would be a strong and independent central bank; collective bargaining was frowned upon, stable inflation and monetary policies were the order of the day. The so-called Freiburg School of economists, retained until this day by the political establishment, sustained ordoliberalism's ideological pre-eminence. Opposing economists were thin on the ground since German theorists were comfortably isolated from international trends, eschewing publication in big Anglo-American journals. Friedrich Hayek, an Austrian-born economist, another hero of the Freiburg School, championed the cause abroad, winning the admiration of Margaret Thatcher and Ronald Reagan.

When the global financial crisis struck in 2008, opinion outside Germany was divided over whether governments should adopt a Keynesian approach, i.e. pump money into the economy to stimulate growth, or focus on debt reduction through spending cuts and tax increases (the austerity approach). When the Greek disaster struck it was no surprise which side of the argument Berlin chose. Ordoliberalism forbade any discretionary intervention, so stimulus was out. Indeed, West Germany had tried a stimulus policy in the early 1970s following the oil shock and the results were disastrous, with high inflation the result (the generation which lived through that period is now the one in office).

Complaints that austerity further deepened a country's recession to the extent that it could even be self-defeating were waved away. Less new debt and spending today meant less tax in the future. Increased private-sector confidence meant more investment. Therefore harsh austerity didn't lead to recession but to a better growth outlook. Chancellor Merkel and Wolfgang Schäuble tended to see difficulties in achieving fiscal targets by debt-laden countries as simply a lack of will.

Finding alternative views in Germany has not been easy. German citizens had major reservations about giving up the Deutschmark which, in the mists of post-war guilt, was just about the only national symbol they could celebrate. Their one demand was that the German culture of rule-based stability would be conferred onto the new currency, and that untrustworthy southerners with their lavish spending and frequent currency devaluations would not be able to ruin it for German taxpayers. Germans took the no bailout rule *very* seriously.

When the very rules they demanded were flouted, a sense of victimhood took hold; the debate which followed provided fertile ground for stereotyping. 'We are looking at layers of deception and victimisation,' explains Ulrike Guérot, a senior associate at the Open Society Initiative for Europe. 'This sense that we Germans never signed up to this. This was part of a very narrow economic debate which was upheld by so many academics that it was easier for stereotyping to emerge. This all came at a moment when we had a rebirth. It was just after 2006 and the World Cup. It was OK to wave German flags again, to feel like a proud nation. It was a national hype, it was Lena [the 2010 Eurovision Song Contest winner], it was BMW, it was exports… It was pretty anti-European in a way.'

Germans, it appeared, needed someone to blame. 'The German mainstream,' wrote Sebastian Dullien of the European Council on Foreign Relations, 'believes the debt crisis in the periphery is the result of overspending by irresponsible governments, exploiting the low interest rates offered after entry into the EMU.' Time and again Germany viewed the crisis in terms of rules being broken (that Germany was the first to breach the Maastricht deficit guidelines was conveniently forgotten). When others spoke of 'solidarity', argued the former ECB board member

Alex Weber, what they meant was help for 'countries which have infringed the rules from those which have applied them… Countries need to take responsibility for their own problems.'

But since eurozone countries in difficulty couldn't by definition print more money or devalue their currency, there was precious little they could do individually. So at European level France and others pushed for Eurobonds, a means of sharing debt through the issuance of common bonds. Again, this was abhorrent to the ordoliberal consensus, since it involved massive intervention and ran the risk of moral hazard. The thrust of German policy relentlessly followed the argument of not allowing countries 'off the hook'.

There are other arguments. Inflation has been frequently invoked as a compelling reason for Germans to cry foul at any talk of stimulating Europe's stricken economies. The experience of the early 1920s, when one US dollar ended up being worth 4,210,500,000,000 German Marks compared to a rate of 4.2 Marks during the First World War, is said to have seared the collective memory. 'My great- great-grandfather,' recalls Guntram Wolff, an economist with the Brussels-based Bruegel Institute, 'had a ship on the River Elba transporting goods from Cuxhaven to the south of Germany. He wanted to retire and settle down on a farm, so he sold the ship in 1921 and with the money he planned to build a house and to use what was left over to start raising vegetables and some animals. Then inflation hit and his money was worthless. My grandmother told me this story when I was a child. These stories are still there.'

Fear of inflation, therefore, has been the powerful, prevailing sentiment in Germany's return to democracy, inured even at a tender age (Otmar Issing, a former ECB board member, is credited with producing a children's cartoon showing inflation as a monster which must be vanquished). The Bundesbank's ruthless determination to keep prices low earned it heroic stature in the eyes of ordinary Germans. In turn its anti-inflationary stance framed the policies then pursed by successive governments.

A survey by the R+V Insurance group in September 2013 found that Germans worried about price rises more than cancer, natural disasters and unemployment, at a time when inflation had been running at just 1.5 per cent. 'The national obsession with price stability has become a stereotype,' noted the *Economist* in May 2013. 'But it is true nonetheless.' No other national media produces as many articles about inflation. After every monthly meeting of the ECB board of governors in Frankfurt the story is reported differently in Germany than in Spain, Italy and France. German academics queue up to take the ECB to Germany's constitutional court in Karlsruhe because they fear it is not sticking to its mandate of nailing inflation. When ECB president Mario Draghi announced two radical initiatives to tackle Europe's seemingly fatal economic crisis – long-term refinancing operations (LTROs) and outright monetary transactions (OMTs) – he was lauded internationally as having almost single-handedly saved the euro. In Germany, however, there were howls of protest from newspapers, and the resignations of two senior ECB central bankers. The reason was that both operations involved the ECB *intervening* in a way that ordoliberalism would have deplored, and that allegedly breached the ECB's mandate. That mandate, as David Marsh points out in *The Euro: The Battle for the New Global Currency* was an entirely German creature: 'On all the key issues regarding the setting up of the European Central Bank – its independence, location, internal structure, monetary instruments and leadership – German views prevailed.'

The monotheistic horror of inflation is, however, being challenged. Mark Schieritz, a correspondent with *Die Zeit*, is another alumnus of the Freiburg School, but he also studied at the London School of Economics (LSE) and as such has pursued a more independent line of questioning. In his book *The Inflation Lie* (2013) he challenges the narrative that hyper-inflation in the 1920s led directly to the rise of Hitler. 'When the Nazis came to power the environment was deflationary, not inflationary,' he says. 'There were 10 years between these two events. Yes, inflation destroyed the middle and upper classes, but the working class wasn't affected that much. Salaries and pensions were increased, but living standards didn't decrease for many working-class families. The newspaper articles and books that were written about inflation were done by the middle class. The working class didn't have a voice.'

This is still a minority view. The official German analysis of what is wrong with Europe was spectacularly endorsed by voters when they elected Angela Merkel for a third term on 22 September 2013. Although the euro crisis barely featured in the campaign, her landslide victory (almost an overall majority) was tacit approval of the German medicine: austerity, reform and competitiveness will in the end lead to market confidence and growth. She may be proved right, and it should not be forgotten that despite (or because of) her gradualist style she has managed to convince taxpayers that Greece, Ireland, Portugal and Spain should be saved.

Her victory also confirmed Germany's risk-averse instincts. In the midst of a crisis, it was no time to change course. She cared little for the impatience of the outside world for Germany to lead: to lead more decisively in the euro crisis, and to lead in world affairs (her decision to abstain on military intervention in Libya baffled and angered allies). Voters seemed to share that indifference.

But perhaps the elections meant something else. A final arrival of the German people at normality? Germany would only ever find normality by embedding herself in a European destiny. After the horrors of two world wars, the years of penitence, the angst over and cost of reunification and then the trauma of the euro nearly falling to pieces, perhaps Germans felt they had finally done enough within that destiny, and that moment may have even begun with the 2006 World Cup, one year after Merkel first became Chancellor. As Roger Cohen observed in the *New York Times*: 'Merkel closed the book on all that. She is the great consolidator. That is why she is loved in a nation weary of self-questioning. Sell cars, balance the books, stay competitive, avoid surprises and live happily ever after.'

* * *

Climb out to the hills that overlook the city of Stuttgart and you will arrive at a smart suburb called Sillen. Turning left off the main street down a quiet avenue, you reach a detached house with a steep pitched roof over a sloping garden. On one side of the path a life-size ornamental goose is poised as if to hiss at any intruders. Spelled out on a dark wooden door is the name of the family who have lived here for fifty years: ROMMEL.

Manfred Rommel, 80-year-old son of the Desert Fox, Hitler's field marshal, Erwin Rommel, opens the door with a bright greeting. Tall and slightly stooped, he is wearing Adidas sweatpants, a T-shirt and a cardigan. With a firm handshake, he announces, 'As a Swabian patriot, I couldn't refuse an opportunity to explain our history.'

The Rommel living room is dominated by bookshelves. Aside from the rows of history, poetry and warfare (including David Frazer's enormous biography of his father, *Knight's Cross*) there are souvenirs and mementos which work their way into a canvas of European reconciliation. They start with a black and white picture of his father taken by the Nazis' photographer-in-chief, Leni Riefenstahl. 'It was taken during the Polish campaign,' explains Rommel junior, referring to one of the most murderous of Nazi invasions. 'She showed my father a gun she always carried for emergencies.' Next is a ballerina figurine presented by a Russian ambassador, a medal from the French Senate and a miniature US flag presented by a US general with the dedication to 'our good friend Manfred Rommel'. As *Oberbürgermeister*, or lord mayor, of Stuttgart from 1974 till 1996, Manfred Rommel hosted 40,000 US troops in nearby bases, over time developing a close friendship with US Army Major General George Patton IV. It was a poignant bond: both men were the sons of the enemy World War II commanders who led some of the greatest and bloodiest campaigns.

As I sit on a leather sofa, he shoos away an enormous slumbering tabby cat. The cat, which doesn't budge, is called Monday. 'It's not my cat at all,' grumbles Rommel. 'It's a deserter. He's the neighbour's cat. He's always sitting on my wife. I have great difficulty in getting him away from me.'

Manfred Rommel is now advancing in years. His long, fine-boned face is alert and bespectacled, but his chin sags below a mouth that struggles with Parkinson's disease. He joined the Luftwaffe when he was 14 years old, and a year later considered joining the Waffen-SS, against the wishes of his father. That same year, his father, who was convalescing after receiving head injuries when his car was strafed by a Canadian warplane, was implicated in the plot to assassinate Hitler. Field Marshal Rommel was never directly involved, but his popularity, and his growing disillusionment with the Führer, drew him to the attention of the conspirators, one of whom even envisaged him as the future president of an independent Germany. When the plot was uncovered, Rommel was regarded as guilty by association. He was visited by the Gestapo and told he would face a public trial and the condemnation of his family, or he could choose suicide. He chose the latter.

Manfred, his only son, then fled the Wehrmacht and surrendered to the French. But before mentioning the war, Manfred Rommel prefers to stick to the Swabians.

'If they want to make something, it has to be perfect. They just hate things being in disorder. There is the joke of the Bavarian and Swabian travelling to France to make some money during the Revolution. The French accused them of being spies and sentenced them to death. The Swabian said the Bavarian came first alphabetically, but the blade malfunctioned and he was let go. Then they took the Swabian, who said, "I'm not lying underneath that until it's been repaired." This is the real commitment to technology.

'Fascism was milder here in Swabia,' Rommel continues. 'It was bad enough, but it was better than in other parts of Germany.'

There is still a certain pride that Stuttgart wasn't totally destroyed by British and American bombers. 'In 1944, Germans produced more weapons and military equipment than ever before or ever afterwards. Bosch and Mercedes were involved in aircraft production, providing engines for 10,000 Messerschmitt planes. The destruction began late because the Ruhr was easier to hit, but after they set up airstrips in France, they fly could further.'

As someone connected by family to the Germany that launched the war and its industrial genocide, but also as a man associated with post-war reconciliation, I ask the Field Marshal's son what he now thinks of the German question. He settles on *fear*. 'Germany had a lucky escape. A very lucky escape. It was an escape from the consequences of the Second World War. What happened here was not so glorious. The Germans were really terrified, when they found out what had happened in Hitler's time, about what might happen under the Russians. It had never happened before. And also the killing of the Jewish people. This was kept secret – of course nobody can kill six million people without leaking news to other places. During the Weimar Republic, the problem was that everyone was in disagreement. Right-wingers didn't want democracy, the Communists were fighting the socialists and wanting to annex Germany to the Soviet Union, there was the dictatorship of the proletariat – all these things terrified German citizens.'

And what of Germany today?

'It is certainly a democratic country. Here there is no chance for extremists from the right wing to win anything. People dislike them, they know their history and this is over.'

And as for his father, the legendary and highly popular wartime commander who led the campaigns in North Africa and against the D-Day Landings, but who turned against the regime and gave his life to spare his family public humiliation: what would he think of Germany today?

'He would be very relieved,' says Manfred Rommel, his voice dipping lower as he contemplates the question. 'He thought maybe Germany had no future except survival. When the Germans found out before the end of the war what had happened in Poland and Russia, they were terrified. They didn't know what to do, they didn't want to surrender because it's easier to surrender if you have a good conscience. But my father said we had no reason to fight on and he had the intention to surrender at the moment of the Anglo-American breakthrough.

'He would be positively surprised, I'm sure. Because he had seen the other side of Germany.'

Chapter 2

France

I can never forgive God for having invented the French.
Peter Ustinov

I'm sitting where Kennedy sat.

By an enormous bay window, curving between sumptuous sandalwood panelling, the President dined at this table with the First Lady in May 1961. It was the spring blush of Camelot, and half a million delirious Parisians had just filled the streets to see them. The Kennedys in Paris was love requited. Jacqueline had spent a year here in 1952 writing for *Vogue*. Now she was back as First Lady, charming President de Gaulle in fluent French, and even, during a meeting with the former resistance leader André Malraux, artfully arranging to have the *Mona Lisa* sent to the White House on loan.

The audacious idea may have crossed their minds as they dined on *Canard à la presse*, the speciality of La Tour d'Argent, and gazed out over the Seine over Île Saint-Louis. When you're the most glamorous ever President of the United States, with a beautiful young wife, what's to stop you having the *Mona Lisa* as well?

Kennedy's seat had already creaked under illustrious buttocks. Winston Churchill, Queen Elizabeth II, Emperor Hirohito, Prince Ferdinand Von Bismarck, Franklin D. Roosevelt, and Richard Nixon were all wined and dined here, as were Clark Gable, Shirley Temple, Salvador Dali, Coco Chanel, Alfred Hitchcock, Kirk Douglas, Charlie Chaplin and Sean Connery. The waiter at my shoulder has personally served Mikhail

Gorbachev, Boris Yeltsin, Bill Clinton, Mick Jagger, Elton John and Diana Ross. Given that we're in the poshest restaurant in Paris, and I'm clearly not a celebrity, the maître d'hôtel should, theoretically, be the rudest man on the planet.

Are French waiters rude?

Rudeness is the most enduring stereotype about the French, and no one personifies it like the French waiter. Poised to sneer, to blank hungry tourists, to whisk away a quarter-full *pression* glass or deny a table, they set the gold-standard on making you feel unwelcome. Some tourists reckon they haven't arrived until a waiter has been rude to them. Travel writers and foreign correspondents testify to the put-downs, the stand-offs, the shape-throwing. Stephen Clarke, whose bestselling series on Anglo-French misunderstandings, starting with *A Year in the Merde*, places the rude Parisian waiter up there among the pantheon of French stereotypes. But are they deliberately and universally rude? Or is it only in the tourist haunts of Saint-Michel, where there's no danger of the foreigner returning for a second meal?

'The job as waiter is to make the moment for the customer unforgettable,' says the very polite head waiter, without apparent irony. 'You must be calm, self-assured. A diplomat.'

Pierre Fernandez, 47, is not really that French. He was born in Paris to Spanish Civil War refugee parents. His mother was a housewife, while his father began his new life as a Peugeot salesman. Growing up in Paris, Pierre dreamed of becoming a master pastry chef, but his future as a waiter was confirmed during two years at the Centre de Formation Apprentis (CFA) on Rue Médéric, the country's main catering school, followed by an internship at Le Meridien. He entered La Tour d'Argent on at the age of 17 and hasn't left. 'There was so much history, four centuries of it. I realised I didn't want anything more.'

Pierre started as a *commis de rang*, the lowest of the restaurant pond life, carrying plates of food to waiters above his station, and bringing back the empties. In those days, the *commis* got nothing in tips ('you have no contact with the customer'), with the spoils being shared between the *chef de rang* and the maître d'hôtel. 'It was a way to test us. You could only rise if you worked hard, and, if you didn't have talent, then hard work didn't do much good. Those who stayed rose through the ranks, the rest quit.'

By 1985, he had become *chef de rang*, later becoming maître d'hôtel. Running the show is a taut balancing act between the twin egos of chef and customer. 'The restaurant is two worlds. The floor and the kitchen. Sometimes the client will ask for a dish that isn't on the menu, so you have to ask the cook. The chef has an ego, he thinks his recipe is perfect and he doesn't understand that the *maître d'hôtel* has to fulfil his customer's desire.'

By now, Pierre, a tall, well-built man with a high forehead and a dark olive complexion, has served every kind of customer, and every kind of ego. In the 1990s there was no shortage of Russian oligarchs throwing money and not too much good taste around La Tour d'Argent. 'They were not my favourite customers,' he says crisply. 'Once someone asked for steak tartare,' he says, frowning. 'It's a rather common dish.'

What if someone asks for steak and chips? President Lyndon B. Johnson is reputed to have done just that. 'We don't sell *pommes frîtes*, we serve *pommes de terre soufflées*,' allowing himself a mischievous smile. 'You have to please the customer even if you don't have what he wants. You have to find a way to make him happy.'

La Tour d'Argent is not a celebrity trough for nothing. Built in 1582 by a hotelier keen to lure knights of the realm to his new inn next to the Seine and the Bernardins convent, it counted King Henri IV as a regular. Stopping off on the way back from hunting, he discovered some Venetian visitors stabbing their meat with small pointed tools. The king liked what he saw, and the fork was formally established in France.

In the 18th century French cuisine was elevated into an art form of which La Tour d'Argent was at the vanguard. It introduced menus for the first time, and its social climbing clientele regarded food as more ceremony than debauchery. Despite revolutionaries ransacking the restaurant and draining the cellars in the 1780s, it was reopened by Napoleon's personal chef, Lecoq, who named his new sauces after some of the emperor's famous victories (Chicken Marengo, for example).

In the 20th century the Terrail family, who remain in charge to this day, took over the management, Claude Terrail managing to brick up the cellar, with it's most precious 20,000 bottles, as the Germans advanced on Paris. It was his *maître d'hôtel*, Frederic Delair, a stern-looking man with ginger chops framing a hairless chin, who invented the house speciality, *Canard à la presse*: the eight-week-old duck is actually *strangled* so it can be baked in its own blood (thighs and breasts removed, it's then placed in the chamber of a silver crushing device and the blood which is pressed out is mixed with cognac, Madeira and consommé, the resulting sauce being reduced and poured over the breast).

Frederic Delair's successor Pierre has spent his adult life in La Tour and will retire there, having worked under three generations of the Terrail family. But being a waiter is a lonely job.

'You have to make a lot of sacrifices,' says Pierre, gazing out as the evening twilight darkens the Seine. 'You are working while people are enjoying themselves. It can be a long day, covering lunch, then a few hours off, and working again till midnight.'

In the afternoon Pierre walks his dog or checks the cinema timetable. He has no family.

'Most families break up. You are working when they are home, and when you are home they are away. The couples who stay together either don't have children, or they both work in the same job.'

* * *

The smell of boiling vegetables and the hard blue tiles suggests a hospital, but this is the laboratory of French gastronomic excellence. It is also where the waiters of the future learn their trade. The École Médéric enrols 700 students annually, and, by the end of their studies, they will carry the torch of French cuisine, table conventions and etiquette across France and into the world. The training can last nine years if the student goes on to complete a Masters. Many start at the age of 16, spending two years learning the basics. These days, they're often from the troubled *banlieux*, the suburbs which exploded into violence in 2005. Waiting tables is one of the few social ladders out of the slums.

The École Médéric was founded in the early 1930s, a rather happy coincidence of the Wall Street Crash: wealthy Americans found that the collapsing dollar suddenly disqualified them from the swanky hotels of Place Vendôme and Rue de Rivoli, leaving an army of chefs, waiters and restaurateurs facing ruin. In response, an association of hotel and restaurant professionals was set up, building on the apprentice system established following World War I (the profession had been decimated by the slaughter of cooks in the trenches). The state agreed to guarantee their running costs, but it also recognised the desperate situation of head chefs, who were surrounded by 'vague persons with no competence in culinary technique'. Waiters, in other words.

Around this time, George Orwell was living in Paris on six francs a day, so hungry that he would eat a slice of bread rubbed with garlic, since its lingering flavour left the impression of having recently eaten. Orwell worked as a waiter in the Ritz on Place Vendôme (where Princess Diana had her last meal), later describing conditions in *Down and Out in Paris.*

> There sat the customers in all their splendour – spotless table cloths, bowls of flowers, mirrors and gilt cornices and painted cherubim; and here, just a few feet away, we in our disgusting filth. For it really was disgusting filth. There was no time to sweep the floor till evening, and we slithered about in a compound of soapy water, lettuce-leaves and trampled food. A dozen waiters with their coats off, showing their sweaty armpits, sat at the table mixing salads, and sticking their thumbs into the cream pots. The room had a dirty mixed smell of food and sweat …

Eighty years later, here at the École Médéric, the would-be backroom slaves of the Ritz are on their toes, whipping sauces, steaming vegetables, manhandling game in and out of furnaces. Barking instructions in impeccable French is the drill sergeant of the next generation of chefs and waiters. Allison Zinder is *American.*

'Younger students like to make fun and there are always references to hamburgers – even my colleagues make references to hamburgers,' sighs Allison, her Richmond, Virginia drawl wafting through the steam. 'It's true in the States we have all that kind of fast food, but we also have it in France. I tell the students, be careful – the obesity rate in France is increasing and we're catching up with the US.'

Allison brought her culinary experience from the States 12 years ago. A one-year diploma on her arrival was designed to appease the suspicion of her French peers. 'The industry is very competitive,' she says. 'In Virginia there was much more solidarity: if you had to turn away some customers, they would suggest another restaurant, but here restaurateurs like to cut the others down. Maybe it's a fear of what other people are doing, that whatever *you're* doing, they might be doing it better.'

The French forever worry about change. While other countries were adding flair and brilliance to local cooking, the French were stagnating. Even the Brits were getting good at it. Some experts believe the student revolt of May 1968 cleaved a generation away from traditional cookery, alienating them from culinary skills and the art of taking time to cook and eat. Obesity levels have doubled in the past decade (although they're still way below British and Irish levels) and diabetes is on the rise. The French have noticed and are worried. There's been a clamour for cookery courses among the middle classes keen to learn what their grandparents knew and how to adapt that knowledge to today's lifestyle.

France now has its own celebrity chefs, and some posh Paris restaurants – Le Meurice, L'Atelier and Black Calvados – have even embraced the burger (albeit made with wagyu beef and laced with 'a ketchup of blackcurrant and blackberries'). But the world of French cuisine is still plagued by that terrible *seriousness*. This is a country where a top chef sued McDonald's for €2 million in damages over a poster that suggested he was dreaming of a Big Mac. Former president Nicolas Sarkozy even launched a campaign, much to the annoyance of Spanish and Italian rivals, to have *la gastronomie Française* recognised as a UNESCO World Heritage treasure. This followed the shock that in Michelin's 2008 guide, Tokyo was awarded more stars than the French capital.

'There's been a tendency for French chefs to rest on their laurels,' says Allison. 'But that's been changing. There are entrepreneurial chefs who are doing more innovative things. There is a fear of taking risks, trying new ingredients, but at the other end of the spectrum – in Provence, for example – chefs *are* taking risks with things, with ingredients, with spices.'

The restaurant business remains cut-throat. Profits in American restaurants are much higher, and even in top-end French restaurants the owners can only expect to make big margins on desserts. It's a 70-hour-a-week slog and there's not always time to experiment. 'That's always the problem in the kitchen,' she says. 'You're always pressed for time, so many things to learn. We're on a hamster wheel.'

But why has France managed to hold onto the mantle of world leaders in cuisine for so long?

That French regions, with their diverse climates, their *terroirs* and *pays*, are blessed with an abundance of fresh produce and cooking styles is only part of the explanation. In fact, until the arrival of Catherine de Médicis from Florence (she became the de facto queen of France in the 1540s), French cuisine was nothing to write home about: it generally relied on thick, heavily spiced sauces disguising the flavour of poor meat. She brought to the French court her Florentine manners and her chefs, versed as they were in Renaissance cookery skills. The Italians had a lighter, more subtle touch: fresh vegetables were introduced and dinner became an event in which the whole family, local nobles, and even servants participated.

But much of the flourishing of French cuisine was, ironically, down to the French Revolution. Although the first upmarket eatery was opened in 1782 by Antoine Beauvilliers, the *officier de bouche* of a Provençal count, it was only after the Revolution, while the nobles were going to the gallows, that their suddenly out-of-work chefs had to quietly reinvent themselves in the new restaurants which were opening up. Within 10 years, the numbers of these *adresses savoureuses* rose from 100 to 600. The word '*gastronome*' first appeared in 1803, while '*restaurant*' entered the Académie Française in 1835. By 1850, Paris had 3,000 restaurants, of which one-quarter were of exceptional quality. Oyster producers from Normandy, market gardeners from Montreuil and beef farmers from Pontoise all profited, while young writers like Honoré de Balzac used the exciting new restaurant culture as a springboard into journalism.

French culinary style rippled across the globe: Antonin Carême became the main chef of Tsar Nicholas and later the Prince of Wales (today he's regarded as the father of haute cuisine). Etiquette and table style flourished as *beaux arts*, while the *maître d'hôtel* could catapult his fame by inventing ever more ornate dishes. On 14 April 1900, no less than 22,250 mayors across France gathered at the World Expo in Paris for an enormous banquet. By then, there were 60,000 gourmet chefs in France. Elitism and snobbery thrived. As the growing bourgeoisie enriched themselves on overseas colonies, their *grandes maisons* needed not just head chefs, but sauce, roasting, pantry, *pâtissier* and iced-lemonade chefs.

Superstars emerged. Georges Auguste Escoffier was the first, earning his laurels under César Ritz at the Savoy, at the Carlton in London and then back at the Ritz in Paris, where one of his trainee pastry chefs was Ho Chi Minh. The Jamie Oliver of his day, he not only invented Peach Melba, but also simplified and modernised the ornate styles of Antonin Carême. He was the first to realise that there was money to be made from tourists, not just the hereditary rich. In London, he created the *Diner d'Epicure*, whose menu was served in 37 cities across Europe simultaneously. He later introduced the à la carte menu, and his *Guide Culinaire* is still a major reference book.

There are those who argue that France may have fallen behind in flashy new styles, but they insist that Escoffier's legacy lays the emphasis on *technique*, and this is what Allison Zinder's impresses upon her students. 'French cuisine *is* the world reference. If you master French techniques, then you can go anywhere in the world and you're going to apply those techniques to local ingredients. What these kids are learning is just the basics, but it's not always very easy. Things which might seem quite simple are actually – in the refinement of the technique – quite complex.'

Does she drill into her students the importance of not being rude? (Restaurateurs and *maîtres d'hôtel* all start in the same channels.)

'I do understand the problem,' says Allison. 'Because there are tourists who come to Paris and don't make an effort to learn a few words of French, or maybe they're asking for things the waiter doesn't know about. I had two friends who came to Paris from the US and asked for a doggy bag. That notion just doesn't exist in France. The waitress didn't know what they wanted, and when she couldn't do her job she felt frustrated and the first instinct was to throw it back at the client. Parisians understand now that tourism has a big role in their economy, and that it's in everyone's best interests to be more polite … Maybe not in the way the Americans would wish – smiles all the time – because that just goes against French nature. The French don't trust people who smile all the time. And I tend to agree.'

The problem is that waiting tables is a profession, a *métier* which is a life's work. Having one's professional principles tested by vulgar customers can by trying, although it's still no excuse – that's the business you're in. Part of the etiquette of service, though, is maintaining a detachment from the clientele; to the professional, it's a respectful *politesse* – waiters tend not to engage in chit chat. Nor do they rely on tips the way Americans do, so they're less inclined to cloying servility. 'The French don't like big tips – it's seen as vulgar, leaving big bills on the table,' says Billy Kylie, an Irish interpreter who's been living in Paris for 20 years. 'Its seen as flashing your cash. It's like having a big chunky watch.'

Fabien Jadraque, a 21-year-old from the suburb of Herblay, a likeable young man with silver-rimmed glass and short dark hair, says that only in the really upmarket joints – like La Tour d'Argent – do waiters earn enough tips to top up their basic salaries, and some do quite well. 'The basic salary is no more than €1,000 [per month]. Some restaurants pay commission, some don't. I know waiters who are 20 and earn €1,300 per month and at the end of the month they are earning €3,000 including tips – but it depends on the restaurant.'

'French waiters are trained, they go to school, and they are proud of what they do,' says Katherine Garnier, an Irish woman who returned from France to work as front-of-house manager in Patrick Guilbaud's restaurant in Dublin for 20 years. 'We tried to get trained Irish staff, but it was so hard – there's no equivalent to the French waiter. They're more formal, they don't like people coming late, looking for lunch after 2 p.m., people drinking their heads off. While the managers might be rubbing their hands with glee, the group on the floor don't like it. They can be impassive, and there is a haughtiness, and sometimes customers don't feel like they're getting through. You have to make a real effort, but soon that façade rolls away.'

According to François Simon, the highly respected food critic of *Le Figaro*, a new generation of waiters has emerged in the new boutique hotels, like Hôtel Costes, Café Marly or Café Beaubourg next to the Pompidou Centre. In the bright and airily minimalist café of the newspaper, François, with slept-in hair and skinny black tie, muses on the rude French waiter.

'Years ago, waiters wanted to be respected. Rudeness was a kind of self-defence. They were simple people, but they couldn't imagine another way to protect themselves from *slavery*. But there is a new generation. The new waiters are very proud of what they do. They are gentle, sexy, there's a new atmosphere, a new mood, but it's only in the past 15 years. In the Saint-Michel area you still have old guys in their sixties, the post-war generation who can be pretty rude. It's a very tiring job, you're working all hours, long days, very difficult for the legs. The French usually stay in their jobs and rise vertically, they don't move around so much as the Anglo-Saxons do. For some waiters, being rude is a kind of sadism, people who use their superiority over those who are under them, who don't know the language. For them, it's a real pleasure.'

At La Tour d'Argent, 21-year-old Nicolas Naudrin, the fresh-faced Apprentice of the Year winner (2008) reflects on the diverse demands on the French waiter. 'You need a knowledge of cheese, floral displays, starters, you need to learn about ingredients. You need to present the menu to the clients and explain everything. But many people can't bear working in a restaurant. They hate chefs because they yell at you, telling you you're not fast enough. People just get depressed and leave. You need to be calm, conscientious, have the right deportment.

'Work is work. When people tell you to do something, you *do* it. It's your work.'

* * *

No country is so ridiculed and adored in equal measure, and no one has so perpetuated stereotypes of the French like the English. 'Excuse my warmth; but my blood boils at the name of a Frenchman,' wrote Lord Nelson. 'I hate the French most damnably.'

Like Nelson, the English have been hating the French since 1066. William Hogarth, the 18th-century satirist, declared that being French amounted to 'poverty, slavery and insolence with an affectation of politeness.' Whether this is a visceral dislike because they mostly met in battle or an enmity based on plain jealousy, either way the bitter blood has coursed through the ages all the way up to General de Gaulle's rejection of Britain's Common Market bid, to the French ban on British beef.

Yet no one loves France like the British. 'The British visit France more than they visit any other foreign country,' writes Theodore Zeldin in *The French*. 'Over a third of them have been to France; but only 2 per cent say they admire the French, and very few indeed would like to live among them.'

That was in the 1980s. By the 2000s, there were few Brits who *wouldn't* like to live among them. In May 2009 the National Expat French

Life Survey of 1,000 expats found that 87 per cent felt happier since moving to France and 94 per cent felt healthier, with most eating better, cooking more, and getting more exercise. They enjoyed better standards of behaviour, stronger family values, more respect for elderly people, less crime and less stress. The village of Eymet in the Dordogne now has more British residents than French ones, and they are not just there for two weeks of the year. 'They come for the quality of life, the scenery, the food and wine, the buildings,' says Charles Hastings, a British estate agent in Montignac. 'They don't buy a home just for holidays, they come and go, sometimes spending six months here. Some have really integrated: they speak French, end up as farmers, play *pétanque* and cook French food. And they find it hard to go back. People say England isn't what it used to be. It's not necessarily that it's less English, but there's some way of life that has been forgotten, and they find that here.'

This love-hate relationship with the French operates both at the grass roots, and in the upper echelons. In the 1990s, another opinion poll revealed that only 35 per cent of the British had a favourable view of the French, while 20 per cent had outright antipathy. That French men are better lovers, French trains run on time, French food is better and French women more attractive only spikes the resentment with jealousy. At the upper level, despite maintaining an uninterrupted alliance since 1900, it so often gets personal. General de Gaulle reduced Harold Macmillan to tears when he blocked Britain's entry into the Common Market in 1962, Margaret Thatcher barely got on with François Mitterand, while the chemistry between Tony Blair and Jacques Chirac was awful.

The Brits naturally passed the stereotypes on to the Americans. American GIs bound for the Normandy beaches were equipped with a booklet entitled '112 Gripes about the French': the French don't wash, the women are loose and French soldiers will surrender at the first sign of trouble. Wind the clock forward to the US invasion of Iraq, and the same slurs were slung. Americans boycotted French goods, the entire population were branded 'cheese-eating surrender monkeys' and French fries were renamed 'freedom fries'. It all added to a climate of injurious stereotyping that both fascinated and irritated the French public. When French historian Balbino Katz found the 1945 era pamphlet in his attic at the height of the Iraq war, and gave it to a French publisher, the print run ran to 14,000 copies within months.

France's presence on the world stage, the size of her culture and the powerfully sensual nature of the French character all keep stereotypes at the forefront of the global mind. 'The great figures of French history have a global dimension,' writes Jonathan Fenby in *On the Brink: The Trouble with France*. 'Joan of Arc symbolises the defiant heroine, and Marie Curie the triumph of women in science, while Brigitte Bardot was the most natural sex symbol the cinema has ever known.'

But that France *feels* herself exceptional – General de Gaulle vowed she must be 'dedicated to an exalted and exceptional destiny' – rarely fails to invite ridicule, and love can turn to hatred very quickly. When Jacques Chirac carried out nuclear tests in the South Pacific in 1995, furious protesters reached for the stereotypes: one Australian mayor urged his fellow citizens to send stuffed cane toads to Paris, while a Dutch MP wrote that France was 'really great, but what a pity it's full of French people'.

But the France as filtered through the prism of stereotypes – beret-wearing, cheese-eating, smelly, lazy – is not the France as understood by the French themselves, and not just for the obvious reasons of subjectivity. It's because defining France as a single, cultural entity has never been easy. President de Gaulle famously told a *Newsweek* interviewer in 1961, 'How can anyone govern a country that has 246 different kinds of cheese?' The point wasn't to stress French devotion to cheese, but its regional diversity (the term 'France' refers originally to Île-de-France, the area now known as the District of the Paris Region). 'Until the French Revolution,' write Jean-Benoît Nadeau and Julie Barlow in *Sixty Million Frenchmen Can't Be Wrong*, 'France was a divided patchwork of nationalities similar to the present-day Balkans. There was hardly any relationship between the Alsatians, the Flemish, the Bretons, the Basques, the Occitans, the Burgundians, the Lyonnais, the Bordelais, the Provençaux, the Corsicans and the Savoyards. They all spoke different languages, lived in distinct geographical areas, and, of course, ate different food.'

That a distinct *French* identity has been forged is down to the ruthless centralism practised by kings, emperors and democrats ever since. But it also means that no one looks in the national mirror more than the

French. They are obsessed with what it means to be French and how that squares with their distinct regional identities, and they're still looking for the answer. The irony is that they're happy to indulge the stereotype.

'The search for the essential Frenchman plays into the hands of the traditional foreign tourist, whose favourite game is to spot how typically *French* the French are,' writes Theodore Zeldin in *The French*. 'The result is that the stereotype is a hoax that the French play on foreigners, but they play it so well that they are taken in by it themselves.'

But where did the French get the idea they was so special? In the 18th century, France was a world power, rich in the arts and synonymous with civilisation. French replaced Latin as the language of educated men; Louis XIV was the Sun King around whom the universe revolved. Through the Age of Enlightenment and the writings of Montesquieu and Voltaire, the French began to see patriotism not as a narrow, chauvinistic idea: being French instead meant you were a citizen of a liberated universe in which people were ruled by reason, principle and altruism.

Napoleon saw France at the centre of a new, egalitarian order, and wanted those virtues to be instilled at all levels. He wanted the Frenchman to be moulded into a common type, where every French child would learn the same piece of Latin prose at the same time and the French person could ultimately be part of the same clear identity.

Dispensing with all those archaic languages, customs and cheeses had to be brutally applied, and extravagantly celebrated by the new State in equal measure. The elevation of grandeur was the binding priniciple, and a visit to Paris is a reminder of how the French do *grandeur* like no one else. 'It evokes power, glory, and moral and intellectual elevation,' write Jean-Benoît Nadeau and Julie Barlow. The society is structured in order to accommodate and promote *grandeur*, so that those who excel are allowed their full quota of greatness. The Académie Française, the Collège de France and the Panthéon (with its recognition of the *Grands Hommes* of the country) all attest to the sacred notion of greatness. This naturally gives rise to French 'exceptionalism', where France regards itself as being above the tawdriness of globalisation (ahead of the EU-US trade talks in 2013, France insisted on keeping the audio-visual sector out of the negotiations in order to protect its films from a Hollywood onslaught). Given that fast-food outlets are everywhere, French towns are ringed by

American-style malls, and Hollywood blockbusts its way to the top of the French film charts anyway, French exceptionalism can be intensely irritating, especially to those with pretensions of their own.

'So why do we still distrust the French?' asks Chris Patten, the former Tory cabinet minister and European Commissioner in his autobiography, *Not Quite the Diplomat*. 'It's largely, I think, because their tired exceptionalism cuts across our own bumptious certainty of our good intentions. How could anyone imagine that *we* are not doing our own best?'

A *Daily Telegraph* headline reads: 'Being Hostile and Rude Is Like Boules to the French', quoting a Japanese psychiatrist who defined a condition among foreigners caused by French rudeness or arrogance. But is the stereotype true?

There is a theory that the peculiar shape of French vowels makes them *look* arrogant. 'Their lips have to protrude when they speak because the French language has more sounds which require the rounding of the lips than other languages,' helpfully explains Theodore Zeldin. 'Nine out of the sixteen French vowels involve strong lip-rounding, compared with only two out of the twenty English vowels…'

Perhaps because of the shocking overthrow of the *Ancien Régime* there evolved in France a more heightened distinction between the public and private spheres, where mannerisms are driven by specific attitudes to personal space, privacy and public relations. It's more subtle than the simple *tu/vous* decorum. A French stranger might perform an act of spontaneous generosity, yet look perplexed when you ask their name. They'll invite you into their home quite willingly, yet stiffen if you ask what they do. At a dinner party, you can freely talk about sex in all its gymnastic forms, but if you want to discuss salaries, there will be an awkward silence. In *French or Foe?*, the American author Polly Platt depicts this ordering of human relations as a series of private and public bubbles: if you know the codes, you can move quietly in and out of each bubble, but if you don't, you might burst the bubble, and that's where the aloofness comes in.

But even in the most banal, fleeting of encounters, the code is there and you risk rudeness if you break it. Entering a shop in France, you need to be quick with your greeting. If the proprietor gets his or her *Bonjour!* in first, the chill factor starts. It's almost a daggers drawn contest as to who gets the greeting out first.

'The first time I realised this was when I was at the railway station buying a ticket,' says Billy Kylie, our Irish interpreter. 'I asked politely for a ticket to Lyon, and the woman said, *Bonjour!* So I said, again, a return to Lyon please, and before doing anything, the woman said, again, *Bonjour!* So I thought, well there must be something to this, so I said, "Is it necessary to say *Bonjour* before I can get a ticket?" and she said, horrified, "Well, yes, it's the least you can do!" '

'It's the *formule de politesse* which is so important here,' says Peter Cluskey, an Irish property journalist recently living in the Dordogne. 'It covers everything in France. Children are trained at school and are given broad brush strokes, not about being polite, but about *behaviour*. The rudeness is partly a formality, the way you address people. There are clients I phone up in England and they'll start using the first name straight away. I now find that rather rude.'

'I wasn't prepared for the aggressiveness of Parisians,' says Jane Lizop, an American writer and journalist living in Paris since 1972. 'It's an urban thing. In shops they're brusque, but they work for a commission so it's like, if you don't want to buy my shoes then go away.'

* * *

I'm on my way to Bar Vavin, a hangout for the gilded youth of Paris just off Boulevard Montparnasse. On the heated terrace at the front, girls sit in groups, smoking and preening each other's iPhones. They are fluffily fashionable in the winter air, have side partings and long hair which is compulsively tucked back behind an ear. Inside, young waiters wear black aprons, white shirts and black ties. Along the swerve of the dark wood bar, they kiss the cheeks of young female customers, who remain blasé at the attention. The boys, thick haired and salon-fresh, wear American university-branded hooded tops. Trumpety jazz meanders brightly against the off-beat of coffee cups on saucers.

I've come to meet Julie (21) and Laure (22), two interior-design students just back from a six-month exchange in Scottsdale, Arizona. They've come to talk about the legendary French stereotype of love. Love, lovers, seduction, relationships, fidelity – the whole *mélange*.

First, how did they find the Americans?

'We couldn't get over the body culture,' says Julie. 'Everyone goes to the gym, the girls are very thin. We were expecting fat people.'

She adds, 'We heard a lot of stories about teenagers getting drunk, having house parties and doing nasty things with several people, but we never saw it ourselves. Alcohol is a huge problem, it's so hypocritical. You can't do anything till you're 21 – you can't even go into a bar and have a coffee. So people get fake IDs or they wait till they're 21 and go crazy. At the same time you can drive and buy a gun.'

And how did the Americans react to them?

'They all asked if we shave under our arms!' exclaims Laure, and Julie nods her head enthusiastically. Why should frat students in Scottsdale think about under-arm hair? It may partly derive from the first encounter Americans had with the French: the Normandy landings. On their way to liberate Paris, American GIs found a countryside crippled by occupation and stripped of food, cigarettes, razors and soap. When they liberated Paris, so great was the demand for stockings and cigarettes that New York firms began mailing large consignments to American soldiers who promptly sold them to the black market. In the euphoria of liberation, US servicemen and Parisian girls were swept up in a wave of mutual attraction. After some time, though, the US embassy noted the 'ardent and often very enterprising' way in which GIs pursued the exotically dressed French girls, who in turn began to complain of *arrogance* on the part of the *Americans*. 'Summoned by a whistle and a proffered pack of "Luckys", one girl earned the cheers of French onlookers by taking a cigarette from the GI, dropping it to the ground and grinding it under her foot,' write Antony Beevor and Artemis Cooper in their book, *Paris After the Liberation*.

Today, given the widespread obscentification of British and Irish culture, through lads' mags and tabloids, notions about sexual availability are confused. 'I went to London and felt very conservative,' says Julie. 'They're so open, so vulgar, the girls are practically naked under their miniskirts.'

For both women, seduction is more important (caution is advised here: in French, '*séduire*' can also mean 'to charm' or 'to attract'). 'If you want to seduce a guy, you have to look nice. Italian girls are the standard. English guys think French girls are cold, elegant cold,' says Laure.

'You seduce by look and by spirit, consciously and subconsciously,' says Julie.

It's an enduring part of our subconscious picture of the French. The idea of the smouldering, sexually intriguing French woman has long played havoc with Anglo-Saxon hormones. French females in English sitcoms (the cloyingly amorous Madame Peignoir in *Fawlty Towers*) struggled to emerge from the caricature of seductress, and French art films often portrayed women as sexually precocious, available and experienced. Yet French women are not necessarily keen on recreational sex: 'If you get off with a French girl,' warns an Irish friend living in Paris, 'their suitcases will be on your landing the next day.' The French male is a different animal and, to the outside world, a not very attractive one (it's no surprise that his anthropomorphic incarnation, the *amour*-mad cartoon character Pepé Le Pew, was a skunk).

Yet love and seduction are an irrepressible part of French life. 'The French haven't changed,' Polly Platt, the American writer, tells me. 'Look at the movies, they're all about love. Look at books, look at TV. Just this week there's an exhibition called *Vive l'Amour*, there's another at the Museum of Science, *L'Amour, Comment Ça Va?* There are ads with a picture of the Eiffel Tower silhouetted against a condom with the caption, "*Paris protège l'amour*". They never get tired of it. For the Americans it's the stock market, for the French it's love.'

But why France? Don't birds and bees exist in other countries?

'Love flourishes in a temperate climate,' wrote Nina Epton in her seminal exploration, *Love and the French*, in 1959, 'where nature is both clement and abundant, where lovers may meet by moonlight without catching a mortal chill, stretch on the hay in the midday sun without fear of sunstroke, and revel in a solitude of birds and flowers, remote from predatory beasts and venomous reptiles. France is definitely in the right latitude for love.'

If love is a latitude, and infidelity a longitude, then France is where they intersect. But for their pre-eminence in the art of love, the French actually owe thanks to the Muslims. In the 12th century, French knights from Aquitaine, returning from Moorish wars in northern Spain, brought back captive Saracens whose womenfolk were custodians of the oral traditions of love which had fluttered like so many butterflies across the Arab world for several centuries. Until then, love as a topic of art or conversation had barely existed in European culture. The songs of these Moorish women were soon picked up by the ladies of the châteaux, developed by troubadours like Duc Guillaume IX d'Aquitaine (1071–1127) and then spread to other parts of France and England by, among others, his granddaughter, Eleanor of Aquitaine.

Thus was born the tradition of *amour courtois*, 'courtly love'. The world of knights and chivalry developed an elaborate set of codes and stratagems, and love took on a mystical power with religious overtones. Knights either loved from afar, wallowing in poetic rejection, or bombarded their targets up close with music and verse; ladies accepted or parried according to an exquisite array of gestures and symbols. Soon, the hallmarks of true love and knightly valour were synonymous. Falling in love was a form of pseudo-religious ecstasy, yet practitioners could also become expert in the *art* of love: 'It is not to be wondered at if husbands are jealous of such an expert artist as I am in the art of love,' wrote Sordel de Goit, a 13th-century Lombard troubadour. 'Because no woman, however prude she may be, can resist the persuasive power of my appeal.'

So 'love' was somewhere between the Platonic ideal and erotic desire. It was a state of grace requiring a long initiation, followed by periods of restraint and moderation. Some troubadours, though, wrote extravagant verse for their ideal love while living a libertine lifestyle on the side. Others tortured themselves with exaggerated notions of chastity (one group of lay monks – this I love – took to sleeping next to naked women to test their endurance). According to the male dominated social order, men were forgiven for moments of passion with servant girls or shepherdesses, and were still deigned worthy of keeping the affections of their truly beloved. Andrew the Chaplain, whose *Art of Courtly Love* was one of medieval France's most well-read treatises, encouraged his knights to take peasant women by force, since gentle treatment and artful sentiment would be a complete waste of time and energy.

In such a climate, the institution of marriage suffered. Popes were forever adjudicating marriages unconsummated, while feudal ladies often had several husbands in a lifetime, since they could be rejected on the flimsiest of pretexts. The Renaissance brought even greater sensual and intellectual delights. The discovery of Greek and Roman civilisations led to a reappraisal of the human body and a new cult of beauty. Styles and trends from Italian courts seeped into French society. Towns were expanding and the gulf between the aristocracy and the masses was narrowing. With the influx of servant girls and ladies-in-waiting, the potential for predatory knights was limitless. Kings too had notorious sexual appetites. François I pursued a host of regal mistresses, writing poems about the difficulty of keeping more than one mistress on the go at any one time.

Following the religious wars of the 16th century, the Catholic Church struggled to improve morals and tighten up marriage laws. Tales of elopements, and their unhappy corollary, forced marriages, abounded (many noble families were so stricken with war-related penury that they married off their children to improve finances). There were numerous unions between young brides and old men, leading to a preponderance of widows. Desperate château-wives who eloped paid for their caprice. The wife of Lieutenant Civil du Châtelet, who in 1521 eloped with her lover, was caught and slung into a convent for three years, where her head was shaved and she was beaten monthly. The only respite was when her husband turned up to claim his conjugal rights. The lady's lover was, needless to say, let off scot-free.

The countryside was littered with bastard offspring who, in keeping with the custom that developed during the Middle Ages, were brought up alongside legitimate children (a curious pseudo-scientific theory held that children born from illicit passion – from hot seed, as it were – were likely to be more gallant, smarter and more courageous than those born within dull wedlock).

But by the end of the Renaissance, the idea of loyalty and chivalry was in decline: men were happier to *live* for love, and see how far they could get, than to *die* for love. They were no longer prostrate at their ladies' feet, spouting love poetry; instead they moved matters to the drawing room, deploying wit and badinage to have those feet raised upon the *chaise longue.*

Court society had few scruples about fidelity. Even as a 14-year-old, the young Louis XIV had a spy-hole into the room where his ladies-in-waiting slept. 'When Louis became king, the greatest ambitions of all the court beauties, married or unmarried, was to become his mistress,' writes Epton. An Italian ambassador noted that such ambition, fulfilled or otherwise, was 'of no offence either to their husband, to their father, or to God'. On the contrary, relatives boasted about it, and the greatest nobles were willing to marry their sons or daughters off to the Sun King's illegitimate offspring.

It was the age of vanity and pomposity, of the fripperies of fashion and the absurdities of etiquette. Marriage, furthermore, was only a means to make money. Young girls were married off to older men provided their dowry was big enough – and if it wasn't, the wretched girls were slung into a convent. The whole cynical state of affairs was bitterly lampooned by Molière. One anecdote told of the marriage of the 90-year-old Maréchal de La Force, who, on his wedding night, had his relatives crowd the nuptial chamber to verify that he'd consummated his vows (it has to be said, though, that overcoming stage fright at 90 to perform is quite an achievement).

Secret marriages and abductions were rife and had to be abolished by royal decree in 1659. Some elopements ended in disastrous marriages, while some abductions ended in happy ones. Males became literal predators: young ladies were known to be kidnapped in broad daylight from carriages in the centre of Paris or from convents (where else?). In some cases, abductions were *de rigueur*, a playful ritual to which young ladies became quite attached (some would have considered it an insult if their suitor hadn't carried them off on horseback). By the middle of the 17th century, the art of French love had descended into frivolous gallantry: men and women of the upper classes were involved in several amorous intrigues at the same time. 'Men entered into a love affair coldly, deliberately, so as to be talked about … Amorous prowess improved one's social status in aristocratic circles,' writes Epton.

But it wasn't just the men who were to blame. French ladies were often as much implicated through their own arts of pretty speech and coquetry, sometimes spending hours in front of the mirror trying out seductive new facial expressions. 'People do not have passions any more,' lamented Pierre de Laclos, author of *Les Liaisons Dangereuses*, 'but carefully calculated designs upon each other. Adieu to tenderness. Debauchery and false love are rife.'

The 18th century was the true age of scandal. There were mixed bathing parties and clubs devoted to salacious tittle-tattle and shock-horror gossip. Secret societies devoted to the pleasures of the flesh were rife. The Aphrodites society met in exquisitely appointed *châteaux* replete with private boxes, upholstered in pink taffeta and equipped with ingeniously placed peepholes. Membership was not cheap – £10,000 for men – and it was limited to some 200 aristocrats and high-ranking clergy.

The Revolution cut through this decadent beau monde like hot buckshot. Vast swathes of the nobility went to the coldest mistress of all, Madame Guillotine. The males, who had strutted their way through high-society bedrooms, carried themselves in the face of impending execution with less grace than the women on whom they had disported. Nina Epton quotes one contemporary witness: 'The Revolution revealed men's weaknesses; they were selfish, fearful and false. The women, on the contrary, discovered their souls in the midst of the turmoil and they risked all to give consolation and shelter to those in need.'

The social changes wrought by the Revolution, however, had a profound impact on French love. With the shackles of church and monarchy slung off, divorce rates soared. The endless leisure and drawing-room badinage which had its roots in *amour courtois* was gone. With Napoleon came the rugged appeal of the military man. Bonaparte himself kept several mistresses, much to Josephine's fury, using them to provide a psychological edge over rivals and subordinates.

But the appeal of chivalrous knights and swooning ladies was only dormant. With the Romantic Movement, from the 1830s, the populace sought relief from revolutionary terror and wars and they found it in nostalgia for courtly love. Blended with the Romantic movement's preoccupation with nature and human passions, French lovers were consumed with theatrical moods and melodrama. Fed on a diet of Walter Scott and Alexandre Dumas, ladies were fainting all over the place; dying for love, long disregarded as a waste of life, was back in fashion. Suicides blamed on 'the impetuosity of passions' were on the rise, while wives were to be found spending all their days 'reading novels in an armchair with a sad, far-away look in their eyes'.

It wasn't surprising. In the real world, engagements were demure and marriages legalistic; it was a buttoned-down culture of notaries and chaperones. Honeymoons were unheard of and the new bride would never appear in public without her husband or mother-in-law in the first year of marriage. Love and marriage *still* didn't go together like the proverbial horse and carriage: marriage was there to create families and tighten the social bonds. In such a hidebound atmosphere, there were real doubts about how many truly happy marriages existed. Balzac blamed both men and women for a lack of imagination (some married couples slept in single beds with wheels, so they could be rolled closer in the event of pelvic stirrings). Women were still sheltered by their parents from an early age and married off against their will. In a landscape of such emotional distress, illicit passions were inevitable (Balzac helpfully estimated that there were 150,000 such liaisons).

Gustave Flaubert's heroine, Madame Bovary, embodied the suffocating disappointments of the age: a provincial doctor's wife (her husband had already been through an arranged marriage and was a widower), she tosses herself into adulterous affairs, railing against the boredom of her bourgeois life and enflamed by the flights of romantic novels, only to find disillusionment with the fading of passions and deceptions of a seducer. It all ends in agonising self-destruction.

Gentlemen thinkers produced thoughtful texts to address the anxieties of the age. Some suggested ways to rejuvenate marriages, others reasoned that marriage could prevent crime, and still more, like Monsieur G.H Prudhon, urged husbands to share details of their business affairs with their wives (he also concluded that in the event of adultery, betrayal, drunkenness or theft, husbands were perfectly entitled to kill their wives).

Within decades, though, such moralising was swept away in the hormonal surge of the *fin de siècle*. Suddenly there was the Moulin Rouge, Toulouse-Lautrec, Manet painting lovers by the Seine, green satin and long black gloves. Women wore corsets and petticoats, and took to calling their lovers by the names of animals and vegetables; men wore moustaches, smoked and rode bicycles and struggled to resist their instincts. 'In our contemporary society,' wrote Paul Bourget in *De L'Amour* (1891), 'to have a mistress outside one's marriage is one of the greatest honours to which a man can aspire, and, conversely, for a woman to be possessed by a man outside marriage is the greatest shame that can befall her.'

Men read books on what to expect when undressing a lady and how to achieve it. 'Every man should have a smattering of anatomical knowledge, ingenuity, tact, strength and above all – patience,' wrote Bourget.

Gentlemen were advised to go for society ladies as their mistresses. 'You must take a married woman,' wrote one expert, 'and a well-married woman… who, because of the ideas current in her class, would never dream of obtaining a divorce.' Husbands were so accustomed to having love affairs that some took to pretending their wife was their mistress – one borrowed his friend's bachelor pad to receive his wife, serving her port and petits fours so that he could 'experience all the tingling excitement of adultery'.

Pornography was on the rise. In 1912, police seized '6,000 kg' of obscene books; smutty postcards were all the rage, and naked dancers appeared for the first time in Parisian theatres. Society lived for pleasure, and spending money on pleasure. It was *La Belle Époque*.

After the slaughter of World War I, the French in the 1920s were determined to enjoy the new cosmopolitanism. There were American soldiers, jazz, opium, long cigarette holders, cocktails, the tango, and Coco Chanel's simple designs. Once again, stable, happy marriages were under pressure. One writer suggested a man might have two wives, another recommended human stud farms where young people could go to 'copulate' twice a week.

Not that these ideas led to greater independence for women: they were still denied the vote, barred from professional clubs and faced discrimination in education. However, by the 1930s, a more mature view of love began to take root. The Catholic Church began to see marriage as an institution built on love, not just procreation, and grudgingly acknowledged that men and women should be on the same personal plane. Mutual attraction and character were discreetly placed above rank and dowry. Couples were becoming engaged on the basis of *camaraderie sportive*, and even the idea of free choice took hold. 'The vital significance of love,' wrote the psychologist Dr Lagache, 'is not procreation or physical detumescence but a liberation from mental solitude … Love is the possibility for two people to be themselves.'

* * *

Looking back over history, long periods of happy and faithful French marriages appear thin on the ground. Certainly among the nobility, and often among the middle classes, unions tended to be mercenary and loveless, and sexual adventurism was the norm. Under Napoleon's *Code Civil*, women had the same rights as children, prisoners and lunatics, forbidden to open a bank account until 1960.

But what about attitudes among today's young women? Back at Bar Vavin, I ask Laure and Julie about their parents' backgrounds. Julie's parents are divorced, while Laure's had her when they weren't married. Her father married someone else, had a child and then came back to her mother.

'My father has married *five* times,' groans Julie. 'My mother has married a second time. I'm doing OK about it now. But I don't believe in love for a whole lifetime.'

'When you start in a relationship,' says Laure, 'you feel sacred, but after a while he knows you so well that you don't really care much any more. You try to keep it going, but it doesn't seem natural. You have a kind of a need for other people in order to feel that desire again.'

These are somewhat depressing observations in those so young. But the figures support the reality that in France (doubtless as in other countries), marriage is on the decline, cohabitation and divorce are increasing, while those who do tie the knot do it later. In 1960 there were 7.0 marriages per 1,000 inhabitants; by 2011 it was almost half that. The number of people getting civil unions has soared from just over 6,000 in 1999 to over 72,000 in 2007. By 2010 there were three civil unions to every four marriages. Nicolas Sarkozy was the first divorced president in the Élysée Palace, and the first to get divorced again once he was in.

Infidelity, that stereotype so perfectly captured in the 'Papa and Nicole' ads for Renault, seems engrained in the culture. The French have even dispensed with the 24-hour clock to insert a code into the lexicon: *le cinq à sept* (five o'clock to seven – the optimum time for an illicit tryst). A recent survey by the polling institute IFOP found that 35 per cent of men and 24 per cent of women admitted to being unfaithful.

'Perhaps it's true that infidelity is less shocking,' says Debra Berg, a Paris-based American clinical psychologist who's been working with French couples for 30 years. 'While it's hurtful, there may be a greater ability to proceed and to handle the problem. People may be less paralysed.'

Not only can French men draw on the example of royalty through the ages, they can point to the behaviour of their contemporary rulers. François Mitterand was a legendary seducer with a string of mistresses (his illegitimate daughter, Mazarine Marie Pingeot, dramatically appeared at his graveside during his funeral). Mitterand's wife, Danielle, once said, 'Which woman can say, "I have never been cheated on," or who hasn't cheated herself?' Roland Dumas, a former foreign minister, had an affair with former lingerie model turned lobbyist for the Elf oil company (he was convicted in 2003 of accepting company favours through his mistress). President Giscard d'Estaing was widely rumoured to have had lovers on the side, while the 2006 book *Sexus Politicus* by respected journalists Christophe Deloire and Christophe DuBois claimed that Jacques Chirac came close to divorcing Bernadette for a journalist with *Le Figaro.*

The French media, long censoring themselves over establishment infidelity, are now revealing all. There to oblige them is a new generation of politicians willing to play out their domestic dramas in public. In 2007 the glamorous Socialist candidate Ségolène Royal announced *on election night* that she was kicking her long-time partner, and father of her three children François Hollande, out of the family home (he only had to wait until June 2012 for his revenge: he won the presidential election and strode on stage for his victory address with his new girlfriend, the former *Paris Match* journalist Valérie Trierweiler). By the time Nicolas Sarkozy romanced and married the model Carla Bruni within weeks of his divorce, the private lives of French presidents had become less of a taboo, but the French were no less relaxed about infidelity. Within a year and a half of *his* presidency, François Hollande was (so to speak) at it again, ditching Ms Trierweiler for Julie Gayet, a 41-year-old actress. The president of the Fifth Republic had been photographed arriving for trysts at a Paris appartment by moped; before covering his first news conference after the story broke I canvassed opinions among the lunch-hour crowd on Charles de Gaulle Etoile and couldn't find one who disapproved of his behaviour.

'Are French men unfaithful? Absolutely,' says Jane Lizop, the American writer in Paris. 'Do they still keep a mistress on the side? Well, who can afford that? The French are less apt to make moral judgements. They don't consider it a reason for divorce. My husband was a serial adulterer.

It wasn't pleasant, and I did a lot of thinking about it. I didn't discover it for a long time, and when I did what really bothered me the most was not so much the fact itself but that he was waving it under my nose, almost hoping that I would find out. I never figured it out.'

But what is it that makes French men stray? Is it simply something in the DNA, a psychological deficit that inclines them to want to fall in love, or at least flirt, with every attractive woman they see?

'There isn't the same battle of the sexes,' continues Jane Lizop. 'I wasn't prepared for this *fantasie* – the imagination men use when they are being complimentary. It's not just the line: they appreciate women because they're women. It's neither bullshit nor is it to be taken too seriously – it's just a pleasure in daily life. I was walking along a busy street and crossing a junction when someone jumped a red light and I nearly got run over. I gave them an earful, I can tell you, made a nasty face and probably said something obscene. Two men were walking past and one said to the other, "A pity, such a pretty mouth." But they weren't being insulting or trying to pick me up!'

But for other foreign women living in Paris, French men have not covered themselves in glory. Over at a café on Rue de Seine near Saint-Germain-des-Prés, I meet 21-year-old Alice, an English student from Oxford, and Cassandra, a 25-year-old politics student from the US.

'I was in a bar in Cannes chatting to the bar manager,' recalls Alice. 'A few days later he phoned and asked would I like to go for dinner. I said yes. Halfway through dinner he was saying, "You know, I really like you, I have feelings for you." I was really surprised – I mean, we had only just met – but I said to myself, well, why not?

'As the evening went on it continued, and I told him, I'm only in Cannes for two weeks. But he insisted – "I wish I could make you my girlfriend." On La Croisette [the promenade in Cannes], he kissed me. It was really nice. The next day he called me. "Listen," he said rather dramatically, "it has been great, but I just can't do this any more! I'm still in love with my ex-girlfriend." I couldn't believe it!'

Cassandra says, 'I was in a bistro near where I worked, when the waiter came over and said, "You've been here before." Later he came back and said, "Listen, I think you're very pretty, do you want to do something later?" We went for a drink and he told me about a big break-up he'd had, and I told him I had one too, and we seemed to share the same pain. So we starting going out, and for three weeks he came to my apartment every night (I had a key hidden at the door which he knew how to find). He invited me to hang out with his friends, having lunch. It was so great.

'But then suddenly there was a change. He disappeared. I saw him a few weeks later. He said, "I'm so sorry, I lost my phone." So he gave me his new number and I phoned him for several days, but again no reply. I went back to his bar and they told me he'd quit his job. A few weeks later I bumped into him again, and I asked what had happened. He said, "I'm so sorry, I lost my job, I lost my apartment, but I really miss you, my life is a mess." But he disappeared again. Six months later I was about to leave for New York. I met him in a café. He came over and said to me, "Remember that conversation we had about how we had this big connection because we'd both just broke up? Well, it was actually a lie. I was still living with my girlfriend."

Later, at Restaurant Paul et Gwena in Montmartre, I meet Pierre, a 42-year-old art dealer and single-ish French male, Elaine, an Irish journalist, Vanina, an Egyptian-American writer, and John, an American film producer.

'Sexism is outrageous here,' exclaims Elaine. 'It's either *madame*, or *mademoiselle*, in the bank, on the street, at work. So you're either married or you're a young lady. If in reality you're neither, you don't officially exist. French men are such idiots! They do everything for themselves. They had their revolution in 1968, but they didn't think to pass it on to their children. We all like to be told we're gorgeous, *charmant*. It's not unpleasant, but it's more like, aren't you really lucky that *I* find you gorgeous?'

'They don't have the dating thing here,' says a somewhat perplexed John, the film producer. 'In America there is a kind of puritanical side to dating, a courtship thing, a general code which means by the third date you at least kiss.'

'Oh, come *on*! The French girls walk around with a toothbrush in their handbag,' interrupts Pierre.

John persists: 'In France a man feels more like he's leading the dance. American women are more direct, more like a guy. But in France you have to keep *re*-seducing them.'

'*Court après moi que je t'attrape,*' says Vanina. (Chase me so I can catch you.)

'I went to the bank for an appointment and the man was 20 minutes late and smelling of smoke,' recalls Vanina. 'I could tell that if I was going to get what I wanted, I was going to have to flirt, but I was so pissed off I didn't want to. There is this pressure to behave like the flirty woman: this is the dance and it's all to grease the wheels. But I just want what I'm after because I'm asking politely and I am a customer. It feels like a dog-and-pony show. It makes me very wary of romantic relationships.'

We continue the discussion until there is finally agreement on one thing. The reason French men cannot avoid the banana skins of passing beauty is that, well, they simple *can't*. Eight centuries of having it all their way have taken their toll.

'In America the attitude is very different,' says Pierre, the art dealer. 'You date lots of people till you meet *the one*, then you marry *the one*, then you have children with *the one* and stay together for the rest of your life with… *the one*.

'In France that sounds like *death*! OK, you meet someone, you marry them, you build a life, you have a family, but your romantic life doesn't necessarily end there. You can fall in love during a Metro ride! Just because you cheat, it doesn't mean you destroy the life you've built with your wife.'

But no one can have epitomised the fatal nexus between power and lust – and have single-handedly given a Viagra-like jolt to a drooping French stereotype – as much as Dominique Strauss-Kahn. In May 2011, at the height of the euro crisis, and when his position as head of the IMF was key to restoring confidence, he was arrested on board a transatlantic jet and charged with the sexual assault of chambermaid Nafissatou Diallo in a New York hotel. Prosecutors later dropped the charges due to the unreliability of the witness, but further accusations emerged of a long history of sexual impropriety, including his alleged involvement in a prostitution ring in northern France relating to a network of businessmen who participated in so-called *libertin* parties with an entrance fee of €10,000.

It was, wrote the *New York Times*, a throwback to the 16th-century tradition of *libertinage*: 'a clandestine lifestyle in certain powerful circles of French society – secret soirées with lawyers, judges, notaries, police officials, journalists and musicians, that start with a fine meal and end with naked guests and public sex with multiple partners.'

Strauss-Kahn's defence was that he didn't know the women were prostitutes since everyone was nude.

* * *

From Bergerac Airport along the Dordogne Valley you drive through some of oldest vineyards in France. Although we're in Bergerac country, the *terroir* here is the same as the Bordeaux appellation, and the locals claim it's older. It was in 1137 that Eleanor of Aquitaine (she who developed the *amour courtois*), at the age of 15, married Henry, Duke of the Normans, becoming Queen of England. The new English administrators put a toll on river boats coming from Bergerac, thus restricting the wine trade in favour of Bordeaux, but in fact Bordeaux wines were improved using Bergerac grapes.

Turning left at Saussignac through fields braided with vines, I approach a hilltop vineyard, Château Haut Garrigue. The estate, dating back to 1737, was originally a lookout post for the nearby château, but these days a cheerful Irish-South African couple, Sean and Caroline Feely, run the 14-hectare vineyard. 'Each vine I'm getting to know,' says Sean on a shady terrace overlooking a field of vines slopping off towards the river. 'Some are as thick as trees. The first year I went at them like a madman.'

Sean and Caroline's journey to Haut Garrigue has been unorthodox. They were both born in South Africa, and moved to Capetown when they met (she was working for IBM and he was a financial journalist). Both had Irish roots: Caroline's grandmother was a French (or Ffrench), one of the Galway tribes, while Sean's grandfather had been a Wexford bank manager who emigrated to the Stellenbosch region to teach but ending up buying into a cooperative vineyard. Wine was, so to speak, in the blood.

Sean's grandmother had left money with the stipulation that it be used to 'get the family home'. When Caroline got a posting to IBM's Irish operation, the wish was granted. Sean got a job with Bank of Ireland's investment arm during the boom and his knowledge of wine qualified him as the unofficial scout for corporate functions. Meanwhile, Caroline set up a consulting firm with two friends, doing night classes in wine and French. They travelled to France at every opportunity to buy or explore wine, finally thinking about getting their own vineyard in 2003.

'The wine business is so difficult, and you can't get a mortgage,' says Sean. 'But they will give you 30 per cent of the value of the property and two full years' running costs. We settled here because we were looking for a vineyard which had the noble grape varietals, a good mix of old and new vines, an historic location, and enough space for a *gîte*. We wanted one where the vines were contiguous to the property – we didn't want to swap one commute on the M50 for another. It was a knock-down price when we bought it. It was such a mess, though. We sold the house in Killiney, and here we are.'

The link between Ireland and wine production is closer than you might think. Sir Walter Raleigh, a one-time mayor of Youghal, landed 1,000 tons of Spanish and Canary Island wines a year in Cork. In the 1700s, Irish merchants, who were able to stave off the worst effects of the Penal Laws, were greater importers of Bordeaux wines than the British. At the end of the Williamite Wars thousands of Irish families loyal to King James followed him in exile to France. Many ended up in Bordeaux, and several hundred entered the wine business – names like Lynch (who had fought at the Battle of the Boyne), MacCarthy, Dillon, Phelan, Hennessy and Barton (of Barton & Guestier fame). Today, Bordeaux has 14 *châteaux*, 10 streets and two wine communes with Irish names (Château Lynch-Bages, Château Phélan-Ségur, Château Pichon-Longueville Comtesse de Lalande, Château Langoa-Barton). The first bottle factory in Bordeaux was built by an Irishman named Mitchell.

Sean and Caroline threw themselves into the vines: 60-year-old Semillon vines which were 'in great shape', 40-year-old Cabernet Sauvignon parcels which needed to be grubbed up, seven-year-old Sauvignon Blanc vines, and wiry Merlot vines rolling off towards the Dordogne Valley. 'It can take between 50 and 100 years to plant vines,' says Sean. 'If you look after them properly, they last a long time, so it's so important which vines you chose, which clone, what varietal.'

But they chose their wine to be organic, so the workload and the constraints on production were mammoth. Not just organic, but *biodynamic*. This could be described as organic plus, or homeopathy for the vineyard. 'We use the biodynamic calendar to plant and harvest,' Caroline explains. 'If you trim or prune vines when the moon is on the rise, you make use of the moon drawing up the sap, and that forms a natural congealing effect around the cut.'

The philosophy also governs composts and sprays. Organic farming can use copper and sulphate sprays to prevent fungal disease, but biodynamic farming goes a step further. 'There are teas made from horsetail – a kind of weed that is very rich in silica. That provides a heat barrier which prevents fungus,' says Caroline. 'Copper, by contrast, creates toxicity in the soil: we only use three kilos compared to an average of eight by our neighbours.'

The work load was a shock. 'The most important thing is the pruning, and you have to prune by hand,' says Sean. 'The level of the pruning determines the quality of the fruit, and you have to factor in the health of the vine. If it's in good condition you'll get 10 buds, if it's tired you might get two. Suddenly I was facing 30,000 vines I had to prune by hand on my own between December and February.

'Then you need to start trellising, tying canes down to the trellis in the spring. That's big work. Then the first fungal treatment starts during April. There are seven treatments starting at 5 a.m. and you can be out all day, weeding, ploughing and doing the biodynamic preparation.'

As a result Haut Garrigue produces only 25,000 bottles a year – around one bottle per vine – while the average vineyard produces 100,000. 'The higher the yield, the lower the quality. We prune very hard, concentrating into fewer batches. It's the same for treating the vines. Conventional growers use 300 different types of fungicides and herbicides, but they strip away the adventitious shoots on the trunk of the vine, so we do it by hand. You don't do organic farming for financial gain.'

Nor do you tackle one of the pillars of French culture lightly. The Feelys' wine story is a useful prism through which we can examine the peculiarities of the French system. Whereas the Anglo-Saxon model is about cutting taxes, reducing red tape, rewarding hard work and rendering welfare benefits an unattractive last resort, the French social model is about high taxes, strong state intervention and comfortable social benefits with the emphasis on a state-guaranteed quality of life. In France, the state, État, is a binding principle, the sole source of legitimate power, not just an administration collecting taxes and organising services. 'In the Anglo-American value system,' write Jean-Benoît Nadeau and Julie Barlow, 'the state is like a back-up. It exists to guarantee individual liberties and to ensure that individuals can reach their full potential. But the French État does a lot more than that. It defines culture and language, runs the economy, dispenses welfare and charity, redistributes wealth, levels differences and defines and defends the common good. It's the skeleton of French society.'

It means the public believes in the state, even if they hate the government, and it also means that France is extremely centralised, relying on five *million* civil servants, nearly one-quarter of the workforce. And it also means high taxes. In 2006, taxes on the average worker represented 50.2 per cent of labour costs; in Ireland, it was only 23 per cent. Public projects can be railroaded through quickly since a government minister takes personal responsibility, knowing he'll be fired if it's not done on time. The system can thus be ruthlessly efficient, and maddeningly interfering.

'When we arrived,' recalls Sean, 'I went to the Chamber of Agriculture. It's run by an army of technicians, analysts and practical people. The head of the wine growers' section met me in his office. He had a classic Chirac face, a long chin. It hit the table three times. He asked me if I had any experience with vines. I said, yes, we had two vines in the back garden in Dublin. He nearly slid out of his chair. He was astounded, but he immediately offered assistance. He has five to six advisors. One lady came out to the house to give advice (there are five to six free visits before you start paying). She came through the first season and the fees were refunded by the French government. They were always very encouraging.'

That was the positive start. Then they tried to hire an extra worker. 'Nothing prepared me for it,' Sean recalls. 'I was keen to do it. I didn't necessarily know how to run a vineyard, but I had a certain familiarity with it. I remember the first day looking at the vines; it was just a jungle of canes. I realised I was in trouble. I called up a neighbour and he came around and we had a great afternoon, and I started to get the hang of it. But I needed another worker.'

The moment you employ someone in France, the state is ready to pounce. If you take on someone at twice the minimum wage – €2,400 per month – you have to pay nearly half that again in social-security contributions, while the employee pays 22 per cent in the same contributions on top of tax. Six and a half per cent goes to the pension fund, 2.4 per cent to the unemployment fund and 5.1 per cent to the social-security fund. All told, a pay slip has 40 itemised deductions.

French unemployment rates are high because it is so burdensome to take on workers (I was once told by the boss of a print company in Paris that it would be easier to set up a new company altogether than to add one worker to the 12 staff he already had).

The next stumbling block was the Mutualité Sociale Agricole (MSA), a kind of farmers' union and social welfare department rolled into one. It provides benefits, training and tax rebates to young farmers, but it also has a surveillance role to prevent farmers from selling on produce (a lamb here, a few eggs there) they haven't declared, and it zealously scours the countryside for undeclared manual workers.

'During the Cold War, France had a huge army of spies,' says Sean. 'When it ended, they all were put in the MSA. Around here, during the plum harvest, a lot of Moroccans are employed. It's perfectly legal. There's one farmer who had five Moroccans working for him, but only two spoke French. The MSA arrived and interrogated everyone. The Moroccans were all shaken up, and that night three of them disappeared even though they were legally employed. They could only bring in half the plum harvest. One neighbour not far from here shot two MSA workers dead and tried to turn the gun on himself.'

Sean believes that the punitive costs of taking on extra staff has put wine producers under enormous strain. 'Five *vignerons* have died within 5 kilometres of here. They were all accidents. But if you can't employ anyone, and you need an incredible amount of safety equipment. and if you pay for it, you'll have no money left, so people cut corners. One guy fell off his ladder. Another guy was asphyxiated by CO2 from wine vats underground. His son jumped in to try to save him and he died as well. Another died in a tractor accident.'

If these obstacles weren't bad enough, France has been undergoing a backlash against alcohol. In 1991, the loi Évin, named after a French minister, set down strict new rules on alcohol advertising, and the state-funded National Association against Alcohol and Addiction (AANPE), began chasing drinks companies for any infringement of the new law. Alcohol promotion is now forbidden on TV, even for broadcasts covering events outside France. During the Rugby World Cup, Heineken was ordered to take down 250 banners in Paris that were related to the tournament (in France the annual Heineken Cup is referred to as the

H Cup). The brewer had already been ordered to shut down its French internet site: the judge ruled that since the internet wasn't on the list of approved outlets for alcohol advertising in 1991 (when the internet as we know it didn't exist), then the website was technically illegal.

When Liverpool played Marseilles in the Champions League in September 2008, they had to drop the Carlsberg logo from their shirts. A ruling in 2004 declared that even the *mention* of an alcohol brand could be deemed advertising. A newspaper was taken to court because an article about Champagne had 'painted alcohol in a favourable light'. The situation has left wine producers in limbo, because following the Heineken case, they have to assume they cannot carry out promotional activity on their French websites, even though *selling* French wine on the internet is legal. The French are even banned from browsing the Orlando Wines site in South Australia, because they are owned by Pernod-Ricard. The site does, however, welcome visitors from Kuwait and the United Arab Emirates.

There's been a massive cultural rethink of alcohol. Between 2000 and 2005, wine consumption fell from 16 litres per person per year to 11 litres, with the figure falling to 8.4 litres by 2011. America, at 140 million litres a year, now produces more wine than France, at 130 million, while in Britain, consumers prefer Australian wine first, American second and French wine third. Many cooperatives producing table wine have gone under due to overproduction. The EU has been encouraging French producers to 'grub up' their vineyards to reduce the growing lake of mediocre wine in the hope that an improvement in quality will help the sector stave off competition.

'For lots of producers it's impossible,' says Sean. 'Many are in their fifties and want a retirement fund, but because of the restrictions they're not getting the sales. They're not equipped to export, don't speak English. There are reforms but they're just putting new rules on top of old rules. There are rules on the width and the height of foliage – these are just nitpicking and irrelevant. Do you think the Australians and Californians give a shit?'

But Sean and Caroline are staying put despite the travails of organic farming, the heart-stopping bureaucracy and the very French style of customer relations.

'The arrogance is an attitude: it's the way they arm themselves,' says Caroline. 'There's no concept of the customer being king. We pay €20,000 a year to an agriculture supplies company. Once we bought a product which didn't work and told them it needed to be sent back to the wholesaler. They said no, we can't be held responsible. You need to deal with the supplier yourselves. He started giving me hell, there was smoke everywhere. It was like he didn't want me as a customer. I said, I'm spending €20,000 a year with you and you're shouting at me about €100 worth of stuff. And he's the owner!

'The concept of the métier – you work hard as a mechanic, a waiter – they take very seriously. A mechanic can treat you like dirt. The first year I felt like a grub. I didn't know how anything worked. But now they're friendly and they're respectful as long as you respect the work they've done. But the arrogance is definitely there – it's an aloofness, like they want to lord it over you. Neighbours keep you at an arm's distance for ages, but slowly you'll be accepted.'

But the rewards are coming. Their Sauvignon Blanc 2006 was rated in the top restaurant in the Dordogne, La Tour Des Ventes in Montbazillac. 'It's been a big hit. The *terroir* is so ideally suited, you get natural aromas and bouquet, great concentration. There's an interesting limey edge from the main fossil rock below,' says Sean. (I take his word for it.)

There's been a melting, too, in relations with the locals, says Caroline. 'They're very welcoming, extremely supportive. There's a real brotherhood, especially around the *vindages* [grape-picking season]. We're all in it together.'

* * *

It's a common axiom that the French are incapable of gradual change. When change does come, it comes through revolution (1789, 1848, 1968). 'There's a huge capacity for innovation, but it's always through pain,' says Sonia Meilke, an Irish woman who's currently head of marketing for BT France. 'It's like childbirth.'

If people in power push too hard for change, those who oppose it can bring the country to a standstill. The truculent farmer blocking British traffic; the air-traffic controller ruining European flight schedules;

the students marching against a rule that might require them to change jobs a few times after college – all have fed into a stereotypical image of lazy French malcontents mired in a social time warp.

Politicians promising change use the most grandiose language, but the promises usually fall flat on implementation. Nicolas Sarkozy ran an entire campaign on the grand idea of a *rupture* – a dramatic breaking with the past. He promised to tackle the entrenched attitudes hamstringing French enterprise, but he really only tinkered with the system. François Hollande promised to combine economic growth with labour-market reform when he came to power in 2012, but amid plummeting ratings he has been lambasted by the right and the left – not to mention the IMF and the European Commission – for his inability to get the French economy going. At the same time France has fallen badly behind Germany in terms of competitiveness and job growth, and this has thrown a spanner into the long-trusted Franco-German motor that used to rev into gear when the European project needed a push.

The France of cafés, Gauloises, accordions, berets, baguettes and red wine is still around, meanwhile, but the symbols have quietly undergone painful change. The wine industry is cowering under the new abstinence and appears alienated from the political establishment. Starbucks challenged French café culture in 2003, and by 2012 had established 63 outlets nationwide (consumers, though, have bloody-mindedly refused to adapt to the takeaway-coffee culture and the company has struggled to turn a profit in France). A survey by the Gira Conseil consultancy in May 2013, meanwhile, found that fast-food chains account for 54 per cent of all restaurant sales, with McDonalds operating 1,200 outlets across the country and even Burger King making a re-entry into the market. Gauloises are owned by the British company Imperial Tobacco and are more likely to be smoked in the Middle East than in France, where a successful smoking ban came into force on 1 January 2008. The French have even improved their driving habits: a radical zero-tolerance attitude introduced by President Chirac saw road deaths fall by half between 2001 and 2011 (8,162 to 3,963). The famous French beret, as worn by Picasso and Jean-Paul Sartre, originates in the city of Pau in the Pyrenees and was originally a Basque headgear. There are only three factories left making berets, and one-third of production goes to the French army.

As for the baguette, it underwent a major decline over three centuries, and it is only now that high-quality, artisanal bread is enjoying a revival. The peasants of revolutionary France ate on average 900 grams of bread a day – nearly a kilo. By the middle of the 19th century it was 700 grams, but a century later the French were eating on average just 320 grams per day, and by 1993 the figure slumped to an all-time low of 150 grams. Today there's been a slight rise, but it's still an historically low 165 grams. In the 30 years up to 1983, the decline in consumption triggered the loss of 10,000 artisanal bakeries.

Even Paris is waking up to the service culture. The widely admired mayor Bertrand Delanoë, has been encouraging waiters, bus drivers, shop assistants and hoteliers to smile more, to speak English if possible and generally be nicer to tourists, who account for 12 per cent of all jobs in the capital.

It may well be that if we factor in the distinctive public-private codes, the ritual of acknowledging whose space you're in, the lack of tipping, the years spent learning the trade and perhaps even all those French vowels that hang around the front of the mouth and force the lips forward, then perhaps French waiters are not actually that rude after all, and that if you're nice to them, they'll be nice back. Of the 15.3 million visitors who visited Paris in 2006, some 97 per cent of them say they want to come back.

Let's return to Fabien, the student waiter from the poor suburbs we met at the École Médéric. If he is the future of French cuisine, then the profession will open itself to the world, and to good manners. 'My ambition is to travel a lot, learn English in Australia, and then to go an Hispanic country to learn Spanish – no problem – and after, if I have a lot of money, open a restaurant in Paris,' he says brightly. 'We rest on our laurels. I know it's a problem. If we see a Japanese person we know he's not coming back. We won't make the same effort we would do with Jean Reno [the French actor] or Zizou [Zidane]. We need to change that.'

And finally, a word about hair.

Do French women have hairy armpits? The cliché has titillated Anglo-Saxon males for an aeon. It's time to put the record straight.

Today a stroll around Paris reveals a growing number of beauty salons, all offering, for a much cheaper price than in the UK or Ireland, a range of épilations. For the purposes of this investigation, épilation is a useful word: it refers in general to hair removal from all parts of the French body, but it allows us to discuss the subject without being too area-specific.

The French, and a growing number of 15–25-year-olds in particular, take body hair very seriously. According to a 2006 survey by the polling institute IPSOS, the vast majority of French people regard being épilée – that is, literally, hairless – as a very important thing. Among women, 77 per cent think it's important in order to be physically *séduisante* (let's say that means attractive), while 74 per cent of men feel the same (about women, that is). Forty-one per cent of women relate it to beauty, 19 per cent relate it to health, while exactly half the male population regard hairlessness as a *beautiful* thing (57 per cent of French men over 35 would *strongly disapprove* if their ladies stopped removing hair).

But French women are also turning against hair on men. Sixty-seven per cent of women would like their men to be *un peu poilu* – a little hairy, but not too much. Forty-five per cent find men who are too hairy 'repulsive', 44 per cent find it 'ugly', while 20 per cent found it 'dirty'. In fact, 55 per cent said they would ask their men to undergo some épilation if they were too hairy (only 5 per cent have actually done it).

It's clearly affecting the young male population: one English student told me the *first three* French men she'd slept with in her three months in France were 'completely hairless'. (This perhaps tells us as much about the English as the French.)

The majority of women over 25 spend an average of one hour and 20 minutes a month shaving, while (paradoxically, I would have thought) 15–25-year-olds spend longer: two and a half hours in total. Most French women regard it is an opportunity to 'look after themselves'. Eighty-three per cent feel the occasion allows them to tend to their bodies, their beauty, even to look after 'other little cares'. (How sweet.)

But then, the killer statistic. Of the 83 per cent of women who remove hair regularly, *three-quarters* of them (73 per cent) also tackle the armpits.

Whatever way you do the math, we can finally put that stereotype to bed. For younger women, armpit hair has figuratively gone to Madame Guillotine altogether. Among 15–25-year-olds, a staggering 89 per cent remove armpit hair. (Just so you know, 82 per cent remove leg hair, 73 per cent sort out the bikini area, and a surprising 19 per cent are done with arm hair.) Finally, the attitude to this very un-French hair-removal business is, nonetheless, expressed in a very French way. Some 81 per cent of women feel 'sweet and light' (*douce* et *légère*) after an épilation, while 65 per cent say they feel more confident.

Whatever about baguettes and berets, wine and Gauloises, Roquefort and rude waiters, lovers and seducers, it appears that the humble human follicle is on the decline in France. French women finally believe they're worth it.

Chapter 3

Spain

May God protect you. One of the Two Spains will freeze your heart.
Poet Antonio Machado's greeting to newborn Spaniards

Francisco Rivera Ordóñez stares down the length of a murderous blade as it runs away from his face. Gripping the *estoque* just below the pommel on its hilt, the right wrist cocked so the sword is taut and horizontal, he presses his elbow into the ribcage. His shoulders are hunched, his neck and head strain forward. He's almost certainly squinting.

The left arm, levered gently away from the torso, grips the grooved handle of a large crimson cape, the *muleta*, which is spread across his waist like an oversized apron. His legs are rigid, and the entire posture is painfully, even comically, concentrated. On his calves are silk stockings, shockingly white against the gold-brocaded suit of deepest purple above. Opposite, staring back in a state of angry bewilderment, stands a 500-kilo Iberian bull. The bull is badly injured but still capable of killing. Everything that has gone before is now telescoped into this chink in the cosmos where the living and the soon to be dead are drawn together in a moment of exquisite intimacy. To Spaniards, it is *momento de la verdad*. The moment of truth.

* * *

It's the night before. Plaza del Socorro is heaving. Teenage girls dance to *Aserejé* (otherwise known as the Ketchup Song) in tight T-shirts covered in the amorous scrawlings of young boys already delirious on sangria and mojitos. *Sevillianas* music pumps from speakers suspended over *casetas*, the impromptu street bars set up with wooden tables and beer taps. La Reyenda Taperia is showing super-8 footage of bullfights from 1964, while Calle Lorenzo Borrego Gomez is a solid mass of drinking and dancing.

I'm in Ronda, a mountain settlement perched on an Andalusia plateau. Over the millennia the Rio Guadalevín has split the plateau in two, creating El Tajo, a vertiginous canyon. Looking down from the safe heights of the Puente Nueva bridge – towering 120 metres above the floor – one can watch birds flying in the canyon below. But it's a stomach-wrenching sight, so the gaze is averted west over olive groves and vineyards, beyond to a gently sloping plain, and, finally in the blue distance past tree-lined ridges, the gaze rests on a jagged, milky-black mountain range whose crenellated peaks are picked out by hard shafts of dying sunlight. Despite the festivities in the town, the panorama is one of melancholy and foreboding.

With the arrival of the Moors in the 8th century, Ronda became an important staging post between the future Emirate of Córdoba to the north and North Africa to the south. By the 15th century, it was still an Arab fortress, but subject to increasing Christian attacks. With the accession of the Catholic monarchs Isabella of Castile and Ferdinand of Aragon, the Moors were swept out of Ronda on 22 May 1485, but both Muslim and Christian history are burned deep into the architecture: the mosques and churches, the palaces, towers and gardens, gateways and minarets, the Arab baths and royal fountains. Ronda is a lavish slice of schizophrenic Spain.

Ronda made a big impression on Ernest Hemingway. In *For Whom the Bell Tolls*, the Nationalist sympathisers thrown from towering cliffs by Republicans in a Castilian village are supposedly based on real events that happened here during the Civil War. The main draw, though, was bullfighting. Hemingway lived here with Antonio Ordóñez, the legendary matador, before they travelled across Spain so the writer could learn the intricacies of the taurine art. Ordóñez's rivalry with Luis Miguel Dominguín in 1959 provided the material for *The Dangerous Summer*, in which Hemingway described the Shakespearian confrontation between the two men – one a flamboyant newcomer, the other emerging from retirement. Hemingway considered it the greatest bullfight he had ever seen.

Despite his gory descriptions, Hemingway was also capable of capturing Ronda's comforts in *Death in the Afternoon*, his meditation on bullfighting. 'The entire town and as far as you can see in any direction is romantic background, and there is a hotel there that is so comfortable, so well run and where you can eat so well and usually have a cool breeze at night that, with the romantic background and the modern comfort, if a honeymoon or elopement is not a success in Ronda it would be as well to start for Paris and both commence making your own friends.'

Hemingway recommended Ronda over anywhere else in Andalusia for witnessing a bullfight. Whether one abhors or adores it, bullfighting remains the primal image of Spain, suffused as it is with the supposed vices and virtues of the Spaniards: bravery, death, cruelty, and, above all, *honour*. Hemingway was fixated with elemental male impulses and he saw honour as the most enduring. 'Honour to a Spaniard, no matter how dishonest, is as real a thing as water, wine or olive oil. There is honour among pickpockets and honour among whores. It is simply the standards that differ.'

Bullfighting is also embedded in the perpetual debate over what is Spain and what is Spanishness. It is a sport (art form, say its followers) that cleaves the country into those who want to keep Spain together, and those regions agitating for ever-greater independence.

I'd caught glimpses of the sport on Spanish television over the years, but could never bring myself to endure the strutting and blood and exhaustion before the animal was dispatched. Like many urban Europeans, I couldn't understand how it could be tolerated in the modern age. The slow death of a bull before cheering crowds – families – was redolent of ancient Rome.

Ronda has been the cradle of bullfighting ever since King Philip II created the Real Maestranza de Caballería (the Royal Calvary Order) there in 1572. The order taught noblemen how to spear bulls from horseback. In fact, the original *torero* was the commoner in front of the bull distracting it before the nobleman killed it from his horse. In the 18th century, the Ronda matador Francisco Romero popularised bullfighting on foot, instead of horseback, and it was his grandson, Pedro Romero Martínez, who became bullfighting's first legend. Pedro Romero spent a lifetime killing bulls, 6,000 in all, introducing the aesthetics which turned it into an art form. Its popularity soon spread among the nobility, while the court painter-in-chief, Francisco Goya, captured it on canvas, and went on to design the *traje de luces* (suit of lights) for Romero's biggest fights. Ernest Hemingway, forever on a quest for true virility, alluded to Pedro Romero in *The Sun Also Rises* as the representation of the perfect male.

It was Hemingway's mentor, Antonio Ordóñez, who suggested in the 1950s that a festival be held to commemorate Pedro Romero's legacy and thus was born the *Feria Goyesca* (Goya-esque Festival). For the very first festival, Antonio Ordóñez wore a *traje de luces* designed by one Pablo Picasso. Today, at the start of every September, the youth of Ronda gild themselves in very expensive period costumes and parade to the bullring in 200-year-old carriages, bathed in the adulation of celebrities, royalty and commoners alike.

This year the Feria would be headlined by Cayetano Rivera Ordóñez, the 31-year-old scion of Spain's most illustrious bullfighting dynasty, whose story is an irresistible blend of tragedy, style and celebrity. His grandfather was *the* Antonio Ordóñez; his father, Paquirri, was killed during a bullfight near Córdoba. He himself had become a high-grade celebrity and, through his modelling work, a style icon (he was also briefly married to a Spanish model). In a frisson of nostalgia, Cayetano asked Giorgio Armani to follow in the footsteps of Picasso (and Goya) and design his suit for the occasion. It was a case of mutual admiration. 'Cayetano has that quiet, sophisticated elegance,' Armani told *Men's Vogue*. 'You immediately sense a man who combines great strength and poise with humility and sensitivity.' Unfortunately, the €70,000 suit, a blend of Goya and bling, with tight-fitting velvet studded with sequins and Swarovski crystals, sent the Italian animal-rights lobby into paroxysms of rage (they had a point: Armani had just sponsored a TV ad campaign urging pet owners not to dump their cats or dogs on the roadside as they headed off for summer holidays).

The protesters had the last laugh. Four days before the fight, Cayetano was gored in Valencia and taken to intensive care in Madrid. The bull did serious damage to his liver, but the fighter survived. The Armani suit was untouched – Cayetano had been saving it for Ronda. As people gather, there is disappointment that he won't be performing, but his brother Francisco is already on the bill.

The night before the festival's climax, I meet Armando Gil, a former bullfighter and now a teacher, in Bar Hermanos Macías. Portraits of Antonio Ordóñez adorn the walls, but there are also pictures of the Hollywood glitterati who followed Hemingway to Ronda. The most illustrious was Orson Welles, who became a close friend of Ordóñez. Today his ashes remain in an old well at the Ordóñez homestead outside Ronda.

'Ronda is the birthplace of the orthodox school,' explains Armando. 'Seville might be more spectacular; here it's more technical, more pure. Elsewhere, if the bullfighter is no good, there are boos and people call names. Here there is silence. It's an honour for fighters to come to Ronda.'

There are around 40 professional fighters in Spain. Perhaps a thousand go forward for training each year, but only a handful make the grade. The ones who do can become very wealthy and very famous, depending on their style. The five *toreros* on tomorrow's bill (there are normally six, but Cayetano is still in intensive care) will be paid around €50,000 each. The current superhero is José Tomás: when fighting in Madrid, his purse can reach €400,000.

Armando is, naturally, quick to defend bullfighting. The Iberian bull – roaming on the Spanish plains since Roman times – is only bred for fighting, he says. If you ban it the breed will disappear, since it's too fearsome to keep as a farm animal. They roam on 360,000 hectares of land, which in turn is host to a range of wildlife. 'They live good lives,' he concludes. 'Much better than farm animals.'

We steal through Ronda's high-end hotels and restaurants – the Parador, the Reina Victoria and the Montelirio – in search of a breeder, or even one of the fighters. We're politely declined at each turn. 'Some of the fighters come for breakfast early at Hermanos's place,' says Armando. 'Get there at 9 a.m. and you might meet some.'

* * *

At 9 a.m. there are no bullfighters at Hermanos's place. I settle for a *café con leche* and Serrano *jamon* on buns of floury white bread. Already there are gusts of excitement and debate blowing through the cafés and bars. I'm still vaguely appalled that all of this is happening just so that grown men can kill animals for entertainment. By the sandstone corals at the rear of the bullring, I meet Antonio Montilla, the bullfighting correspondent for *Diario Sur,* Málaga newspaper. He leads me through a wooden gate and into a cobbled courtyard, before climbing a staircase to a square walkway from where we can look down into *corales.* A dozen bulls glower up. Dusted with sand, their chestnut hides heave in a collective mood of black irritation. In the air is the thickness you get before a street fight. 'They should provoke respect and fear,' says Antonio. 'They're strong, athletic, muscular.'

There is a flurry of excitement among the aficionados and officials. Francisco Rivera Ordóñez, Cayetano's younger brother and grandson of Antonio Ordóñez, has just appeared. Dressed in casual designer elegance, he has the centre-of-attention gait of a David Beckham arriving at the training ground. A documentary crew swivels and ducks in fawning motions as he glides around the walkway. Before he leaves I introduce myself, and in smooth, accented English he agrees to talk to me later.

Francisco's arrival here is one of the first rituals of many. Bullfighting is a religion, with its own liturgies and sacraments. He meets his team and officials in the courtyard. They gather in a huddle, talking rapidly. It looks as if they are scrawling something on cigarette papers, with each paper then rolled up and dropped into a sombrero, on which is placed the bullfighting rule book. There is a solemn hush, broken by whispered prayers and signs of the cross.

I have not the faintest clue what's happening.

The book is lifted off and the cigarette papers unrolled. There is much shouting and animation and the group disperses. Francisco goes back up to the walkway over the pen and I follow. Above is a commotion of hurried negotiation and gesticulation. Francisco approaches. 'You must leave.'

Back in the courtyard, Antonio explains what's happening. Each contestant will fight twice, so the animals are paired off to combine a more aggressive-looking beast with a docile one in order to make the contest as fair as possible (for the fighters, that is). The pairs are drawn from the hat so each fighter knows which bulls he will confront a few hours later. Far from this being a local or recent tradition, Hemingway describes the exact same ritual in 1939 in *Death in the Afternoon.*

The bulls are then separated into individual pens, where they will remain until the fight. It's done slowly so as not to frighten them – and to prevent them from attacking each other. From where I'm standing, it doesn't sound like a gentle canter. These are tightly wound coils of aggression, 500 kilos of bad-tempered muscle. From behind the walls there are shouts and bellows, a general alarum through which hide crunches against wall and rump thuds against timber. Something isn't right. As the dust and roars rise above the *corales*, I'm reminded of the scene in *Jurassic Park* where the dinosaur, about to munch the live goat, is unseen, but is quite capably represented by the furious lashing of foliage. I later discover that one of the bulls was attacked by two others and killed.

Bulls have sophisticated memories. During training, matadors must work with females since the young bulls will remember them later. Once in the ring, a fighter recognised by a bull will be at a frightening disadvantage.

Francisco Rivera Ordóñez reappears and we have a conversation. He grew up in Ronda and Seville, although he was born in Madrid. He's now 32, at the peak of his craft, and the apex of the bullfighting aristocracy. His first wife is the eleventh Duchess of Montoro (full name María Eugenia Brianda Timotea Cecilia Martínez de Irujo y Fitz-James Stuart). Although the couple divorced in 2002, Francisco maintains a good relationship with his former mother-in-law, the Duchess of Alba, Cayetana Fitz-James Stuart (so broad are her estates that it is said she can traverse the country from north to south without leaving her land). Her children, however, have publicly denounced through the glossies her own desire to marry a man 24 years her junior (she's 82). Later she will be chauffeur-driven to the bullring, the crowd (clearly relaxed about her nuptial plans) surging forward to shake her hand through the backseat window. Francisco, meanwhile, is currently dating his ex-wife's cousin.

First I ask about his brother.

'He's doing OK,' he says, 'getting better every day.'

Does the goring of Cayetano affect him?

'I'm nervous, nervous … more nervous. Scared, worried about everything, because it's a very special day for me. I'm worried that the fighters have good bulls. I feel so sad about it, when I think of my brother. I'm going to miss him a lot today, but when I'm in the ring I'll try to have fun and feel this moment.'

With that, his entourage, and the documentary crew, sweep him along and away, out through the timber gates of the *corales*. The rest of his afternoon will be devoted to more ritual. There is a chapel next to the *plaza de toros* where fighters pray before the contest. Francisco will eat a very light lunch – perhaps just fluids – so that if he's injured his stomach will be empty. Some fighters are so consumed by nerves before the fight they occasionally use the large red cape (*muleta*) as a shield behind which they might throw up what little remains inside.

I meet Antonio Hidalgo Pérez, at 68 the most famous *aficionado*, or supporter, in Spain. He proudly shows a picture of himself with Luis Miguel Dominguín and Antonio Ordóñez, the rivals immortalised by Hemingway, taken in Málaga in the 1950s. Followers of *la corrida* are impetuous, passionate, spoiled and cantankerous, making imperious demands on both man and bull.

'It's the national culture of this country,' says Antonio, slapping the back of his right hand into the creviced palm of his left. 'It's a deep tradition for Spain. The animal is specifically raised for this moment. The bull has the opportunity to fight for its life and can even save its life. The man puts *his* life at risk and so does the animal and there are two doors: the Great one and the hospital. It's a fight to the death for the animal and the bullfighter.'

This is an argument I hear a lot as I move through the crowds. On Plaza España, a handful of government ministers amble across the square through the crowds, enjoying the attentions of the paparazzi (no qualms here about patronising a blood sport). On Carrera Espinel, people gather outside the Churreria Taperia while hawkers sell fans, baseball caps, Stetsons and sombreros, roasted almonds and fake Marlboro cigarettes. The cafés are filled with casual spectators, locals and aficionados who've travelled from around Andalusia; many paid for their tickets a year in advance. They're working their way through *morcilla de Burgos* (black pudding with rice), *gambas* (giant prawn), *croquettes, jamón de bellota, chorizo Serrano, puntillitas fritas* (fried baby squid), *boquerones fritos* (fried whitebait) and *morcilla de cebolla* (black pudding with onion). Flamenco song erupts here and there. As five Iberian bulls await their certain deaths in the enclosures at the bullring, the party outside is swinging. I hate to say it, but this feels *extremely* Spanish.

Spaniards who support bullfighting compare it to ballet or sculpture. Critics pen their reviews for the culture, not the sports, pages. Its rules are governed by the Ministry of Culture, which also issues prestigious annual awards. It is funded not just by the government but also gate receipts and TV rights. Sponsorship is minimal – it's regarded as too rarefied a cultural expression, and the *traje de luces* has no room for garish logos. 'In principle it's not the blood itself, or the aggression,' one supporter tells me. 'It's the aesthetics of it, the artistic part. It's one of the ancestral activities which survives in today's culture.' Another adds: 'You also have the elegance, the art, which is more attractive than the blood. That's what attracted Goya and Picasso, Lorca, Antonio Machado, Hemingway and Orson Welles.'

It's 5:30 p.m. The fight begins with a horse-drawn procession snaking its way through the roaring crowds which have filled Calle Virgen de la Paz. First come the ladies in powder-blue and baby-pink 18th-century gowns, replete with mantilla head-dresses. They are in their late teens and are the cream of Ronda society: the costumes are made specially, never rented, and can cost up to €6,000 (it's acknowledged that not everyone in Ronda can afford to take part). Throughout the festival, they're chaperoned by an older female minder who ensures that no mischief takes place. Gazing down from their 18th-century carriages, these debutantes are, after all, meant to represent the feminine counterpart to the very male world of the bullfight.

Next appear Francisco Rivera Ordóñez and the other *toreros* leading their *cuadrillas*, or teams, all wearing the brocaded velvet suits of Goya's time. They're looser than the contemporary *traje de luces*, which are extremely tight fitting to avoid horn snagging.

Inside the ring, I take my seat on the second tier, looking down into the circle of apricot sand. The Ronda Plaza de Toros was built in the late 18th century next to the cliffs overlooking the canyon. All summer long, vultures would wheel balefully over the town as the carcasses of horses that died during *la corrida* would be hurled into the depths below. In those days, and up until 1917, on average two horses were killed per fight; they were no match for the bulls, who would toss them in the air or pierce their hides so that their entrails littered the sand by the end of the fight. The loss of so many horses wasn't just bad for bullfighting's image. 'It can cost €40,000 to €50,000 per horse,' Armando says. 'They need five years of training, so it doesn't make financial sense for horses to die in the ring.' These days, better training and the thick, quilted mattress-like covering they wear, called a *peto*, keeps them (mostly) alive.

All around are cigar smoke and upper-class plumage. People locate each other with mobile phones, and the two girls on my left, in their early twenties, wave excitedly when they spot friends across the ring. The spectacle opens with the sound of trumpets. The *Alguacils* enter first and trot regally around the ring, two riders in period uniform from the reign of Philip II, the defender of Catholic Europe in the 16th century. They represent the police who once cleared town plazas where the fights used to take place (the ring was introduced because the spine of the bull is so tough it can't make sharp turns and prefers to run in arcs).

The *toreros* and their teams enter, parading before the audience, and bowing to the *corrida* president, who is installed in the royal box next to the festival queen and local dignitaries. There, too, is the Duchess of Alba (a representative of the royal family is always present at a bullfight).

They clear the ring and the three 'acts' begin. The first is the *tercio de varas* ('the lancing third'). At this point I'm wrestling with curiosity, a sense of dread and some kind of excitement I'm not at all comfortable with. Out springs the bull from *la puerta del miedo*, 'the door of fear' (every aspect, every technical detail, is made livid with melodrama). Cooped up all afternoon in an unfamiliar pen, pent-up rage propels him across the ring (sometimes they reach 50 kilometres per hour). The beast first charges the pink and golden cape and tosses in vain as team members, led by Francisco Rivera Ordóñez, side-step their thrusts. These opening moments, the *suerte de capote*, allow the matador to observe the bull's behaviour and attitude, especially which of the two horns he prefers to use.

Music pipes up again. In come two *picadors*, men on horseback each carrying a long lance, or *vara*, with a sharp steel tip. One of the *picadors* gets close enough to the bull to stab the *morillo*, the enormous muscle at the back of the bull's head and shoulders. By this time, the bull is going hell for leather at the blindfolded horse, which seems ludicrously out of place. Around the action, the *cuadrilla* piles in to distract and direct the bull.

Within moments, to the sound of trumpets, the horsemen have left the ring. The first 'third' is over: at this point, the bull has displayed either his cowardice or bravery. With the start of the second act, the *tercio de banderillas*, or 'third of flags', the bull is still charging whoever is closest. Yet, when he is motionless blood is seen pumping in waves from the wound on his neck, so that his left leg is crimson. He is angry and confused, looking from left to right.

By law, a bullfight shouldn't last much more than 15 minutes, 20 at the most. To keep the customers entertained, it must be as fast moving as possible. This second act involves three *banderilleros*, each of whom must plant two barbed sticks (*banderillas*), from which trail coloured paper tresses, into the flanks, ideally as close as possible to the where the *picador* has already wounded. If the job is done well, then only two are needed, but if they're sunk into the wrong part of the flank, then up to eight can be used. These add to the bull's growing anger, whatever about the pain inflicted. He tries to toss the *banderillas* away the way people sometimes flick annoying hair out of their face.

On cue, it's now the final phase of the fight, the *tercio de muerte*, 'third of death'. The *banderilleros* have left, and the action is now focused on the *medios*, the dead centre of the ring. It's high noon between the *torero*, Francisco Rivera Ordóñez (his *cuadrilla* is safe behind the *barreras*, or timber barriers) and the bull. The beast is now debilitated by blood loss. Ordóñez grips the *muleta*, the scarlet cloak that is lighter than the *capote* of the first two acts. It's a common misconception that the red colour raises the temper of the bull. The animals are colour blind; the red colour simply masks the animal's blood as it's absorbed during the fight.

By now, the bull's head has sunk, the culmination of the *picadors'* and the *banderilleros'* earlier handiwork. Weakening the *morillo*, or goring muscle, brings the head down for the final confrontation. In the tight circle, the two are drawn together in a dance of death, a pas de deux to the accompaniment of a morbid paso doble. To my untutored eyes, the bull seems to have become fixated by the *muleta*, and as such Francisco is toying with him, making pass after pass with the cape, the bull lurching forward mechanically each time to toss the man, but instead tossing cloth into air. Once or twice he missteps so that a hoof buckles into the sand. There are *olés* and applause, oohs and aahs, but the crowd seems lacklustre. A moment of silence, in which Spain's ancient culture is unfolding with sacramental pathos, is punctured by a mobile text message, quickly smothered. I'm bemused by what exactly tickles the crowd's fancy and what draws their contempt.

Then, after numerous feints and manoeuvres, Francisco strikes the pose which brings us back to the *momento de la verdad.* There is a hush around the ring as man and beast lock eyes. Francisco sights the bull. The agonised silence is broken as he leaps forward and sinks his *estoque* deep into the goring muscle.

The bull doesn't fall immediately. In the following seconds, limping and bleeding heavily through the mouth, he is surrounded by the *cuadrilla.* They have enough space to flap their capes in his direction, yet are close enough to be gored. But the bull is cornered, and his head hangs heavy, twisting this way and that towards his tormentors. In a matter of seconds, the bull buckles and crumples to the sand. For an instant it's like he's reclining in a summer field before the rain starts. But these are his final breaths. One of the team, the *puntillero,* steps forward to plunge a dagger (*puntilla*) into the bull's brain. The body spasms and lies still.

The girl to my left says '*Hola*' in a voice that carries an unimpressed impatience. It sounds like, *There you go*, or, *Well, thank God that's over.* The middle-aged, cigar-chomping man to my left concurs. '*Poca fuerte*,' he says, shaking his head. 'No good, not much strength.'

'He does not want to fight today,' says the man's son disdainfully (as if the bull will want to fight on another occasion).

It's all over quickly. Three liveried horses are led into the ring and the stricken bull, attached to a yoke, is jeered as it's dragged out of the ring. The *monosabios* promptly rake the sand and scoop up the congealing blood.

It's time for the next fight.

* * *

To outsiders, bullfighting reflects some kind of primal Spanish obsession with death, with extremes. 'There are two things that are necessary for a country to love bullfights,' wrote Hemingway. 'One is that bulls are raised in that country and the other that people must have an interest in death.'

I asked Francisco Rivera Ordóñez if there was some truth in this. 'It's very difficult to explain to someone, even to someone who goes to the ring. Only another bullfighter can understand it. Bullfighting is a way to express yourself. There's nothing like it in the whole world. It's a Spanish thing. I don't think it's cruel. The bull is part of the man: the bull is giving his life to the man, but the man has to be ready to give *his* life too. I know I'm here today, but I don't know what's going to happen tomorrow.'

This tendency to fatalism, suggests Armando, is why the Spanish are more likely to carry organ-donor cards. 'See how many transplants there are in Europe,' he says. 'And then look how many there are in Spain. When you know you're going to die you're better off making it possible for someone else to use your organs. Life is here today. That lamp might fall on your head, and it's *adios*. Life is just life – you can have it or just lose it. You don't know where you'll be tomorrow.'

'Certainly the Spaniard does cherish a particular view towards death itself,' according to the travel writer Jan Morris in *Spain* (1964). 'The death of the bull is the moment of truth; the death of a man is the climax of life – an unwanted climax to be sure, but something that expresses a kind of fulfilment for a people unfulfilled in history and environment.'

But what exactly did Jan Morris mean by Spain's 'unfulfilled' history?

The year 1492 is usually taken as the critical point in assessing this history. The Islamic Moors from North Africa had conquered the Christian Visigoths on the Iberian Peninsula in 711 ad and ruled for the next 800 years. It wasn't until 1492, when the two Christian rulers from separate Spanish regions, Isabella of Castile and Ferdinand of Aragon, marched into Granada, that the Moors were finally vanquished in the *Reconquista.*

The new Spain was characterised by the authoritarian values of Isabella's Castile and the formidable power of the Catholic Church. Both forces were backed by a ruthless army. 'The connection between Church and the army remained close during the rapid growth of Spain's empire when the crucifix was the shadow of the sword over half the world,' writes Antony Beevor in *The Battle for Spain*. 'The army conquered, and the Church integrated the new territories into the Castilian state.'

Within two generations, this new Castilian reality forced its way on to the European stage with the Spanish Inquisition and the conquest of South America. But both the Inquisition and Spain's colonial adventures were to have profound effects on how the country developed right up to the Civil War in 1936. Coinciding as they did with the Reformation and the rise of Protestant England, they also shaped foreign perceptions of the Spanish and brought stereotyping into play. During the conquests of Mexico by Hernán Cortés and Peru by Francisco Pizarro, there may have been admiration in Europe at their genius and heroism (how so few Spanish soldiers managed to overthrow the Inca and the Aztecs), but their brutal treatment of the indigenous populations horrified the European imagination. When the writings of Bartolomé de Las Casas, a Spanish Dominican priest who campaigned against the genocide of South American Indians, were translated into English, the Spanish reputation for barbarism spread. Some English travellers even saw the imminent decline of Spain as punishment from God.

The Spanish Inquisition tended to reinforce this view: initially intended to investigate the sincerity with which Spanish Jews were converting to Christianity after the *Reconquista*, the Inquisition became a wildfire of cruelty by which the slightest suggestion or whisper could lead to the wholesale condemnation of innocents, who underwent the *auto-da-fé* ritual of public humiliation, before being burned at the stake. An anti-Spanish pamphlet in 1624 quoted a Spaniard admitting that, 'Cruelty is natural and inherent to our nation, for except that our victories be drowned in blood we cannot taste them.' (Taken from Patricia Shaw's *The English View of the Spaniard, 1590–1700*, quoted in *Beyond Pug's Tour*.)

The Spanish were sensitive to these perceptions. In the early 20th century the writer Julián Juderías coined the term '*La Leyenda Negra*', 'the Black Legend', to refer to the anti-Spanish literature that fuelled the myth of Spanish fanaticism, superstition and cruelty.

Stereotyping, meanwhile, was further inflamed by the long maritime rivalry with Britain culminating in the defeat of the Armada in 1588. Grotesque Spanish caricatures took root in the English mind: they were vain, cruel, vengeful, amorous, lascivious and boastful. In Christopher Marlowe's *Lust's Dominion: Or the Lascivious Queen* (1599), the evil Spanish queen is willing to kill her own son in order to give her Moorish lover satisfaction. Besides cruelty, Spaniards were lampooned for their sobriety and gravity, their piety and devotion, even pomposity. Samuel Pepys, in his *Diary*, held forth about the endless 'ceremoniousness' of the Spaniards, while Shakespeare's Don Adriano de Armado in *Love's Labour's Lost* is long-winded and pedantic. James Howell, in his *Instructions for Forreine Travell* (1642), blames the extremes of climate, suggesting that the Spaniard's brooding, overly ponderous and unchanging nature was reflected in the blistering heat: 'the violence thereof lasteth a long time without intension, or remission, or any considerable change…' Compared to the French, the Spanish were 'Speculative and saturnine … slow and heavy'. While merry England was dancing around the maypole, the Spanish were serious, sober and forever wearing black.

The Protestantism of England also contrasted sharply with what was perceived as the indolence of the Spanish. People basically assumed they lay around in the sun all day drinking wine. The roots of this perception lie in how the Spanish empire exploited its dominions. Spain's primary target was bullion, and the tons of silver and gold gouged from her territories was a sugar hit of wealth. The country splurged on magnificent cathedrals dripping with gold. It failed, however, to invest in industry or agriculture. No mercantile class developed which might have instilled a reputation for energy and enterprise. Furthermore, thousands of Jews had been expelled in 1492, trade with North Africa had slumped and the zealously Catholic establishment continued to denounce usury long after it was accepted in the rest of Europe. It was no surprise, then, that Spain emerged in the 19th century as an extremely backward country, with a façade of ecclesiastical wealth. In 1788, some 50 per cent of males were unemployed; the country was moribund under the weight of the Church, the army and the nobility. Francis Willughby, the English ornithologist who visited Spain in 1664, attributed the backwardness of Spanish agriculture to 'the wretched laziness of the people … walking slowly, and always cumber'd with a great cloak and long sword'.

Yet Spain was famous for its battles, its soldiers, its martial decorum and its castles (Castile is named after them. While the English talk of castles in the air, the French synonym for daydreaming is 'to build castles in Spain'). Spanish infantry were regarded as the best in Europe; Miguel de Cervantes was an infantry soldier and a member of the naval elite corps before writing *Don Quixote*, while Fr Ignatius of Loyola, the founder of the Jesuits, was a soldier enlisted by the Duke of Nájera. Lord Byron wrote of the Spaniards, 'Back to the struggle, baffled in the strife, War, war is still the cry, War even to the knife!' When Spain produced Habsburg monarchs, the Spanish were to be found all over Europe fighting for the Catholic cause. Spanish troops in the Low Countries in the 17th century were revered for their infantry in the same way the French were for their cavalry, and the English for their navy.

Such a reputation, though, was a pallid consolation during the empire's decline. Continual religious wars and the War of Spanish Succession (where European powers fought to prevent Spain and France from uniting under a single Bourbon monarch) took their toll on the country's resources, while Spain was further hammered by the Napoleonic wars (1808–13). But as the Industrial Revolution was blackening the skies with soot and despoiling the European landscape, Spain began to hold a romantic appeal for a new breed of traveller, precisely because she was so underdeveloped: Washington Irving, who later became US ambassador, Richard Ford, a British writer who produced *A Handbook for Travellers in Spain*; and George Henry Borrow, were all drawn to Spain's bleak, anachronistic beauty. Borrow's *The Bible in Spain* included the tale of the Roma girl who worked in a cigar factory, a character later immortalised in Bizet's opera *Carmen* (Bizet had never set foot in Spain).

For these and later writers – Ernest Hemingway (*For Whom the Bell Tolls*) and George Orwell (*Homage to Catalonia*) included – Spain was a land of extremes. 'Spaniards were presented as black and white,' explains Tom Burns Marañón, a former correspondent for *Newsweek* and the *Washington Post* and writer of several books on Spanish society. 'You either loved or hated them. They were fantastically generous or cruel, hugely proud or not giving a damn, warlike or indolent, immensely religious or ferociously secular, lying around in the sun or fabulously heroic. Even the climate seemed to carry these extremes – it was bakingly hot in the central plain in summer or incredibly cold in the winter. You have flat lands and mountain ranges, fantastic gorges with a bridge and no river underneath, huge rivers with no bridges. You had these wonderful cathedrals and buildings where *nothing happens*. It was like a kind of Jurassic Park for travel writers: you could come and see what your own country looked like 200 years previously.'

* * *

In 1959, there was a minor scandal in a small fishing village on the Costa Blanca, when the local mayor fell foul of both the Church and the government. The source of the scandal was the bikini, and the fishing village was called Benidorm.

The first tourists had just begun arriving at Valencia Airport from northern Europe. When their skimpy beach attire was noticed by the archbishop, he promptly threatened Mayor Pedro Zaragoza Orts with excommunication for permitting bikinis on a public beach. Such an order would have meant social death, so Zaragoza got on his Vespa and drove to Madrid to plead his case before General Franco himself. When he explained that Benidorm badly needed tourist revenue, the General was impressed. Within a week Franco's wife, Carmen Polo, visited the village, later returning several times. The excommunication order was quietly dropped, and the bikini was to begin its long reign over the Costa. More tourists arrived, bringing an erotic openness sharply at odds with the repressive Catholicism of Franco's Spain. 'The tourists more importantly had the power to out face the Church,' writes Giles Tremlett in *Ghosts of Spain*. 'They brought not just money, but the seeds of change. They also brought the fresh air of democracy. There was no turning back.'

In 1947, the British novelist Rose Macaulay could describe a road trip along Spain's Mediterranean coastline as one of emptiness and the odd staring local. Suddenly, between Mrs Franco's visit and 1973, the number of visitors to Spain rose from 3 million to 34 million. Today, Spain attracts 53 million tourists a year.

The shock of hyper-development (until then, these rocky, unwanted shorelines had been characterised by thrift and deprivation) was such that by 1971, some 90 per cent of all non-chronic mental illnesses in the province of Málaga were among teenage males who had gone to work in the tourism industry. 'Overnight,' writes John Hooper in *The New Spaniards*, 'its inhabitants were confronted with a new way of life in which it seemed as if the men had more money than they could cram into their wallets, and the women walked around virtually naked.'

For the hordes of British, Irish, Dutch, German and Scandinavian tourists, it was simply sunny Spain, a land of *sombreros* and *sangria*, sunburn and paella, bullfighting and flamenco, macho men and donkeys. The stereotype repertoire was easily absorbed, since the official preference was to ensure that interaction with the real culture of Spain, the real lives of the people, was kept to a minimum. For Franco the fewer the disparate regional symbols, the easier it was to promote a unitary Spain (a 1950s Iberian Airlines poster, for example, showed a Spaniard playing guitar on a donkey with a flamenco dancer beside him, and an Iberian Airlines plane flying overhead). Hence our view of Spanishness was skewed in favour of a limited geographical range: Andalusia, Murcia and Valencia, the Balearics and the Canaries. To the Romantic writers of the 19th century, Andalusia was actually the wildest, most mysterious and least 'European' part of the Peninsula, but for the tourists of the 1960s and 1970s it was a generic land of sun, sand and sex. The authorities were happy to import bullfighting into areas where it had never previously existed, just to reinforce the official idea of Brand Spain.

So when Spaniards are confronted with stereotypes of Spain, they are usually amazed and irritated: flamenco, bullfights and paella are mostly the preserve of the south and south-east. The rest of Spain is overlooked. Spanish identity – or rather, *regional* identity – is a much richer and profoundly more controversial paella.

To understand it, we need to go back again to that pivotal year, 1492. Events then created a fracture that led ultimately to the bloodletting of the Spanish Civil War, and the fracture remains a running political sore to this day. It even explains the furious rivalry between Real Madrid and Barcelona.

The union of Isabella of Castile and Ferdinand of Aragon wasn't just a marriage. It signified, for the first time, the full union of Spain. Since Roman times, Spain had been a plurality of regal entities whose inhabitants enjoyed more individual freedoms from the local kings than most in the Europe of the time. León, Navarre, Asturias, Galicia, Aragon and Catalonia all maintained their own armies, legal systems, treasuries, parliaments and civil service. Even when principalities came together under the Castilian monarchs, they still called themselves *Los Reyes de las Españas*, Kings of the Spains. So when Isabella and Ferdinand marched into Granada and sealed the end of Moorish Spain, the new country was to be Christian, unitary and forged in Castile's image.

As it built its empire abroad, Castile sought to entrench its authoritarian, centralising power over a feudal system that was becoming out of date in the rest of Europe. To ensure that the wealth coming back from the New World didn't enrich – or empower – Spain's old regions, citizens of Aragon and Catalonia were banned from engaging in commerce there. Successive rulers continued to concentrate power in the Castilian centre. Philip II made Madrid its capital, choosing a spot in the dead centre of the Spain that had no harbour and few geographical advantages. When the empire went into decline, however, Castile failed to notice. 'Castile had the unbending pride of the newly impoverished nobleman who refuses to notice the cobwebs and decay in his great house and resolutely continues to visualise the grandeur of his youth,' writes Antony Beevor in *The Battle for Spain.*

Inevitably, the old regions rebelled when they saw their rights and traditions trampled over. Already in 1520, the uprising by the *Comuneros* against Isabella's grandson, Emperor Charles V, was partly due to the dismissal of local traditions. The Catalans were next. They had once enjoyed their own empire over the Mediterranean – the Balearic Islands, Corsica, Sardinia, Sicily and the Duchy of Athens – so were none too happy about being under the cosh of Castile. In 1640, Catalonia and Portugal rose up against Philip IV, pledging allegiance for a time to Louis XIII of France before Barcelona fell in 1652. The Catalans later supported England, before their laws and institutions were harshly reduced by Madrid in 1714.

But other European trends were to have a destabilising effect on Castile's centralising impulses. The influence of the Enlightenment and the French Revolution prompted reforms which reduced the powers of the clergy and engendered the rise of a liberal middle class. Social progress, though, was postponed with the arrival of Napoleon in 1808. The Spanish War of Independence against the French lasted six years and ripped the country apart, with insurrections against both the monarchy and the invaders. The regions, normally abhorring any notion of a single Spain, nonetheless fought ferociously against Napoleon's armies (the War of Independence gave the world the term '*guerrilla*'). When the French were finally pushed back over the Pyrenees, the country was in ruins. The nascent liberal parliament (Cortes), taking refuge in the southern city of Cadiz, seized the initiative with a new constitution in 1812. It was a breakthrough for middle-class liberalism, seeking as it did to end Spain's absolute monarchy and the power of the Church. The 1812 constitution may have inspired later legal systems in Europe and Latin America, but at home it institutionalised the confrontation – to date unresolved – between what has become known as *las dos Españas*, the two Spains. One liberal and secular, with an emphasis on devolving more power to the regions, the other Roman Catholic, conservative and dedicated to a unitary, royal Spain.

The new constitution was short-lived. It was scrapped by Ferdinand VII in 1814 and the remainder of the century was a long, tortuous struggle between traditionalists and liberals. As the middle class grew in wealth and confidence, the monarchy sank into corruption. But the political stalemate meant the generals took on a more robust role, with 37 coup attempts between 1814 and 1874. In 1873, following the abdication of King Amadeo I, the first Spanish Republic was proclaimed. It only lasted 23 months, brought down by army intervention.

By the beginning of the 20th century, Spain was in a gruesome state. Its empire was lost, while in a humiliating defeat by the United States in 1898 Spain lost the Philippines, Cuba and Puerto Rico. At home, poverty abounded. In the end, the trinity of Church, army and monarchy held sway, but they presided over a country in which life expectancy was 35, illiteracy averaged 64 per cent and two-thirds of the population worked on the land. The social polarisation, simmering over four and a half centuries, finally came to the boil with the hate-filled cataclysm of the Spanish Civil War.

The international situation in Europe widened the conflict and deepened the suffering. The Republican government – left wing, secular, in favour of more regional autonomy – was supported by Russia and Communist sympathisers across Europe. The Nationalists – authoritarian, centralist, Catholic – were supported by Hitler and Mussolini. Some 600 Irish Blueshirts under General Eoin O'Duffy fought on Franco's side, while the 80-strong Connolly Column fought for the Republican XV International Brigade. The British and French governments, although alarmed at the rise of fascism, sat on the fence. General Francisco Franco's victorious Nationalists are thought to have murdered 200,000 opponents; the Republican side 38,000.

* * *

In 2007, I visited Madrid to report on a new law to provide financial and practical support for families wishing to uncover mass graves from the Civil War. In Madrid's Almudena Cemetery, I met Emilio Silva, a 36-year-old journalist, next to the monument to *Las Trece Rosas* (the Thirteen Roses). I asked Emilio who they were. 'They were young women, leftist sympathisers. They were shot by Franco.'

I found the execution of 13 young women instantly shocking. Yet Emilio's own story opened the door to the Civil War's horrifying legacy a little wider. In 1936, his grandfather Emilio had been working in his costume shop in Priaranza del Bierzo in the northern province of León when men from a right-wing militia entered. He was loaded onto the back of a lorry with 14 others and driven to a roadside spot outside the town. He and the others were shot and thrown into a mass grave. His crime was to have lobbied for a secular school.

Decades later Emilio found the grave. With the help of friends and some forensic scientists who had worked in the former Yugoslavia, they were able to identify his grandfather's bones through DNA. Emilio gave his grandfather a proper burial in the local cemetery, but his quiet activism started a debate which ultimately led to the new Historical Memory Law.

But he was the first. Until that moment, the so-called *pacto de olvido* (the pact of forgetting), had prevailed. It was the deal between the right and the left that effected the transition to democracy after Franco died in his sleep in 1975. The pact kept a firm lid on the atrocities of the Franco era, but, nearly 30 years later, as the left and right began to polarise, people began to ask what had happened to their grandfathers, uncles, mothers, fathers and aunts during Franco's terror. It turned out that Spain was littered with abandoned mass graves on roadsides, down country lanes or on hillsides (an estimated 40,000 in Andalusia alone). There had been atrocities by the Republicans too, of course, but their victims had been given Christian burials in consecrated cemeteries. 'It's important that Spain, like France and Germany after the Second World War, remembers what happened so that we can build some kind of justice for the victims,' said Emilio.

That a request for the respectful burial of Spaniards executed in their droves 60 years previously should have been a cause of controversy seemed barely believable, but the new law, from the centre-left government of José Luis Rodríguez Zapatero, was bitterly opposed by many on the right. The People's Party (PP), the democratic successors to Franco, grudgingly agreed, having previously blocked any attempt at giving Franco's victims too much prominence. 'It's Zapatero's way of really trying to make the [centre-right] People's Party extinct in Spanish politics,' says Professor Pedro Schwartz of the San Pablo University in Madrid. 'Since it was the Francoist politicians who opened up the way to democracy, it was seen as the best thing to say: let's forget about the crimes of the Franco era, let's also forget the crimes committed by the Republican side during the Civil War, and let's start again from the beginning.'

Descendants of Franco's henchmen were also against the law. 'There are many people who lost relatives, me included,' Carlos Giron de Velasco, whose father was Minister for Works in Franco's cabinet, told me. 'But this was solved a long time ago, it's not necessary, and there aren't so many people who demand these rights.'

It's true that it hasn't been universally desired by the left either. The family of Federico García Lorca, one of Spain's great 20th-century poets and dramatists, shot by Nationalist troops, has long declined to exhume his grave near Granada. The problem is that mass graves are mixed, and bones are often unclaimed. But with democracy Spain is still coming to terms with the bloodletting. In a Europe that is shocked by the massacre of 8,000 Muslims in Srebrenica in 1995, it's chilling to check the roll call of mass shootings that characterised Franco's advance on Madrid and his vindictive repression after victory in 1939. Under democracy, Spain has quietly put away the visible reminders of Franco, renaming streets and plazas and removing statues (the last statue in Madrid was only removed in 2006, while one remains in the North African Spanish enclave of Melilla). The *pacto de olvido* may have held fast in the first decades of democracy, but the left see it has an imposition by the right, who were still in the driving seat after Franco's death.

* * *

Under Franco, Spain was the most rigidly centralised country in Europe. He was from Galicia, rather than Castile, yet his commitment to a unified Spain was absolute. During and after the Civil War, Franco aligned himself with the Catholic Church – even though he wasn't particularly religious – in order to reinforce this single identity. When Franco died, regional nationalism went through a slow-motion explosion (accepting devolution for Catalonia and the Basque Country was the price the right had to pay for the *pacto de olvido*). Over time his legacy so tainted the concept of a united Spain that following his death, politicians on the left struggled with euphemisms to avoid actually using the word 'Spain'. Regional nationalism (if that's not a contradiction) therefore muddles how we conceive of Spain and Spanishness. Politicians and academics fret about it, and the Basque separatists ETA give it a murderous edge.

Spaniards themselves are too busy poking (sometimes unpleasant) fun at each other to be bothered with how outsiders view them. In 2000, the Madrid government standardised licence plates so that drivers could no longer identify where other motorists came from (the notion being that it would stop them swearing at a Galician or a Valencian for cutting them up in the traffic). Some regions responded by prefixing licence plates with a regional abbreviation. And when the black silhouette of the bull, which had stood on hillsides around Spain, was co-opted from a sherry company to become a new symbol of Spain, Catalan separatists adopted the donkey as their symbol, even erecting a risqué billboard showing a donkey mounting the famous bull.

The Catalans regard themselves as a separate nation. It had its first parliament in the 11th century, has its own language (which spread as far as Sardinia and even Florida), its own regional government, its own icon – the black-skinned Virgin of Montserrat – and in Barcelona FC, its own 'national' team. Catalan nationalism blossomed in the late 19th century when they felt constrained by the backwardness of the rest of the country. It had a broad prospect on the Mediterranean, was next door to France, and was ahead on new currents and trends. It was among the most industrious parts of Spain, and it maintained strong links to Cuba from its days of empire (the Bacardi family had Catalan roots). So when Spain lost Cuba to the US in 1898, it was the last straw. Those Catalan virtues, which have helped make Barcelona one of the most prosperous cities in Spain – hard working, entrepreneurial, deal-making, censorious – have also created the image of the tight-fisted Catalan.

By contrast, the Galicians have been moulded by extreme hardship, including frequent famines, widespread poverty and emigration. Battered by Atlantic storms, as far spiritually from the Mediterranean as you could imagine, the Galicians are seen as superstitious, mistrustful, canny, religious, morose, depressed and unassuming. Rarely visited by tourists beyond the centuries old *Camino* pilgrimage to Santiago de Compostela, it took the *Prestige* tanker disaster in November 2002 to properly put that corner of Spain that overhangs Portugal on the map (a devastating train disaster in July 2013 also brought the world's media in droves). An obsession with death and the afterlife, and with little spirits who live on hilltops, hint at Galicia's (disputed) Celtic origins. Its seaboard culture boasts legends, pirates and shipwrecks, and their fishermen are the hardiest on the high seas. They're renowned for investing simple phrases with layers of hidden meaning through a skill known as *retranca* (the posture of grim inscrutability by prime minister Mariano Rajoy over whether or not Spain would seek an EU-IMF bailout in the Autumn of 2012 was regarded as quintessentially Galician. Spanish *pride* no doubt also had a part to play). 'Meeting a Galician on a staircase,' writes Giles Tremlett in *Ghosts of Spain*, 'it is impossible to know whether they are going up or down.'

As early as the 14th century, *Galegos* migrated to Andalusia, and later to all parts of the Peninsula, and from the 18th century until the 1950s they left in droves to Latin America: 900,000 in the 19th century, nearly 1 million in the 20th. They settled in Uruguay, Argentina, Venezuela and Cuba (Fidel Castro is of Galician extraction). In South America today, a *Galego* is a derogatory term for a Spaniard – it is even synonymous with the village idiot, or the corner-shop owner in Argentina – and it's galling for a Catalan or Basque holiday maker to be within earshot of the pejorative. For centuries, Galicia provided cheap labour for the rest of Spain. Today, though, it is famed for being home to Amancio Ortega, the billionaire inventor of the perennially popular Zara brand, and for having the third most seizures of cocaine shipments in the world (after Columbia and the US).

We know the Basques through ETA, but their relationship to the other regions is much more complex. Their language – Euskara – is excruciatingly complex and sets them miles apart from France and the rest of Spain, between which they are geographically sandwiched. The age of the language, thought to have been around before (even long before) the Indo-European languages took root, and the lack of wholesale migration, suggests they have been where they are today for a very long time. Anthropologists even worked out that they tend to be taller and more muscular than their neighbours. They have always been the recalcitrant residents of the Peninsula, the last or slowest to be conquered, and always winning more local rights and privileges than anywhere else. Although Basque nationalism in the 19th century was a reaction *against* modernism (the opposite of the Catalans), economically the region became one of the powerhouses of Spain (they are the richest citizens per capita), thanks to its huge reserves of iron and timber.

Industrialisation brought thousands of poor migrant workers from the south. That fuelled stereotyping no end: the father of Basque nationalism, Sabino de Arana y Goiri, launched a doctrine of hatred against the southerners in 1892: 'They come up here bringing with them their bullfights, their flamenco songs and dances, their "refined" language so abundant in blasphemous and filthy expressions.' In the struggle between liberal and traditional Spain in the 19th century, Basques were on the side of the latter, so puritanical was their brand of Catholicism. But, torn between their religion and their hatred of centralism, they chose to support the Republicans rather than Franco during the Civil War, and paid for it with the bombing of Guernica by German warplanes, an atrocity immortalised on canvas by Pablo Picasso.

Despite the recent (violent) adversity towards the Spanish state, Basques have always been key, often popular, players in Spanish history. Admired for their strong, silent qualities, many were employed as sailors by Philip II, including Juan Sebastián Elcano, the first person to circumnavigate the globe in 1522. In Chile, the most sophisticated urbanites will let you know how Basque they are (the more Basque they are, the whiter they are). 'Ironically, until the appearance of ETA in the 1950s, the Basques were extremely popular in Spain – they were seen as reliable, honest, unpretentious, somewhat stubborn,' says Charles Powell, historian and professor at San Pablo-CEU University in Madrid. 'That's why the emergence of ETA took people by surprise.'

We should know the Andalusians best, yet they retain a mysterious, dangerous, wild beauty. 'For half the world the image of Spain is the image of Andalusia,' wrote Jan Morris in *Spain*. 'The huge slab of country, mostly mountainous, that begins where the tableland is bounded by the southern Sierras ... There are no half-measures in such a place, so close to the earth, so perilously near the frontiers of caricature.' Whatever about the harsh delights of the region to foreigners, the Andalusians are seen by other Spaniards as superficial in their Catholicism. They're into the trappings and the ritual – think of the Holy Week processions with the *nazarenos*, those folk with the Ku Klux Klan-type hoods – but not great ones for the substance. They are sneered at by the Basques, who are more austere in their Catholicism, more into the substance, but less drawn to the ritual.

Castilians are seen as dour, serious, hard working and reliable. Their most prominent cheerleader (if that's the right word) has been José María Aznar, the former Spanish prime minister. He self-consciously identified himself with these Castilian virtues to win votes, but also because he wanted Spain to be seen as a more serious country, in contrast to the flamboyant Felipe González, the outgoing Socialist prime minister from 1982 to 1996, who presided over a liberal social revolution. Aznar was fiercely anti-federalist, believing that the devolution of education to regions like Catalonia and the Basque Country was leaving children historically brainwashed.

Valencia, meanwhile, is quintessentially Mediterranean Spanish, fun loving, outgoing and noisy. The Fallas de Valencia fair in March, a tribute to St Joseph, is a no-holds-barred fireworks display lasting sometimes weeks, bringing 100,000 people onto the streets. Over the past 25 years, *Valencianos* have been engaged in a linguistic dispute with their Catalan neighbours. They speak a language they refer to as Valencià (which Catalan speakers understand perfectly); Valencian nationalists, who tend to be conservative, insist it is *not* Catalan, no doubt because they resent the traditional wealth and arrogance of their Catalan neighbours, while left-wing voters have no trouble accepting that it is, in fact, a variety of Catalan.

* * *

Spain has undergone breathtaking change since Franco's death. Between the collapse of empire and the rise of the dictator, the country had slumped into a bad-tempered, schismatic, poverty-stricken, inward-looking land. But with Franco gone, Spaniards embraced *La Movida Madrileña*, the get-up-and-go revolution that they have furiously clung to ever since. Within a generation, they shook off the stiff, black corsets of small village life, of uncompromising Catholicism and of authoritarian Puritanism. In its place was a free-for-all. The villages emptied and the cities expanded. EU funds poured in following membership in 1986, rail and road networks stretched out in all directions, and tourism and property boomed along the Costas. World-famous architects were lured in to build the most breathtaking, experimental designs: the Guggenheim in Bilbao by Frank Gehry, the Alamillo Bridge in Seville by Santiago Calatrava, Arata Isozaki's indoor Olympic sports stadium in Barcelona, Norman Foster's new Metro system in Bilbao, and the new Madrid Airport by Richard Rogers. 'This love of modernity hides what Spaniards sometimes call *huida hacia delante*, or "running away forwards", this time in its cultural form,' writes Giles Tremlett in *Ghosts of Spain*. 'These façades of "brave new world" buildings hide a certain disrespect, even contempt, for the old.'

Spain was reinventing itself at a furious rate. For centuries, the establishment had defined the country in terms of what it was not: it was against the French, and its Christianity was a bulwark against the Moors. When the country swung to the left after Franco, Spain had to decide what it was actually *for*. She embraced EU membership, since it provided some breathing room from the perpetual struggle over region versus nation. Under democracy, a multiplicity of agencies has promoted the new Brand Spain across the planet. Subsidised cinema produced filmmakers like Pedro Almodóvar who uses bright, garish images with provocative, irreverent themes to subvert the values of old Spain. In the year 1992 alone, Spain hosted the Olympics in Barcelona, the Expo in Seville, the

European Capital of Culture in Madrid and the 500-year anniversary of the discovery of America. There were world-beating banks, telecoms companies and airports. Spain invested heavily in its old colonies: travel to Chile today and the airport, the motorway which takes you into town, the petrol station you stop in, the hotel you stay in and the mobile-phone network you use are probably all Spanish owned or built.

Under the Socialists in the 1980s, the country seemed to dive headlong into hedonism. Anything that someone wanted banned was instead embraced (when Italian prime minister Silvio Berlusconi banned any Italian newspaper from publishing photos of topless models at his villa in Sardinia, *El País* was the first outside Italy to do so). A 2004 report revealed 20,000 prostitutes working in hundreds of brothels whose owners had their own national association. Spain became Europe's leading consumer of cocaine, while Ibiza led Europe's club and ecstasy culture. In 2001, Spain was drinking more than the EU average, although Spaniards rarely binge drink. Drug addiction and AIDS were among the bigger social problems in the first decades of democracy (in 1992 Spain had the highest AIDS rate in Europe, with two-thirds of heroin addicts contracting the disease). In a still largely Catholic country (80 per cent, according to the polls), divorce was legalised in 1981 and gay marriages were later introduced (under Franco, homosexuals were jailed). In 2004, the Socialist government relaxed the rules even further on abortion. Late-night porn and sex chat lines are standard on several national and local channels. 'While the bishops huff and puff, the gulf between the Vatican's teachings and what Spaniards do continues to widen,' writes Giles Tremlett.

In this post-Franco era, defining Spanish identity has become increasingly troublesome, whatever stereotypes outsiders have of the Spanish. The tension was already there in Barcelona in 1992, when local politicians used the Olympics as a showcase for *Catalan* culture and achievement, much to the annoyance of Madrid, which wanted Spain promoted. Politicians and academics have anguished over whether Spain is a nation at all. Is it a state filled with different nations, such as the Basques, the Catalans and the Galicians? Is it even a nation of nations? Allegiance to a strong, definable sense of Spanishness is hard to come by – and some regions have less of that sense than others – but it isn't as clear cut as the debate makes it sound. A survey in 2003 surprisingly discovered that a Spanish identity was weaker in the region of Extremadura than in either the Basque Country or in Catalonia. For some observers, the official drifting of regions away from a central Spanish identity has been undermining the hope that greater devolution would actually make the country stronger. Observers have spoken of a regional turning inward through stricter language policies, even a sense that regional governments were subtly trying to keep other Spaniards out. Among Castilians there has been increasing resentment that the national language – Castilian (*castellano*) – is being marginalised in the Basque Country and Catalonia, where even French and English are sometimes more favoured.

* * *

'Spain Rocks!' was the heady *Time* Magazine cover in March 2004. It celebrated the recent strides in the country's global presence through food, architecture, business and culture (centre-right prime minister José-Maria Aznar's support for the US invasion of Iraq also meant that Spain 'rocked'). During its 14 year boom Spain created one quarter of all new jobs in the eurozone. Most of them, we now know, were based on cheap credit and ruinous construction policies. As such the euro crisis has been particularly cruel on Spain. Unemployment has soared (26.3 per cent by June 2013, the worst in Europe after Greece, with youth unemployment at 55.2 per cent), emigration and poverty rates have increased, while a sharp rise in mortgage defaults and evictions have seen families literally put on the streets. The Madrid stock market nose-dived, while Spanish bond yields rose to 550 basis points above German *bunds* from a position of just 8 basis points in 2007.

National self-confidence has suffered. 'We used to be the European miracle,' observes Gildo Seisdedos, professor of marketing at IE Business School in Madrid, 'growing and creating employment as one of the world's leading economies. We built a strong economic fabric with a high degree of recognition, with companies in every sector – banks, utilities, services. We were competing with the highest standards in the EU and beyond. The perception of high unemployment has revised this idea. Now we are looking to the dark side.'

Spain fell into the acronymic PIGS club. Dutch dock workers in Rotterdam asked a *New York Times* reporter why they should have to work hard just to pay for Spaniards to take siestas. The Spanish government, fretful of the damage to a global image which had been carefully managed since the transition to democracy, set up a programme to monitor how Brand Spain was doing in the eyes of Americans, Brits and Germans. The initial findings were not encouraging. 'Twenty years ago,' says Javier Noya, the academic charged with running the observatory, 'the Spanish government commissioned a survey of Germans, asking if they thought Spaniards worked hard. Eighty percent agreed. Today the figure has fallen to 40 per cent. Spain scored positively on sport, culture, heritage and so on – but Germans now think we're lazy. This has a direct bearing on Spanish companies trying to win German investment.'

In April 2012, Richard Boucher, the deputy secretary-general of the OECD, told a NATO parliamentary assembly in Marseille that 'nobody wants to be like Spain today … it is only good for flamenco and red wine.' This was a direct linking of a country's economic fall to reductive stereotypes. The apology demanded by the Spanish foreign minister (and received) was of little comfort. Some accused successive governments of not doing enough to sell Spain's qualities beyond simply being able to transition from dictatorship to democracy. 'As a result,' wrote William Chislett, a journalist and author living in Madrid, 'the old stereotypes of a country of fiesta and siesta have re-emerged with a vengeance.'

In the Pew Research Center's Global Attitudes Survey in May 2013, Spain was well regarded in most of the countries polled, usually by around 70 per cent or more (in Germany it was a surprising 75 per cent), suggesting that outsiders were capable of differentiating between the country's economic mess and the cultural virtues of its people. However Spaniards had a lower opinion of *themselves* in general. The crisis certainly hammered people's faith in hitherto well-respected institutions, such as the Bank of Spain, or the nationwide web of savings banks (*cajas*), which took huge gambles on the property market (and lost). Political parties didn't help the general mood of angry decline: the Partido Popular was dogged by a slush-fund scandal at a time when voters were grappling with falling living standards. The monarchy, normally seen as above the fray, was badly damaged by King Juan Carlos's decision to go on an elephant-hunting trip in Botswana while his son-in-law was being invested for tax fraud and embezzlement.

But the effect of the crisis has had a profound – and confusing – impact on the question of regional automony. On the one hand, as Spain imposed harsh austerity to reduce its runaway deficit, the price of autonomy was being questioned. 'In some quarters,' notes Charles Powell, a director of the Elcano Royal Institute, 'the existence of 17 autonomous communities is increasingly being seen as an expensive luxury that Spain can no longer afford (assuming it ever could). It has thus become commonplace to accuse politicians at the regional and municipal levels of spending well beyond their means in their never-ending efforts to curry favour with voters.' Such spending levels led to what observers called 'culture envy'. One region sees a spectacular airport or arts centre (the Guggenheim Museum in Bilbao is an example), and they want something similar. While some projects were completed, others drove the region deeper into debt with cost overruns.

By the same token, Spain's richer regions began to bridle at any attempt by Madrid to impose austerity on their budgets. Catalonia was the most truculent region of all. Its debt was €41.8 billion, but that, complained Barcelona, was because it received €18 billion a year *less* than it put into the central government's coffers (embarassingly, Catalonia then had to seek a €5 billion bailout from Madrid). When Madrid refused to grant the region its own fiscal independence (such as that enjoyed by the Basque Country and Navarre) the situation boiled over, with over a million people taking to streets of Barcelona to demand independence. A regional election called by the governing (until then mildly separatist) CiU party under Artur Mas became a virtual plebiscite on outright separation from Spain. In the event the CiU won 50 seats and 30 per cent of the vote, but not an overall majority. In January 2013, the new parliament issued a 'declaration of sovereigny', effectively signalling Catalonia's long-term intent to secede (the Spanish constitutional court later effectively ruled out that idea), while a group of lawyers and academics were appointed to draw up a blueprint to cover every legal and practical aspect of creating a new country.

Even as regions themselves have struggled to boost their economies, their efforts can be undermined by the region/state tension. The launch of the Brand Spain initiative angered regions that wanted to promote their own symbols of excellence. When the government of Castilla and León (known in Spanish as the *Junta de Castilla y León*), sent a trade mission to New York, there was no mention of the word Spain on its promotional literature. As a result many people mistook the word *Junta* for a Latin-American military government.

In 2010, as Spain's economic crisis was escalating, a seismic event revived hopes that Spaniards of whatever 'nationality' were capable of uniting around a common destiny. That moment was the 116th minute of the World Cup Final in Johannesburg when the midfielder Andrés Iniesta (Castile-La Manchia-born but a naturalised Catalan playing for Barcelona) scored the winning goal against the Netherlands, sending Spain into raptures of celebration. At a time when the centripetal pull of regional separatism was growing, public euphoria was seized upon by observers. Outpourings of national pride had, in the past, been divisive, and Spain's long-suffering failure to rise to the world-class potential of its players was often blamed on the Catalan or Basque contingents not pulling behind the national team. Indeed, until his death in 1975, Franco infused international fixtures with as much high-temperature nationalism as could be mustered (the team's style, dubbed *la furia española*, boasted classically Spanish virtues of virility and machismo). But on this occasion the World Cup Finals in South Africa invited a more wholehearted fervour for the national team than ever before. There was a greater preponderance of Spanish symbols and flags in the Basque Country and Catalonia. The morning after victory, newspapers gushed with praise. 'The Spanish team is a metaphor for what Spain can be!' declared the conservative, Madrid-based *ABC* newspaper.

In the event, the World Cup win in 2010, while part of the process of drawing the Civil War toxins out of the national team, signalled more of a compromise than outright victory for those hoping for a nation reunited through football. At the final whistle, Xavi, the Barcelona midfielder, ran around the pitch with the *Senyera*, the Catalan flag, and when he and Charles Puyol arrived on Spanish soil with the victorious team, they were spotted with their belongings draped, again, in the Catalan colours. 'These people were not binning their regional identities,' wrote Simon Kuper in the *Financial Times*. 'Rather, they felt both Basque and Spanish, or Catalan and Spanish.'

* * *

José María Manzanares is next into the Ronda bullring.

A fighter from Alicante, he's more flamboyant than Francisco River Ordóñez. His white *traje de luces* has a striking black brocade. His bull, too, is more aggressive, so the crowd is enjoying the spectacle, rising to their feet to wave pristine white handkerchiefs after it has been killed.

'*Mucho mejor!*' (much better!) says the cigar-chomping man to my right.

Míguel Ángel Perera, from Barachos in Extremadura, is next. By the third phase, the bull is again mesmerised by the *muleta* but has to be coaxed, much to the annoyance of the crowd. Perera's passes and manoeuvres are so intimate that his white suit is smeared with blood. In the third act, he holds the *muleta* behind his back, swinging it back and forth, teasing the bull into a trance. The animal is now just centimetres away from Perera's crotch, his powerful horns virtually dovetailing into Perera's hips. At the end of a series of passes, the *torero* turns his back on the bull and walks slowly and contemptuously away. 'This is *desplante*,' Armando explains later. 'Turning one's back on the bull to show self-sufficiency and pride against an animal ready to kill you.'

When it's all over and eight bulls have been slain, there is more pageantry and trumpeting as the crowd make their way out of the ring; the fighters are borne aloft on Goya-esque carriages and off to a reception. The alleyways and streets are again a mass of people as the evening begins. Beer, Rioja and tapas are in big demand. I meet Armando in a bar near Plaza España. Over fava beans and Andalusian sausage, he's eager to explain more of the mysteries. We start with the moment of truth.

'The goring muscle, the *morillo*, is the centre of importance. It's 20 centimetres thick and it controls all the movement of the head – up, down, left, right. The heart is behind the shoulder,' he explains, drawing an aerial image of the bull's neck and shoulders on a beer mat. 'You can't kill a bull from the side – the shoulder bone protects the heart. You need to make him bring his head down. The more the *morillo* is damaged, the lower the head and the more the muscle opens up.' This explains the opening wound by the *picador*'s lance and the further wounds inflicted in the same spot by the *banderillero*. Not only do they weaken the muscle and lower the head, they also incite the bull's rage to make him attack more aggressively, while weakening him through blood loss.

Once the head has been lowered, the matador is presented with a narrow target, a soft focal point which opens up between the shoulder blades. This point is called *la muerte*.

'It's one metre from there to the heart,' says Armando, almost romantically.

In that split-second thrust, the *estoque* cuts through veins, muscle and arteries, eventually finding, like a persistent lover, the heart or aorta. The bull dies of a haemorrhage, and if not the *punterillo* is called in to finish the job.

'You can't kill a bull sideways. The sword jumps off the bone. You have to do it face to face, with elegance. Otherwise, to the spectators it's *adios*,' says Armando. 'You have less than half a second to kill the bull, but it can throw you over the wall given half a chance. And if you miss, the crowd boos and you can be called a butcher, the worst kind of insult. It's the moment when most bullfighters who get killed can die. It's an animal fighting for its life.'

These are the arguments used to win over opponents, and they do carry a curly kind of logic. The artistry the fans adore is not art for art's sake, but art for *pity's* sake, since a badly timed move can increase the bull's suffering. Sometimes the crowd gets so indignant (at the suffering of the animal, so it is argued) that they hurl cushions at the ring. Ultimately, the bull's suffering is perceived within the following moral framework: it has enjoyed a free-range life on the plains, instead of being factory farmed, and all he is asked for in return is a 15-minute death – a death in which he can technically defend himself – instead of an instant death at the abattoir.

'Why should the life of a fish be worth less than a bull?' asks Armando. 'People eat good steak. Do they ever ask about the condition of the animal before it was killed? Another thing,' he adds, forcing a last forkful of fava beans into his mouth, 'if the bull was returned alive to the breeding farm, he would kill the mother and calf. Bulls are extremely territorial and they need to have enough of their own grazing space.'

These arguments cut little muster with opponents of bullfighting. Fernando Alvarez, a biology professor, wrote in the spring of 2008 in *Público* newspaper: 'Bulls suffer and die during the bullfight, but have no way of escape; the bull doesn't enjoy a happy life or a dignified death. If we stopped breeding bulls to kill, there's no evidence that wild bulls or their habitat would become extinct. The artistic and traditional aspects of the bullfight cannot justify its sadistic component.'

In 1991, a new law, *Ley de Espectáculos Taurinos*, defined bullfighting as a cultural tradition and introduced a new rulebook. It lacked any move to reduce the animal's suffering, but the new rules did tackle the question of the horses, which, in order to make life easier for the *picadors*, had become much sturdier. Under the system, the lance-head had to be smaller, while the lance, the horse and the *picador* had to be lighter. At the first festival in which it was introduced in 1992, the bull was less weakened than normal and he promptly killed the *banderillero*, Manolo Montolíu The matadors called a strike and the government backed down.

Another alleged practice is the 'shaving' of the bull's horns. Critics – opponents and fans of bullfighting alike – claim that the horns are shaved, or trimmed, in order to throw the animal's balance and to affect his judgement of distance. This is emphatically rejected by Armando. There is some tempering of the horns for the *caballeros*, he says, the bullfighting still done on horseback. 'The horns are made blunter to save the horses since they are so expensive to train and maintain. But for the men, the horns are actually sharper.'

Many aficionados also believe that the fighting spirit has been bred out of the bulls due to commercial pressures. After the Civil War, when herds were badly depleted, finding enough bulls of the right quality and temperament to replenish the top breeds was difficult, so ranchers were breeding animals that looked fierce but were actually docile. By the 1960s and 1970s, bulls were increasingly falling over without putting up much of a fight. 'Through selective breeding, stud farms can change the temperament of the bull, make it more of a docile collaborator rather than a fierce enemy,' one bullfighting analyst told me. 'Fighters like this, and it can make them more money. The problem, though, if you go too far is that you can end up with a cowardly or weak bull.'

More and more bulls are falling down before the *coup de grâce*. Some are overweight because of their diet in the stud farm (breeders *are* making more of an effort to exercise the bulls to prevent this from happening). There have also been numerous allegations of doping. Most bulls are given some kind of tranquiliser when they arrive at the *corales* to calm them down, and some people believe it often hasn't worn off for the three or four days between the arrival and the fight.

The image problems may explain a sudden controversy surrounding Francisco Rivera Ordóñez in early 2009 when he was awarded the prestigious Fine Arts prize from the Culture Ministry. The award, for his 'more aesthetic, poised and deep' style, prompted José Tomás to return his own medal in disgust amid claims by rival fighters that Francisco Rivera was actually boring, more noted for hitting the scandal magazines than his bravery in the ring (Francisco's brother Cayetano, by now recovered from his goring, refused to enter the ring with another bullfighter who had added his disparaging voice to the debate). Critics saw the affair as a nostalgia among Tomás and others for the visceral rivalry between fighters that was part of a bygone era.

Indeed, bullfighters used to come from the ranks of the rural poor; full-blooded characters, sometimes gypsies, who survived (or didn't survive) multiple tossings and gorings. Now many come from well-to-do families and have university backgrounds.

An oft-cited poll in *El Tiempo* newspaper in 1985 showed that 51 per cent opposed bullfighting, while 35 per cent supported it. A 2002 Gallup poll found that nearly 70 per cent had 'no interest', while the remaining 30 per cent had 'some' or 'a lot' of interest. The poll also found that the over-65s were more likely to support it than the 25–34 age group. Bullfighting schools and fan clubs only emerged in the early 1970s, but they have spread with the help of public funding. The official attitude, though, remains curiously contradictory: the city of Madrid sponsors six fan clubs with the money it makes through bullfights, yet it also funds a number of anti-bullfighting organisations.

But even this bastion of raw Spanishness has not been spared the blade of the financial crisis, nor the increasing defiance of the regions who reject the idea of Spanishness. The numbers of fights rose during the new tourism boom of the 1950s and 1960s and, despite a slump in subsequent decades, enjoyed a revival during the debt-fuelled boom of the 1990s and 2000s. But the tradition is now being squeezed by a triple alliance of animal-rights activists, regional 'nationalism' and the economic crisis. Following 20 years of small-scale, localised opposition, Catalonia introduced a full ban in 2010, which came into effect in 2013. In the Basque city of San Sebastian, the city authorities declared there would be no further bullfights until 2016. As the recession has bitten deeper, numbers attending *corridas* have fallen steadily. The government pushed up prices thanks to a sales tax on cultural events, while disputes between promoters, matadors and creditors over wages have become increasingly bitter and public. With promoters paying less for bulls, breeders have started to shed their stock – or send them to the butcher instead. Meanwhile, one of the principal showcases for bullfights – the week-long celebrations of local patron saints – have been drastically underfunded. Local authorities subsidised them partly through the property sales taxes that rolled in during the construction boom; now that tap has been turned off. As the crisis has worsened, more and more Spanish bullfighters have gone to fight in Peru where the wild, mountainous tradition of the *corrida* and the ruthlessness of the bulls – if not the size of the purse – provide the attraction.

* * *

In Ronda I saw eight bulls tormented, outmanoeuvred into exhaustion, then stabbed to death. The ritual and expertise are breathtaking, but the reality is that, whatever about the aesthetical genius of the *torero*, the odds are pretty much stacked against the bull from the start. With the rather imperial preening of the well-heeled audience, I came away with more distaste than admiration.

Despite the economic crisis and growing hostility in some regions, the art form, sport – call it what you will – seems likely to survive, especially if the Spanish economy recovers. It is likely to remain an intrinsic part of Spanishness, however that concept may be defined, and however inimical it appears to the Spain of chic architecture and free-and-easy modernity. 'It affects the elections and the power system. Parties wouldn't come to power if they banned it,' says Armando. 'No government would dare to forbid it.'

Chapter 4

Italy

In this beautiful country one must only make love; other pleasures of the soul are cramped here. Love here is delicious. Anywhere else it is only a bad copy.
Stendhal

Pasquale Marrandino, aged five, was still asleep in the car when his mother, having just unloaded the shopping, realised and rushed out to retrieve the sleeping boy. Five minutes later the car was racked with machine-gun fire.

The boy's granduncle, 69-year-old Pasquale Marrandino, had just done something few of his neighbours would dare: he had reported the Naples Mafia, the Camorra, to the police. The machine-gun attack was their matter-of-fact gesture of displeasure. When neighbours began refusing business and a barn sheltering the family's water buffalo was burned down, the Marrandinos knew what was next. For three years after the shooting, every trip the family made, including little Pasquale going to school, required a police escort. In 1999, Pasquale the elder died, aged 71. 'He died under the pressure put on him by the Camorra,' said Paolo, his 48-year-old son, who now runs the family mozzarella business.

My visit to the farm began in Naples's Piazza Garibaldi, where the morning gladiators were in full swing – the thrusting Fiats, chopping taxis, slicing Vespas, head-butting buses, flailing pedestrians. Joining the stampede of traffic out of the city, I was soon driving past the slumbering hulk of Vesuvius, now wreathed in a gathering haze of sea mist, and bearing north towards Castel Volturno. All around were saturated fields and canals – land, it turns out, perfect for the mud-black water buffalo that produce mozzarella cheese. The buffalo's hide is so dark that their internal temperature can hit 42 degrees Celsius in summer. With so much water around, they stay cool.

Pasquale Marrandino bought a handful of buffalo in 1947, gradually building up the herd, and selling the milk locally, as the docile, furry beasts gorged on the dark locally grown *oietta* grass. By the 1970s he was converting the milk into mozzarella and soon selling the fat globules of delicate cheese across Italy, and later the world. By 2003, demand for the family's mozzarella was at an all-time high. The Camorra were naturally curious: they first wanted ownership, then a straightforward cut of €150,000 followed by €50,000 in monthly protection. Paolo's father refused. 'We were planning to leave, when my father said, "We've built this place up from nothing, why should we leave?" ' recalls Paolo.

* * *

To understand the origins of organised crime we must look, of course, to Sicily. The island was ruled by outsiders for centuries – Arabs, Normans, Spaniards, Austrians and Bourbons – and since rules were imposed from abroad, they were routinely broken. Banditry was endemic, so landowners resorted to vigilantes to maintain law and deliver justice. Over time, though, deals were brokered between bandit and vigilante, and territories violently marked out. The landowner – often absentee – looked the other way.

Writing in *The Italians* in the 1960s, Luigi Barzini offered two definitions. Lower-case 'mafia' was a moral code by which Sicilians learned from birth that the world was divided into friends and enemies. The code required scrupulous attention to honour and dignity, the avenging of insults and a merciless secrecy. Upper-case 'Mafia', on the other hand, refered to the actual crime networks, not strictly organised into hierarchies, but more like 'an ant colony or beehive'. Members did not see themselves as criminals; rather, violence, extortion and murder were dressed in the garb of honour, loyalty, valour – even honesty – so long as the code was adhered to. If one lived by the code, then family honour had to be defended using whatever means; votes could be garnered for politicians with a gentle threat of violence; businessmen would be quietly advised, with an apologetic humility, that tributes should really be paid to *amici* (friends). The varnish of respectability was theatrically observed by all, from peasant to archbishop. The bosses were paragons of respectability: lawyers, surgeons, country proprietors. 'They have spotless records,' writes Barzini. 'Their manners are ingratiating, they use diplomacy rather than force, speak in a low voice and prefer to employ old-fashioned forms of address.'

Today, however, the Neapolitan branch of the Mafia, the Camorra, cares little for hushed respectability. Since 1979 the network has caused the deaths of 3,600 people. Its activities have been brought to the public's attention by *Gomorrah*, the bestselling book by Roberto Saviano, an undercover reporter from Casal di Principe, not far from Paolo Marrandino's farm.

Gomorrah's thesis is this: so comprehensively has the Camorra insinuated itself into the official economy that the economy has itself become dependent on organised crime. It begins with the mountains of real and fake goods imported from Asia. According to Saviano, almost half of the 2.6 million tons of Chinese goods entering through Naples are unregistered and Camorra controlled, costing the Italian exchequer €200 million every six months. This cash mountain has spread Camorra influence into virtually every sector of the economy, a hidden presence protected by a global web of blind alleys, decoys and shelf companies.

In sweatshops dotted around Naples, thousands of Italian and Chinese workers have converted unregistered products into actual consumer goods destined for Italy's top fashion houses or for high-street stores (or even West African street vendors) as well as reaching the global market through a network of retail outlets, even shopping centres, which have all the appearances of normal traders. This shadow economy has its own rules, order books, auctions and work contracts, its overriding imperative that goods must be produced ever faster, ever cheaper.

The profits are staggering. A crime family can have an annual turnover of €300 million. Money is invested everywhere, from China to the next neighbourhood. The flexibility of the new global economy demands small and medium-sized operators, and they in turn enhance the whole process. What the Camorra system offers is advantageous pricing rather than intimidation; the allure of profit, rather than fear of the gun.

The same principles have been applied to drug trafficking: small 'investors' pour a nest egg into cocaine and see it ripen in such a way that the wealth accrued outweighs the risk involved. The Camorra's stranglehold on cement companies, meanwhile, provides access to every part of the construction process. According to Saviano, at every level of local administration in Campania – land-zoning, sanitation, construction – the Camorra has had a hidden hand. Since 1991, seventy-one local authorities have been dissolved because of Camorra ties.

But it's the Camorra's involvement in waste disposal that brings us back to Paulo Marrandino and his water buffalo. It's estimated that the Camorra has earned €44 *billion* through illegally shifting industrial and municipal waste which, say environmental organisations, if gathered together would be nearly twice the size of Everest. Much of it is toxic, shipped down from the industrial north: fertiliser, printer toner, aluminium, asbestos and sludge from tanning factories, all dumped in farmland, quarries, swamps. The Camorra simply made it cheaper to do it their way, sidestepping those irksome EU waste rules in the process. Respectable middlemen provided a blind link between legitimate companies in the north and the illegal-dumping operators in the south.

The Marrandino family may have defied Camorra threats, but the side effect of their activities soon brought them to their knees. In 2008, high levels of cancer-causing dioxins, caused by illegal dumping and the burning of waste, were found in some mozzarella exports (the Campania region already has higher than normal levels of liver cancer). Japan and Korea quickly banned the cheese, and France threatened to follow suit. When the European Commission threatened an EU-wide ban, the industry went into a tailspin. Italy's reputation as a producer of fine foods was severely dented. Paolo's farm was hit hard.

'We lost €300,000 overnight,' he says.

It wasn't a new problem. Already in 1994, Naples was producing more garbage than it could dispose of thanks to a shortage of landfill, no incinerators and no recycling. The Camorra had moved into transporting waste, at the same time frustrating attempts to expand landfill, build incinerators or develop recycling. In May 2007, fifteen thousand tons of rubbish were stockpiled in the suburbs, and a further 3,000 tons in central Naples and in the slums. By July 2007, the US embassy was advising Americans not to travel to the Campania region to avoid the health hazards of toxic fumes and the dangers of angry demonstrators.

Within a year the problem was back and dominating the general election as 350,000 tons of uncollected waste rotted across the region. The right and left blamed each other for the mess (even though voters suspected politicians on all sides connived with the Camorra-led waste business). 'It's been created out of nothing by politicians on the left and the right,' said Paolo bitterly. 'They're either trying to get more votes or trying to damage the opposition, so they've created an irreversible problem and damaged the whole region for nothing.'

'We are completely abandoned,' said Gaetano, a shop worker in Pianora, a working-class suburb in the hills. 'We have a store here, selling food, and for the customers it's not a pretty sight to see rubbish piled up just opposite us.'

The level of despair and public cynicism was depressing. 'Now we can't even drink the water,' said a student outside Gaetano's shop. 'Even the local politicians are making money from the waste we were bringing down from the north, so why should they try and stop it happening?' In March 2008, the president of the Naples region and former left-wing mayor, Antonio Bassolino, as well as 27 other officials, were investigated for irregularities in the waste management system. Charges against all 28 were eventually dropped by Neapolitan prosecutors in November 2013 under Italy's statute of limitations rule.

* * *

Hollywood has had a long love affair with the Mafia. From the shadowy intensity of *The Godfather* to the high-octane humour of *Goodfellas*, to the everyman angst of *The Sopranos*, each generation has its favourite. So engrained in the culture is the celluloid portrayal of Mafia power – with its executions, wisecracks, family intrigue – that life has come to imitate art. *The Sopranos* crackles with references and in jokes about Hollywood depictions of mobsters, and in turn real-life *Mafiosi* are quoted on FBI wiretaps as saying how *The Sopranos* are just like them. It's nothing new:

Mario Puzo's fictional Godfather, inspired by the Neapolitan Alphonse Frank Tieri, ensured that the term *Padrino* (Godfather) became common parlance instead of *Compare*, the traditional word for a clan leader. Al Capone used to turn up on the set of a 1932 movie to observe the character (Tony Camonte) upon whom he was based. The argot, sartorial style, even architectural designs, have been copied from what modern gangsters see on the screen. Roberto Saviano describes how in Casal di Principe, a Camorra stronghold outside Naples, clan leader Walter Schiavone built a replica of Al Pacino's mansion in *Scarface*, complete with the marble staircase and balcony on which Pacino's Tony Montana character dies in a hail of bullets.

Having all that power no doubt encourages Camorra gangsters to live out pseudo-historical fantasies (one family named its offspring after Roman emperors, another kept a collection of books on Napoleon). But they know how to separate real life and make believe when it matters. On the one hand, local members were delighted to advise director Matteo Garrone when he was filming a version of *Gomorrah* in their neighbourhood (one actor, Giovanni Venosa, who played a Camorra boss, was himself convicted of extortion just months after the filming stopped), while thousands of pirated copies of the DVD were on sale in Naples, all with Camorra connivance. On the other hand, they weren't so keen on Saviano's book on which the film is based. He's been under police protection since October 2006.

By the sun-kissed marinas of seafront Naples, I'm due to meet a gentleman who prefers his movie stars to be above board. The tourist quarter, with its UNESCO World Heritage stamp of approval, has been cleared of rotting garbage, but the damage has already been done. Hotel bookings are down 30 per cent on the previous year, and down 40 per cent since 2004. In his leather-bound office, Sergio Maione, director of the €300-a-night Grand Hotel Vesuvio, is not happy. The roof garden and restaurant, overlooking the Bay of Naples, and both named after the legendary tenor Enrico Caruso, have just closed (Caruso lived and, on 2 August 1921, died in the Hotel Vesuvio). A few weeks before my visit, the restaurant received just 16 bookings over an entire weekend. Sergio blames not just the Camorra, but the entire sclerotic system of governance (as he speaks, he presses a button and within seconds a tuxedoed waiter appeares with fresh espresso). 'I can remember Bill Clinton, François Mitterand, Claudia Schiffer, Sophia Loren, Alfred Hitchcock, all staying here. Now the tourists are staying away,' he says sadly (it is a somewhat bitter irony that the fictional Tony Soprano, no stranger to waste management, choses to stay at the Vesuvio during his trip-to-the-old-country episode). 'It's not just politics. Whoever gets into government will have to deal with the lobbies and there are all kinds of lobbies in Italy – the professions, the unions. The lobbies are against any progress or modernisation. The garbage crisis is the last straw. It makes Italy look like the Third World. It is *shameful*.'

* * *

Italy as a Third World country? What a fall from grace. Twenty years before the garbage crisis, the poet Leonardo Sciascia wrote: 'We will continue to fall, without ever hitting the bottom.'

And yet the mental image is so different. 'Italy is a soft drug peddled in predictable packages,' writes the Italian commentator Beppe Severgnini, 'such as the hills in the sunset, olive groves, lemon trees, white wine and raven-haired girls.' We think of the food, the fashion, the cars, the footballers, the opera, the art, the climate, the cappuccino, the *trattorie*. We think hills in Tuscany, gondoliers in Venice, Gregory Peck in *Roman Holiday*, Helena Bonham Carter in *A Room with a View*. The Italians have been wading, just like Anita Ekberg in the Trevi Fountain, waist high through *la dolce vita*.

The drug has never ceased to draw visitors south. In Roman times it was the Barbarians, in the Middle Ages a stream of pilgrims yearning to visit the seat of the Holy Church. Traders, crusaders, theologians, knights, scholars, princes and gentlemen all slogged over the Alps, lured by vague desires, holy obligations or intellectual pursuits. 'They liked the mild climate but feared it,' writes Luigi Barzini, 'as they liked but feared at the same time the Italians' elegant life, easy pleasures, adaptable morals, intricate reasoning, wines, women, the harmonious landscapes, the feeling of being immersed in history and ennobled by it.'

During the Renaissance, which began in Florence in the 14th century, the pull of Italy increased as Michelangelo and Leonardo da Vinci reshaped the way Europeans looked at themselves, at beauty, at the world and at God. But below lay darker forces. John Addington Symonds, the Victorian scholar of the Renaissance, wrote: 'Beneath the surface of brilliant social culture, lurked gross appetites and savage passions, unrestrained by medieval piety, untutored by modern experience. Italian society exhibited an almost unexampled spectacle of literary, artistic and courtly refinements, crossed by brutalities of lust, treason, poisonings, assassinations, violence ...'

So early on a disconnect between the high ideals of the Holy Roman Church and the reality of Italian lives was planted in European heads. While Italy's sensual pleasures entranced Milton, Goethe, Byron and Shelley, the Italian *character* was frowned upon. Early stereotypes of Italians focused on duplicity, intrigue and murder. Much of this was inspired by the writings of Niccolò Machiavelli, the Florentine diplomat whose experience of war, conspiracy and political murder drove him to investigate the ruthlessness that motivated rulers to discover how it might be best harnessed – or avoided – to strengthen the ruler's position. It was about how politics *was* run and not how it *should* be run; and his conclusions, sometimes cynical, sometimes despairing, took shape in *The Prince*, published in 1532. Although Machiavelli sought more efficient governance, when his views travelled, he was only remembered for advocating ruthlessness. Elizabethan theatre bristled with duplicitous, cunning and amoral Italians: in Webster's plays, Italian characters poison their victims in *four* different ways. And once Britain went the way of Protestantism, prejudice was conflated with an abhorrence of popery.

The Jesuits didn't help Italy's image. The Society of Jesus was set up in 1539 as a reaction against the Reformation and the scandals with which the Church had become synonymous. It stood for discipline, obedience and prejudice. Although established by a Spanish priest, Saint Ignatius Loyola, it was later expanded by the Italians and their assertive, regimented ways – not least their alleged involvement in conspiracies and assassinations – all added to the negative image.

Young gentlemen, though, were still encouraged to travel to Renaissance Italy (to Dr Johnson, an Italian education was indispensable). Italy became Europe's finishing school, with graduates affecting Italian mannerisms, fashion and conversational skills. Their heads were filled with classical verse and the marvels of antiquity, but little of real, contemporary Italy. After World War II, travellers, artists and writers kept coming. Despite the ravages of war, it was a place of affordable culture and beauty. Fashionable Americans enjoyed *la dolce vita* in the nightclubs of Rome's Via Veneto, following in the footsteps of the dazzling, profane and ultimately shallow characters of Federico Fellini's 1960 film.

There was a lot of traffic in the other direction. Tens of thousands of Italians migrated to the United States. The majority came from Sicily and Calabria, forming the febrile ghettos from which the American Mafia emerged. But these southern Italians, who tended to be poorer, shorter and darker, also engraved on people's minds a very specific Italian type, so when Americans visited Florence in Tuscany, they were surprised to find blondes.

* * *

Today, Italians cling to Brand Italy. She is still famed for her fashion designers, her Ferraris, her lamé models and lacquered footballers. However, the future beckons. The future is called China.

In 2006, I travelled to the city of Prato to the west of Florence. Here over 700 square kilometres of factories once produced the fabric for Italy's fashion houses, employing 50,000 people. It was even acknowledged by Hollywood in the shape of Oscars for best costumes – Ridley Scott's *Gladiator*, Mel Gibson's *Braveheart* and Martin Scorsese's *Gangs of New York*. All the costumes were made with fabric from Prato.

But by the time I arrived, the fabric industry was being decimated. Competition from China, Turkey, North Africa and Eastern Europe had seen one-third of textile companies close down, with the loss of 15,000 jobs. Prato has been the centre of Italy's textile business since the Middle Ages. The yarn was produced here, woven into quality fabric and then sent to the designers. Nowadays, most of that is already done in China for a fraction of the cost. Prato must produce extremely high-end stuff to survive; otherwise, it's just 'improving' the fabric that comes from China, a last-minute link in the chain of production so it can qualify for the 'Made in Italy' badge. Prato's family businesses are run by ageing parents whose offspring are often no longer interested. 'China is growing very quickly,' says Franco Millotti, the president of Milior, a family firm just about surviving by producing very high-quality fabrics using unorthodox materials. 'We are afraid that in a short time they will produce part of our product and give us a very big problem.' He hopes his 28-year-old son will take over the business, but he's not sure.

But the Chinese threat wasn't just from afar. It was right there in Prato: 60,000 Chinese people (half of them thought to be illegal) working – and sometimes sleeping – in sweatshops. The ghetto encounters little, if any, curiosity. They fill vast storerooms with cheap, mass-market clothing for the European high street and send the money they earn back to China – in 2008, this amounted to €1.6 *billion* in remittances. Ironically, they may even be keeping Italy's indigenous fashion industry alive: the labour is cheap (the Chinese claim conditions are better than back home), and the industry benefits because it keeps wages down. And it means that every garment they finish carries the coveted 'Made in Italy' label.

* * *

Italians still die for their labels. It is, after all, the home of Versace, Ferragamo, Zegna, Dolce & Gabbana. When David Beckham signed for AC Milan, Victoria must have felt she was coming home. 'I'm fed up with the exaggerated importance they give to how they're turned out,' says Deirdre Doyle, an Irish professional living in Milan. 'Everything – clothes, cars, shoes, sunglasses – has to be designer. They're so aware of how much money they spend on themselves to look that way and that annoys me.'

'Appearance is everything, especially clothing,' says Fiona, an Irish woman married to a Sicilian. 'We go skiing in Bergamo every year where we have an apartment, and every time I meet some new women there they ask the same three questions: what does your husband do, what kind of car do you drive, do you have any other properties. Italians are very superficial. How the house looks and how beautiful their daughters look are the most important thing. Italian men are very aware of their appearance, always have the right aftershave, worry about how their hair looks.'

Such cattiness may be forgiven when you realise how visual the culture is. Life in Italy is a photo shoot. In a climate that produces so much light and brilliance, people need to look their best, and admitting they're succeeding evokes no embarrassment. All is spectacle, gesture, animation, visual stimuli. Orson Welles said that Italy is full of actors, 50 million of them; only the bad ones were on TV. In a country with the highest density of classical treasures, the beholding of beauty is a relentless activity. Eroticism is rampant, lingerie shops appear at every corner, mainstream television is filled with stunning 'show girls' prettying up the middle-aged presenters. And in its infatuation, the European high street can no longer cope without its macchiato coffees, its panini or its Dolce & Gabbana handbags.

La bella figura – cutting an attractive figure – is a highly cherished concept. But it is more than superficial; it is to succeed in appearing *appropriately* attractive. What you're trying to sell will be immeasurably enhanced if you look good while you're doing it. During the election campaign in 2006, I visited Fabio Violente, a Bari public relations executive, who was dressing up to the nines with his girlfriend, father, mother and sister, for an election rally by Silvio Berlusconi. 'Berlusconi has a beautiful cinematic face, a Hollywood face,' explained Fabio. 'This should not worry people. On the contrary, it does politics good. With this image he succeeds in bringing contentment and goodwill towards his political programme.' To Fabio, image enhanced content.

His hero's mission, meanwhile, has been to elevate *la bella figura* into a political meditation. Where other European leaders are reluctant to flaunt their wealth, Silvio Berlusconi is canny enough to know that cavorting on a yacht appeals to the innate celebration by many Italians of material beauty.

'He represents the Italian mind, the good and the bad, the pathologies,' says Beppe Severgnini, the author of *La Bella Figura: An Insider's Guide to the Italian Mind.* 'The pathology of sympathy, for example, is very Italian. He can sell you everything, he is very loyal to his friends, very much an Italian character, very much obsessed with appearance. If you don't know Italy and the Italian character, you don't quite grasp the charm and appeal of Mr Berlusconi.'

Personal vanity is thus no venial sin: Berlusconi disappeared from view in 2004, later resurfacing with a face lift and a hair transplant. (When he appeared with Tony and Cherie Blair at his villa in Sardinia wearing a rather medical-looking bandana, the favourite left-wing joke was that he had been circumcised.)

Berlusconi started out in property in the boom years of the early 1960s, culminating in a project to build 4,000 gated apartments in Milan. Against considerable odds, the project – Milano 2 – was a runaway success. For Berlusconi, it was a parable of the entrepreneurial David against the Goliath of bureaucracy. For his critics, however, the whiff of corruption was there from the start. For such a straightforward enterprise there was a Byzantine web of Swiss bank accounts and shelf companies (Berlusconi's name disappeared from the project in 1968, not resurfacing until 1975). The suspicion, never proven, was that Mafia cash was used to bankroll Milano 2.

The limitations of property prompted Berlusconi to diversify. Television was tailor made for his hunger for profit and his desire to see dreams realised more swiftly. Until the 1980s, Italian television was not unlike Ireland's: risk free and closing down at 11 p.m. But thanks to a close friendship with Bettino Craxi, the Socialist leader, he spotted an opening in new broadcasting laws. Within months he bought up every local TV channel and established his first national channels.

When magistrates ruled that he'd breached local broadcasting rules, his commercial channels were partially blacked out. But the outcry from a public just getting hooked on *Dallas* and *Dynasty*, and the swift intervention of his friend the prime minister, meant Berlusconi's TV dream – now under the umbrella of Mediaset – was very much alive. Throughtout the 1980s the dream transformed the relationship between Italians and television. Mediaset broadcast an unapologetically American diet of films, quiz shows, cartoons, soap operas and variety shows. The overriding principle was popularity, while the female form was elevated to new importance (a trend that spread to the public channels RAI1 and 2). 'Mediaset's programmes were heavily sexually oriented in a way that stopped just short of nudity,' writes Paul Ginsborg in *Silvio Berlusconi: Television, Power and Patrimony*. 'Every middle-aged compère was, and still is, accompanied by scantily dressed soubrettes. Cameras zoomed in upon them from below and behind, emphasising anatomical detail whenever possible.'

Berlusconi, meanwhile, had his own advertising company (Publitalia), so he could offer thousands of small and medium-sized firms a 'golden chain of connection' from the goods they produced to his advertising company to his programme makers to his broadcasters and on to consumers. Advertising was rampant: in 1984, RAI, the public channel, showed nearly 50,000 ads worth over 330 hours; commercial television, on the other hand, was showing *half a million* ads, all adding up to 3,500 hours. And the ads were not subtle. 'Italian commercial television advertisements in the 1980s were a noisy, endlessly repetitive, frontal attack upon fledgling consumers,' writes Ginsborg.

In 1986 Berlusconi brought the same principles to bear with the purchase of AC Milan. Decisions delivered with enough fanfare and style would compensate for what they lacked in substance. It was a brilliant strategy. He introduced the flair of Dutch football, signing Ruud Gullit, Marco van Basten and Frank Rijkaard. Within three years they had won the Italian league and the European Champions' Cup. The success of his team came on the back of Italy's World Cup win in 1982. Everything flowed into television, and television was increasingly controlled by Berlusconi.

Politics naturally beckoned. After the 'Clean Hands' investigation uncovered rampant corruption and sparked the collapse of the Christian Democrats in the early 1990s, Berlusconi stepped into the vacuum, moulding disparate political and business elements into a new centre-right movement, Forza Italia (named after a football chant). In 1994, the party won 21 per cent of the vote. Berlusconi promised to run Italy like a profitable business and, indeed, 50 of his MPs were employed by his advertising company. That same spring, he became prime minister, and AC Milan won the European Cup.

His first turn as prime minister lasted six months. He was out of his depth in the bear pit of Italian politics and his coalition partners, the right-wing Northern League, pulled out over pension reforms and indications that Berlusconi himself was being investigated as part of Clean Hands. In the meantime, he faced accusations of illegally financing political parties, bribing the financial police, tax fraud, false accounting and corrupting judges. In court appearances, he defiantly rejected the charges, and in pubic he repeatedly spoke of a 'Communist' conspiracy among magistrates. Forza Italia MPs with shows on Mediaset delivered a stream of invective against the judiciary.

The big word in Berlusconi's political vocabulary was Freedom (in 2008 he changed the name Forza Italia to People of Freedom). It meant, however, freedom from bureaucracy, regulation and stifling control. Voters responded to the mantra. Fifty-four per cent of shopkeepers and the self-employed voted for Berlusconi, as did 44.8 per cent of housewives who were bombarded with ads every 15 minutes of the daytime schedule (given the low female participation in the labour market, that meant a lot of voters). Italians were now watching more TV than anybody else with viewing time increasing by a full hour a day during his broadcasting reign. 'Programming was seamlessly integrated with advertising… A programme is interrupted for a "promotional message" and news items are there to plug a product,' writes Tobias Jones in *The Dark Heart of Italy*.

Berlusconi wasn't ramming party political broadcasts down the throats of his viewers, but critics suggested the effects were subtle and cumulative. Since advertising created the sense of longing that feeds modern consumerism, the values of that advertising could, over time, create an idealised version of family life. 'These imagined families belonged to Berlusconi,' writes Paul Ginsborg. 'They are neat, well turned out, sporting, joking, computerised, pro-American, globe-trotting, business-oriented and privatised … [Berlusconi] presides over the imagination of a significant segment of the population.'

In this rapture, the population, part of it at least, has been mesmerised by the Berlusconi fable: the wealth, the escapism, the sporting victories, the *bella figura*, the cunning avoidance of tax and regulations, the sexual braggadocio. On one rather artless level, Berlusconi had become the living embodiment not just of Italian virtues or vices, but of Italian *stereotypes* which lie close to the surface. 'A leader,' to quote Alessandro Meluzzi, one of his disciples, 'who will be chosen because everyone can recognise something of themselves in him, can identify themselves and that which they would want to be.' But as always in Italy, there is a darker side to the superficial stereotype that Berlusconi embodies. Between 2011 and 2013, his interminable legal problems were dominated by a sex scandal that was incredible, even by his standards, and which triggered mass demonstrations by Italian women convinced that Berlusconi's antics had for years given sanction to a growing and official misogyny, which had, in the words of one critic, turned Italy into a Whore-ocracy…

In reality, Silvio Berlusconi's macho histrionics are not new. For years he had laced his self-made myths with tales of sexual adventure (he once boasted that he seduced the secretary of the president of a major pension fund so that he could lobby for a possible investment into his housing development in Milan). His dinner parties at Arcore, the 147-room country villa near Milan which later became synonymous with his notorious *bunga bunga* parties, were spiced with lurid stories, the telling of which were sometimes accompanied by nude pictures of his wife Veronica.

Even his off-colour remarks to (or about) fellow world leaders (his wiretapped reference to German Chancellor Angela Merkel is unprintable), were for a while tolerated with a sigh, or a shake of the head. But his insatiable appetite for girls nearly one quarter his age eventually became no laughing matter.

'On the one hand,' writes Alexander Stille in *The Sack of Rome*, 'Berlusconi is a traditional Italian macho, the kind of guy who can be found bragging about his sexual prowess at the local bar in most towns across Italy. On the other, there is something new and subversive about Berlusconi's attitudes toward sex… He has introduced sex into whole new areas of public life – television, sales meetings, press conferences and encounters with world leaders.'

Whether Berlusconi thought that popular tolerance of a stereotypical form of the ageing male sex drive would shield him from an eventual comeuppance is hard to say. But from 2009 on, a steady drumbeat of allegations and revelations began to take their toll. First, his wife divorced him, issuing a public accusation that he had been "consorting with minors" (namely an 18-year-old lingerie model called Noemi Letizia). Then a call girl, Patrizia D'Addario, alleged that she had been recruited to spend the night with the Italian prime minister (his robust denial included the notion that he couldn't possible have sex with a woman if there was no conquest involved). Soon there were further allegations of prostititues spending the night at Berlusconi's Rome residence Palazzo Grazioli.

However, the full spotlight into Berlusconi's private life would not be shone until an obscure police incident in Milan on 27 May 2010. A 17-year-old Morrocan girl called Karima El Mahroug had just been arrested by police in in connection with the theft of €3,000 when the police station received a phone call from none other than the prime minister himself, Silvio Berlusconi. According to court records he ordered the hapless police officer in charge to release the girl since she was related to the then Egyptian President Hosni Mubarak.

In fact El Mahroug had no connection to Mubarak. She was a belly dancer and illegal immigrant who had been working in night clubs under the name Ruby Rubacuori (Ruby the Heartstealer) and who had been introduced to Berlusconi by Nicole Minetti, a former dancer and later dental hygienist who was, to the astonishment of the political class, given a high-ranking political job by Berlusconi in Lombardy. By the time a criminal case was assembled, a picture had emerged of a lurid procurement network run by business associates to provide a supply of young girls for erotic *bunga bunga* parties in Arcore.

Many of these girls were allegedly recruited from the ranks of so-called showgirls or *Velline*, teenage starlets who aspired to appear on Berlusconi prime-time variety shows (as described by Paul Ginsborg above).

At the height of the Ruby scandal I visited the Alpha Model Agency in Rome where a dozen or so would-be showgirls were being put through their paces to learn how to appear on television (all of them, when undergoing a mock interview, described their hobby as 'shopping'). I asked Federica Boldrini, the instructor, if the girls in her class could find themselves channelled through the variety show scene into the arms of Mr Berlusconi at Arcore? Her answer was more instructive about the status of women in Italy than about the then prime minister's sexual appetite.

'Of course one uses one's own body these days to earn money,' she said. 'That's how it works. Everyday it's something we in the industry talk about. Of course it's not up to me to judge if some girls have done something to reach a certain level – the girls here tell us they would never dream of it – but I don't know what happens elsewhere. But here they have to work hard.'

Morgana, the mother of Sharon Gallo, who was one of the more promising students, said somewhat ambiguously, when I asked her if she was worried about what her daughter was getting in to, 'Absolutely not, I'm not worried. We have a saying: if you plant seeds well, then good things will grow…'

On 24 June 2013, a court in Milan found Silvio Berlusconi guilty of paying Karima El Mahroug for sex between February and May 2010. Since she was underage, this was a serious crime. He was also convicted of abusing public office for the telephone call to the Milan police station. For both convictions he was barred from holding public office and given a seven-year jail term. Because because he has two options to appeal, few observers believe he will ever serve a day in jail.

* * *

The Italian male is a complex character. All doe-eyed and vulnerable in the chase of his inamorata one minute; playing the macho rooster the next. To find out more, I have come to the Drunken Ship in Campo de' Fiori, a popular drinking quarter in the centre of Rome. In the 17th century, it was where Giordano Bruno, philosopher, priest, cosmologist and occultist, was burned at the stake for heresy. His hooded statue today broods in the direction of the Vatican, and Campo de' Fiori still has a whiff of anarchy about it. On the night Pope John Paul II died, while the rest of the world was plunged into sadness, customers in Il Nolano bar cracked open a bottle of champagne.

In the Drunken Ship, Clare from Ohio has just picked up a small shot glass, and in less than a second a creamy jewel of alcohol disappears in a hard, professional swallow. Her drinking friends are fellow students, mostly getting drunk, and quite a few have plunging necklines. In zoological terms, they are gazelles. Surrounding them amid the static charge of predatory heat are the cheetahs, young Italian males. Massimo has chosen the grazing uplands of Campo de' Fiori well: these females have been sprung loose from the alcohol-restricted campuses of Midwest America. Here in Rome, on a five-month semester to study Italian film or English poets, they can drink themselves senseless. Massimo finally nods to his fellow cheetahs to make themselves scarce: he is going in for the kill.

I'd heard about this from my friend Enrico. 'You'll find them at the Spanish Steps, hitting on American women. Some of them will try to chat up 10 girls. They'll ask for a light, or the time of day, and say something like, "Ciao, we've met before!" They think that because they're American, they'll be an easy lay. But Italian girls are not like that.'

I had arranged to meet Enrico and his wife, Chiara, that afternoon to find out. The tourists on Piazza di Spagna were posing for snaps with Roman Centurions, queueing for the *carrozzelle* horse-and-carriage rides, or gazing up at the house where Keats died. The Dior, Missoni and Yves Saint Laurent boutiques were bustling. Chiara, it turns out, has a good handle on Irish and Italian men. A native of Rome, she spent five years in Dublin. 'Irish men are completely lacking in confidence. They're only really confident enough to talk to you when they're drunk, and that's when they're at their *least* attractive.'

Enrico quickly points out our candidates: a cluster of boys looking too cool to do anything that might unruffle the studied bravura. For the moment, they've made only a few cursory moves, so I make my own. I approach two attractive young females. Have they been hit on by the Italian male? Serena, a brunette, is actually Italian, but she moved to Toronto when she was 19. 'When I went to Canada I thought, I can breathe! I can walk the streets without being hassled. I actually began to think I was ugly!'

Catherine, a redhead French-Canadian living in Germany, said: 'I got hit on the moment I got off the plane. It's either, *Ciao bella*! Or *Complimenti a tua mamma*! I'm totally against it, but after a while you think … well, it's kind of nice, as long as they don't want something from you. You get comments about your hair and skin. Foreigners getting hit on are kind of scared, but Italian women are so used to it.'

Later, back at the Drunken Ship, Claudia, a 25-year-old special-effects producer from New York, says Italian boys are the worst. 'They *chase* you!' says Claudia. 'In Florence I got *chased*! Then at the Coliseum they kept jumping in front of my camera, offering to take photos of me. They're very aggressive. I was once hit on in a hotel lobby in Mexico by an Italian hockey player and he invited me to Milan. The guy was a 28-year-old marketing executive for Giorgio Armani and he said I could stay at his place. I was expecting a really cool apartment, but he was living with his mother!'

Some hate it outright: 'If it was America, it would be sexual harassment, no doubt about it,' says an architecture student from Boston.

Back to Massimo, who is zeroing in on Clare from Ohio. After a while, they're in deep conversation. She seems interested.

'Italian men *are* beautiful,' says Claudia, looking on somewhat dreamily.

We're joined by Mia, also from the Midwest. She is, however, scathing. 'They're creepy! They think American girls are easy. My friend was jogging in Rome and as she was waiting at a red light, a guy pulled up beside her on his Motorino, grabbed her arm and said, "Marry me and run away with me!" Poor girl! And her mother's Italian!'

Suddenly, it's 2 a.m. and the gazelles, sniffing the air for danger, decide to leave for Scholars Irish Pub. Clare from Ohio pulls away.

'Where are you going?' cries Massimo.

'Um, we're leaving, we have to leave,' she says.

'I come with you!'

'I'm leaving, we have to leave.'

'But I come with you!' Desperation is creeping in.

'Uh, I don't care. I have to leave.'

Later, Scholars is heaving. The sports screens around the walls reinforce the sense that this is a trading floor, and we're in a bull market. All around, young American exchange students, Paddies, Brits and Jocks are in the extra-time drunken denouement (this is an environment in which sober Italian males – Massimo included – are not comfortable). I run into Clare from Ohio. So what about Massimo? 'Oh him, I wasn't really interested,' is the darted response before she rejoins the gazelles. Poor Massimo.

* * *

Italians have elaborated seduction into two branches, the trivial and the melodramatic. Both are part of a complex, often joyful, art. In Fellini's *La Dolce Vita*, journalist Marcello Mastroianni is seen hovering in a helicopter over the roof of an apartment complex trying to solicit a phone number from a group of bikini-clad sunbathers. The rejection is taken with an amused shrug. It's the pleasure of this, the frivolous braggadocio, but also the knowledge that statistically he will eventually get lucky.

But when they fall for a girl, Italian men can be extremely inventive and romantic in the pursuit. While Irish teenagers cross the seduction bridge after several pints, Italians engage in *fare la corte:* the girl is pursued with a flower, a necklace, invited for an ice cream. It can take a long or short time and has its echoes in the *amor cortese*, the courtly love rituals learned from the French in the Middle Ages which ran through Dante, with his Beatrice, and Petrarch with his Laura. One Italian friend tells of how as a teenager, a boy who was pursuing her discovered she would be visiting a museum in Venice a week after he was there. 'When he was in the museum, he wrote that he loved me on a windowpane and made sure I was directed to it when I went there. This went on for years.'

Irish women enjoy the attention when they travel to Italy, and it drives Irish males to distraction. 'Irish girls find Italian boyfriends usually in the first month, and then they're hooked,' says Tom, a twenty-something Irish professional in Milan. 'Then their Italian comes on in leaps and bounds. One girl I know met her boyfriend at the lost-luggage counter at Bergamo Airport the *day she arrived*. Irish girls are not too hard to talk to and Italian males are pretty direct, so you can see how that works. But Irish guys are not as confident or persistent and Italian women can be quite standoffish, even if they don't mean it. So Irish guys take rejection literally and as a result often end up stuck on their own.'

Embedded in the Italian male psyche is an attitude dating back to post-war morality when they saw foreign women – usually from the north – as more available. 'In the 1950s and 1960s, women were very much under the kosh of the Church and the Communist Party,' says Massimo Canevacci, Professor of Cultural Anthropology at Rome's La Sapienza University. 'It was a difficult time for pheromone-charged males who associated foreign women with easy sex. I used to meet with my friends in the 1960s and we would say, "*Andiamo a stranieri*", which more or less meant, let's go chasing foreign women.'

Some foreign women enjoy it, others are intimidated. 'Because they have a feminine side, Italian men connect very easily with women,' writes Clotaire Rapaille, the international marketing guru and author of *Culture Codes*. 'Italian women love them for it. In fact, even foreign women respond differently to Italian men than they do to men of other cultures. Largely this is because Italian men make it clear that their attentions are in fun and neither threatening nor salacious in any way; their strong natural connection to women makes it easy for them to convey this.'

Within Italy itself, the trouble begins when cultural tolerance is given legal weight. In the late 1990s, a court decided that a single or 'sudden' slap by a man on a woman was acceptable if it was 'isolated or impulsive'. Then a driving instructor in Potenza had his conviction for raping an 18-year-old student overturned because she was wearing jeans (it was, ruled the judge, impossible to remove someone's jeans without their consent). There was outrage: female MPs wore jeans to parliament in protest, and a sexual abuse helpline was flooded by callers worried about the judgment's implications.

The ruling was later rescinded. Indeed, other cases have shown that wayward attitudes to sexual decorum are less tolerable. In a case that sought to end unwanted physical encroachment in public spaces, an appeals court jailed a 58-year-old man for patting the behind of a girl as she worked in her parents' ice-cream shop.

The stereotype has deep roots, but in literature, Italian seducers get their comeuppance, or are marked by some kind of failure or other. Giacomo Casanova, the 18th-century adventurer, diplomat and seducer of 200 women, who died penniless, remains the embodiment par excellence. Born in Venice in 1725, he lived a life of adventure, scandal, fame, intrigue, duelling, swindling and gambling, inveigling his way in and out of the beds of nuns, princesses, teenagers, wives, duchesses and – at one point – the six daughters of the mayor of Geneva. His irresistable charm, combined with his endurance skills, enhanced the prototype of the Italian stallion. 'His physical capacity to satisfy the most exacting mistress,' writes Luigi Barzini, 'by renewing his homages to her a practically unlimited number of times through the night and the following day, with only short *entr'actes* between the exertions, is not as surprising as the feat of psychological endurance: he was never bored, never embittered by experience, sincerely admired one woman after another.'

According to Giuseppe Manica, who has run the Italian Cultural Institute in numerous capitals for the past 30 years, we need to look south, to Sicily. 'Arab culture left a strong impression. The Arabs were there since 827. Many of the ideas of the macho sense of honour, of strength, of being able to face any challenge, of placing oneself above women – I suspect these came from the Arab influence.'

In the 20th century, Vitaliano Brancati explored themes of male sexual delusion on his native island. In *Don Giovanni in Sicilia* (1941) and *Bell'Antonio* (1949), he portrays a Sicily 'filled with ambitious and foolish

Don Juans, failed rakes defeated by life, who live in a world of sensual fantasies and amazing erotic adventures', as Alfredo Sgroi writes in the *Encyclopedia of Italian Literary Studies*. 'In a Catania beaten by the sirocco, which numbs and blocks all vital impulses, his characters often fall into a condition of total inertia, metaphorically represented by long afternoon siestas and vain gossip, the sole subject of which is women.'

Today, the Latin lover's sexual performance still grabs flashy headlines in the glossies, but beneath the hyperbole there is an undercurrent of angst. According to the leading sexologist, Professor Chiara Simonelli, Italian men are disorientated by their loss in status and the growing emancipation of women. 'In Mediterranean countries, there's always been a deep separation of roles. A woman was supposed to be shy and uninterested. Their virginity was protected by the grandmother and the male would come along and be the dominant partner. These stereotypes used to be complimentary, but not any more. In the past 40 years, women have changed, within families and within the culture. Women are more independent, more sexually assertive, and men are not happy.'

The changes are happening where they matter most: in the bedroom. A study by Professor Simonelli found that 40 per cent of Italian couples were not having sex, partly due to a decline in the male sex drive, and the male's growing preference for the internet and prostitution. In the past, the Italian male was expected to have had some sexual experience (from a prostitute or an older woman) before proposing to his *fidanzata*. These days, even girls as young as 16 have had some kind of sexual encounter, and when it comes to the wedding night, she is often more experienced than her husband. 'I've had so many emails from men who say they've claimed to have had experience, but in fact they haven't. It's because they're lacking confidence,' says Professor Simonelli. 'And so they're spending more and more time getting sexual gratification on the internet, where they aren't judged. Or they are taking girlfriends from Eastern Europe who they see as more passive, who don't speak Italian, and who are more impressed by their power. Compared to them, Italian women seem too demanding.'

In 2006, of the 20,000 Italian men who married foreigners, one-fifth of the brides came from Romania (Ukraine, Poland, Russia, Albania and Moldova were all in the top seven). It's not surprising that Romanian women are on top: following Romanian accession to the EU, thousands took up domestic jobs in the Italian marital home. Many men have divorced their wives and married Romanians instead.

* * *

Why do Italian men appear so confused? According to the stereotype, they are either image-obsessed, appallingly lecherous or mother-fixated wimps who live at home until their thirties. Or an unattractive blend of all three.

'There are many Italian men,' says Mara Tognetti, a sociologist from the University of Milano-Bicocca, 'who still want women with a traditional sense of family, women who know their roles as mothers, wives and homemakers. I call these men "B-men" [as in Serie B, or second division in Italian footballing terms], who either have a failed first marriage, or who have been living a long time with their parents, and so are strongly under the influence of the family.'

This overbearing influence of the family may be more specifically the influence of the famous Italian Mamma. 'The Italian mother figure was so connected with her sons, and they were so immersed in this love, that they transferred it to an erotic version which they applied to young women,' says Professor Canevacci at La Sapienza University. 'The mother would sacrifice her life for her children, especially her male children.'

The influence of *La Mamma* is not to be underestimated. Why else would the expression *Mamma Mia!* have become so enduring? It is the universal response to disappointment or emergency. In *Mamma Roma* (1962), an achingly stark portrait by Pier Paolo Pasolini of those who survived the Fascist era, Anna Magnani's character is a metaphor for Rome itself, but also for the suffering of Italian mothers during the war and Italy's post-war hunger. She puts herself through prostitution in order to bring up Ettore, her 16-year-old son, yet her limitless love is still not enough to prevent his prison death. Italian history is riddled with wars – wars between families, cities and regions, wars against the invaders – and throughout, women made enormous sacrifices to keep the family intact, even while the paterfamilias reigned supreme. 'The man is the titular head of the family, but by no means the monarch,' observes Luigi Barzini in

The Italians. 'Men might run the country, but women run men. Italy is, in reality, a cryptomatriarchy.'

That was written in 1964. Are things still the same?

There have been enormous social changes since then. Under Mussolini's edict, only 5 per cent of women were employed outside the home. Today, more are in full-time employment, but attitudes to their role remain. The average female salary is 35 per cent lower than a man's, and the percentage of women in parliament is the same as that of Morocco. The sanctified position of the Mamma, too, is slow to change. Mothers still pamper their sons, while scrupulous housekeeping propaganda is drilled into the daughters, and so the cycle is repeated. As a result, Mamma maintains a hallowed, sometimes intimidating presence in the private lives of Italians.

'The mother-in-law won't come first, but nearly first,' says Deirdre Doyle, our Irish professional living in Milan. 'A lot of foreigners find this difficult. I had a very intelligent mother-in-law who got what she wanted but she did it in a very tactful, diplomatic way. But I have a friend who's married to an Italian man and he rings his mother every day, and he won't make any decision without consulting her first. It drives his wife crazy.'

My Roman friend Chiara says, 'I knew an Englishwoman who was starting a very promising relationship with an Italian man. One day they were caught in a thunderstorm and when they got back to her apartment, he asked to borrow her hairdryer – for his *shoes*! He said his mother would kill him if his shoes were ruined. She ended the relationship immediately.'

Not just because of the shoes, one suspects. Italian mothers are rarely pleased with the choice of daughter- or son-in-law.

'Italian mothers are extremely jealous and possessive,' says Fiona, a Belfast woman who has lived in Italy for 30 years. 'I'm lucky in that my mother-in-law lives in Sicily, but when we were getting married she announced they were going to arrive the day before our wedding and stay for a *month*. I reminded my husband that we were going on honeymoon to Thailand immediately after the wedding. He was very reluctant to tell his parents, so I said, "Well, I'm going on my own and I'm not sure if I'll be coming back." '

'It's amazing how the family is still so close,' says Paul, an Irish executive working in Milan. 'I tell my Italian friends I only phone my parents once a week or once every two weeks and they can't believe it. They'll call their parents every day, even twice a day. When they're going out they'll meet up with cousins, whereas an Irish person wants to start from scratch and leave the family network behind.'

* * *

In Rome's Termini Station there are towering black-and-white posters advertising Emporio Armani. Some of the travellers this June morning look like they've stepped off the billboards to dwell amongst us. The young fashionistas, however, have to queue up like everyone else, flicking hair and blanking out the world behind aviator shades. I'm here on the trail of another kind of beauty – one defined by wisdom and grace – in order to examine the phenomenon of the Italian family. I'm going to the birthday party of Rosa Di Paolo. She's just turned 100. Her grandson, Enrico, is bringing me along. Everyone will be there.

Rosa was born on 30 May 1908 in Fiuggi, a medieval hilltop village in the Lazio region. The town was once a staging post between Rome and Subiaco, where St Benedict established his 12 monasteries which became the cradle of the Benedictine Order. But Fiuggi became more famous for its thermal waters after they cured both Pope Boniface VIII and Michelangelo of kidney stones ('the only stone I could not love', according to the latter). Royal families across Europe began clamouring for *Acqua di Fiuggi*. By the turn of the 20th century, large hotels had sprung up and generations of wincing Italians began making the renal pilgrimage.

These days, however, the miracle waters have not lived up to their potential. Poor business decisions and a disastrous foray into the sparkling-water market have seen tourism decline. But for Rosa Di Paolo, a regular dose of *Acqua di Fiuggi* plus a glass of red with lunch and dinner have been her secret. We meet her at the Forum Restaurant, where generations of Di Paolos are arriving. Backs are slapped, cheeks are pinched and multiple conversations are in full flight. There are Magdalenas, Felicitas, Maria-Fatimas, Cristoforos, Sophias, Beatrices, Giovannis and Lauras. Rosa's daughters, Lea, Lisa, Rita, Gloria, Vittoria and Dora, and her son, Nello, are all fussing around her. There are cherubic priests with tumbling curls, and toothsome great-grandchildren. The men are all hugs and arm grips. Alessandro, one of Rosa's 35 grandchildren, is incapable of talking to another male guest without lovingly straightening his tie. After a meal of *fettuccine alla ciociara*, asparagus and saffron risotto, roast herbed pork, all helped along with Prosecco di Valdobbiadene and a Cesanese del Piglio Hyperius red, there's no better time to reflect on the stereotype that launched a thousand pasta sauces: the big Italian family.

Even by the exacting standards Italian women set themselves, Rosa looks great. Steady enough on her feet, her silken-grey hair swept back and her skin the colour of gingerbread, she could pass for 75. She greets me warmly, although I'm mistaken for a grandson. Her short-term memory is not so good and she'll be known to wonder where her husband is (he died in 1975). But later, Rosa will recite by heart, without a stumble and with rhetorical flourishes, poems and prayers she learned when World War I was just starting.

Rosa kept the family together during two world wars and probably around 70 governments. As a young girl during World War I, she wept next to the cast-iron fountain on Piazza Piave as news of local casualties were passed around. At nine, she was looking after her ailing grandmother, who, just before she died, saw the Virgin Mary pass through the room. Rosa always felt sore at missing the apparition. 'Having spent all that time looking after her grandmother as a young girl, she felt that she at least should see the Virgin,' says Enrico. 'I remember her as a very strong figure. When I was a kid, if we didn't salute my father when he came home from work, she would get very upset.' Even into her seventies, Rosa spent every summer cooking the big evening meal for the extended family of 15 nephews and nieces, and seven sons and daughters.

She spent long periods apart from her husband. Filiberto was a prosperous local who'd entered the family coach-and-horse business, operating a service back and forth to Rome. His father, Gaetano, taught him how to smoke when he was 12 so he wouldn't fall asleep at the reins. But much of his time was spent in America, the details of which are rather coyly released as the meal progresses. Filiberto, it seems, had a short temper. He shot a park ranger attempting to seize the timber Filiberto had illegally gathered in the local forest (I'm assured the ranger was only *slightly* wounded), fleeing to Scranton, Pennsylvania. Rosa and her seven children endured one spell of his exile that lasted 20 years. She never complained or questioned his absence. Even back home, Filiberto's impatience got the better of him: trying to load his donkey with bales of straw, the beast would stubbornly tip the load to the ground before Filiberto had the time to balance it. After four attempts, a frustrated Filiberto took out his pistol and shot the donkey on the spot.

Now, decades later, such details are gently wafted into history. After the meal, the sprawling extended family gathers around Nonna Rosa in a blanket of love. And, as she blows out the candle with the help of her youngest great-grandchild, the entire assembly breaks into a paraphrased version of 'Donna Rosa', an old Italian standard. It's a wonderful moment.

'I love it! To see the children like this brings tears to my eyes,' says Dino. 'What they do for their mother and grandmother, the respect and love they show.' Dino Lucarelli was born and raised in Cleveland of Italian parents and is a nephew of Rosa. His second wife, Angelina, who's now on the floor being spun around in a *tarantella*, is also Italian. 'In America, a lot of people don't respect the elderly or take care of them. So many of them end up in retirement homes,' Dino tells me solemnly as Angelina returns breathlessly to her seat. 'It's good to be able to go back to your family, to where you live.'

* * *

The Italian family has been the only reliable institution, more so than the Church, and certainly more than the state. Since history decreed that Italy be raped, pillaged, and fought over by almost every European power, it was natural that no set of laws could be trusted with one's allegiance. 'The first source of power is the family,' writes Luigi Barzini. 'The Italian family is a stronghold in a hostile land: within its walls and among its members, the individual finds consolation, help, advice, provisions, loans, weapons, allies and accomplices to aid him in his pursuits. No Italian who has a family is ever alone.'

These rules were more rigidly adhered to in the south than in the industrialised north, but they compel themselves through all facets of Italian life. Being a family member is a constant push–pull of favours enjoyed and demands required, hand-me-downs and pick-me-ups. 'The

Italian family,' writes Beppe Severgnini in *La Bella Figura*, 'is a market where nothing is sold, lots of stuff is given away, and everything is haggled over.' Italian family members will happily lend huge sums of cash to each other rather than trust a bank (which is why Italy was better placed to cope with the global financial crisis in 2008–2009), but all the honesty, reliability, obedience and generosity demonstrated within families are the very qualities thrown out the window when it comes to the public sphere, to fellow motorists, to tax collectors and so on. While foreigners tease Italians about their public chaos, their corruption, their queue-jumping, their government-a-year politics, you should see how clean, orderly and disciplined are the insides of Italian apartments, their bathrooms, their bedrooms. (Try putting a suitcase on the bed after you've come home from a trip.)

But the family itself may now be paying for this state of affairs. Social observers largely agree on one thing: the country's problems – the fact that it couldn't unify itself until 1879, the rise of the Mafia and of Mussolini, the endemic disorganisation of society, its corporate scandals, even the garbage in Naples – are all explained by a recurring theme. Loyalty to a the central government takes a back seat: family first, then Church, then secret society, then company, then village, then city, then region, and so on. When adherence to the law is a concept so universally derided, then it follows that corruption, economic mismanagement, criminality and tax evasion are given safe passage. The economy suffers, clientelism increases, old men hang onto their featherbedded corporate positions for years, and somewhere down the line young people find it extremely hard to get into jobs and into property.

The reality is that Italy, so long associated with big, happy families, is no longer having big, happy families. In the 1990s, Italy had the lowest birth rate in the world, crossing what demographers call the 'lowest-low' fertility threshold, the rate at which society can replace itself. That rate is 1.3 children per woman, and if it prevails for too long, the population can fall *by half* within 45 years.

Foreigners have always been amazed that such a deeply Catholic country produced so few babies, especially when divorce was so rare. The reason is the economic conditions which keep women out of work and discourage them from having children. They simply put off settling down because they can't afford it. And if they *do* enter the labour market, child care is extremely expensive, and Italian men are still reluctant to pull their weight in the home.

Let's look more closely at this. In 2001, a total of 81 per cent of Italians felt that a child would suffer if its mother was at work. That simply reflected official and cultural attitudes, since the number of women working is still among the lowest in Europe. A study by the Max Planck Institute polled 3,500 Italian couples in 2008 and found that only 11 per cent of the women had received a third-level education. This is important since those with higher education tend to *want* to have more children; for the poorly educated, having more children just seems too expensive.

Traditionally, Italy's welfare system favoured families over individuals; or rather, keeping families together instead of encouraging women to work. Ironically, that failed to stir women into having more children, and has, as we've seen *lowered* the birth rate. The tax breaks for children and child care are negligible (why should the government waste money on child care when there was always a Nonna at hand to do the job for free?); public spending on families amounted to 1.1 per cent of GDP, compared to a 3.4 per cent average for the pre-enlargement EU15. And because the family is such a refuge, there is little incentive to flee the nest when times are tough. So people delay the transition into parenthood, and the longer women wait, the fewer children they have.

More than any other country in the developed world, Italian young people live in the parental home the longest. The average age of men hanging onto Mamma's couch is 36. They're called *mammoni*, pampered males for whom the outside world is just too uncomfortable. In 2007 the finance minister Tommaso Padoa-Schioppa even offered *mammoni* financial incentives to join the real world and leave the parental home.

It's no laughing matter. The pampered male also keeps the birth rate low. According to the Max Planck Institute study, 70 per cent of Italian women do 75 per cent of the housework. This reduces their desire to have more children – most are just too tired. Combining the pressures of the day job with the 'second shift' of housework – while Giovanni applies his moisturiser as he watches AC Milan on TV – means the appetite for more *bambini* suffers.

For many young people, though, Italy's fall down the economic league tables forces them to stay at home. By the mid-2000s, they were called the thousand-euro generation because that was what they earned a month. The power of the unions, lobbies, and political patronage has meant that a meritocratic upward mobility is impossible. 'I'm very angry at my country at the moment,' Paola Olivetto, a graduate in foreign languages who was studying for a Masters degree, told me in 2006. 'It's not just the money, it's just that you can't get a meaningful job that reflects your qualifications.' At 31, she was working as a secretary in a law firm for €960 per month before tax with little prospect of advancement. She was still living with her parents, since renting somewhere was well beyond her means.

To the problems of privilege and prejudice add inflation. When the euro replaced the lira, retailers rounded prices up to neat figures, fuelling inflation as salaries stagnated. Between 2001 and 2005, Italian families reduced their savings by 40 per cent, while salaries rose by only 13 per cent. Everyone was feeling poorer and even pasta was boycotted when prices rose by 20 per cent. For a country so dedicated to *la dolce vita*, it was hard to swallow.

When the family stepped in, it was often grandparents who stumped up the most. According to a report by the Observatory of the Elderly (l'Osservatorio Anziani), Italian grandparents give as much as €7.5 *billion* to their grandchildren, not to mention the emotional support and practical help of babysitting. But, again despite the stereotype, the love and support isn't necessarily being requited. Pensioners now make up 19 per cent of the population, and many are living – and dying – alone.

In 2005, a story appeared that seemed to crystallise the decline of the big, close-knit Italian family. Giorgio Angelozzi, a kindly old man, put an ad in *Corriere della Sera* offering €500 to any family who would adopt him as their granddad. His dear wife had died, the pupils he taught had forgotten him, and he was living alone with the cat. White-haired Giorgio was suddenly on prime-time television, musing on how Italians were losing touch with family. That an old man could be adopted touched a very raw nerve and a bout of intense national soul searching followed. He was duly adopted by a family living near Milan.

This would have been the perfect ending, but …

Within months, Mr Angelozzi had conned his new family into paying for operations he never had, then left them with a €2,900 dental bill. When he was detained by police after stealing a chequebook, it was revealed that his dear wife had divorced him in 1971 and that he had a criminal record that ran to seven pages.

Whatever way you look at it, there is something not quite right about the Italian family. Its role as a haven from and bulwark against the unruly state outside is still as important as ever, but economic woes appear to have weakened it. The tableau of Rosa Di Paolo and her legion of children, grandchildren and great-grandchildren is not a dying image, but a less common one. These days hundreds of thousands of immigrant workers from Peru, Equador, Romania or Albania look after single elderly Italians, because the family no longer has the time nor the inclination to do it.

Demographer Francesco Billari, from Bocconi University in Milan, has concluded meanwhile that couples who *don't* marry are actually *more* likely to produce more children. Births outside marriage are going up (18.6 per cent of all births in 2006), while marital births have fallen. Cohabiting at 25, concludes Billari, will have the same effect on fertility rates as getting married at 27.

No Italian government would deliberately pursue a policy of encouraging couples to have children outside marriage. Governments don't think like that – certainly not Italian ones – but demographers do.

* * *

Italy is among the few countries whose stereotypes reverberate with that all-important kernel of truth. They really do love ice cream, adore food and talk incessantly. On a beach in Viareggio, I fell asleep to the sound of four women talking and gesticulating simultaneously. I awoke an hour later and they were still in full, quadraphonic swing. 'A meeting in Ireland would have a particular agenda, a structure and a goal and you would try to avoid phone calls and interruptions,' says Sean Lynch, a business consultant living in Italy for 20 years. 'In Italy it's a free for all, just a big excuse for everyone to rant and rave at the same time. I remember coming out of the first meeting I attended asking, can anyone tell me what was agreed, who does what, and where do we take it from here?'

Pasta is still the staple, but the cuisine is so profoundly regional that Italians are irritated by foreigners' inability to look beyond pizza and spaghetti (it's just one of 350 shapes). Italian fashion still rules the catwalk, even if globalisation has snaffled up much of the actual production.

The country remains a prisoner to corruption and political patronage. Locals have given up complaining – it has been thus for centuries. 'Politicians are appointed to everything – health authorities, hospitals, administrators, even surgeons can be political appointees,' says Michael Poole, a Belfast lawyer working for an international legal firm in Milan. 'In any of the nationalised industries, every time a new government is formed they have to sack everyone who was appointed by the previous government. I work in town planning. As soon as a politician gets involved, that's the end of it.'

The Mafia are still slithering through economic activity: in 2007, the association of small businesses, Confesercenti, published an 86-page report concluding that the Mafia was Italy's biggest company. Revenue from extortion, loan-sharking, burglary, theft, counterfeiting, contraband, kickbacks and control of public contracts delivered an annual turnover of €90 billion, or 7 per cent of Italian GDP.

* * *

Our final trip through Italian stereotypes includes a visit to the home of Francesco Schiavone. It's not actually his real home, and we won't find him in today, but it is a plot of land he once owned. Francesco is currently in an Italian prison, but getting him there was a long and murderous process. Mr Schiavone was one of the Camorra's top godfathers, the head of the Casalesi clan, worth a reported $48 billion. He was eventually sentenced to life imprisonment in June 2008 after a 10-year legal process during which five people involved in the case, including one interpreter, were murdered.

On a bright day in June, I drive down the Pontina highway to Latina, the coastal province to the south of Rome that forms part of the Lazio region. The area includes the Pontine Marshes, drained under the orders of Mussolini in the 1920s and settled by families from the Veneto region in the north, people with unimpeachable Fascist credentials. Today, Lazio retains, especially among its football supporters, far-right tendencies.

I've come to meet Dario Campagna, a former narcotics officer of medium build, prematurely grey, his goatee beard and Ray-Ban sunglasses lending the appearance of a ski instructor. Dario has done something that, to any sane individual, appears extraordinarily foolish. He has taken land off the Camorra. 'There are always worries, because you are dealing with organised crime,' he says with disarming understatement. 'You can never be safe.'

The land Dario has taken is an 11-hectare vineyard, now basking in breezy afternoon sunshine. The vines hang with heavy clumps of Trebbiano bianco grapes, a tractor rakes the ground between the rows, while workers prune the upper branches. These volunteers work for Il Gabbiano (The Seagull), a charity run by Dario to rehabilitate former felons. They're here on Schiavone's soil thanks to a government plan to confiscate Mafia land and put it to good social use. It's part of a quiet, determined revolt against the Mafia by ordinary Italians. What is now a promising vineyard, producing 10,000 bottles of fruity table wine a year, had been used by the Camorra as a dumping ground for all sorts of things (it is close enough to Campania to be within the Camorra's reach). When Dario began to plant vines, he was surprised to dig up thousands of bank notes, which fluttered about him in the breeze. Unfortunately they were lire and therefore useless.

Restoring the land was never going to be easy. A few days before the first harvest in September 2006, intruders entered and cut the wires that held the vines, and their fruit, in place. Almost the entire harvest – €50,000 worth – collapsed. With the rains that accompanied the vandalism, most of the grapes were destroyed. Dario was undeterred. 'We want to give a strong message to the community. We will never stop, we will keep fighting for this, and we'll be ready to call the police when there is the need for them. We'll keep working on this piece of land.'

To their credit, the neighbours, who would have known who the previous owners were, came to help when news of the catastrophe spread. Three hundred turned up to salvage as much of the crop as they could. 'They helped us rebuild, they keep an eye on the land, and they let us know where to get the products we need to grow the vines,' says Dario.

No one has been apprehended for the sabotage, but Dario is convinced it was Camorra sympathisers. 'It's in their interest that this land stays untouched,' he said. 'It's a sign of power.'

Dario's first vintage was called Campo Libero (Free Field).

The initiative is bearing fruit elsewhere. In Palermo, the Sicilian capital, €600 million worth of Mafia property was handed over in 2008 alone. Villas were being converted into *agriturismo* operations (country B&Bs focusing on local produce), while Mafia farmhouses were becoming organic restaurants. Near Corleone, the house belonging to Salvatore 'Totò' Riina, once the boss of bosses, thought to have personally killed 40 people, was opened to the public in November 2008. Another initiative, named after Placido Rizzotto, a land-reform campaigner murdered by the Mafia in 1948, identifies the companies which refuse to pay the Mafia *pizzo*, or protection money, so that thoughtful consumers can shop there (80 per cent of Sicily's businesses still pay the *pizzo*, netting Cosa Nostra €100 million a year).

In the face of so much political impotence, ordinary consumers, at least, feel they can shake a small fist at the Mafia. In Rome, I visited the *Libera Terra* (free land) store just across from the Roman Forum at the corner of Piazza Venezia. Inside, Antonio Dell'olio was tending to late Friday afternoon customers. On neat shelves were bottles of olive oil, pesto, an array of 'anti-Mafia' pasta products, red and white wines, seeds, flour and chickpeas. All organic, and all from land taken from the mob. 'This is an opportunity to rehabilitate territory and people,' says Antonio. 'We have created an option for young people in areas where the Mafia are most present.'

But he struck a warning note. 'This is not just an Italian problem. The Mafia are buying up land in Romania, and property in Berlin and Brussels and all over Europe. The 'Ndrangheta [the Calabrian Mafia] are buying property and shares in companies all over Germany. There are Russian Mafia, Eastern European Mafia, Albanian Mafia. It's a European problem.'

As a customer turned away with her jar of *Libera Terra* pesto sauce, Antonio paused. 'We are trying to set an example for Europe. We have the longest anti-Mafia tradition. Here in Italy, we are the primates of the Mafia world.'

Chapter 5

Denmark

A clean little country with able, honest partisans, proud of their skills. No military, no thieves.
Iboja Wandall-Holm, Slovak refugee and concentration camp survivor.

Henning Nielsen, stonemason, is carving sand-coloured bricks on a noisy cutting machine in the doorway of a 12th-century white-washed Lutheran church.

With an unruffled, good-natured mien, Henning's look of satisfaction in labour has settled into a mild grin. His salt-and-pepper hair and grey beard, which girds chin and jaw line but rises no further, give him the look of a pilgrim just off the *Mayflower.* Each block of stone, streaming with mustardy water, is gripped by both hands as it's pressed against the treacherous blade. Under his guidance, the block falls open in sudden silence to form two bricks. Each he tosses into a white bucket. When he switches off the querulous machine, ravens caw and sparrows twitter in the trees that ring the churchyard.

'People are saying,' he says, 'that it's a very tiresome situation for the country and for those workers involved.'

I'm in Bislev, a tiny village in Jutland, surrounded by grey stubble fields. Smoke drifts from farmhouse chimneys, drizzle swells into fat drops that sag from wintery twigs. In the distance lies the Limfjord, a shallow, irregular-shaped sound that separates the island of Vendsyssel-Thy from the rest of the Jutland Peninsula. The distant murmur of geese flying in low formation over the liquid aluminium waterway deepens the air of profound, even desolate, tranquillity. Yet here we are at the latest front in a very deadly clash of civilisations.

'I'm really sad so many people in the world are angry about this – we know it's also costing lives and that makes me sad,' says Henning, before reaching for another block.

Not far from the church, hunkering down with its dark silos and processing units, lies Arla Foods, a cooperative plant owned by 10,600 Danish and Swedish dairy farmers. Every day milk is turned into butter, feta, cream cheese and milk powder. It's a successful, rural enterprise, but the company's horizons stretch a little further: Arla Foods now owns subsidiaries in the UK and US, and for years it's been expanding in the Middle East, recently investing €55 million in cheese-spread production in Saudi Arabia. It's paid off: growing affluence has pushed the Middle East turnover to an annual €300 million – one-third of Denmark's total dairy exports.

But then, in September 2005, an unlikely catastrophe struck when the Danish newspaper, *Jyllands-Posten*, published 12 cartoons. The images depicted the Prophet Mohammed in terms which could been seen either as playful or deliberately provocative. Since Muslims believe that *any* depiction of Mohammed is blasphemous, a local controversy escalated, then exploded across the Middle East and beyond. By February 2006, there had been violent demonstrations in Syria, Lebanon, Egypt, Saudi Arabia, Indonesia, Pakistan, Afghanistan, Nigeria, Iran, India and the in the Gulf. Nearly 140 people were dead. Danish embassies were attacked in Damascus, Beirut and Tehran. Muslims vented their fury, while politicians in the West railed against the assault on free speech.

Saudi Arabia led a boycott of Danish goods, and the rest of the Arab world quickly followed. Soon Arla was losing €1.3 million a day. The company repatriated staff working in Saudi Arabia and laid off some of the 800 local workers as production was halted. Here in Bislev 125 workers were laid off, including Jana Nergaard, who'd been working at Arla for 10 years. I sat with her father, Edvard, the local gravedigger at Henning's church, in his living room in a modest bungalow. Wearing a thick plaid shirt and sky-blue dungarees, Edvard said he just couldn't understand it.

'I know a young man who just got a job over there and he's lost it already. That's a real shame. He hasn't worked long enough to get unemployment benefit. What can he do?' Edvard says, his eyebrows raised in persistent surprise. 'Jana hasn't really reacted – she never reacts. She takes things as they come – always. She's been fired but she's not the only one. They were told that the other day … Of course, it's sad, but we don't talk about it. We're like that. We don't get mad at other people. We keep things to ourselves.'

The crisis started with a Danish children's book, *Koranen og profeten Muhammeds liv* (The Koran and the Life of the Prophet Muhammed), written by 50-year-old journalist Kåre Bluitgen. He was having problems in finding someone to illustrate the book, having been turned down by three artists uneasy about depicting the Prophet – even for a children's book. One referred to the murder of the Dutch filmmaker Theo van Gogh, while another alluded to the attack on a Danish university lecturer after he'd read extracts of the Koran to non-Muslim students.

Bluitgen's dilemma was picked up by Denmark's *Politiken* newspaper, which ran an article about it on 17 September. Almost accidently it turned into a public debate about self-censorship, democracy and Islam. *Jyllands-Posten* culture editor Flemming Rose decided to invite 40 cartoonists to provide their own depictions of Mohammed. This time, 12 responded, including three from the newspaper's own staff. The images they came up with were to become the most destructive cartoons ever drawn.

To the non-Muslim eye, they appeared harmless enough, even if dealing with serious issues. One depicted a bearded man with a turban from which sprouted a bomb fuse; another had Mohammed standing in front of two Muslim women in full *niqab* dress; a third showed Mohammed in heaven informing recently arrived suicide bombers that they couldn't enter. The images carried captions with in-jokes incomprehensible to non-Danish speakers.

In an accompanying article, Mr Rose wrote that Muslim demands for special treatment within a secular society was 'incompatible with contemporary democracy and freedom of speech, where you must be ready to put up with insults, mockery and ridicule.' That did not mean, he added, 'that religious feelings should be made fun of at any price.'

The cartoons were noticed by members of Denmark's 200,000-strong Muslim community. First, a number of imams complained to the government. Then ambassadors from 12 Muslim countries sought an urgent meeting with prime minister Anders Fogh Rasmussen. In their letter, they also complained about other perceived anti-Muslim sentiment, specifically naming former soft-porn actress Louise Frevert (who had compared Muslims to cancer cells), and the culture minister, Brian Mikkelsen, who was reported to have said Danish culture could be used as a 'tool' against growing Muslim influence. The ambassadors asked that the cartoonists be 'taken to task ... in the interests of interfaith harmony, better integration, and Denmark's overall relations with the Muslim world'.

So far, perhaps, so reasonable.

Anders Fogh Rasmussen replied that freedom of expression had a wide scope and the government couldn't influence the press. 'However,' he wrote, 'Danish legislation prohibits acts or expressions of a blasphemous or discriminatory nature.' In other words, the Muslim community could go to court if they wished.

The ambassadors said they didn't want the newspaper to be prosecuted, just somehow held to account. The Egyptian foreign minister entered the fray, writing to both Rasmussen and the UN Secretary General, Kofi Annan saying, again, no prosecution was necessary, just some kind of official statement calling for respect for all religions. Rasmussen replied that even a non-judicial intervention would be impossible within the Danish system. Despite the polite tone, things were escalating.

On 27 October 2005, a number of Muslim organisations did file a complaint under blasphemy and discrimination laws, but on 6 January 2006 the regional prosecutor dropped the investigation. Danish case law, he declared, extended to editorial freedom in such instances. While freedom of speech had to be balanced with protection against discrimination, no violation of the law had occurred.

The decision angered the clerics. They had already compiled a 43-page dossier of alleged insults against Islam. The dossier included the 12 cartoons, but it also included newspaper articles, alleged hate mail and other more inflammatory photographs and cartoons. One picture showed a contestant from a French pig-squealing contest, another portrayed Mohammed as a paedophile, while a third depicted a dog next to a Muslim at prayer. This latter material was not, however, published by a Danish cartoonist, nor did it appear in any Danish newspaper.

In December 2005, a month before the criminal case was dropped, the imams took the dossier on a tour of the Middle East. The material received a wide airing, appearing on numerous TV channels, including Al-Manar, owned by the Lebanese militant organisation Hezbollah. The imams wrote that they didn't want to appear 'narrow and backward' and that Danes shouldn't be accused of 'ideological arrogance'. But the conflation of the two sets of images convinced critics in the West that the imams had a deliberately radical agenda.

Jyllands-Posten published a guarded apology in Arabic and English. 'The 12 drawings were sober. They were not intended to be offensive, nor were they at variance with Danish law, but they have indisputably offended many Muslims for which we apologise.'

The cartoonist responsible for the 'bomb in turban' picture explained that the image had been misinterpreted, and that it was simply a comment on fundamentalism. But by this time the finer arguments on both sides were lost as controversy raged. While embassies burned and protestors died in the streets, other Western newspapers reprinted the cartoons in solidarity. It was now an international crisis. Two radicals in Germany saw the cartoons as a legitimate reason to carry out a bomb attack during the World Cup finals, while four British Muslims were jailed for incitement to murder during a demonstration in London. In America some right-wing sympathisers were reported to have bought Danish goods like Bang & Olufsen stereos and Lego, with imports increasing by 17 per cent.

Denmark was in a state of deep anxiety. Some, including a number of Danish ambassadors, felt the government should have apologised sooner and that the whole thing was badly handled; others were outraged at the sight of Danish flags being burned on the Arab Street. Martin Krasnik, a journalist and author of a book on radical Islam, told me, 'The Muslim community in Denmark has failed completely in creating a moderate leadership. It's a completely miserable failure. The Muslim leadership are now willing to compromise and settle for goodwill, but only because the government and the newspaper did too much, backtracking completely before all demands, both for Muslims and the cheese eaters of the Middle East. It's been a complete climbdown.'

A Muslim MP, Naser Khader, set up the Moderate Muslim Network, and within days it was claiming 500 members. Well dressed and intelligent, he appeared the very picture of Muslim moderation. I met him at the Danish parliament. 'We don't want the Islamists to take over the agenda,' he said. 'We want to live in peace, and we want to integrate. We want democracy, we want to look forward. Danes argue that the majority of Muslims are thinking about the pictures, but it's not true – the majority are dreaming about getting a job, about their children, about their health – just like Danish people.'

A short time later I met the 60-year-old cleric at the centre of the crisis, Ahmad Abu Laban, in the study of his Islamic centre in Dortheavej, an immigrant neighbourhood in Copenhagen. He was the co-author of the 43-page dossier and had led the delegation of clerics across the Middle East. Born in Jaffa, Laban's family had emigrated to Egypt in 1948, where he later graduated as a mechanical engineer. He worked in the oil industry, but took further studies in Islamic theology before settling in Denmark in 1984. He came with a track record of radical views, suggesting variously that foreign tourists killed in Algeria 'might have been spreading AIDS in the same way Jews were spreading AIDS in Egypt', refused to condemn September 11, or the stoning of a Nigerian woman for adultery. He described Osama bin Laden as a 'freedom fighter'.

He began our interview in a surprisingly moderate tone, admitting the violence that erupted in the Muslim world had been counterproductive. The delegation had gone to the Middle East to get Muslim academics to shed light on the issue, he said, 'not for riots or demonstrations.' The whole controversy was all about culture and intellect, not violence.

'I used to speak positively about the prime minister! This man was elected in a democratic way to maintain and safeguard Danish values. The Danes are kind people, but he should have met the ambassadors. We want Europe to be more open, to accommodate us and give us reasonable status, not as intruders, not as occupiers, but as humble citizens,' he said. But when I mention Naser Khader, Laban's face darkens and his voice swells. He had already referred to Khader and his ilk as 'rats in holes' during Friday prayers. 'This man is playing a very nasty game,' Laban thunders. 'He is cheating his own country. He shouldn't get public money: we pay taxes for MPs to do a good job. It's not the imams. Let people say these are radical imams, they are narrow minded, we take it, no problem. Let [Khader] open his eyes. If he cannot see it at this moment; he should be honest enough not to cheat Denmark any more. There are one billion Muslims in this outcry, male and female, poor and rich, educated and illiterate. He's just a third-class politician.'

Twenty minutes later, I'm in bar-lined Nyhavn, one of the most picturesque harbours in Scandinavia. Outside the plush Hotel D'Angleterre, thick snow is folded around the ice rink and a hard winter light gilds the upper façades of the 17th-century townhouses. Young children skate around, cheerfully oblivious to the shock the country is experiencing. Thinking about Laban's interview, it's hard to reconcile his reasonable-sounding demands for inclusion with his views on the West and his visceral hatred of 'moderate Muslims'. But was there something to the belief that immigrant alienation had been allowed to fester, and if so, what does it say about the Danes, and Danishness?

For Henning Nielson, the stonemason, Danish 'mentality' is a world away from what he watches with sadness on his TV screen. 'We're not like that here in our culture. Maybe we have a special kind of humour that we think everyone else has, but maybe they don't have it. It was only a joke, those cartoons.

Edvard Nergaard, the gravedigger, adds. 'What they're doing, it's completely mad. Maybe it's the underclass, people without education. They want to change the world to their way of thinking, and they're using this situation. At the same time, it's not necessary to insult other people – that newspaper should have thought about that. Think about it! Those countries down there, they take 70 per cent of our cheese. They didn't think about that.'

Maybe it's the stolid, Shakespearean wisdom of the Danish gravedigger, but, even given his ability to see both sides of the argument, there's something in Edvard's incomprehension at the cartoons crisis that is indicative of a wider anxiety gripping Denmark for some time.

* * *

What do we know about the Danes?

We tend to lump them in with the other Scandinavians. Blond, good natured, liberal and tolerant. When we think of Denmark, we think of

Brigitte Nielsen and Hans Christian Andersen's *Snow Queen*, we remember Lego (it comes from the words '*leg godt*', 'play well') and Danish pastries (called *wienerbrød* in Denmark). It's the land of elegant design, and (probably) has the best lager in the world. We recall when the plucky Danes, only qualifying because Yugoslavia had been kicked out of the tournament, beat the Germans in the final of Euro '92 (the Danish team was on the beach when they found out they'd actually qualified). Eduardo Galeano, a Uruguayan football correspondent, wrote, 'The German players came from fasting, abstinence and work. The Danes came from beer, women and sunbathing … Germany, who ought to have won, was beaten by Denmark, who owed nothing to anybody and who played as though the game was a continuation of their games on the beach.' Everybody loved how Danish fans painted their faces with the national colours – the first fans to ever do so.

So, according to stereotypes, the Danes should be one of Europe's more likeable families. Our perceptions may not have started well. The Vikings raped and pillaged, ransacking our monastic settlements. Over the centuries, visitors encountered a hardy, windswept place of rugged manners. 'Jutland is the most dreadful region,' wrote Monk Adam of Bremen in 1060. 'The land is scarcely cultivated anywhere and hardly suitable for human habitation.' Yet even then travellers found a rare egalitarianism. 'We know not of jealousy on this island,' a Viking queen told Jahja Bekri, a Moorish diplomat in 845. 'With us, a woman's relations with a man depend on her own free will, and when she no longer likes him she goes her own way.'

Denmark was put on the map by Shakespeare, who'd come across the story of Hamlet, the Prince of Denmark, through Saxo Grammaticus' 13th-century Danish chronicle *Gesta Danorum* (the Deeds of the Danes). He also knew about Kronborg Castle in Elsinore (Helsingør in Danish) since English ships passing through the Øresund had to pay a sizeable toll to the Danish Crown. An early stereotype of the Danes focused on their drinking habits, and Shakespeare didn't hesitate to use it. Hamlet even complains about how foreigners stereotype the Danes as drunks, overlooking their other achievements: 'They clepe us drunkards, and with swinish phrase/Soil our addition.' Hamlet, though, doesn't actually *question* the charge.

By the 17th century, Denmark's capacity for drinking was well established. Charles Ogier, secretary to the French envoy, described the wedding of King Christian IV's son in 1634. 'After the arrival of the Holsteiners and the Saxons,' he wrote, 'such a great amount of beer and wine was consumed that both refectories, bed chambers, vestibules and entrance halls were actually awash. And to drain dry these lakes, equidistant everywhere were placed vessels and barrels into which the inebriated and befuddled topers could more easily rid themselves of their abundance and pass their water.'

Later visitors frowned upon the quality of Danish food, recoiled at the poverty of Copenhagen, marvelled (again) at their appetite for getting drunk, and blushed at their predilection for taking their clothes off. During the wars with Sweden in the late 1650s, Jan Pasek, a Polish officer fighting on the Danish side, wrote: 'They sleep naked as their mother created them and see nothing shameful in this, but undress and dress in the presence of each other. They do not have any hesitation in the presence of a stranger, but take off all their clothes by candlelight.'

The Irish diplomat Robert Molesworth (1656–1725), during his time as British ambassador, was less shocked by nudity as he was by the drinking: 'The liquors that are most in vogue… are Rhenish wine, cherry brandy, and all sorts of French wine. The men are fond of them, and the fair sex do not refuse them.'

So much for what outsiders felt about the Danes. What about their fellow Scandinavians? We tend to think of Scandinavians as a fairly uniform bunch, but as Thomas Hylland Eriksen, a social anthropologist at the University of Oslo, writes, there are significant differences. 'Foreign stereotypes tend to depict Scandinavians as wealthy, enlightened, rational and bored Protestants with strong welfare states, lax rules of sexual morality and an institutionalised yearning for nature and simplicity.' Yet, he adds, despite the fact that their languages are so similar as to be mutually intelligible, there are key differences, and the Scandinavians haven't always got along (the historical friend-enemy rivalries between Norway, Denmark and Sweden mean that each country sees itself in relation to its neighbours: 'The Swede is always depicted as a rich and arrogant child of the Enlightenment, the Dane as a slightly decadent hedonist, and the Norwegian as an uneducated, often stupid, country bumpkin,' writes Eriksen).

For Denmark, the 17th century was a defining era in their relationship with the Swedes. Basically, they took on the powerful Swedish kingdom and lost three wars on the trot, in the process losing the provinces of Skåne and Blekinge and never getting them back. The long period of Swedish-Danish rivalry only came to an end with a peace treaty in 1720 when Russia began to threaten the balance of power in the Baltic. Yet Denmark has always been out of kilter with the Scandinavian mainstream. Its location on the northern tip of Europe made it a more *southern* country. Danes see themselves as the Nordic Latinos: easy-going, tolerant, urbane, sociable and relaxed. To Swedes and Norwegians, Copenhagen, with its liberal alcohol and drug rules, is a kind of sin city. What has evolved is an increasingly patronising attitude towards the Swedes, whom the Danes see as humourless slaves to state control, and who therefore *lose* control when they come to Denmark on drinking trips. According to the *Xenophobe's Guide to the Danes*, even English hooligans are more tolerated. 'The sight of an Arsenal fan halfway up a lamp-post swilling beer from the anus of an inflatable rubber pig caused little more than some shaking of heads. A German or a Swede would have been arrested and heavily fined.'

It's true that Swedes tend to see Denmark as one big off-licence. In Helsingør, a short ferry ride from the Swedish side, I noticed on Bramstræde Street a barricade of beer, whiskey, vodka, sherry and schnapps outside a drinks outlet, and a sign in Swedish reminding the visitors they could bring home 10 litres of spirits, 10 litres of port/sherry, 20 litres of wine and 110 litres of beer. A story in the local press had just referred to a Swede who was so drunk that he followed a police car all the way to the station and went in to complain that the car had turned right three times without using its indicator.

'I think Swedes are getting a little more offended by the attitude of Danes towards them. It's not malicious, probably more like boorishness,' observes one expat journalist living in Copenhagen.

Yet Denmark shares the distinctly Nordic social model: high taxes, but wonderful social benefits. Was this always the case, and if so, how did it come about?

In the beginning of the 19th century, things weren't going at all well for Denmark. The British attacked in 1807 to prevent Napoleon getting his hands on the Danish fleet, and, when Denmark allied herself with Napoleon, Britain pounced again, taking control of the straits between Denmark and Norway, a loss that led to the country going bankrupt. A painful defeat later against Prussia in 1864, in which Denmark lost the cherished provinces of Schleswig and Holstein, was one too many: Denmark became neutral, a status that continued until World War I.

But it was during the momentous years of 1848–49, and the pan-European revolution against the absolute power of monarchies, that pivotal social change occurred. King Christian VIII could see that absolutism's days were numbered and he recommended changes which ultimately formed the June Constitution of 1849, a document well ahead of its time guaranteeing as it did civil rights and a two-chamber parliamentary system which was signed by his son, King Frederick VII, after Christian's death.

At the same time, Danish agriculture was undergoing big changes. More land was cultivated, and farmers made the lucrative switch away from crops to livestock. Soon butter, bacon and eggs accounted for up to 90 per cent of all exports – much of it to the UK. In a quiet revolution, farmers with small and medium-sized holdings set up a network of dairy and bacon cooperatives, developing their export skills. As part of the process, farmers and workers forged an unusual consensus, both strengthening their political clout as a result.

So, due to the relative prosperity in the countryside, the extension of the vote, the emergence of consensus between former rivals, and the fact that compulsory education was already in place (Denmark was the first country to introduce it in 1814 and illiteracy was abolished by 1850), progressive politics were on the march. Towns expanded, new arrangements were agreed between employers and workers, new services led to the growth of salaried workers, and women began to enter the workforce, all before the turn of the 20th century. In 1870, a number of women's associations were formed; by 1908, they could vote at municipal level, and by 1915 at national level. 'The whole struggle was more peaceful because of the cooperative nature of society,' says Karen Sjørup, head of the Equality Research Unit, Roskilde University.

That general spirit of cooperation bore fruit elsewhere: a deal between the Conservative Party and the Agrarian Liberal Party established a universal, tax-financed pension scheme for the over-60s (it wasn't reformed until the 1980s); in 1892, voluntary health insurance was introduced; in 1901, the Liberals, supported by the Social Democrats, brought in unemployment insurance for the first time. The close bonds between the Lutheran Church and the state meant the Church would take on social responsibilities at parish level (today, 83 per cent of Danes are members of the Church and they all pay a church tax). The benefits were basic, and welfare was on the understanding of eventual self-reliance through work, but they set the tone for a more dramatic social system in the century to come.

But Denmark first had to endure the high unemployment, bank crashes and financial crises of the 1920s before it was bold enough, in 1933, to launch the most radical welfare vision the world had ever seen. With unemployment pushing the 40 per cent mark, the Social Democrats introduced a far-reaching reform bill commanding broad political support. The world was taking notice. The Nordic model suddenly seemed an attractive third way between the extremes of capitalism and communism, both of which had been badly discredited by the stock-market crash and Stalin's purges. It seemed to show that democracy – despite the unstoppable appeal of totalitarianism – *could* actually work. Even Britain seemed to take notice. 'The Scandinavians are the very best sort of people,' wrote Anthony Blunt, the future Russian spy, in *The Spectator* in 1938, 'who seem to have all the advantages of being progressive without any of the unpleasantness.'

Although it often evolved in a piecemeal way as a result of awkward compromises between opposing political parties and interest groups, the Danish system ended up as *universal*: everyone gets a slice no matter what their family or employment situation. The benefits are given to the individual, not a couple, with profound implications for the independence of Danish women. Even if sickness and unemployment payments depend to some degree on employment contributions, the state still pays the biggest share through general taxation. The welfare doesn't always come in the form of cash; instead, services – such as health and education – are free. According to the Heritage foundation, Denmark has the second highest level of tax revenue as a percentage of GDP in the world, just behind Zimbabwe.

There were discretionary changes in the 1970s and '80s, but benefits levels are still substantial and Danes remain proud of the system (foreigners who live there complain and marvel in equal measure). Bill Bryson once said you could cast a Pepsi commercial in Denmark in 15 seconds, but Danish pride is driven as much by its generous social system as its blond and beautiful people. According to the *Xenophobe's Guide*, 'The Danes' mission in life is to help the rest of the world to see just how wonderful Denmark is. They feel sorry for all the poor souls who aren't Danish, have never visited the country, or otherwise live in heathen ignorance of their land of milk and honey.'

The Danes regularly top those happiness surveys. In the Map of World Happiness in 2006, Denmark came first after Switzerland (the Irish came in 11th), while, in 2008, *Monocle* magazine declared Copenhagen the world's most 'liveable' city. Danes describe their country as *Smørhullet*, 'the butterhole'. It was explained to me thus by an expat journalist: 'Danes create a hole in the middle of their rice pudding and fill it with butter. To them, their country is like that, a privileged, perfect society that is like the butterhole and everything outside is just boring rice. Foreigners just want to come and get their fingers into the butter.'

Strolling around (wonderful) Copenhagen you're at the centre of the butterhole. The shops are bright, the streets are spotless, the people are blond, design is everywhere and the transport system is first class. The Tivoli Gardens manage to be a harum-scarum fun-fair but without the tack: there are roller coasters, bumper cars, rifle ranges, bandstands, pagodas, a lake with a life-sized pirate galleon, bagel bars, juice bars, Italian restaurants, Balkan-themed bars. There is no litter, the queues are long but orderly, and if you're not blond the sunlight will catch your hair and turn it into chestnut honey.

Here too is where you feel '*hyyge*', the difficult-to-translate concept conveying 'cosiness', or conviviality and contentment (if *hyyge* isn't happening, Danes reach for candles to conjure it up: candle sales are enormous in Denmark, and people love to fill their cafés, bars and living rooms with the things). If butter is the taste, then *hygge* is the feeling.

Despite the happy glow, however, the Danish family has undergone sharp changes. Marriage has declined steeply and couples are getting married older (36 for men, 33 for women). One-fifth of all couples living together are unmarried and one-quarter of children at home don't live with their biological parents. Because of the independence achieved by women, working mothers mean the numbers of children in day care is considerable: in 2011 97 per cent of all children aged 3–5 were looked after by day carers or in day-care institutions. In other words, the family, and the dynamic between men and women, has changed considerably.

* * *

To get a Danish perspective, I take the train along coast of the Øresund towards Hamlet's place. The 10:31 for Helsingør leaves Copenhagen Central at 10:36, a five minute delay which, in Scandinavia, doesn't feel quite right. The trains themselves, though, are hushed havens of social awareness. Icons indicate all the social categories resolutely welcome on board. There are special seating areas for the disabled, cyclists, mothers with small babies and people with dogs. At every stop, passengers disembark and immediately start cycling, rollerblading, or skateboarding away – every kind of motion, it seems, except two-legged. The female ticket collector stamps my five-times machine-endorsed ticket with an affirmative that sounds like 'Yips!'.

Lone Kühlmann and her Danish yard dog, Trine, meet me at Humlebæk Station, a small, well-to-do commuter village of 8,000 cycling, skateboarding, rollerblading souls. 'Did you have to change?' she says with evident alarm. 'They're doing works on the tracks!'

This, I learn, is a very Danish impulse. Danes demand, and largely get, high standards in public and private services. They want them delivered with care and are quick to complain if the service comes up short. And, thankfully, those who receive the complaints do so without complaining (this is what keeps standards high). Lone, pronounced 'Loh-ne', a writer and broadcaster in her sixties, agrees. 'Everyone around here is going absolutely *mad*! They consider it a personal insult! They can talk about it for *days*!'

She lives with her Norwegian journalist husband in a pleasant and much-extended clapboard house, with dark chocolate wood and burgundy window frames, surrounded by a furious yet orderly growth of herbs, flowers and shrubs. Inside are bookshelves weighed down with yellowing volumes of Danish and European writers, the walls decked with paintings and photographs. The home has the aura of a busy, bookish and actively cheerful family. Beyond the rear garden, steps lead down to a charming wooden deck being buffeted by winds slithering across the Øresund. Lone's son Joachim, a 26-year-old student, shows me around. On either side of the Kühlmann pier are moored swish-looking yachts. 'We'll have to get one to keep up with the software millionaires who've moved in,' moans Joachim.

That the Kühlmanns don't have a boat is unusual. Most Danes are no more than an hour from the sea and the country is made up of 406 islands. Along the coastline, one little harbour follows another, each filled with shiny new yachts with names like *Lady Amiable*. Lone *is* a member of the local rowing club, a stylish wooden structure with clean, even lines and not a hint of the detritus and oil stains you might expect. Inside the house are chic pieces of modernist furniture, including the *very* Danish Arne Jacobsen chairs from the 1950s. Out front there is another jetty, this time designed by a famous French architect (remember, this is only a *jetty*). 'He wanted to extend it all the way to Hveen!' Lone laughs, gesturing to an island across the sound that used to be Danish, but is now Swedish.

When Danes aren't boating, they are soaking up modern art. Not far from Lone's house is the Louisiana Museum of Modern Art, a shrine to all that is so tasteful, artful and so very *modern* about the Danes. 'It's a symbol of all that's best in Danish culture,' she beams. The museum used to be the manor home of Knud Jensen, who inherited a huge dairy business and then sold it to the Americans for a fortune in 1959, just before he established the museum. Locals called him Oste Jensen, or Cheese Jensen, an epithet old Knud, understandably, didn't take to. Littered with sculptures by Henry Moore and Alexander Calder, the facility became the highbrow playground, even rite of passage, for the town's bright little buttons. 'All the sons and daughters used to go and work there. It was usually their first job.' Today, Humlebæk citizens still come in their droves to enjoy the art-drenched lawns and leisured pavilions of Louisiana. If you're wondering why the museum was called Louisiana, Cheese Jensen's three wives were all called Louise (which meant, I guess, they were always introduced as 'Cheese and Louise').

Further along past the harbour is a row of tastefully restored fishermen's dwellings, built in 1905 when the manor released building lots, and all now costing a fortune. Each has a flagpole and today they are flying long, thin, heraldic-looking Danish flags. This is something foreigners notice about the Danes; some find it a little too smug, though others, like Erich H. Jacoby, German-Jewish refugee who fled to Denmark in 1933, love it. 'I remember the first Sunday outing with them,' he wrote of his adoptive family, 'when I could not get enough of observing the peace and happiness of a healthy people, the waving flags in the gardens along the Sound and the untroubled quality of life.'

Lone explains: 'These flags are just to indicate they're home. But if they have a party or a birthday, they'll run up the full Danish flag. Then everyone else on that row does the same. It's *so* pretty!'

Back home over Danish sausage, honey mustard and rye bread, we discuss what it means to be Danish. 'We're not German and we're not Swedish,' broods Joachim, a reflex answer that is not meant to start a discussion. The poor Germans. Germans are expressly forbidden to buy property in Denmark unless they live there all year round under a law enjoying an EU exemption which dates back to the 1950s, when Danes were worried that what the Germans couldn't do by war, they would do by real estate. It's a remarkable piece of Danish hypocrisy, notes Joachim, since most MPs have summer houses in the south of France.

'I remember going on holidays with my parents in the 1950s,' recalls Lone. 'We were camping in France and Germany was a country you had to go through. We stopped in an old pub on the Rhine and there were some men singing German drinking songs. My father nearly had a heart attack! We had to leave before he started a fight.'

Lone has just written her second book, *Vi Bliver Ikke Yngre* (*We're Not Getting Any Younger*), a scruff-of-the-neck salvo directed at Danish women who feel sorry for themselves. Her first book, which sold 100,000 copies, was called *Lev Selv*, loosely translated as *Live Your Own Life*. It's another come-on-girl-get-it-together clarion call that tries to 'urge Danish women that the time is now and you shouldn't wait around for life to start or for someone to make you whole'. Her new book is aimed at women in their fifties and sixties who are turning bitter at a common occurrence in modern Danish society.

'There are a lot of women who kicked out their husbands when they started having kids, because they felt their husbands were basically useless,' explains Lone, spearing a large Danish sausage. 'It was very common for women to do this because they were so well looked after by the state. Now they get upset when, ten, fifteen years later, they meet their husband with his new kids which he's had with a blonde young enough to be his daughter. I mean, you *can't* be bitter. The only one you hurt is yourself.' she says.

This is a real phenomenon. A large number of Danish men – perhaps as many as 10,000 – have actually moved to Thailand. Some observers, like Anders Agger, a documentary-maker, believe it's down to male disorientation at the thorough independence of women. 'These are men in their forties and fifties who simply couldn't stay in Denmark,' he says. 'They felt there was so much equality that they needed to go somewhere where there was still a kind of old-fashioned hierarchy of the sexes. One man I spoke to said he asked his wife, who was in the kitchen, if she could bring him in a cup of coffee and she came in to the living room and said, make it yourself!'

Despite the declared happiness of the Danes, the resolute independence of women, the candlelit lifestyle, the sunlit design, some expats find life curiously frustrating. Take children, for example. Rolien Créton, a Dutch journalist married to a Dane and living in Copenhagen for the past 10 years, tells me: 'The child is at the centre of everything and is taken everywhere. In Holland we have babysitters, but here the children are taken to the restaurants. They're encouraged to make suggestions about what the family does and what they eat. In Danish culture it's very important that the child learns to think for themselves.'

But in a very Danish way, new mothers are expected to be just as fulfilled in their social as well as in their working lives. 'New mums all meet for a coffee and leave their babies outside,' Rolien says. 'I was shocked! In the summer, and even in winter, you find a row of prams outside the café while the mums are drinking coffee inside, and they have alarms connected to their prams so when one alarm goes off, everyone reaches for their monitor.' Denmark was one of the first countries to organise mum-friendly cinemas: the mums leave their babies in the foyer and are given a number and a beeper. If their baby wakes up, they're informed and they bring it into the cinema (if more than one wakes up at the same time, the auditorium can be filled with the slurping noises of breast-feeding babies).

The new Danish family arrangements – Mum and Dad separated – have created other patterns. One Irish professional explains: 'The kids are up at 6 a.m., eating their cold porridge, then it's snowsuits on and into the pitch dark, when mums cycle them to the kindergarten, where they stay until three or four. Then they're collected by their father. The Danish housewife is dead and the welfare system facilitates it. The social pressures to work are huge.'

Danish conviviality – *hygge*, even – has long impressed foreign visitors, and is in sharp contrast to the more reserved Swedes, and the much more reserved Finns. The former RAF officer Richard Adams, who went on to write *Watership Down*, spent some time in post-War Copenhagen: 'Most Danes are, by contrast with the English, light-hearted and pleasure-loving, good at merriment and without the self-consciousness and rather chilly disposition of so many English people. One marked aspect of the surprise was the drinking capacity of the Danish girls. They didn't at first glance strike one as seasoned drinkers. The Danish girls, even those no more than 19 or 20 years old, were quite accustomed to "one lager, one schnapps; one lager, one schnapps" in almost indefinite succession. This rattled our men, who found they simply *could* not do it.'

But some foreigners find that the upfront conviviality disguises an invisible barrier. 'I thought Danes were more open than they actually are,' says Charles Ferrall, an American correspondent for *Newsweek*, who's been living in Copenhagen (and married to a Danish woman) for 30 years. 'If you're here on a *visit* and you go into a bar, you'll have a good time. People will talk to you, you'll have a sing-along, and so on. But if you *live* here, when you meet those same people on the Monday morning, the barriers are up. They're thinking about their lives, their jobs, their families – this may be universal, but even though they do really have a sense of contentment, and really appreciate the joys of life, if you *live* here it can be difficult to share that with them.'

The generous welfare benefits also amaze expats. How about the Bone Express? For six years, the health system chartered a plane every winter, filling it with doctors and nurses and flying it off to the Alps, scooping up the Danes who had broken their legs skiing, then flying them back home. For the authorities, it made more sense than having hundreds of individual Danes all going through their travel insurance. The practice only ceased in 2008.

Clare McCarthy, a journalist from west Cork who's lived in Denmark with her Danish-Hungarian husband, Paul, for 23 years, describes the following experience. 'When I was nine months pregnant, and had a three-month-old girl, I was in Cork and I started noticing some bleeding. I was worried I was going to miscarry, so Paul contacted our doctor in Copenhagen and they said, right, we'll send someone over. They sent a nurse over, with Paul, they flew first class, arrived in Cork, got me on a plane and flew me back to Denmark. Then they provided a babysitter for 20 hours a week free of charge so that I could recover.'

This brings us back to our examination of the Danish social model, and how we need to understand the Mohammed cartoons crisis in this context. Danes are famous for, and pride themselves in, a progressive, politically correct view of the world. It's drummed into them from an early age: a law on primary education obliges schools to 'familiarise pupils with Danish culture and to contribute to their understanding of *other* cultures and of mankind's interaction with nature'. That's not *encourages*, but *obliges*. But squaring off this worldview with an immigrant population whose numbers increased spectacularly over a short period of time has proved difficult. This is the identity crisis gripping Denmark.

The country had significant unemployment problems in the 1950s, so emigration was more the norm, but in the 1960s some 18,700 immigrant workers were required to service a growing economy. Unlike in Sweden, where immigrants were granted full citizenship, in Denmark they were regarded as 'guest workers'. By the 1990s, with conflicts raging in Somalia, Yugoslavia, Afghanistan, Iraq and Kurdistan, the numbers rose to 130,000. Yet Denmark kept its liberal asylum policies: between 1990 and 2002, it allowed family members to join and took in a higher proportion of applicants than any other industrialised state.

For a country that had been relatively homogenous, such numbers were bound to cause problems. 'I moved here in the late 1970s, when Denmark was 96 per cent homogenous,' recalls Charles Ferrall, who was teaching at the time. 'There was one religion, one ethnicity and the remaining 4 per cent were other Scandinavians. I taught in different schools. There might have been three, four kids whose parents were guest workers. The teachers had no clue. There was no one to teach Danish as a second language. In the 1970s, these people were invisible. They were pushed into a corner and started ghetto building. Then, in the 1980s and 1990s, there was an influx of refugees – Somalis, Afghans, Pakistanis. There were language issues and unemployment. Then the kids in the class were becoming bigger in numbers, so you had gangs forming. And they were saying, we're not going to take it any more, to be ostracised, where our parents are coming home from work upset because some remark was said to them.'

The problem with Denmark, Mary Hilson writes in *The Nordic Model*, was that it had a strong tradition of 'civic nationalism'. Loyalty to the state overrode loyalty to ethnic identity. At the same time, there were strong centralising and conforming instincts within that state, and these would inevitably encourage assimilation rather than multiculturalism. Put bluntly, visitors would have to become more like the Danes rather than maintain UK-style distinct cultural neighbourhoods.

In 1998 Denmark introduced the Integration Law. It framed the debate in economic terms: immigrants and their dependents should be integrated to such an extent that they could become *economically* self-sufficient. The key to integration would be employment, and the new law foresaw government-funded training and education in the Danish language, but also in 'Danish values' such as 'tolerance and respect'. This was developed further by a new law in 2005 which placed even more emphasis on individual duties and responsibilities.

This all seems reasonable, but once they were given a political edge, perceptions changed. The year the Integration Law was introduced, the far-right Danish People's Party (DPP) elbowed its way into politics. Its aims were to reduce immigration drastically, oppose 'Islamicisation' and promote the assimilation of foreigners. They supported Anders Fogh Rasmussen's Liberal and Conservatives coalition in return for their policies to be made mainstream. Since 2001, therefore, the official attitude has been that while Denmark should *understand* immigrants, the onus was on *them* to adapt and become more like Danes. The problem was defining what Danishness was – it was more than just 'meatballs and gravy', as Rasmussen said. 'Politicians were forced to fall back on very general values – respect for human rights, freedom, equality and democracy – that were more understood as universal principles rather than essentially Danish characteristics,' writes Mary Hilson.

The outside world noticed this change of tack, especially after the 2001 elections when the DPP increased their vote. Both they *and* the mainstream Liberals were accused of using xenophobic imagery to win votes. It seemed to fly in the face of the notion of a liberal, tolerant country. When the new government introduced a law imposing a minimum age of 24 for Danes wanting to marry a foreign spouse (the government claimed immigrants were marrying spouses from their home country at an early age to get them into Denmark), it was publicly criticised by Ruud Lubbers, the UN's High Commissioner for Refugees. In Sweden, where a more multicultural, pluralist approach to immigration had taken root, it wasn't liked very much at all. 'Sit there on your elongated bit of Germany,' raged the Swedish tabloid *Aftonbladet*, 'and munch open sandwiches by yourselves. Sit there with your moustaches and drink Tuborg till the cows come home. Sit there, you inbred cavemen. But don't come crawling over the Öresund Bridge for sympathy when you get fed up with isolation – because you won't find it here. Danish bastards...'

Strong, and, dare one say it, very un-Scandinavian stuff (perhaps all that alcohol-related teasing had built up resentment).

It's no surprise, then, that relations between Sweden and Denmark were further soured by the Mohammed cartoons. The Swedish press accused the Danes of being intolerant and xenophobic, while the Danish press accused the Swedes of being self-censoring and politically correct.

But what was behind this very un-Nordic crisis in Danish politics? There's no doubt that people were starting to feel insecure about their welfare model. The country had worked hard, and people paid very high taxes, to have a social and health-care system that was the envy of the non-Scandinavian world. Now these foreigners wanted to come and just take what they could get.

Anders Aggers, the documentary-maker quoted earlier, broadcast a five-part series on being Danish entitled *And It Was Denmark* (a line from the national anthem which migrated to football terraces). He interviewed dozens of Danish people living abroad who were now looking back at their home country. Most were concerned about what was happening, concerned, that is, about the swing to the right. 'Denmark is now a society where people think, we have enough in ourselves, and we have built up this society after all these years, and we have all these goods which we export, and yet we're not taking care of outsiders or the outside world. There's a feeling that something is missing,' he explains. For Danes at home he detected a deeply troubling mood. 'It's easy to say there's a looming racism, but I don't think that's necessarily true. We're not racist, but there is a kind of surprise that people want to come and take our goods, and to benefit from our social model. Danes are just not sure that they have to deliver and take in people from another country. It's like, we're very content, and we're just not ready to share.'

So Denmark is struggling with a growing contradiction between its liberal, tolerant traditions and world-famous humanitarian record on the one hand, and its discomfort at perceived abuses by those they've invited on the other. 'The country is split between those who are globalised, work for Caritas, foreign aid, and those who are basically anti-foreign,' says the Irish journalist Clare McCarthy.

Perhaps Denmark's tradition of self-reliance may not sit comfortably with a dependency culture, whether perceived or real. Denmark's economic success is built on indigenous small and medium-sized businesses, and it has never been in hock to multinationals that come and go. James Mellon, British ambassador from 1983 to 1986, put it thus: 'The Danes are conscious that it is new ideas that make a living in a smart, competitive world, and, from this increasingly educated population, comes bubbling forth a constant supply of new, small companies.'

Expats, though, are divided in their conclusions about living in Denmark. Some, like Tim Ferris, the author of *The 4-Hour Workweek*, are just delirious about Copenhagen's sensual pleasures. He writes on his website: 'Right up there with Argentina, Denmark has a jaw-dropping number of gorgeous people. The truly beautiful part, and unusual differentiator, is they appear blissfully unaware of the fact. There is little LA-style pretension unless you go to a social-climber magnet like Club NASA, which helps to pull the mirror gazers off the streets. Go in the spring or summer and there is no need for catwalks – the sidewalks at Nyhavn are good enough.'

To others, like Clare McCarthy (who nevertheless has stayed for 22 years), the conformism in Denmark gets too much. 'You'll never starve to death in Denmark, but you can be bored to death.' This sentiment is echoed by Rolien Créton: 'I cycle ten metres down a one-way street to avoid a huge detour, but every time there's always some person wagging their finger and saying, you're not allowed to cycle in this direction.'

As for the cartoons crisis, the repercussions are still being felt. Further threats were made against the moderate Muslim MP Naser Khader, and, in October 2007, a conspiracy trial heard that Flemming Rose, the culture editor of *Jyllands-Posten*, was the target of an intended car-bomb attack. In 2010 Kurt Westergaard, who drew the picture of Mohammed with his turban shaped like a bomb, was attacked at his home by an axe-wielding Somali, while another conspiracy to behead journalists at the newspaper was foiled by police. Inevitably the affair spawned a rise in demagoguery on the other side: Lars Hedegaard, a journalist and historian, came to prominence after he set up the International Free Press Society, and disseminated allegedly insulting articles about Muslims. In February 2013 an attempt was made on his life by a gunman posing as a postman.

* * *

On a warm, sunny July morning, blond joggers pass along the landscaped dock of Kalvebod Brygge. I'm heading for Hans Christian Andersen Boulevard, which takes me across the water to the old wharf quarter of Christianshavn, where old brick depots are converted into media and couture offices – Kenzo, Dior – and luxury apartments on Overg. Oven Vandet, overlook the canals. But by the time I reach Prinsessegade, the gentrification has petered out. Sedentary drunks are on their second bottle, staring in wonder at the world. It is 9:30 a.m.

Soon one of the last redoubts of the alternative society announces itself on an overhead archway: *Christiania.* This morning Christiania looks like it's recovering from a severe night on the tiles. On Pusher Street signs of life are either of the canine, or of the slow, ageing human variety. Next to a doorway sits a black water-filled bucket on which the word 'HOUND' is scrawled. Outside Café Nemoland on red-painted picnic tables, empty beer bottles left overnight grow warm and sticky. At one table an elderly male is still asleep, upright. Dogs move with plodding fatigue, tails twitching at the passing of each familiar resident.

All around, curmudgeonly old heroes of the revolution are biding their time. Sitting at coffee tables, they gesticulate amid blooms of hash smoke turned silver by the strong morning sunshine. Above them, hanging on the eves, old Tuborg ice buckets host fresh young cannabis plants arching languidly towards the sun. Status Quo is, somewhat appropriately, playing in the background.

As the morning inches forward, residents pass more briskly. People appear and disappear on bicycles (cars are forbidden). The first tourists arrive, one walking down the entire length of Pusher Street with her arms folded. Under a huge *trompe-l'œil* mural, which will fascinate the hash smokers as the day wears on, I meet Ulle Lykke Andersen, one of the district's official spokesmen and a resident of 29 years standing. He's wearing a fresh white shirt, and shoulder-length sandpaper hair. 'This whole area,' he says, 'used to be the military barracks, part of the old defence system of the city. In 1807, the Brits carried out the first ever terror bombing here. They lobbed new firebombs over the walls, burning one-third of the city. They went for the civilians and ended up taking the entire Danish fleet. They didn't want Napoleon to get it.'

In the 1960s, the 84-acre site now known as Christiania was abandoned by the modern military just as quickly. The city was still pondering the area's future when members of a hippy commune, seeking to establish an alternative society around a music festival in Jutland, saw an opening. When a reporter from an underground magazine sprayed the words 'Emigrate with Bus Number 8' [to Christiania], the idea took off. 'It was on September 26, 1971, that was really Christiania's birthday,' explains Ulle. 'Suddenly it set fire to the hippy movement, and next thing there were 700 people here.'

The pioneers took the authorities by surprise, securing a three-month stay of execution. Over time, Denmark's instinctively non-confrontational approach meant they were left to pursue their quaint social experiment in peace. Christiania evolved with its own flag, anthem, and mission statement into a free-wheeling, non-conformist state within a state. The 1960s dream of a Utopian society had a final, Danish outpost.

'Within the first few weeks, the ethos was established: you can do whatever you like as long as it doesn't interfere with what other people do,' Ulle recalls. 'It was very easy going, very optimistic, ideals were high. This was undisputed anarchic liberalism: the more far out it was, the better.'

It was bound to come unstuck. 'By the late 1970s, every kind of hard drug was available,' says Ulle. 'Heroin, cocaine, speed. When I moved here in 1979, ten people had already died from heroin use. Out of 700 residents, 150 were dependent on it. It was like a shooting gallery in Harlem. But we changed it from the inside. We cooperated with the treatment institutions and eventually got rid of the hard drugs.'

But the hard drugs were replaced by soft ones, with disastrous results. Hash being a bigger cash crop, dealers poured in from the outside, since the authorities were launching crackdowns elsewhere. The market was soon violently divided by rival biker gangs and, by the '80s and '90s, Christiania had become a major clearing house for the cannabis trade. Cartels were investing in hash cultivation in Thailand, Afghanistan, Morocco, Libya and India, while dealers display the yields in a prodigious array of hash stalls. 'There was a pride,' says Ulle, 'in having as many different types of cannabis for sale as possible.' By the late 1990s, the trade was worth half a billion Danish crowns. It wasn't for local consumption: the drugs brought in from abroad were traded through Christiania to the European market.

By 1991 Christiania was out of control. The authorities knew that a drug-fuelled hippy dream occupying public land was simply not on, but a total shutdown was unrealistic. A compromise was reached: the residents would maintain the properties and pay utility bills in exchange for not paying rent, and taking on the task of cleaning up the drug operations. A new sense of responsibility set in, says Ulle. People built and maintained their own houses and set up small businesses. A communal fund attracted 2,000 crowns a month from each resident, with workshops, cafés and restaurants paying more. Of 20 million crowns gathered into the hippy exchequer, 11 million would cover electricity, water, waste management and ground taxes. From 1997 the enclave even had its own currency, the Løn. There were blacksmiths and ironmongers; an antiquated-looking bicycle, based on the old Dursley Pedersen model, was developed and sold out of Christiania. Tourists appeared, drawn to Christiania's mischievous notoriety, and the city was airily content that it all added to the Copenhagen brand.

When a resident died or moved out, the rent-free accommodation would be advertised in a weekly newspaper. Successful candidates plucked from the queue of would-be residents had to prove a tangible connection to the quarter to be voted in, in a kind of reverse-Big Brother process. 'You work your way in,' explains Ulle, partly proud, partly frustrated by the obdurately democratic nature of the process. 'We don't have votes. It's always consensus. Everyone has to have a say about everything, so it's really hard to get to a decision. But that's what we stick to.'

In March 2004 the government discarded 30 years of tolerance. The arrival of the Danish People's Party coincided with a crackdown on persistent drug dealing, by then estimated to be worth one billion Danish crowns (€134 million). The government, says Ulle, was spoiling for a fight. A 10-hour raid, involving 200 riot police, was led by a police chief just back from training Iraqi police in Basra. Locals built barricades and pelted officers with rocks and Molotov cocktails. The authorities made 50 arrests, saying it was an assault on the drugs trade, but others saw it as being driven by economic realities. 'The police have always hated Christiania. It represents a challenge to the state's monopoly on the use of force,' historian Jes Fabricius Møller told the BBC at the time. 'But if you live on expensive land, you have to pay for it.'

The enclave was prime development land, and the government had drawn up a multi-million kroner plan to split it into a cultural centre, apartments and retail outlets, a 'normalisation' scheme which would force Christiania into the 'real' world.

Yet some on the left insisted Christiania, despite the drug menace, was a social success. In its own unorthodox way it has taken in those marginalised by society and given them a home, a community, a chance to get involved in work or in the arts. There are currently some 40 Greenlanders living in Christiania, a segment of Danish society prone to alienation and discrimination. 'It's only here that they don't feel they have social problems,' says Ulle.

Others might dismiss this as fanciful. Christiania is still plagued with drug problems: as the cannabis market in Copenhagen fragmented, rivalry for the Christiania market turned violent. One man was killed by machine-gun fire outside Café Nemoland in 2005 and another seriously injured in a grenade attack in 2009.

In May 2009, following five years of wrangling, evictions, court appeals, riots and police raids, the Eastern High Court ruled that the government was entitled to press ahead with its development plan. While it envisaged Christiania residents remaining, the years of rent-free living would have to go. Many felt that the dream was finally over.

'It's a symbol of Denmark's humanistic liberalism,' says Ulle without hesitation. 'It's the Danish way of talking instead of fighting. It's a tradition we are pretty proud of, a system of looking around and taking the time to decide something. We have two gods: Thor, the god of weather, and Loke, the god of trickery. It's the basic Danish understanding that everyone should listen to Loke as well as to Thor. It's an ideal.'

I ask Ulle if even now he thinks Christiania can survive. His cigarette gently nuzzles the edge of the ashtray. 'It will take a miracle,' he says. As the ash falls away, leaving a reddish pearl of burning tobacco, he smiles. 'But we have already experienced quite a few miracles here.'

In the event the miracle materialised. In 2012, after a successful legal battle, the state agreed to the creation of a community-based foundation which, on the back of government loan guarantees worth €30 million, was able to take control of the site, including the listed buildings, and rent them at cheap rates to Christiania residents.

* * *

As I leave Ulle and the Woodstock Café, a group of Danish schoolchildren, all wearing reflective waistcoats, is being led by an anxious-looking teacher down Pusher Street. The children look at the locals, drunks and hungover Greenlanders, who in turn look back. It's a surreal spectacle.

As I pass under the overhead arch on my way back to the normal world, a sign says, 'Welcome to the EU'.

Chapter 6

Sweden

One shouldn't commit suicide out of fear of death.
– Swedish proverb

I'm crossing the Öresund, the broad breastplate of water separating Denmark from Sweden, having left the great Danes behind. In the distance, a pastel ribbon of land is Sweden. As the ribbon draws nearer, Scandinavia's tallest building, looking like a badly rolled-up magazine, shimmers into view. On arrival at Malmö station, my host takes me directly there through the city's well-ordered and unfeasibly graffiti-free streets.

It was in 1999 that the local chairman of a housing association was so impressed by a white marble sculpture of a twisting human being by the Spanish architect Santiago Calatrava that he asked him to turn it into a skyscraper. You could do this kind of thing in a prosperous, design-savvy country like Sweden. So it was, in August 2005, that Sweden's leading architectural jewel, the Turning Torso, was inaugurated: nine segments of five-storey pentagons turning gracefully as they rise.

Despite its cutting-edge design, the building was actually chosen to replace a very blue-collar symbol of Malmö. The Kockumskranen was a huge crane that had been part of the skyline during the city's shipbuilding heyday until the industry went bankrupt. But the Turning Torso represented a brighter future. It won the 2005 Emporis Skyscraper Award, beating the Q1 Tower in Queensland and the Montevideo Tower in the Netherlands.

But before I can admire its frozen athletic grace, my host and driver, Dr David Eberhard, shakes his head. 'It's ridiculous,' he fumes.

Dr Eberhard is not a dissenting architect, but a clinical psychologist and head of the psychiatric emergency centre at St Göran's Hospital in Stockholm. 'None of the windows open,' he grumbles.

The reason, according to Dr Eberhard, is to prevent suicide. It's hard to see why a far-sighted safety measure should infuriate a medical man, but Dr Eberhard is adamant. Sweden is suffering from a debilitating neurosis, he says. A compulsive fear of everything.

'Actually, I'm looking at it from a psychiatric point of view, except I'm psychoanalysing not a person, but a country. You can define something called panic syndrome. You identify the symptoms and come up with a cure, and the most effective cure is cognitive behavioural therapy. The method is: don't avoid the panic, learn to think about it, evaluate the risk, then change your behaviour. That's what you do with a patient. I'm trying to do it with Sweden.'

What started out as a one-man mission has gripped Sweden's chattering classes. Dr Eberhard has angered many, but has also won the support of colleagues and members of the public. With neighbouring countries encouraging his crusade, partly because they love to mock the conformist Swedes, his fame has spread throughout Scandinavia. But he genuinely thinks Sweden is a special case. 'We have this thing about the Germans and their sense of order, *ordnung, ordnung*. But Sweden is worse.'

It began with an opinion piece he wrote for the leading daily, *Dagens Nyheter*. He challenged Swedes to realise that living on planet Earth can be a dangerous business. Letters and emails flooded in, and the editor encouraged him to write a book. *In the Land of the Safety Junkies* was a publishing sensation, selling 40,000 copies in the first year. Dr Eberhard argued passionately that Sweden's safety culture had encroached on every part of living, from bicycle helmets to exaggerated fears over paedophilia. Fear of dying was strangling the joy of living.

Dr Eberhard has as much reason as any other parent to look askance at the big bad world. He has two boys and two girls, but he makes sure they practise what he preaches. The eldest, 12-year-old Cornelia, shocked fellow pupils, teachers and parents when, as a 7-year-old, she turned up at school alone and on foot. 'People were scandalised. They were wondering what kind of father I was,' Dr Eberhard recalls.

The problems patients were presenting with at St Göran's in Stockholm convinced Dr Eberhard that Swedes had become over-cosseted. 'People tended to be more afraid. They weren't coping with normal things, like if their dog died, if their boss was in a bad mood, if their girlfriend left. I treated a young couple, both around 20. The boy had decided to end the relationship, so the girl took a lot of tablets and tried to kill herself. She was in a terrible state. But the boy – the one who was *ending* the relationship – he *also* tried to take an overdose. He couldn't cope with what he was doing. And yet neither of them had any previous history of psychological problems. Ten years ago, you were never getting cases like this. Now I was getting them four or five times a day. You can't just tell them, "Get a grip!" Some of them are in a bad way. But you try to get them to cope with the relationship by going to friends and family instead of seeking psychiatric help.'

To Dr Eberhard, overregulation and the hail of opinion polls were enfeebling Swedish society. 'I saw a survey asking Swedish citizens whether it was a good thing that 15-year-olds should not be allowed to watch football because of the risk that they might become hooligans. One-third actually thought it was a good idea!'

The Arbetsmiljöverket (the Swedish health and safety executive) appeared to be accruing more powers and issuing ever more bizarre laws. The kid gloves seemed to be permanently on. 'There is a suburb of Stockholm called Täby,' he continues. 'Bus drivers began to complain about the speed ramps, that if they drove over them too quickly they would get a backache. So instead of telling the drivers not to drive over them so fast, they rearranged the entire bus route so that they would actually *avoid* all the speed ramps!

'We all die of something. If we don't know that, we come off worse. But society in Sweden is beginning to believe that if we regulate everything, control everything, then nobody will die, at least not until they're 85.'

Dr Eberhard admits that, especially as a doctor, it's not something he can easily campaign against. 'If we have zero deaths on the roads, then who am I to say that's a bad thing?' he says. 'And we should be proud of that. But we spend 20 million Swedish crowns [€2 million] on every life saved on the roads. Compare that to what we spend on the health service for every life saved. It's probably just half a million Swedish crowns [€50,000]. Is it money well spent?'

* * *

Professor Claes Tingvall would say yes. He is director of traffic safety at Vägverket, the Swedish Road Administration (SRA), and regarded as the father of the most radical transformation in road safety anywhere in the world. The Vision Zero concept, introduced in 1997, wasn't short on ambition: the reduction of *all* road fatalities and serious injuries to *zero* by 2020.

Its authors set out to change the entire perspective on road deaths. Vision Zero is all about shifting responsibility away from the driver, and instead spreading it across a spectrum of 'stakeholders': road designers, car manufacturers, schools, hospitals, the police and legislators. Human life, the reasoning goes, takes priority over the objectives of road traffic, so safety should be given the same centre of importance it's accorded in aviation and employment. 'For 70 years, every country has had a rule that it was "forbidden to crash". That created a mindset that the road user was the problem,' says Tingvall. 'But if you took the approach that is used for aviation safety, in the energy sector, in the workplace, then the system *itself* creates safety. The first thing to recognise is that the user is fallible and is expected to make mistakes. Stakeholders have to integrate that fact. You wouldn't get the aviation sector saying that we have done a cost-benefit analysis and therefore we can get prices down to this level if only *x* number of passengers die, nor would you get a company saying our product will be cheaper if we only kill this amount of workers.'

Vision Zero means bad driving is factored into road construction and the technology that surrounds it. Drivers are not relieved of their responsibility as such. But the new attitude is that, traditionally, road accidents, serious injury or death punished bad drivers *unfairly* for their error: now the burden would be shared between those who build the roads, those who use them and those who police them. The fatalistic maxim that we all could be knocked down by a bus tomorrow simply does not fly in official Sweden: under Vision Zero, we are philosophically entitled *not* to be knocked down by a bus (even if the bus driver has a bad back from all those speed ramps).

'An accident that results in serious human injury means that the components in the road transport system are not functioning well together,' says the Vision Zero manifesto.

But Vision Zero doesn't just mean zero fatalities, it also means zero serious injuries. This necessitates a calculus between accident and serious accident. The system, for example, works out how much the human body can withstand in a collision: since humans can survive at 30 kilometres per hour, but not at 50 kilometres, then the survivability factor becomes the absolute priority, dictating where you put roundabouts and how you design cars.

Huge swathes of Swedish suburbia have duly been switched to 30-kilometre per hour zones (that's just 18.6 miles per hour) and roundabouts have sprouted at every turn in built-up areas. There may be fewer accidents at traffic lights, but due to the angle of impact and slower speed, accidents on roundabouts are less serious and therefore more desirable. Median barriers, now ubiquitous, can actually lead to more crashes, but they kill or seriously injure very few people. 'It's all about controlling energy,' says Tingvall. 'You can do that with median barriers. But if a car crashes head on into a truck, you have no way to control that energy.'

So drivers shouldn't be punished unfairly for crashing, and petty collisions are tolerable if they reduce more serious smashes.

But much of the radical thinking is where car manufacturers and road designers get together. This has led to what some regard as in-car nannying: those annoying sensors that remind you that your seat belt is not fastened or that the alcohol on your breath means you shouldn't be driving (one device activated by blowing into a monitor before your ignition will start is now actually regarded as too much work for the driver, so a more passive control system is being developed). Another system, using cameras and radar, along with more sophisticated road markings, envisages the car 'steering' itself *back* into the correct lane if the driver drifts into the wrong side of the road. Volvo, long synonymous with pioneering safety, has rejoined the fray. The company was bought by Ford in 1999 and, according to Tingvall, drifted from its historic association with safety (Volvo had introduced safety belts in 1959, child locks in 1972, rear-window brake lights and dual-stage airbags in the 1980s, and side-impact airbags and whiplash protection in the 1990s). But Volvo is back on mission: the XC60, which rolled out in February 2009, comes with a laser sensor behind the windscreen to monitor traffic up to eight metres in front. If a collision looks imminent, the brakes will automatically be applied. Insurance companies promise to cut premiums for XC60 owners and, in September 2008, Volvo declared that by 2020, *no one* would be killed or seriously injured in, or by, one of their vehicles.

These are grandiose claims. Tingvall insists this kind of collaboration is the only way to radically cut road deaths. He accepts there's been criticism that the zero targets cannot realistically be met, that the whole enterprise is too expensive and that too much responsibility has been taken away from the individual road user. But he is unrepentant.

'People complain about the nanny state, but this is a very strange way to discuss it,' he says. 'You wouldn't be creating a better society if you had more dangers in the workplace, so why on the roads?'

Vision Zero is work in progress. Dozens of research programmes are under way and the authorities are constantly trying to get everyone involved, encouraging commercial fleets and trade unions to purchase 'safety-forward' vehicles. Once certain solutions are deemed effective, they become the optimum model – even an ISO standard – with which all new roads and road users must comply. And Sweden is now exporting Vision Zero to countries around the world.

Has it brought results?

The preliminary findings are positive. In 1997, there were 541 deaths. By 2006, the figure had fallen to 431, making Sweden among the safest in the industrialised world. In 2007, there was a 6 per cent increase, although 2008 saw the figure fall again to around 400. By 2012 the trend had continued with just 286 road deaths.

Sweden has, of course, set very high standards for itself. It introduced mandatory daytime running lights in 1978, and compliance is now so automatic (it's actually 100 per cent) that surveys and enforcement are 'no longer necessary'. In 1990, the drink-driving limit was lowered to 50 milligrams of alcohol per 100 millilitres of blood, cutting deaths by 10 per cent.

But Tingvall is disappointed. By 2009, the authorities were still well off their target. Some €150 million per year is spent on adapting country roads, and even though the cost of saving a life has been reduced to one-twentieth what it was in 1997, motorists are still driving too fast (Tingvall dismisses the joke that the thing you are most likely to die of on Swedish roads is old age). 'We are not at all getting close – it's a long journey,' he admits. 'We are getting into something which was designed 100 years ago. The only thing we can do is to improve a little each year.'

But why has Sweden led the way?

Professor Tingvall says it's the ability for a society to organise itself around modern ideas. On 3 September 1967, in a spectacular *coup de modernité*, the Swedes pulled off a trick almost as breathtaking as Ireland giving up smoking in pubs. On Högertrafikomläggningen Day, Sweden switched from being a left-hand drive country to being a right-hand one (*Högertrafikomläggningen* means 'right-hand traffic diversion').

It was a daring act, but because it worked it marked Sweden off as a special kind of society. Although Swedes had been driving on the left since 1736, bizarrely the vast majority of cars were actually *left*-hand drives. The reason there weren't more head-on collisions during overtaking was because the Swedish countryside was blessedly short of people. Even though most of Europe and all of their Scandinavian neighbours were driving on the right, Swedes had repeatedly rejected the switch, even voting against it in a referendum in 1955. But the government decided enough was enough, and in 1963 the Riksdag (Parliament) approved the changeover.

'Sweden started on the left because it wanted to be Anglo-Saxon, but then in the 1960s, the government wanted to be more American, and more in tune with those around them,' says Professor Tingvall.

The whole operation was very Swedish. The government, like a benign but firm parent, decided what was best and then prepared citizens for the change (there was a four-year lead-in period that even involved the use of psychologists). The safeguards were comprehensive and observed by all. On the day itself, workers across the country peeled the black plastic off the traffic signals that directed Swedes away from their misguided Anglo-Saxon aspirations and on to the true Euro-American path. Non-essential traffic was banned from 1 a.m. to 6 a.m.; any vehicles on the roads during that period had to come to a complete stop at 04:50, then carefully change to the right-hand side of the road and stop again before being allowed to proceed at 05:00 (one can just imagine the tension in the control centre). The whole operation was a resounding success: 125 reported traffic accidents, compared with 165 the previous Monday, and no fatalities. Strict speed limits as low as 10 kilometres per hour probably had a major impact; road deaths returned to their normal rate within two years.

'It was very successful,' says Professor Tingvall. 'People predicted a catastrophe, but there were very few accidents. There had been a long planning process: every citizen got involved.'

* * *

Citizen involvement, an orderly transition, no shocks or surprises...

That a country could execute so radical a social change in a matter of hours with no pandemonium was the kind of image Sweden enjoyed projecting. Sweden generally gets good press. How could it not? This is the country of ABBA and IKEA (two of the most comforting commodities modern humans could ask for), a land in which tolerance, equality and promoting human rights are virtues that appear unquestioned. While 20th-century Europe swung violently between capitalism and communism, Sweden steered a successful in-between course. Citizens embraced high taxes to enjoy world-class public services and a high quality of life. Society seemed to outsiders to be efficient and orderly. A country which embraces environmentalism more effectively than most, Sweden reduced carbon emissions by 9 per cent between 1990 and 2006, even though its economy grew by 44 per cent. It regularly beats all comers on giving money to the Third World. All told, Sweden sets a standard of modern living of which the rest of us can only dream.

It was not always thus. Tacitus spoke of the Suiones as a powerful tribe with longboats. Swedish Vikings may have fought, traded and pillaged their way across Europe, but throughout the Middle Ages, Sweden remained a poor, sparsely populated land. It wasn't until the 16th century that they were united under one king, Gustav Vasa, rediscovering their colonising instincts in the process. He built an empire stretching from the Baltic to Munich, terrorising Poles, Lithuanians and Germans along the way. Sweden even had a 17th-century colony in New Delaware, which they had to surrender to the Dutch. Eventually, though, repeated wars took their toll: Sweden was soon eclipsed by the rise of the Russian Empire and, in 1807, it lost Finland to the Tsar. In the 1860s during the *Svältår*, the starvation years, poor harvests, hunger and disease decimated the population. Between 1850 and 1910, 1 million Swedes, mostly the very poor and the very young, emigrated to America. Every second child died in infancy.

The origins of Sweden's very modern democratic serenity are often related back to this period. The loss of empire prompted a period of inward-looking reflection on liberal reforms. Ultimately the policy-makers who would transform Sweden from a very poor society to a very rich one in the 20th century accepted the imperative of progressing beyond mass hunger and emigration through the rational, scientific ordering of society.

But in truth, Sweden had democratic traditions going back to the middle ages. The parliament, or Riksdag, can be traced back to 1435, and by the 16th century its four chambers represented farmers, the clergy, the bourgoisie and the nobility. The King often favoured the farmers as a way of curbing the influence of the nobility, and so to ordinary folk the monarchy was a relatively accessible, even benign entity ('to go the King' was an expression of local empowerment).

Swedes too were anxious to avoid the polarising effects of the industrial revolution, whose excesses were only too evident in Britain. Industry was spread to avoid grim urban ghettos of exploited workers, while liberal factory and mill owners poured money into schools, medical insurance and churches in the pursuit of socially responsible capitalism. The rigourous application of Lutheranism, which involved Bible reading for everyone in the villages from the early 1700s, meant that no matter how poor Swedes were they could still read and write.

In 1889, the Social Democratic Party, the political movement that would come to dominate Sweden throughout the 20th century, was founded. What made Sweden different was that this movement didn't embrace the class conflict of Marxism; instead it was based on an inclusive idea of trade unions, religion and temperance, thus ensuring a tradition of consensual politics. The Social Democrats also carefully nurtured the old traditions of the benign king at the head of a centralised state, so ordinary Swedes were comfortable with the idea of a 'caring' government in the capital.

Even in the 1890s, when IKEA was barely a twinkle in anyone's eye, Swedes were encouraged to own their own homes. They also had the highest per capita phone ownership in the world. The privations of life in rural Sweden meant women and men shared the burden, so gender equality was established early. In 1921, the '*folkhemmet*' philosophy was introduced by Per Albin Hansson, the much-loved leader of the Social Democrats and a future prime minister. 'The term loses a lot in translation,' writes the maverick Swedish journalist Ulf Nilson in *What Happened to Sweden?* 'Literally it means the people's home, but what it really suggests is a great tent for everybody, the great society. It is a country where the citizens, all for one and one for all, look after each other, like members of a good and loving family, where the head, which is the government, decides what is good for everybody.'

Per Albin Hansson himself described it thus:

> The good home knows no privilege or neglect, no favourites and no stepchildren. There, no one looks down on another, no one strives to gain advantage at the expense of others, the strong do not repress the weak. In the good home, equality, thoughtfulness and helpfulness prevail. Applied to the great people's and citizens' home, this would mean the breakdown of all social and economic barriers …

But there was an undertone of exclusivity, a pre-condition at the entrance on the doorstep, as Göran Rosenberg, the Swedish author and journalist notes. 'The Swedes were anti-authoritarian, cooperative, independent, strong-minded, consensus prone, with an innate sense of justice, sharing the "instincts" of an ancient people. Swedishness was a home-grown quality, owing very little or nothing to foreign influences and "imports".'

It was a stirring vision, and the Social Democrats were given a decades-long run in implementing it. When they took office in 1932 they would not relinquish power for another 44 years.

The impact of the movement cannot be understated. Their transformation of Sweden was radical, turning a once hierarchical and formal country into something quite different. 'The Social Democrats had set out to remake Swedish society almost completely,' writes the journalist Andrew Brown in his meditation on Sweden, *Fishing in Utopia*. 'They had inherited a poor, patriarchal and formal society, and turned it into a rich, feminist and fiercely egalitarian one.'

The Lutheran Church had been a powerful force, so neither it, nor rural conservatives, would give up without a fight, and the final conflict was over jazz dancing. In the 1940s conservatives led a major moral panic over jazz dances in rural dance halls, and whether they led to unbridled sexual behaviour among young people. The *Dansbaneeländet* (dance ban) was the last big rearguard action by the Church in Sweden before it was brought into line by the *folkhemmet* ideologues.

To the Social Democrats, a welfare state and capitalism were not mutually exclusive. It was up to the state to use *both* to shape society according to its aspirations. 'High and stable rates of economic growth (*tillväxt*) were a prerequisite for high levels of welfare (*trygghet*), but the opposite was also true,' writes Mary Hilson. 'A stable economy required a comprehensive welfare state.'

What helped Sweden pursue its utopia was its neutrality during World War II. It may have been a highly qualified neutrality (8,000 Swedes went to fight alongside the Finns against the Soviet Union, while the government allowed Germany to transit 2 million troops through its rail network to Norway), but Sweden's industries and resources were pretty much intact by the end of the war. Free from the constraints of religion, superstition and poverty, the Social Democrats set about their transformation of Sweden. It affected everyone: how people worked, where they lived, what happened in their private lives. 'All the doors are open,' wrote Henrik Stenius, the Finnish historian, 'to the living room, the kitchen, the larder, the nursery, not to mention the bedroom – and they are not just open: society marches in and intervenes, sometimes brusquely.'

* * *

Did this social transformation lead to one of our favourite Swedish stereotypes, that of the blond, sauna-loving, sexually liberated Swede?

There are several clues as to its origin. The first we find in a 1955 article in *Time* Magazine. Although Sweden had been staunchly Lutheran, the Church was now officially part of the state – almost a government department – and as such bishops were more constrained in launching moral crusades against permissive behaviour.

An episcopal letter complaining about the 'alarming' levels of abortion, birth control and promiscuity prompted a backlash from Swedish newspapers which thundered that the Church had no business meddling in people's affairs. The bishops retired, shaken, to their churches, but the story was picked up by *Time* Magazine. 'In its efforts to please the government,' frowned the report, '[the Church] has become so watered down as an institution that to the average Swede it has lost most of its spiritual meaning.' In shocked tones, *Time* listed off the abortion rates in Sweden (5,000 a year), and the numbers of unmarried mothers (27,000 in a population of 7 million). Worse was the attitude to sex education in schools: the authors said they 'blanched' when a teacher admitted telling teenage pupils that sleeping together was fine so long as they were 'in love'. That promiscuity was being promoted by *teachers* was too much for American sensitivities (this was 1955, after all), whatever the very Swedish rationale behind it. 'Young people sleep together everywhere,' a local psychologist had told the magazine. 'We don't frown and tell them that it is sinful and expect that that will prevent it. Since they're going to do it anyway, we try to give them training and teach them to be honest.'

That Sweden's political system was dangerously close to socialism added to the distaste with which the US was beginning to regard Sweden. In a 1960 speech to Republican supporters in Chicago, President Dwight Eisenhower spoke of the dangers of a 'socialistic' system: higher suicide rates, alcoholism, loss of ambition. He didn't name the country (Swedes, naturally, thought he was talking about Denmark), but on a visit in 1962, the President told Swedes he had been badly informed and apologised.

But other elements fed into the stereotype. In Spain, *La Sueca* became a stock figure in the new risqué movies produced when Franco relaxed censorship rules in the 1960s. She was the tall, available blonde who descended from the snowy north to reveal all on Spanish beaches (she usually ended up chasing the *macho español*). Other cinematic vignettes, from the celebrated director Ingmar Bergman, of Swedes swimming naked in the Stockholm archipeligo, further contributed to the impression of carefree hedonism; while actress Anita Ekberg – blonde, voluptuous, with a sexual allure complicated by an icy demeanour – completed the caricature. In films, Ekberg's figure was as important as her character (Bob Hope famously commented that her parents had won the Nobel Prize for architecture), with her performance as Silvia, uninhibitedly wading through Rome's Trevi Fountain in Federico Fellini's *La Dolce Vita* (1960), a symbolic high point of the stereotype.

Then in the early 1970s dimly lit American cinemas were filled with the mewings of imported 'Swedish' pornography; only the films weren't Swedish. 'I remember being a 17-year-old student in Mineapolis in 1972,' recalls Rolf Fredriksson, a correspondent for Sweden's public television (SVT), 'and going into a cinema advertising Swedish porn. But when I watched it the actors were speaking *Danish*, (well, what few lines they had), but it was still called Swedish porn.'

It's a notion that has been hard for Swedes to shake off. It's true that the more rational approach to post-war social planning meant that the authorities took a pragmatic approach to sexual issues (the approach which so horrified *Time* Magazine readers), but it largely related to how they could get women into the workforce while still allowing them to have children at the 'right' time. Today, though, young Swedish women are probably no more or less inhibited than their British or German (or, heaven forbid, Irish) counterparts. Discussions on sexuality are more frank and less squeamish, a reflection of the longstanding gender equality, but when they turn up on Mediterranean beaches, Swedish women suffer more invasive male attention for their presumed availability (Swedes also have to correct the notion that men and women enjoy communal saunas – they do, but rarely outside families). In fact, Sweden is rather less tolerant of male hedonism than many other countries, thanks to the strong feminist lobby: campaigners successfully convinced hotel chains to remove pornographic pay channels from their bedrooms, and Swedish MEPs even lobbied that any officials travelling on EU business did not stay in a hotel which carried such channels. In 1999 a new law shifted criminal responsibility in prostitution cases entirely onto the shoulders of the male client, while the women themselves were regarded as largely blameless.

* * *

So rather than Sweden being the free-and-easy, liberal, tolerant country the stereotype conjures up, social control has been important, if not central. The Social Democrats had tools which were already in place. Since 1686, the Lutheran Church had been in charge of the local population registry in every village and, after 1946, it gave the government a key weapon. It recorded every piece of information on who lived where, owned what apartment, was married to whom. It kept tabs on who had children in and out of wedlock, on who was paying tax and who wasn't. To its supporters it ensured the most effective policies; to opponents it was the tyranny of control.

As we have seen, the *folkhemmet*, or people's home, was ordered around a highly paternalistic state, which left little to individual discretion. Part of this rather panic-stricken approach was inspired by an academic husband-and-wife team who had a resounding influence on the Swedish welfare model. Gunnar Myrdal, a Nobel prize-winning economist, and his wife Alva, a sociologist and later Nobel Peace Prize laureate, wrote *The Crisis in the Population Question* (1934), which warned of the Swedish population declining to an alarming degree within generations (the mass emigration of the 19th century was not such a distant memory).

The Myrdals' ideas inspired the state to encourage women, especially in working-class areas, to enter the labour market through gender equality, child care and subsidies which were decades ahead of their time. The ultimate imperative was to ensure the right population balance, but critics now argue that the Myrdals' orthodoxies simply encouraged the state to direct citizens' every movements.

'We were supposed to die out in Sweden within a few generations,' says Mattias Svensson, a writer who has explored the subject in his book

Glädjedödarna (Killjoys). 'Everything had to be rigorously controlled, there was no room for one's own discretion, so it came down to the state providing furniture, food stamps, everything. Nothing too big or small could be spared petty regulation.'

Ordering the good society also necessitated some rather nasty practices. In the 1930s eugenics was a respected science in Sweden – not just in Germany – and an Institute for Racial Biology was established in Uppsala in 1922. Between 1935 and 1975, nearly 63,000 sterilisations were carried out under a new eugenics law (other Nordic countries had their own laws) and the legislation was only abolished in 1976. Preventing women (or at least forcefully persuading them) from having more children was not inspired by the *racial* ideology of the Nazis, but by ideas about what made society more economic and efficient. Considerable numbers of women, often gypsies, social 'undesirables', or those with a suspected genetic predisposition, were forcibly sterlised. It was a taboo subject only properly investigated in the 1990s.

Alcohol was also heavily controlled. Five regional monopolies merged into the Orwellian sounding *Systembolaget*, literally the System Company. It allowed the state to control the sale of alcohol with the strictest of conditions. From the 1920s until the 1950s, individuals were even given quotas on alcohol depending on their age, sex, marital status, occupation and social standing. The system required home inspections, and a bureaucracy based on espionage. The state decided how alcohol should be sold, even how it should be displayed (if one beer was refrigerated, all beers had to be refrigerated). There had been a tradition of restricting alcohol use going back to the great temperance movements in the 19th century, yet under the new Social Democrat system the attitude to alcohol was *not* going to be radically liberalised. Konrad Adenauer, the first post-war German chancellor, once remarked that you couldn't get a schnapps in Sweden if you wanted it at a time of day the authorities deemed unsuitable.

While the whole regime seems terrifying to Irish sensibilities, there was a less than sinister rationale: in the people's home drunkenness should be prevented, and alcoholics be taken off the streets, because the state was there to *care* for people.

There have been challenges. In the 1970s *Tritmba*, a nightclub in Stockholm which was repeatedly raided by police because of its late opening hours, was the focus of a campaign to relax the rules. Today, the *Systembolaget* is still the only retail outlet permitted to sell alcohol above 3.5 per cent volume, and alcohol remains a political hot potato (one politician recently wanted mandatory measurements for bag-in-box wines, while Belgian beer was long forbidden because it was too strong).

* * *

Trying to contrive the happiest, most provided-for of societies runs the risk of inviting despair. It was reflected in the work of Ingmar Bergman whose themes of mortality, loneliness, faith and despair painted a competing picture of the Swede as sexually liberated yet mentally depressed, even suicidal. By the late 1960s, Sweden had reached the pinnacle of social progress, yet fulfilment seemed to be missing. The Social Democrats had presided over an economy and welfare system that was the envy of the globe. In all the indicators – health, education, life expectancy – Sweden came out near or at the top. Intellectuals noted their country was cleaner, more law abiding and more tax paying than those unreliable (Catholic) countries from the Mediterranean (it wasn't surprising that Sweden stayed out of the EU until 1995).

Yet something didn't feel right. On the left there was puzzlement over lingering inequality after two decades of unparalleled growth. The government had built 1 million new homes in a radical construction programme in the late 1960s (they were modern, bright and well furnished), yet they 'came to stand not for the rational, efficient and cosy people's home, but as a concrete and brutal symbol of social alienation', as Mary Hilson writes in *The Nordic Model.*

The sense of a slow-motion rupture started with a series of wild-cat strikes in the iron mines of northern Sweden in 1970, and continued with the oil crisis of 1973. The Swedish right began to articulate misgivings about moral permissiveness, about a welfare system that seemed to inhibit individual freedom, and about the monolithic nature of the state. The right complained that the unions and government conspired in a stiflingly perpetual consensus. The *Arbetarrörelsen* (Workers' Movement) organised the accommodation you lived in, the holidays you took and the evening classes you signed up for. Everyone was in a union.

The government's response was to press ever harder for equality. Gender was top of the list: from the early 1970s, benefits lured thousands more women into the public sector (80 per cent of public servants in Sweden are now women); husbands and wives had their salaries taxed separately rather than as one income. In 1973, only 16 per cent of children went to a nursery, but by 1989 it had risen to 64 per cent.

When shocks came, they were truly shocking. Olof Palme was prime minister and the towering presence at the head of the Social Democratic Party. When he was gunned down in front of his wife on a Stockholm street on the night of 28 February 1986, the carefully woven membrane behind which Sweden had tried to construct the most equal, prosperous and safe society in the world was shattered. Palme had, naturally, no bodyguards: the last political assassination had been in 1792.

Conspiracy theories swirled. Palme had enemies on the right and left. He had annoyed the Americans and was also a strident critic of Russian Communism. Sweden had carved out an international niche of diplomatic outrage over injustice, setting herself up as the conscience of the world. In the end, a local alcoholic, Christian Pettersson, was tried on the basis of Mrs Palme's testimony. He was convicted of murder but later released on appeal. The murder weapon was eventually found in 2006, but it was too late to link it conclusively to Pettersson. In 2004 he had fallen drunk off a park bench and died.

* * *

The disorientation of the 1970s and 1980s led Swedes to a bout of soul-searching. The idea that Sweden had a *culture* just like a country such as Gambia had been anathema to academics. If Sweden had an ultra-modern, rational society, then what need had it for culture? Culture was all about old customs and irrational beliefs. Sweden was a homogenous, white, introverted country. In 1984, the European Values Study revealed that 40 per cent of Swedes said they preferred to be with people whose values and opinions they shared – much more than other Scandinavian countries, and far ahead of countries like Spain and Italy.

But by the late 1980s, Swedes were beginning to ask questions about themselves and what kind of people they were. The country was no longer homogenous: for two decades, Sweden had absorbed nearly 1 million refugees and economic migrants. Against the backdrop of the Palme murder, researchers began to explore notions of Swedishness. Professor Åke Daun's seminal study, *Swedish Mentality*, was published in English in 1996.

He set about examining the Swedes as a people, comparing them with other cultures and trying to work out their national character through testimonies from a growing population of foreigners living in Sweden. He concluded that Swedes were regarded as cold, reserved and inscrutable, a trait personified to an exemplary degree by the tennis star Björn Borg. This shyness was an obstacle to visitors. Getting invited into a Swedish home was hard work. 'If a foreigner needs directions, Swedes will be very friendly and helpful, but they won't speak to you on a train or on a bus,' he told me by telephone from Stockholm. 'They entertain very few people, they have small numbers of friends and they tend to stick to friends from childhood for a long time.'

Lack of spontaneous interaction is something many expats find puzzling, especially the Irish, who have made an Olympic sport out of it. 'You could be walking down a quiet street and go by a couple of Swedes and they will do all they can to avoid making eye contact,' says Colm O'Callaghan, a former Irish broadcast journalist and manager of an information services company, 'because the thought of saying hello is just ridiculous to them. Even walking in a forest, people will walk by and ignore you.'

Why do they do this? Professor Daun studied levels of shyness among Swedish and American university students. Swedes were more competent in conversation, but less willing to initiate. 'English-speaking guest lecturers are sometimes astounded at the silence in the auditorium when the discussion is left open for comments or questions from the floor,' he wrote.

Swedes, he discovered, tended to speak in a low voice and to avoid eye contact, often alternating their attention towards something else (Professor Daun quoted an American bank director trying to hold a conversation with a Swedish client who was so determined to look past her out through the window that eventually the American turned around to see what the client was looking at).

The important thing, Professor Daun observed, was that shyness for Swedes – certainly compared to Americans – was not a negative characteristic. It showed empathy, willingness to listen, unpretentiousness. Yet it bothered a lot of Swedes. 'What they say is interpreted as a sign of who they are, and consequently everyone should think carefully before he or she says anything,' says Professor Daun. 'This takes time and leads to pauses, and it is assumed that those listening do not interrupt and use the pauses to take over a conversation … In contrast to the French and many other nationalities, typical Swedes never express opinions they do not hold in order to incite a discussion or to shed light on the other side of a subject.'

The roots of this shyness go back to Sweden's rural past, where people lived in small, often remote communities and remained largely homogenous. 'Swedes expect similarity, they like people who are like themselves,' says Professor Daun. 'That is an obstacle for foreigners. It's difficult to come close to Swedes. You enjoy good relations with your workmates, they're friendly, but it doesn't go beyond that.'

And yet, when Swedes travel they feel liberated and are more likely to let their hair down. 'Before moving to Sweden I believed that most Swedes were similar to those that you meet on your travels who are just as boisterous and sociable as the Irish,' says Hugh McCarthy, an executive with Enterprise Ireland in Stockholm. 'The reality is a much tamer society than I had envisaged, coupled with an almost German-like efficiency in daily life.'

But Swedes getting drunk in Mediterranean bars is not entirely about using alcohol to lower inhibitions – it's the very act itself that gives them that liberated feeling. 'What matters to the drinker is less the physiological effects of alcohol than the "cultural ticket" to a freer and more irresponsible pattern of social interaction,' writes Professor Daun.

Shyness necessitates an avoidance of conflict, and Swedes will strive for consensus at every stage of social and business interaction. But it can have curious consequences. Expats comment that when you're invited for dinner, the host puts enormous energy into where guests are placed. They work out who is interested in music, who is interested in sport, who are teachers, who are accountants. Make sure they're seated in the correct pairings, and consensus will be guaranteed. Where possible, controversial conversation pieces are to be avoided.

'If you're at a dinner party in the UK,' says James Savage, an English journalist living in Stockholm, 'you can spend the whole evening having a real difference of opinion and people can end up agreeing to disagree. But in Sweden, everyone is striving to find the point of agreement and if anyone breaks the consensus, and doesn't keep up the pretence of everyone agreeing, then there's a really awkward atmosphere. Disagreeing is just not the done thing, even on relatively trivial matters.'

This avoidance of conflict is magnified in business. 'The level of consensus in Swedish business can be off-putting at times,' says one Irish executive. 'Sales cycles consist of relationship building and a meticulous attention to detail, so they are generally longer and more protracted than in most other countries. However, if your company is accepted by a Swedish organisation, you generally find you have a partner for life.'

Again the striving for consensus and the fear of eccentricity reinforce the sense of conformity. 'The strangest thing about Sweden, to an English eye,' writes Andrew Brown in *Fishing in Utopia*, 'was always its tremendous conformity. It did not matter what the orthodoxy might be: the point is that everyone knew what was acceptable and proper to believe.' For example, '*Lagom*' is one of those difficult-to-translate words, which means something between 'great' and 'terrible'. In a buffet, you should take a *lagom* amount, i.e. not too much but not too little. 'Swedes seem to strive to do everything moderately,' says Colm O'Callaghan. 'I run quite a lot for the average person and compete in long-distance running, so I'm doing about 60 to 70 miles a week. This is kind of frowned upon. If I did nothing at all, it would also be frowned upon.'

This idea that moderation can be taken to an extreme is something that has preoccupied Fredrik Lindström, a comedian, broadcast journalist and linguist. He produced a TV series on the Swedish language: how it's used differently across the country and what it reveals about Swedish culture. He soon realised that through language, he could divine what makes Swedes *Swedes*. He turned his conclusions into a stand-up comedy routine called *Swedes Are People Too*, a wry look at how Swedes see themselves and how foreigners see them. Lindström discovered they were a lot more mixed up than we thought.

'When I started to look at international perspectives of the Swedes, I realised that while foreigners looked at Sweden as a mainstream, liberal country, in fact it was a country of extremes,' he told me. 'The obsession with modernity is extreme. Tradition is ugly, modern is good. I discovered something of this through translations. The word for "human error" in Sweden translates as "human factor". Yet "human factor" is actually a technical term for the way humans relate to machinery or technology. So to make it synonymous with human *error* means that the human factor is always negative. So self-confidence in Sweden lies in technology, in things we can measure. Human values are rated as low.'

Lindström argues that the terrible poverty and emigration in the late 19th century hard-wired the primacy of technological modernity into the Swedish mindset. 'Our self-confidence comes from our engineers. There was a survey of different countries asking people what – out of 25 things – made them most proud of their country. In Russia the first was the army, the second was their literature and culture. In Sweden those were the last two. What Swedes were most proud of was their nature, and their *technology*. Swedes think their society is almost perfect. In the 1960s we had a fantastic economy; we were on top of our self-confidence. We saw other countries as way behind. There they beat their kids and watch dubbed TV shows.

'Every country's language can be traced back to when their country was on a high. For the English it was the 19th century, for the French it was the 17th century, for Swedes it was the 1960s. The term "hello" is "*hej*" – pronounced "hey!" – Swedes use it all the time, but it's really a word from the sixties. That was when we really tried to build up Sweden in a modern way. We started to lose titles. You wouldn't say someone was the boss, you wouldn't have such formality or visible hierarchies.'

Lindström believes that Swedes have traded tradition for modernity in a more ruthless way than other Europeans. They have less use for family, an institution not so rigorously protected by the constitution, as in Ireland, or so fundamentally important, as in Italy. One study showed that 70 per cent of Swedes were content to be away from friends and family for a while. Swedes move on average 10 times in their lives, much more than most other Europeans. They find their sense of belonging not in families but in a wider and looser social group. By conforming to what the big group does, they feel secure. 'You always have to check that you're just inside this group, so for example you can end up having these absurd discussions about immigrants,' says Lindström. 'You might have one person who has spent years working with immigrants, and then he says one thing which might be perceived as racist, and he's out in the cold. Then you have another person who has done nothing practical for immigrants but is careful that he always says the right thing, so he's then inside the group.'

And they find more security in the comfort of numbers. 'We have values in modernity and numbers, things which are measurable. We all know our personal codes, we know how much the alcohol content is in drinks, we know the birthdates of our friends and even colleagues, we know the exact size of our apartments in square metres, even the exact measurements of the apartments we used to live in. I tell my audience, outside Scandinavia *no one knows* the exact square metres of their old apartments.'

Lindström argues, in fact, that the essential Swedishness of IKEA is not that it has all those sleek, Scandinavian lines, but something else. 'If you have a society where modernity is highly valued and where tradition has a low value, then change just drives itself. You can't turn back to tradition once it's gone. If you want to have a pub in the UK or Ireland, everyone knows what a pub is supposed to look like, and it will look like that in 25 or 30 years' time. But in Sweden there's no traditional way, so after five or 10 years you have to hang the pub on the latest trend. That's why pubs and restaurants are forever getting torn down and refurbished. It's no coincidence that the most famous Swedish exports – IKEA and H&M – reflect this. Both are founded on the idea of replaceable modernity. If you don't like it after a few years, you just throw it away and get the latest stuff.'

* * *

Perhaps Sweden is somehow like the teenager who has just gone to college. He loves the sudden freedom but misses his mother picking up after him. This brings us back to Dr Eberhard and the land of the safety junkies. Why are Swedes so obsessed with safety and so worried about what the outside world might inflict (during the Asian tsunami crisis in 2004 there was a debate in Sweden about whether or not it was the government's responsibility to bring Swedes home if they encountered trouble abroad)? Critics would argue that over time the cradle-to-grave welfare system has cosseted the population into an unrealistic expectation of what the state can protect the citizen against. Throw in the security that people feel in numericals – as Fredrik Lindström points out – and you begin to see where this safety mania comes from. If you bombard people with figures on the harm that can be caused by some natural or man-made phenomenon, then there is the reflex to make a law to protect against it.

Most people with small children, for example, know that bangs on the head are an irksome but unavoidable part of toddler awareness. In Sweden, a significant number of parents are not convinced. At the Babyland store in downtown Stockholm, I came across a range of *indoor* helmets. Retailing at 169 Swedish crowns (€15), they are specially designed cotton helmets for little Svens and Erikas aged between nine months and two years so that they don't hurt themselves indoors. 'Sweden is the safest country,' says Richard, the helpful attendant. 'Babies fall, hit their heads. So they need to be protected. They're very popular.'

The indoor child helmets are manufactured and distributed by NG Baby, a small company in Emmaljunga in southern Sweden. The director, Marie Ståhl, says they sell 6,000 every year (they're also distributed in Norway, Finland and Denmark, but they're not quite so popular there). Sales are increasing every year. 'They were designed because of demand from parents who wanted their children to feel more safe and secure.' But aren't these kinds of things going a little too far? 'I agree in some respects,' she says, 'but some children run around all day and parents feel that if this helmet helps them to stop hitting their heads, then that's a good thing.'

A new term has been coined for people who buy indoor helmets. They're called 'curling parents'. Taken from the winter sport where competitors furiously brush a pathway along the ice to guide a polished granite stone towards its target, it's a metaphor for parents who believe no obstacle should inhibit the progress of their children. The term was coined not by a Swede but by a Dane, Dr Bent Hougaard, a child psychologist in Copenhagen.

He came up with the idea and turned it into a book in the mid-1990s, having studied the 800 families who had gone through the divorce courts in Denmark. He was, of course, talking about Danish parenting. 'The point I was making,' says Dr Hougaard, 'was that you can't give a child too much love and care, but if you turn it into a service you are doing the wrong thing and you will get very demanding kids. Now you have kids aged six who are telling their teachers in school, "I don't have to listen to what you say." This attitude is not falling down from the sky. They're getting it at home. It looks as if we have thrown away old rules but haven't replaced them with anything better than freedom and democracy. But you can't teach a three-year-old democracy! It's absurd, it's an illusion. You end up with families sitting down having dinner and discussing with the child what kind of food they would like to eat, or when they would like to go to bed. A three-year-old doesn't understand the clock.'

The book received modest attention in Denmark and it might have stayed that way, but in 2004 it was picked up by a Swedish journalist who wrote an article about Dr Hougaard's work. 'Suddenly all hell broke loose,' he told me. 'I had five or six newspaper editors contacting me. There were magazine articles. I was on television and radio. They translated my book into Swedish and it sold 20,000 copies. Suddenly you had Swedish government ministers confessing that they were a curling parent too.'

You start to notice these things in Sweden. On the Arlanda Express from Stockholm to the airport, a plasma video screen displays an elaborate presentation on the safest way to bring your luggage onto the escalator. How much damage, I wondered, could I have done to myself by wheeling my suitcase onto the moving stairs? Many Swedes accept that overweaning fussiness is becoming a problem, but it's a sensitive subject.

To Dr Ann Heberlein, a philosopher and theologist, the retreat of God and the predominance of the state have sapped Swedes' ability to take responsibility for their lives and manage suitcases on escalators by themselves. 'People don't believe in God, but they do believe in social democracy. We're in a state where God is not part of daily life, and doesn't have a presence in people's conscience.'

Where did God go? Sweden was actually one of the last countries in Europe to convert from paganism to Christianity. In the 16th century, Lutheranism replaced Roman Catholicism and it then held unchallenged, sometimes puritanical, sway for four centuries. But the arrival of the Social Democrats brought about far-reaching changes. By 1951, Swedes could for the first time choose *not* to belong to any religion, and in 2000 Church and state were formally separated. Until then, Swedes had automatically become members of the state Church at birth (1.6 per cent of taxable income actually went directly to the Church). Swedes today use the Church for the big life events (baptisms, weddings, funerals), but not much beyond that. A 2010 Eurobarometer survey showed that only 18 per cent of Swedes agreed with the statement 'I believe there is a God' – down from 23 per cent in 2005 – putting them second last in the EU.

It was as a university lecturer that Dr Heberlein began to notice how Swedish teenagers were taking less and less responsibility for their lives. 'A lot of students felt that if they didn't get the correct grades it was not their fault. Then I started to see it in society as a whole. If you're unemployed it's not your fault, it's a lack of education. Life is unfair, it discriminates against gender, race, etc. If you meet the wrong person it's not your fault, it's because your father didn't love you enough. We're being fed this stuff and we buy it. We've become a nation of wimps.'

* * *

'My Swedish stereotypes before moving,' says Hugh McCarthy, our man with Enterprise Ireland in Stockholm, 'revolved around blondes (with pigtails), ABBA, porn, massages, frolicking in the snow and the Swedish chef from *The Muppet Show*. A crude list in retrospect, but one which was certainly shared by nearest and dearest back home.'

Away from the vexatious arguments about social control, people outside Sweden do tend to hold a positive image of the place. No discussion about road safety anywhere in the world is complete without a reference to Sweden's advances. A Google search prompts an avalanche of references to blondes, au pairs, legginess, blue eyes, ABBA and Volvo, beautiful nature, conservation, a cold climate. ABBA, for years Sweden's second biggest export after Volvo, picked up where Anita Ekberg had left off. Throughout the 1970s their dominance of pop charts allowed the stereotype of the happy, harmonious, blond Swedes to reach global maturity. The appeal was constantly updated through a rotational cycle of album re-releases, as well as cinema and theatrical tie-ins (*Mamma Mia* and *Muriel's Wedding*). 'Before ABBA, people just thought of neutrality, long winters, timber and steel when they thought of Sweden,' says Thomas Johansson, ABBA's promoter, producer and tour manager from 1973 until the band stopped touring in the early 1980s. 'It was ironic, since they were so focused on writing songs that sounded like the Beatles. We were never conscious of creating a Swedish image.' In fact, ABBA were hardly taken seriously in their native Sweden by the music press, but once their fame spread the government realised they had an unbeatable Swedish brand on their hands. 'Suddenly ABBA was a Swedish export,' says Johansson. 'Overseas, the Swedish embassies came aboard. Everywhere we went, the embassy or consulate was ready to host a party and look after the band. They did the same for sports stars. British embassies never did anything like that. By the late 1970s, ABBA and Björn Borg had become synonymous with Sweden in a way which didn't harm the country's image at all.'

Politically, Sweden is admired and envied for political moderation. During the financial crisis in 2008–2009, Sweden was often cited as the model economy, even offering the world a model in bailing out banks during a 1992 financial crisis. 'Sweden is always trendy for political reasons, whether you like the country or dislike it,' says Maria Rankka, president of the conservative think tank Timbro. 'But there are a lot of misunderstandings. Michael Moore [the polemical American film director] likes Sweden, but he likes his particular version of Sweden, i.e. that it has a totally publicly funded health-care system. But since the late 1980s and 1990s there have been reforms.'

Some Swedes now look back at the 1970s as a decade of welfare excesses (even though many of the benefits remain untouched). Unemployment benefits were increased and fewer questions were asked of those who couldn't find work. More and more people retired on generous pensions as the retirement age was lowered. There were improved educational benefits and longer paid holidays. From 1980 onwards, men and women were made equal by law. Laws were also interpreted as *obliging* municipalities to provide families with lodging, TV, food and clothing, health care and education if they couldn't provide for themselves. Even 25–35-year-olds were able to *retire* if the state decided they were sick or disabled, so they were being paid for life for not working. It's the same today: if you're unemployed, you'll received

80 per cent of your salary for 200 days, 70 per cent for the next 100 days and 65 per cent for the next 150 days. Should you remain unemployed after that period you'll still receive €1,100 each month after tax (that doesn't include all the other housing, health and education benefits). To get these benefits you need to be part of a voluntary insurance scheme that costs around €13 per month.

Parental leave has other Europeans gasping with envy. You can take *a year and a half* off work as a male or female parent (and not just after the birth of a child) and still receive 80 per cent of your salary. In 1992, some 52 million parental benefit days were taken by women. The number fell to around 30 million in 2000, but by 2012 it was back at around 51 million days. In 2012 Swedish parents were compensated for 5 million days taken off to tend to a sick child.

Sweden is unique in that its education and health systems are completely paid for by the public sector, whereas most other countries have some kind of hybrid scheme, so it's not surprising that public-sector employment has been expanding all the time: in 1964 it employed 526,000 people, but by 2001 that had doubled. By 2001, public spending on social services reached 29 per cent of Sweden's gross domestic product (GDP), the second highest in the developed world, after Denmark.

With the winds of globalisation howling around the Baltic, though, something was going to have to give. Could Sweden continue to tax her citizens so punitively when companies were moving to India and China?

Changes have been coming by stealth. In the early 1990s, a school voucher system was introduced so that parents could send their children to an 'independent' school (to call them private would be going too far) and public funds would follow the child. Today, some 15 per cent of parents send their children to these schools and it has brought about a measure of competition. 'Parents and pupils are more empowered, and the quality has improved,' says Maria Rankka.

In the mid-1990s, the Social Democratic government and the opposition agreed on a strategy to get more people to pay for private pensions so that today – unlike other European countries, such as Germany – more money is *not* being taken out of the pension fund than is put in.

In 2006, the generosity of the system dominated the general election. The Social Democrats, led by prime minister Göran Persson, were defeated by a coalition of conservative parties under the Alliance for Sweden umbrella (still in power in 2013). They won partly because the electorate was fed up with the incumbent party, but also because the jobless figures were at odds with the booming economy. The unemployment rate of 4.8 per cent, it turned out, had disguised perhaps 1 million workers (out of 8 million) who were on permanent sick leave, studying or on early retirement.

* * *

There are, of course, upsides.

Terry Greenwood, a Stockholm-based publisher who arrived in the early 1970s, recalls a land of efficiency with the price of drinking and eating out the only real drawback. 'Sweden was pretty much like I expected it to be – cold, sparsely populated, politically stable, peace loving, well organised, clean and efficient. It was also expensive and, yes, it has to be said, had more than its fair share of blondes. Everything worked. Trains and buses arrived on time. The underground was not daubed in graffiti or vandalised and breakdowns were rare. The postal service was reliable. Banks were efficient. Personal ID cards made paying bills and drawing cash very easy. The health service was admirable. State-run crèches enabled women to work. New mothers took a year's maternity leave with full pay. No one smacked their kids, at least not in public. People generally put their rubbish in a bin instead of in the streets. There was a general appreciation for nature and the environment.'

Thirty-seven years on, the strains are showing. Swedes now often mourn a loss of innocence, where crime has risen, immigration has led to social tensions, and the social fabric, for all the professed equality and benefits, is beginning to fray. This malaise is explored through the fictional character of Kurt Wallander, a brooding, overweight detective who inhabits a world of broken marriages, international terrorism, child pornography and parental neglect. In an interview with the *New York Times*, his creator Henning Mankell recalls growing up in small-town rural Sweden in the 1950s, where poverty existed, but where the government 'gave a lot of power in making political decisions to local communities, through politicians who lived right in the villages'. The growing remoteness of the state from rural life, as the Social Democrats pursued its grand experiment, led, he said, to the deterioration of the criminal justice system.

'These days, violent crime is a daily occurrence,' concurs Terry Greenwood. 'The trains no longer always run on time. The city is dirtier and has its fair share of graffiti. The health service is straining under the weight of demand. The economy has become progressively worse as an increasing number of multinational exporters have been sold off and swallowed up. Unemployment is rising steadily, and not just because of the recession.

'But by and large, the changes have been positive. Immigration and active membership of the EU have made it a more interesting and vibrant place to be. The city of Stockholm is truly cosmopolitan and the entertainment scene has undergone an amazing transformation. The nightlife now stands up to that of any other European capital. On any given day downtown, you'll hear many languages being spoken, from French to Ethiopian, Iranian to Czech. Dialects are spoken on every corner by peoples of non-Scandinavian origin. New culture blends, new music, new attitudes. The stereotypes of tall, blue-eyed blondes are fading fast. Football stars have names like Zlatan rather than Sven. The streets are no longer as safe as they once were. You have to be as streetwise here as anyone else in Europe.'

But Sweden still functions well.

'Swedes are orderly,' says Colm O'Callaghan, the former Irish broadcast journalist who's been living in Stockholm for 10 years. 'I really notice this every time I return to Ireland. Swedes have processes for everything and, annoying as they are about sticking to these processes, they do seem to work. Things function here without a hitch. If someone says they'll come out to you to fix something, they always arrive when they say they will and tackle the problem. If you change address, you just have to inform the tax authorities and everyone else will be automatically informed (banks, telephone company, electricity companies). It's that kind of process-oriented society that the Swedes have.'

But the official thoughtfulness means that we can't only speak of curling parents; Sweden is the curling *state*. Roads are equipped with pressure pads near traffic lights so if there's no other traffic around it will be green when you get to those lights. Airports and train stations never seem to be jammed and overcrowded. The authorities predict growth and create an infrastructure on time. While in Dublin the airport and the M50 have constantly struggled to keep up with demand, in Sweden they build roads to *anticipate* demand. A tunnel on the north side of Stockholm is already being built to cater for future demand; it will take drivers around the entire north of the city without ever hitting a traffic light (granted, Sweden is a big country for its population size, so cities have room to expand).

A curling state, though, still needs to ensure that its citizens glide in the *right* direction. On a Swedish driver's license is a barcode which includes social security information, so when purchasing something with a credit card and providing your driving license as the mandatory ID, when the license is swiped along with the credit card the information is stored about what you just bought. In January 2009 a deeply controversial new law came into effect allowing the Swedish intelligence services to monitor virtually all electronic data – telephone, text, fax and email messages – passing in and out of Sweden without a court order or warrant.

Sweden is still widely noted for its liberal immigration policy. Whether it's down to a kind of neutrality guilt or a desire to spread social democratic tolerance around the world, Sweden has taken in more refugees than any other country. Södertälje, a small town south of Stockholm, received more Iraqi refugees than the US or Canada *combined.* That tradition, of course, doesn't necessarily mean harmony between Swedes and immigrants. Many have been placed in high-rise suburbs, neatly separated from mainstream life. While there have been successes in integration and multiculturalism, especially in sports and entertainment, there have been numerous cases of discrimination and ethnic tension. Immigrants are more likely to be convicted of rape and murder, and, in such a conformist society – even one which professes a passionate belief in equality – it can be difficult for foreigners to feel accepted. 'It seems to me that one of the distinctive marks of Swedishness is the ability to feel completely excluded from the society around you, precisely because it is so conformist and closed,' writes Andrew Brown in *Fishing in Utopia.*

In May 2013 Sweden was shaken by a week of rioting in Husby, a district of Stockholm with a large immigrant community, following the killing of a local man by police. The burning of vehicles and buildings spread to other districts and beyond the capital. The general response of the international media was, 'How could this happen in *Sweden*?

But in terms of social attitudes at least, Sweden remains an extremely tolerant, nonjudgmental kind of place. In January 2009, three out of four of the centre-right coalition parties approved same-sex marriages. Divorce rates are high (around 50 per cent), but are so commonplace that they rarely attract social stigma. Gender equality is directed into every corner of social legislation so that the fear of penury among women is hardly a reason for staying in an unhappy marriage. The result is a broad variety of mixed families, ad hoc constellations of children, stepfathers, stepmothers, and stepsiblings, some even leftovers from two relationships back.

Swedes, naturally, deal with these Brady Bunch families coolly. 'The reality in Sweden is that we don't need each other except for emotional help,' says Tilde de Paula, a Swedish TV presenter who wrote a guidebook for these new families (*Gummimammor, plastpappor och bonusbarn: Handbok för styvföräldrar*, or, in English, *Rubber Mommies, Plastic Daddies and Bonus Children*). 'We don't need each other for money, we don't need each other for a career, for a house, for children. We have a very equal society: men and women are able to work, have a family, earn money and support themselves. But emotionally we do need someone.'

De Paula herself has been through two break-ups involving three children. When she met a new partner who didn't have children himself, he couldn't find any books about how to deal with this situation, so she decided to write one for him. It became an instant bestseller, with the first print run of 6,000 sold out overnight. 'When you have children you prepare yourself, you read about the pregnancy, the birth, you prepare the home. But there are people who suddenly go into a ready-made family and they need to know how to do it.'

Her idea was to help these fragmented families make life as stress free as possible for the children. 'For a child it's always best if their parents are together, but it doesn't have to be a bad thing if you grow up with stepfathers and stepmothers as long as they put children first. It's better to have four happy parents who always see you and make you feel loved than two parents who aren't happy. It's not like we're promiscuous. But we accept families who look different and we treat them with respect.

'Stepmothers tend to try harder to involve themselves in the children's lives. The stepfather tends to be more peripheral, not as eager and less interested in changing their lives as much as the stepmother does. Many have more problems with the new family than they intended to have. They have a picture of it being easy. But it's a shock, so there is first a reaction, then acceptance.'

De Paula is thoughtful about contemporary Sweden, about the state as the ever-present guarantor of social happiness, and about the elusive nature of personal fulfilment, especially given the heightened sense of choice to which the web-enabled, globalised and ultra-modern Swede is exposed.

'I had two break-ups and three children and it's something I do see as a failure. If I had a choice I would have stayed in one relationship,' she says. 'The amount of people we meet in our lives, the amount of travelling we do, the number of people we can meet on the internet – the search area becomes so much bigger and it's hard to appreciate what we have. The grass is always greener. You have to remind yourself that you have a choice and you chose to be with this person and you also have to remind yourself what parts you appreciate. When we don't feel the passion maybe we still care for each other – but we don't have that feeling of being in love. You've had kids, and the life you knew is upside down and you're no longer the centre of your world. Some people just don't believe it's going to be good again, and so they leave only to discover that the same thing can happen in another relationship when it's too late. Sometimes they forget to hold on to something. When we're so self-sufficient, it's harder to remember why we did this. If it was good and fun and pleasant all the time it would be a very strange life, it would be strange if we didn't have sadness now and again.'

Chapter 7

Finland

Nothing separates a Finn from a Finn,
Nothing except death and the police.
Jorma Etto, Finnish poet

On 7 November 2007 18-year-old Pekka-Eric Auvinen entered Jokela High School in the small town of Tuusula, 40 kilometres north of Helsinki. Carrying a legally held .22 calibre gun and 500 rounds of ammunition, he moved between classrooms opening fire methodically but at random. By the end of his shooting spree, he'd shot dead five of his schoolmates, the headmistress, a teacher and a nurse (at least one of the victims was shot 20 times). He turned the gun on himself and later died in hospital.

Auvinen had been described as either odd, quiet, or diligent; teachers had noticed an interest in the Nazis and Stalin. But on YouTube that morning he broadcast a tortured rationale for the massacre he was about to commit. Describing himself variously as 'a cynical existentialist, anti-human humanist, anti-social social Darwinist, realistic idealist and god-like atheist', he promised to eliminate all he saw fit (or unfit). 'You might ask yourselves, why did I do this and what do I want. Well, most of you are too arrogant and closed-minded to understand.'

Auvinen was right about one thing: the killings left many unanswered questions. 'It's incredible that something like this has happened in Finland,' said Jokela history teacher Kim Kiuru. This kind of thing was supposed to happen in America, not Finland. But to visitors, certain statistics emerged which were greeted with disbelief. At 56 guns per 100 people, Finland actually had the *third highest* gun ownership in the world, after the US and Yemen. It also had a very high murder rate. In time, well-established stereotypes seemed to add themselves too easily: Finns drank too much, they were depressive – all those long winter nights must have something to do with the high suicide rates – they were uncommunicative and prone to outbursts of violence.

I arrived in Tuusula around midnight at the Lutheran church where a help centre had been set up. I met a group of students huddled under a dripping birch tree. 'Everyone panicked,' said one student between nervous drags of a cigarette. 'It was chaos, unreal. I can't really handle my feelings yet – one of those killed was a friend of mine. I just can't believe it happened *here*. [Auvinen] had always been a strange person, but I never believed he would do anything like that. Everyone thought it was just some kind of joke. It's going to be hard to realise that some of our friends aren't here any more.'

The next day, students gathered outside the lakeside high school, clutching each other tearfully, and laying flowers and candles at the inevitable shrine. Hearing me speak English, a middle-aged man with a black leather coat zipped tightly against the cold approached, suddenly launching into a tirade against an article in the London *Times* that morning. The article had insulted Finns and disgraced the name of journalism, he said.

The article had been written by Aki Riihilahti, a professional footballer, of all things, who played for Crystal Palace and the Finnish national team (on his website, he describes himself as a 'motor of midfield, writer, a bit of a legend'). In the article he drew attention to a fading innocence in his home country, a disappearing world of unlocked doors, where the prime minister could shop without security, and where the quality of life was so good, people thought they'd 'won the lottery of life'.

But then, Riihilahti wondered, perhaps Finns had been naïve to the truth. In reality Finns were 'reserved and unsociable, so loners have never been considered that different or a threat to society'. Depression and loneliness were endemic in a population spread out over remote distances with short winter days; suicide, at 21 per 100,000, was three times the British rate. 'Nor can you avoid meeting alcoholics; some of my younger friends are proud of their ever heavier drinking habits.' Riihilahti stopped short of concluding that a combination of these truths meant Finns were now predisposed to mass murder: this was a once-off massacre that could happen anywhere (the conclusions were shared by most other Finnish observers, while the police report concluded that Pekka-Eric Auvinen had acted alone).

Then it happened again.

Within a year Matti Juhani Saari, a 22-year-old student at Kauhajoki School of Hospitality, 180 miles north-west of Helsinki, walked into a classroom during an exam, and opened fire, killing 10 people, before turning his .22 calibre pistol on himself. In 2010 the Finnish parliament was forced to act, introducing tough new restrictions on gun ownership, raising the age limit, introducing both a new test for applicants and the possibility of medical clearance certificates.

So what is going on in Finland? Psychoanalysing school massacres is beyond the scope of this book, but I'm interested in the stereotypes alluded to in trying to explain them. They are well known. The *Helsingen Sanomat* newspaper even has a tongue-in-cheek guide: Finnish plastic bags are the strongest in the world, so they can take the weight of all those vodka bottles; when someone smiles at you on the street, you assume he's (a) drunk, (b) insane, (c) American; Finns rarely talk to each other except during Midsummer's festivals, when they holler at each other across lakes. There are variations on the theme of drunkenness, references to the 105 ways to eat herring and the necessity of having boiled potatoes in their jackets on every dinner table during every meal.

'We like to think the stereotype is changing,' says Renne Klinge, a diplomat at the foreign ministry. 'But it persists with some of our closest neighbours. We say Finnish people keep quiet in many languages – that's not totally wrong. We aren't afraid to give our opinions, but we reflect more, and don't show our hands. Swedes are traditionally more open, but they don't let you get close. Finns take a long time to open up, but when they do they become very close.'

Let's start with murder. Despite our notion that Scandinavian countries are intrinsically peace-loving places, Finland's murder rate *is* high. According to the National Research Institute of Legal Policy, it's one of the highest in the EU and higher than all the other Nordic countries.

Every year, three Finns per 100,000 are killed by people they know, with the vast majority of murders taking place during quarrels between drunk, unemployed and middle-aged men. 'The classic Finnish homicide is of someone knifing his best friend after an argument on a drunken fishing trip – and then, remorse-stricken, handing himself in to the police,' Aki Riihilahti observed in the offending *Times* article.

In 71 per cent of all murders between 2002 and 2006, both the killer and those killed were drunk, while in 85 per cent of the cases, at least one was drunk. More often than not, men were the killers, and the killers were drunk. Women were less likely to be under the influence, but even 61 per cent of them *were*. The most common method is to stab with a sharp instrument (a kitchen knife more often than not), while seventy-two per cent of murders took place inside apartments.

How did Finns get like this? Medieval Europeans had an image of the Finns as 'primitive hunters, practitioners of magic and sellers of wind to stranded seafarers,' according to *A Concise History of Finland*. They lived on a heavily forested and sparsely populated territory stretching from the Baltic to the Arctic Sea, with lakes and drumlins gouged and deposited by the retreating ice. An early legend told of a visiting English bishop, Henry of Uppsala, murdered by a peasant on a frozen lake in the 1150s at the bidding of his spiteful wife. Thus emerged the first image of the 'wild' Finn.

From the 13th century, Finland was ruled by the Swedes, within whose worldview the Finns were uncultivated brutes. Finnish farmers trading butter, skins, dried fish and livestock to merchants in Stockholm and Tallinn evinced a rather simple, humble piety: wealth was frowned upon and poverty held to be a virtue. Travellers commented on the meagreness of the Finnish diet, with one French writer settling down to bread made from dried fish bones and ground birch bark.

As Sweden became an imperial power, Finland bore a high burden of her military adventures through conscription and taxes. Peasant uprisings were few – it wasn't easy to muster angry hordes in such a sparsely populated landscape – but were brutally suppressed. Finns naturally felt hard done by. Their language was disregarded by their Swedish overlords to the extent that by the 17th century, the administrative and judicial system barely acknowledged the Finnish language or culture at all.

Towards the end of Swedish rule, at the turn of the 19th century, changes to inheritance and property laws prompted landless peasants to move across eastern Finland and southern Ostrobothnia. Against a backdrop of war and disease, the production of alcohol (*viina*) thrived among the disenfranchised rural population. With the Swedish judicial system tilted against locals, violence and murder flourished (securing a murder conviction required two witnesses and a confession, and getting those were well-nigh impossible in the wild forest). The authorities banned *viina* in 1756, both to curb the violence and because grain was in short supply. The producers, though (i.e. farmers), rebelled since it was a valuable commodity that underpinned social status. Already, drinking habits notorious in the 20th century were becoming ingrained in northern and eastern Finland.

By the end of the 18th century, the Finns were tiring of their subservient role; after the Swedish King Gustav III launched an attack on Russia in 1788 and lost, Finnish nobles and army officers suggested to Russian Empress Catherine the Great that Finland become an independent state under Russian protection. The Kremlin, anxious to weaken Sweden's position and busy with its own wars against the Turks, was only too happy to oblige. In March 1809, Finland became a Grand Duchy within the Russian Empire under Alexander I. To many ordinary Finns, they were simply swapping one master for another; to the Swedish-speaking minority, it was a disaster. To Russians, on the other hand, the Finns weren't worth the trouble of absorbing. 'They have nothing of their own,' wrote Carl Johan Walleen, a member of the Russian Committee for Finnish Affairs in 1813. 'Nothing that is characteristic, which distinguishes them from other peoples, and on the whole they possess so little true attachment for their fatherland, their language and their government, that they surely within a fairly short time will completely disappear and be absorbed into their conquerors.'

This the Finns were determined not to allow. 'Swedes we are no longer, Russians we cannot be, so let us be Finns,' wrote the exiled Finnish academic A.I. Arwidsson in 1811. In the University of Turku, on Finland's south-east coast, a group of academics argued that a budding national identity could never fully blossom until the elite started using the language. They travelled into Karelia, a vast province to the east and one historically fought over by Finland, Russia and Sweden. Karelia, they believed, was the cradle of pure Finnish culture, one preserved by simple folk and not tainted by Germans or other Scandinavians. The Russians were happy enough with this state of affairs: anything that drew the Finns away from Swedish clutches couldn't be *that* bad.

With Finns asserting their separate culture and language, the *Kalevala* – an epic that to Finnish minds rivalled Homer and Ossian – was published in 1831 and inspired Jean Sibelius, the (Swedish-speaking) Romantic composer to explore Finnish identity with symphonies like *Finlandia*, the *Karelia Suite*, and *The Swan of Tuonela.* Suddenly, the peasantry was portrayed in glowing terms: no longer drunken layabouts (a Swedish mental image), they were instead simple custodians of the purest culture. (Some writers were disappointed, however, when the peasants failed to conform to the new ideals of sobriety.)

Claims of an ancient Finnish culture were, naturally enough, derided by the Swedish establishment who still felt slighted that Finland had chosen St Petersburg over Stockholm. But after the revolutions of 1848, the Russians, too, who until that point seemed to go easy on the Finns, began to crack down on *too much* Finnishness. They imposed severe restrictions on Finnish students and censored new literature in the Finnish language. Life soon got worse for everyone: there was a catastrophic famine in the 1860s which many Finns saw as punishment for deviating from the honest life of the peasant. But there was also rapid industrialisation, and the movement of landless peasants to the cities caused murder rates to soar once again (elsewhere in Europe, they were actually decreasing). Meanwhile, as political turmoil gripped the Russian Empire, St Petersburg was rolling back Finnish autonomy, stirring further nationalist agitation. The Swedish minority, still sizeable in numbers, was wary of both Finnish nationalists and Russian Bolsheviks, reminding the Finns that *they* were the true standard-bearers of the Enlightenment: freedom-loving, individualistic, coastal-dwelling and looking West for inspiration. The Finns, on the other hand, 90 per cent of whom lived in the countryside, were dreamy peasants whose roots came from somewhere in Asia.

Ironically, cracking down on alcoholism was seen as an intrinsic element of Finnish nationhood. Lutheran austerity had sunk muscular roots and prohibition was a constant focus of wrangling between Swede and Finn, with Finns accusing Swedes of blocking moves to sober everyone up, while the Swedes argued that since they had greater self-discipline (sobriety) they didn't need prohibition. Old habits were still dying hard, though: Sibelius, a known frequenter of Helsinki's pubs, was rumoured to have got up one night to travel to St Petersburg to conduct a concert, only to return to the pub two days later to find the same people on the same seats.

After World War I, Finland gained national independence for the first time, but not without a civil war between radical Social Democrats and a right-wing government in exile, which left tens of thousands dead. In the 1920s, Finland began the painful process of nation-building, and part of that discourse was alcohol and what it meant to be Finnish. A fresh attempt at prohibition triggered a boom for illicit distillers and, with waves of migrant workers drifting north to join the logging boom, the combination of widely available *viina* and the universally owned sheath knife, or *puukko*, the potential for deadly violence was considerable. From 1921 to 1932, when prohibition ended, three-quarters of all recorded crimes were alcohol related. During the same period, the murder rate was three times higher than it is today.

Bowing to the inevitable, the authorities held a referendum in 1931 and 70 per cent of Finns voted to abolish prohibition. Control would henceforth be enforced by a state alcohol company, and to keep the working classes away from drink taverns were made as unwelcoming and limited as possible (such conditions probably encouraged Finns to drink even more heavily). After 1947, murder rates fell, but only until the supply of alcohol was once again liberalised. In 1969, 17,000 grocery stores were granted the right to sell beer: once again alcohol-related murder soared, and it remains three times that of the rest of Western Europe to this day.

* * *

On a Saturday morning in October 2004, I'm on a helicopter flying over the Baltic from Helsinki to Tallinn, the beautiful old Hanseatic capital of Estonia. Below us, steaming across an apricot sunrise, two enormous passenger ferries are headed to Tallinn for pretty much one reason: to buy cheap alcohol. By the following afternoon, the passengers will have bought enough to fill a sizeable quarry. It's a surreal form of repatriation: most of the booze bought in Estonia was brewed, distilled, fortified and packaged in *Finland* in the first place.

Finland has always dealt with alcohol problems through taxation or prohibition. Drink is either banned, or made so costly that it's hardly worth the trouble. Neither option has worked. In the years after Estonia gained independence from the Soviet Union, Finns travelled to Tallinn to stock up with as much cheap vodka as Finnish customs would allow. But now, with Estonia having joined the EU (and its single market), there is theoretically no impediment to Finns, as EU citizens, buying as much as they want, since they are buying it from *other* EU citizens.

The government has responded with the old reliable: taxation. But this time, taxes have been cut, with duty on spirits slashed by 40 per cent to try to dissuade the booze cruisers. 'The situation is bad, but the alternatives are worse,' government advisor Ismo Tuominen tells me, with an air of desperation, in the Health Ministry in Helsinki. 'If we don't act, there will be massive infiltration of alcohol and a massive grey market in beverages. Is it right or wrong? No one knows right now, but the main thing is we must keep the alternative of having alcohol taxes as a way of decreasing alcohol problems.'

But a visit to the Liviko off-licence in Tallinn indicates it isn't working. The Finnish weekend-trippers are spending a fortune to the delight of Raynar Kits, the store manager. 'Sales here have risen four times,' he says. 'A bottle of vodka here is three to four times cheaper.' The Finns largely ignore Estonian products, like the 80 per cent-proof vodka Viru Valge, in favour of their own brands. 'The alcohol is actually produced in Finland,' continues Raynar with satisfied amusement. 'It's exported to Estonia, Finns travel over here and just bring it back. They're a conservative people and they like to buy the same brands they buy at home.'

In Helsinki the government is naturally horrified. 'We already know from alcohol research that the reduction of prices leads to more harm,' broods Ismo Tuominen. 'Already there is some indication that drink-driving, assaults, homicides are growing.' The government is caught in a bind. Failure to reduce tax on spirits will trigger job losses at home, but even when they do lower taxes, the population has taken no notice. Happiest are the Swedes, who have flocked to Finland to buy spirits now cheaper than at home. Discussions have been held between the Swedish and Finnish prime ministers with no outcome. 'Somehow we have lost the possibility to have our own alcohol policy, and that is a shock,' says Esa Österberg of Stakes, the National Research and Development Centre for Welfare and Health.

At five o'clock on Sunday afternoon the weekend booze cruisers arrive back at Tallinn's ferry port, some stumbling out of taxis, most laden down with wine, beer and spirits. Others are wheeling flip-open carts, specially designed by an enterprising Estonian. One passenger wheels six cases of gin as nonchalantly as it if were a Samsonite hard case. 'Here we paid €160,' says one couple, gesturing sheepishly to a filing cabinet-sized consignment. 'In Finland we'd pay €360 or more for this!' But the binge spending doesn't stop on dry land. The tills on the on-board off-licence are ringing with an alarming through-put of beer, wine and spirits, all sold at, you've guessed it, Estonian prices. Some customers stare at the shelves as if in a trance (one tells me he's driven four hours from his home to Helsinki, spent the weekend in Tallinn, and will make the four-hour journey back home the moment we dock). As we set sail into the Baltic, a fellow passenger, bottle in hand, sways and sweeps the air with an expansive ballad which he sings all to himself.

The Finns eventually took the issue in hand when they assumed the EU presidency in 2006, forcing neighbouring states to agree to raise their alcohol taxes. Estonia raised its own duties by 20 per cent, but that caused knock-on problems for the poor Estonians: in November 2008, police discovered a 2-kilometre *underwater pipeline* running through a reservoir on the Russian–Estonian border, built to pump 6,200 litres of illicit vodka into Estonia. The authorities arrested 11 men and seized 1,159 litres of untaxed alcohol hidden in a truck in Tallinn.

Eventually Finland restored the taxes on spirits which were cut back in 2004. No prizes for guessing the result: the weekend cruises simply got busier, with the amount of alcohol being purchased increasing by 10 per cent between January and August 2008, including a 16 per cent increase in hard liquor (there was a corresponding decline in drink sales in Finland). Finns *are* changing their drinking habits. City dwellers are drinking more wine as they try to follow cosmopolitan European trends. But a UNICEF study shows that one in three children aged 11 to 15 says they have already been drunk several times. This is one stereotype that is not going away just yet.

* * *

I've come to Lapland. Or rather, I've come to Lapland by mistake.

Instead of a winter wonderland, it's late July and 33-degrees Celsius. The sun is like chilli sauce on my skin. I *should* be here in the depths of winter if I want to explore how Finns in the northern latitudes cope with seasonal extremes of light and darkness. But thanks to scheduling difficulties, here I am in Rovaniemi, the Lappish capital, just a few weeks after the midnight sun rolled along the horizon and drifted back up into the sky.

I expected Lapland to be an enchanting place, frosted into crystalline brilliance, with moose frolicking under the Northern Lights. Instead, on the corner of Poromiehentie Street and Koskikatu Street it feels like a Nevada suburb. I can see the Las Vegas Bingo Club, Scan Burger, McDonald's, Intersport, Cohico Bar and Restaurant, and Xiang Long's Chinese restaurant. Further down the street is H&M, Subway and Mama Rosso Italian Restaurant. And it's very, very hot.

The next morning, I'm collected from the Clarion Santa Claus Hotel by Tuija Laine, a local guide, who drives me through heavy rain out of Rovaniemi. To the very unseasonal sound of slapping windscreen wipers, she provides a snapshot of how the Laplander copes with the annual division of light and darkness, where for two full months (December and January) the only light is a dim glow to the north, yet where from June 6 to July 7 the sun shines 24 hours a day. 'It's a myth that we're very depressed. We just recharge our batteries, or people go south,' she vouches. 'Some say we are very quiet, but when you get to know us we are very lively. In winter there's nothing to do, it's so dark and cold that we just relax. It's harder in the villages. You might only have 50 people. Two hundred max. There is a lack of activities,' she explains as we climb out of Rovaniemi. 'We're very happy in the summer. We don't sleep a lot because we don't need to. So when autumn comes I'm so tired, I want to sleep.'

From Ounasvaara Hill, we gaze down at Kemijoki River, Finland's longest waterway, which runs 500 kilometres north before emerging into the Gulf of Bothnia. Beyond are the gentle quartz hills that ring the town. In the distance, the forest rolls peacefully off to the horizon (I'm wondering if I could cope with the circadian rhythms here, or if they would drive me to drink).

The term 'Lap' is thought to mean 'people who live apart'. As Finns migrated from the 11th century onwards, they could only expand to the east or north. The pattern of settlement was slash and burn: forests were cleared, trees set on fire, and the settlers fenced themselves into farms. Finns caricature Laplanders themselves for being 'slow'. Although Rovaniemi has Sámi roots (more on them later), the Hämäläinen tribes that arrived in the 12th and 13th centuries have had, it's thought, a lasting impact. According to Irina Kyllönen, a researcher on the tribes of Finland, 'The Hämäläinen … are slow in speech and hence slow in thinking; slow at work and in making decisions. Even the dialect of the Häme region is said to be slow and rambling. Nevertheless… it implies that the Hämäläinen are deliberate in their actions, and this deliberate nature means they will do their job well, and that is a compliment of the best kind in Finland.'

To the innate characteristics of the tribe, add human solitude. Lapland is 94,000 square kilometres of wood and lakeland, yet home to only 190,000 people, 57,000 of whom live in Rovaniemi. The living density is 2.1 people per square kilometre, a fact which alone may explain a taciturn predisposition. 'For 500 years, Finns had to constantly move north,' Finnish MEP, writer and filmmaker Lasse Lehtinen tells me. 'It was a brutally tough existence. The result of razing forests was that Finns settled on individual farms, away from each other, and avoided the settlement of villages contiguous to the land. That meant there was an ingrained isolation, jealousy, competitiveness and resentment of the neighbour. There were always some quarrels over a boundary or waterway. People became suspicious but also very self-sufficient; they were like the frontiersmen of old Western movies. You tended to create your own law. It was different on the coast. There, there were Swedish speakers, who formed cities, opened schools and provided education.'

I'm hoping to meet a frontier Finn living in the woods, but first, says Tuija, we have a rather important person to meet.

Santa Claus.

Twenty years ago, the hotels in Rovaniemi were closed for Christmas, but some bright spark realised that Santa Claus was a marketing opportunity to die for. The first charter flight was a Concorde that took off in 1980, and the Santa industry has been booming ever since. Today, there are 250 charters a season from the UK alone. Each Christmas, 70,000 visitors stay overnight in Rovaniemi and a further 10,000 arrive on day trips. By 2016, Rovaniemi expects tourist revenue to reach €474 million. The greater number of tourists are British, Irish, Italian, Japanese and German, nationalities which all evidently still believe in Santa Claus.

Tuija drives me towards Santa Claus Village, but on the way we pass Santa Claus Park. It's the competition. How do we square that one with the kiddies? Two Santas? 'The children are reassured that there's a 2-kilometre underground tunnel between the two if they ask awkward questions,' Tuija reassures me solemnly. In fact, Finns used to tell their children that Santa Claus lived in a cave on Korvatunturi Mountain, 180 kilometres to the north near the Russian border. But the narrative changed to suit the Santa industry, and he decided to come down to the Arctic Circle to see children every day.

Right on the Arctic Circle, Santa Claus Village is a fully fledged Disney-style theme park. Even in high summer there is a crowd of tourists ambling through the souvenir shops and the post office, where the authorities have made a poignant display of all the letters (12.5 million from 200 countries) sent by children every year. There are letters from every country, even Iran, Iraq and the Palestinian territories. 'Often children from these countries don't send a wish list,' says Tuija. 'They just ask for peace and health in their country…' Kids from the UK and Ireland? 'They just give a list of the presents they want,' says Tuija.

Meeting Santa, it turns out, is no problem as a child, but as a journalist, I might as well be interviewing Michael Jackson. I'm dressed in a special Santa Claus sleeveless Official Press fleece before filling in a media consent form. A publicist asks rather sharply when the interview will be published, thrusting me her business card and insisting that I let her know in good time. As global brands go, Santa Claus isn't a bad one; no one around here is going to let the image slip. A peremptory announcement in six languages reads: 'Do not use your own camera: the photographer-elf will take a picture of your meeting with Santa Claus which you can buy. You're welcome!'

We pass through a darkened tunnel with piped cave-like sound effects, 'granite' walls, simulated ice and snow, and green and purplish lighting underfoot. I imagine that for a small child it might be quite frightening. Tuija agrees. Up and down we travel, until we arrive in a high-ceilinged timber chamber with an enormous pendulum swinging 50 feet from its roof mount. This is the Time Wheel, designed to confound the clever kids who ask how Santa Claus can deliver presents to millions of children around the planet on one single night. 'Santa Claus can slow down time so he can make all the deliveries,' says Tuija. She's not smiling.

Finally along a red-carpeted anteroom, I'm led into meet Santa Claus himself. Resplendent on his throne, the real Santa pulls no surprises. He has hands like shovels, a red waistcoat over an enormous white tunic, dark green breeches, thick red and blue legwarmers, and a luxurious beard down to his navel. A tiny rectangle of face peers through grey gushes of hair and beard. On shelves behind him are 'old' tomes, amulets and potions, while on the wall is an old two-piece telephone. Despite the fairy tale, lo-fi trappings, these meetings are streamed live on the internet from December 1 each year.

On cue, Santa invites me to sit closer, and an instruction is barked by a photographer-elf in the gallery above: 'Smile, please.' I have time for just a few questions. First I want to establish that the real Santa Claus is, in fact, Finnish. A stream of Finnish, sparking laughter from Tuija and the photographer-elves on the gallery follows. I haven't understood a word. 'So what are the Finnish people like?'

'The Finnish people are very peaceful. They think and they think and then they decide. When we do something, we plan it very carefully, then when we do it, it's done perfectly!'

'What is it like to be Finnish in 2008?'

'It's a nice place to live! There are no catastrophes, no wars, we live in peace, we live together and we are happy. There are not so many foreigners living here…'

My *God.* My heart runs cold. Santa Claus is a *racist*? How am I going to explain this one to all the boys and girls who've been so good all year round? But Santa Claus continues, thankfully changing to a more politically correct tack. 'Ahem, we see foreigners in Rovaniemi, and we all speak together, and there's no conflict!'

Santa shakes my hand and the next family is ushered in. As I'm whisked out, proof that I met Santa is already on a plasma computer screen in the corridor. It's mine for €25. In fact the entire journey through the tunnels and up to Santa Claus, has been 'captured' by the video-elves and is now *already* being offered as a DVD for €29. It must be quite a little earner every Christmas. 'Yes!' says the cashier-elf. 'There are four of us here just doing the till. It gets *so* busy.'

I'm feeling somewhat disenchanted by the hard sell, but I'm sure European and Japanese children love it, and I suppose Rovaniemi needs all the revenue it can get. Driving away from Santa Claus Village, Tuija discusses global warming, a worrying development for the Rovaniemi brand. 'People need snow here. You have to have it. We've had no trouble yet, but you never know. We're very worried about it.' The first snows of Lapland arrive in the beginning of October and turn into permanent snow by the end of the month. But in recent years the permanent snow isn't guaranteed until just before Christmas. Some tourists are already making the nine-hour drive to the North Cape for guaranteed snow.

As we continue through the woods, Tuija keeps an eye out for reindeer. There are more reindeer than people in Lapland: 200,000 roam through the forests and plains. 'In the summer they like to come through the trees to the road. It's because of the mosquitoes: when the cars go past the draft relieves them from the insects. It causes so much trouble, because drivers hit them. Then in winter it's so hard to stop quickly because of the ice. They come to the road in winter because of the salt put down by the city. They love it!'

It strikes me that reindeer must be fairly intelligent creatures to work out – en masse – the benefits of traffic-generated wind drafts and municipal road salt. But most people, according to Tuija, just think they're stupid. 'They just stand there and stare at you. You can't hurry them off the road.'

We arrive at the homestead of a man who knows his reindeers. Ari Kangasniemi is a 50-year-old hunter-craftsman who turns reindeer antlers into handicrafts at his pine-built workshop not far from the Ounasjoki River. There are 35 different species of reindeer, all with different antlers, which are shed in October and November. The farmers are happy to sell them on, but they don't come cheap. Ari shows me one set from a Sakeasarvi male: together they weigh 10 kilo and Ari might fork out €12 per kilo. 'Only 5 to 8 per cent of reindeer have such good horns,' he explains.

Ari has swept-back fair hair, a bushy moustache, and a polite and reserved smile which makes him instantly likeable. He comes from a Inari, a town 300 kilometres to the north. It's Sámi country, the oldest indigenous people of what is known in ethnographic terms as Northern Fennoscandia. Today 70,000 Sámi straddle the northern wildernesses of Norway, Finland, Sweden and the Kola Peninsula in Russia. Their true origin is unknown: DNA tests suggest they go back 15,000 years, predating the last Ice Age, while another theory is that they are related to other Arctic settlers. They were portrayed by Tacitus in *Germania* as the Fenni, primitive hunters 'happy in their simplicity'. Until the end of the 17th century, all Sámi owned reindeer, but the slash-and-burn methods of the settlers endangered their existence. Today they are regarded as a distinct ethnic group with rights and privileges.

Ari's forebears are Sámi, and he still makes witch drums, an ancient Sámi instrument looking and sounding like an oval *bodhrán* with reindeer instead of goatskin. Ari's wife, Irene, is from Kemijärvi, now on the Russian side of the border. She's in charge of marketing and selling: antler chandeliers, carving knives with goat willow and antler handles polished to the smoothness of mother of pearl. Another favourite is the *kuksa*, a smooth-handled wooden cup seen hanging from the belts of rural Finns to be used for coffee or vodka when they're hunting or searching for blueberries, lingonberries or cloudberries (the latter has the vitamin C of eight oranges). The cup derives from the thick skull-cap canker found on a silver birch; Ari carves out a spoon-shaped piece from the wood and the canker, boils it for 24 hours in salted water, then soaks it in paraffin before fashioning it into a light, durable cup.

Ari spends much of his time fishing and hunting. He fishes mostly white fish known as *siika*, but the salmon which used to be abundant no longer swim upriver from the sea because of the hydroelectric plants. He'll think nothing of travelling 330 kilometres north to fish for two weeks, camping on his own by the lakes and generally losing himself in nature, before bringing back 100 kilograms of fish for the winter.

We get onto the subject of alcohol. 'Years ago, we used to make our own. At the time it was forbidden to buy or use it, so we made a liquor called *pontikka* … very Finnish. *Very* strong, made from wheat. But we don't do it so much nowadays. Alcohol is legal and available now, but it's expensive. So when Finns go to Russia or to the Canaries they just drink and drink and drink. But at home I think it's changing. It's not nice for us any more. We've changed our behaviour, become more international. Before one of the reasons we drank so much was there was nothing to do. It was so dark. The big drinkers might be bachelors, men who were very lonely, who had no family so they had no responsibilities. Now we've become more modern. We drink, but not to get quite so drunk.'

Ari's passion is nature. 'The forest is a church for us. You can sit by the fire all day, thinking about life and nature.' And the shy, taciturn Finn? 'The typical Laplander was very unsure of himself, very self-conscious. Maybe my father and grandfather were the same. But we've learned. When we want to talk, we can be very tender. It's different if you know each other, but if you meet a foreigner you might take two steps back and you don't look in their eyes. But after talking and talking, you feel relaxed. Finns do have a wall, a brick wall. But when you break it you have a long-lasting friendship.'

We leave Ari in his log cabin, complete with smoke sauna and pine décor. I couldn't help be impressed by his bond with the forest, although the figures suggest Finns have some way to go before reforming their sometimes destructive relationship with vodka. Living in Lapland has never been easy. It was always beyond the pale due to its distance from Helsinki, and the vast stretches of forest were inimical to the rule of law. The pioneers who settled here ran up against the Sámi culture, corroding it as they went but also taking on some of the Sámi influences in how they ate, dressed and spoke. During the 1920s and 1930s, when Finland was enjoying its independence from Russia and trying to fashion a national identity throughout the realm, they had a tough time of it in Lapland, so poor were the communications and road networks, and so recalcitrant the locals. At the same time, the migrant workers drawn to logging were hardy pioneers spending days alone doing back-breaking work in a hostile environment. They forged a distinct northern identity that attracted the ideologues of both Communism and religious revivalism. (One fundamentalist sect which remains there to this day is so puritanical, I'm told by a Finnish colleague, that it orders custom-made washing machines complete with frosted glass doors so that underwear cannot be glimpsed spinning around inside.)

During World War II, Finland fought two heroic but losing battles against the Soviet Union: the Winter War (1939–40) and the Continuation War (1941–45). After Hitler invaded the Soviet Union, Finland had looked to Germany for protection, effectively granting German troops a Lapland base for operations against Russia in exchange for weapons. The arrangement backfired badly for Finland: as part of the eventual armistice with Russia, Finland not only lost their precious cultural heartland of Eastern Karelia, but they also had to disarm the Germans and eject them from Lapland. As they retreated, the Germans left only seven buildings standing in Rovaniemi.

* * *

But are Finns made melancholic by all that absence of daylight? Across the Jätkänkynttilä Bridge over the Kemijoki River in a riverside bungalow lives Dr Antti Liikkanen, a silver-haired 62-year-old clinical psychiatrist at Rovaniemi hospital. He has spent his life exploring the nexus between daylight and human moods. Finns, he explains, are deeply prone to seasonal variations, right down to the texture of snow. 'There are four aspects to Arctic Personality Disorder (APD),' says Antti. 'When we hunt, we're very greedy. We defend what we've got so we're stingy; we make love only in April in order to have babies in January; and we need to know, so we're obsessed by information.'

There are, in fact, five million inhabitants in 30 countries north of the 16th latitude, but half of them live in Finland. While the rest of us have four seasons, Laplanders have *eight*. 'That's a lot of work for serotonin systems,' says Antti with a frown. 'The brains, stomachs, bodies. They are all affected by light, temperature and social surroundings.'

These aren't just Antti's notions. Most Laplanders adhere to them. His own guide to the eight seasons is as follows:

> 1. *The Frosty Winter:* January begins with powdery snow and the period of 'polar night frost': people do their best to endure the long darkness and cold in the calm following New Year's festivities.

2. *The Crusted Snow:* March and April, following Shrove Tuesday, have an incredible amount of light in the air, even though the nights are still dark and cold. It's a time when love is also in the air, says Antti – a time for blossoming and fertilisation.

3. *Departure of the Ice:* The breakthrough of spring: nature starts to awaken, though snow can still be found on the ground. People are not yet ready to wake up, but the reindeer are already birthing.

4. *The Midnight Sun:* The sun no longer sets, and the mosquito arrives, feasting on birds, woodland animals and people. Nature flourishes in 'round-the-clock ecstasy'.

5. *The Harvest:* With the flowering of the willow herb, the harvest arrives – a time of coming down from intoxication, hangovers, lack of money and the hint of autumn's impending fatality.

6. *Brilliant Autumn Colours:* Ice and snow are on their way, while the labours of summer revert to the telling of tales in winter. With the fishing and hunting finished, father searches for work in forestry, road building, factories, away from home and family.

7. *Black Snow:* After the glorious autumn colours, it snows, and these first downfalls of snow melt with the mild weather. Buck reindeer have already sired young deer, but with the frost freezing the melted snow the supply of food for the reindeer declines.

8. *The Christmas Period of Polar Night:* Continuous darkness draws attention to the starry skies and Northern Lights, and to the fables told through the ages to the next generation. It's a period of rest, eating and reflection, following the

> frenetic activities of summer. Christmas is a festival of rebirth, light and of surrendering what is old. Protecting the family from cold and darkness is the priority.

These are quaint, even folksy, definitions, but Antii is serious about their effects. 'Each season has a different depressor, and all Finns have some season by which they are depressed. For males it's April – crusted snow, a lot of light, the serotonin system can't stand it. Women get depressed in October and November, the season of Black Snow.'

Overall, though, Laplanders have been better equipped than southerners through the centuries. 'In Helsinki the climate is as harsh as in Rovaniemi, but in Lapland we have a better relationship with winter.' It's the same with Seasonal Affective Disorder (SAD). 'It's a milder depressive episode. As a clinical term, between 2 to 3 per cent of the population suffer it, but sub-clinically, 40 per cent suffer it. Again, there is more in Turku than in Lapland, more in New York than in Halifax, more in Switzerland than in Sweden. It's because over 10,000 years, we have become adapted to it. Getting used to all eight seasons has given us *sisu* – tenacity, stamina, perseverance.'

The problem for the modern Laplander is that the psycho-climatic, life-preserving equilibrium developed over thousands of years is out of kilter thanks to mass industrialisation and the modern information society, starting with mass logging in the 19th century. 'Only now,' he says, 'can we see signs of how the fine control of this adaptability has failed. The character of these failures can be a warning for mankind.' Laplanders should *tailor* their activities to the exacting schedules of the eight seasons. During the polar night, or twilight time, Laplanders should stick to night-time activities, sleeping as much as possible, staying at home, 'telling old stories around the fire, or meeting with friends, having a few beers. People should work as little as possible. The Sámi people have learned it: they don't work very much during the winter. They turn inwards towards themselves and leave the reindeer in the woods.'

In spring Laplanders should surrender completely to the sexual and fertility impulse, whose human fruit born in the Autumn will need to be provided for. This provision is done, naturally, during the summer when the Finn should behave 'like a maniac, round the clock, without any pause and eyes glittering with Lappish madness and the feverish search for gold'. These are extremes of activity (or lack of it) but that's what the northerners are accustomed to over the millennia, says Antii.

How tempting to have whole seasons devoted to sleeping, drinking beer, telling stories, and having procreative sex, I'm thinking, but there is a serious side. Antii insists that Lapland's mental equilibrium has been unhinged not by lack of daylight, but by the disruption of primal rhythms by modernity, and that this is reflected in the homicide figures. The murder rate is highest in Lapland, Northern Karelia, Päijät-Häme and Kainuu, all parts of northern and eastern Finland. The lowest murder rates are found in the southern and western coastal provinces and, in the past decade, the gap has widened.

'We've been having a lot of trouble here since the middle of the 19th century, and it's been getting worse,' says Antti. 'Psychosomatic illnesses, suicide, depression, murder, heavy drinking. It's the same with some of the other Arctic people, like the Inuit. The unemployed actually do better because they get social security and they can go hunting or fishing. But for the rest of us, we should work as little as possible in the winter and as much as possible in the summer, but it goes totally against Western capitalist philosophy. And the government are not sympathetic to this idea – they're too busy with EU rules and the rules of the market. And the problem with Lapland is that there are more guns here for hunting than anywhere else. We are killing each other with guns. We're just like the Americans.'

In his office in Brussels, the MEP Lasse Lehtinen argues that most Finns, whatever about the Laplanders, are moving beyond the stereotype, which has been largely perpetuated by the Swedes. 'During the 1950s and 1960s, some 350,000 Finns emigrated to Sweden to work for Volvo and Saab. They went straight from the backwoods, without first becoming accustomed to city life in Helsinki, and that defined Swedish stereotypes of the Finns. At one point every second person in Swedish jails was from Finland. They couldn't communicate, they drank, they committed petty crimes.

'The two wars we fought during the Second World War created guerrilla thinking. For every Finn killed, 13 Russians were killed. We lost 90,000, they lost nearly a million. The Finnish way is to be self-sufficient, resourceful, do your own thing. So if you get an order, you go and do it in your own way and you don't keep referring back to your commander. It's a fact that Anglo-Saxon NATO generals in Afghanistan are constantly frustrated by this attitude from the Finns.

'There is still a Lutheran work ethic. Finns measure themselves by what they do, not how much they earn. The police are valued as the first or second most trusted professions. There's next to no corruption and Finnish policemen are proud if they can give a traffic fine to a superior,' he says. The school shootings, he believes, are a symptom of a malaise among young males, perpetuated by the very ambitious curriculum, with teenage girls performing better and tending to favour relationships with older boys, whereby younger adolescent males are often left isolated. 'Girls rarely drop out,' says Lasse. 'By contrast, within a couple of years the young men are lost, sometimes for the rest of their lives, ending as case files for the police and social services.'

* * *

On a clear summer's day I'm on the last part of my journey through Finnish stereotypes, in a taxi heading north from Helsinki on a sunlit motorway, flanked by silver birch, spruce and pine. It's time to focus on the bright side of the Finns.

Finns have evolved as world-beaters in cool design. In the 20th century Finland seemed to outperform everyone in minimalist and functional style. Nokia became a global telecommunications behemoth and a byword for hushed, hi-tech design (although these days, it's controlled by the Americans). Part of Finland's reinvention is due to the collapse of the Soviet Union: during the Cold War, Finland exported one-fifth of its goods to Russia, so when the Soviet economy imploded exports fell to 5 per cent, sending Finland into a steep recession. With unemployment skirting 20 per cent, painful reforms were implemented, especially in the banking sector, while Nokia, which started out making cables and rubber boots, made the spectacular switch to mobile telephony (Finland's experience in the early 1990s, plus the fact that it has a Triple-A credit rating, has allowed the government to grab the moral high ground in advocating fiscal discipline during the euro debt crisis).

Now I'm on my way to meet someone whose has both defined and subverted Finnish design. I arrive at 26 Lamminpääntie Street in Veikkola, a non-descript low-rise dormitory village of neat clapboard homes, slumbering amid the pines. A rambunctious 76-year-old with the looks (but not the whisper) of David Attenborough bounces off the children's swing and lopes over past the Porsche. It's Eero Aarnio, possibly the coolest designer on the planet.

'Come in!' he beams. 'My wife and daughter are shopping! I'm on holiday!'

Eero looks more like a Brit on his first day by the pool, a man determined to enjoy himself. He's actually an epoch-defining designer, an alchemist who turns modern plastics and big colours into the iconic wonder designs of the 1960s and 1970s. Today he remains the toast of interior glossies from Manhattan to Tokyo. His self-designed 300-square-metre lakeside home is spread effortlessly over three levels; open spaces, flooded by natural overhead light, evolve naturally into each other, and hum with contemporary connectivity. There are big splashes of colour against the smooth white timber, his never-matched designer stuff – lamps, chairs, shelves, brilliant plastic toys that appeal to children and adults alike – are everywhere.

Eero dips rhetorically in and out of one award-winning design after another, still clearly enthralled by his own handiwork. Then we're out into the terraced garden, through patios exploding with surfinia, following wooden steps down to the Lamminjärvie lake. By the water's edge there is a traditional smoke sauna, or *löyly*. Finns bemoan the replacement of the *löyly* by those small electric units crammed into any home or apartment. The smoke sauna is wood burning: a 200-kilo layer of stones is heated to 100°C by a wood fire below, and when water is applied the steam is more gradual rather than overwhelming. When early Finns were on the move, they relied on the *löyly* for cooking food, preserving hygiene, and giving birth, thanks to the antibacterial tannic acid contained in wood smoke. Finns have realised there was something in the time and care needed (a warming-up process starts in the morning and lasts all day) which rendered the *löyly* a more authentic experience, and have revived it.

Eero agrees. 'We sit in for five to 10 minutes in 100 degrees, then go down and jump in the lake, then we do it again, three times in all, then we open a beer and talk about philosophy and ask how the stars are made! The combination of warm and cold is so good for your physique! It's so relaxing! My friends do it in wintertime. They cut a hole in the ice and come out of the sauna and jump in.'

Then the world-famous designer wants to get me naked. 'We have a swim! Clothes aren't needed! Look, the water is 22 degrees!' He pulls a thermometer out of the lake with the joy of a child who has just proved something to his parents. I suggest we have a swim after the interview, and with a bound, Eero is back indoors.

Eero Aarnio was born in Helsinki in 1932, and was 11 when Russian bombers forced him to dive into the basement. It was in copying his brother's papier-mâché models of cowboys that the young Eero displayed his early talent (his parents sold them to Stockmann, Scandinavia's best-known department store). As an architecture student in the early 1950s, his poor showing at maths held his ambitions in check, but his knack with models and drawing led him to the Finnish school of interior design, coming first in 150 applicants in a competition for places. After his military service, Eero spent two years in different design offices before landing a job with Asko, Scandinavia's biggest furniture company, in the winter resort of Lahti.

One of his first designs was the Ball Chair, an iconic wonder – fun, sexy and simple – which he produced in 1963. 'I wanted to do something new, something special which would be *seen*. The boss said if they sold even one he'd eat his hat. We produced 100 and in one week they were all sold in 30 countries.'

But it was the buyers who launched the Ball Chair's iconic appeal. Bing Crosby, Sammy Davis, Jr., the Shah of Persia, Princess Grace of Monaco were all collectors and, overnight, Eero Aarnio put Finnish design on the world map. The Ball Chair was updated to the Bubble Chair, two of whose prototypes, designed in 1966, I'm thrust into. They look as if a huge bulb has been sawn in two and the two resulting Perspex hemispheres are hung from the ceiling by a chain (they still have celebrity appeal – Kylie Minogue, Kevin Spacey, are but a few of the modern owners). 'People said it was a space thing, something inspired by Yuri Gagarin. But I just loved plastic, and the best shape for plastic was the round shape – that's when it's strongest. There was no mould for this one. We just heated an acrylic sheet, fixed a metal ring to it, placed it over a hole in a big table and then blew air into the hole.'

Due to its see-through design and pod-effect, the Bubble Chair became an erotic prop for sex kitten photoshoots the world over. Eero springs out of the proto-Bubble and slides open a door from main wall cavity. Displayed are dozens of magazine covers (three *Playboy*) featuring Bond-girl starlets curled up inside. In a touching retro innocence, a 1960s edition of *Man's World* headlines an exposé on 'Unusual Oral Sex Practices!' This is the essence of Aarnio's *oeuvre* in its natural place and time. 'The girls follow the lines of the material,' he says with a shrug.

Eero specialises in designs that are functional and funky, simple and playful (and never inexpensive). His home displays rows of piggybanks, freestanding plastic trees, a collection of puppy designs (nine in a row in bright green, produced with children in mind, but ordered in bulk by an Italian bank). He's still as prolific as ever. A cubed soft leather armchair Captain Kirk would die for is just two weeks old. 'I don't have a name for it. What shall we call it?' he wonders. Then over to his latest invention, the Swan reading lamp, with their plastic stands in black, red or yellow, resembling a swan's neck. It's so obvious you wonder why it hasn't been done before.

In 2008, Eero was awarded the Compasso d'Oro, the highest accolade accorded by the Italian design industry. 'Italians are surprised that this kind of design is from Finland. I've often been described as an Italian designer, partly because my name sounds slightly Italian. They associate Finland more with wood. They don't expect plastic. When my show went to Mexico City the mayor asked me, why go for bright colours? Yours is a dark country, there's snow and night, it should be pessimistic. But I like bright colours yet I appreciate the Finnish landscape so much.'

Finns indeed can thank the harsh climate for their pre-eminence in design. While southern Europe had the luxury of year-round design, Finns didn't. 'In Finland you needed to be quick and function-oriented,' explains Anna Valtonen, a senior designer with Nokia. 'We didn't have too much of the gilded stuff in our history, so we tended to go for the functional and the minimalist. Finland has always been squeezed between big countries, so since the 19th century we had to use design as a way to assert our national identity. While the rest of Europe was going through art nouveau in the late 19th century, we had our National Romantic Style, which meant using big rocks and anything which placed an emphasis on nature and the climate.'

By 1917, Finland had been building a national identity for 30 years, much of it focused on art and design. When the Olympic Games were held in Helsinki in 1952, the functionalist stadium designed by Yrjö Lindegrenin and Toivo Jäntti was the star of the show. In the 1930s, Eliel Saarinen designed the Helsinki railway station, while Alvar Aalto, who rebuilt Rovaniemi, produced the Paimio Sanatorium, whose design brought maximum light and air to patients. Inside, his bentwood chairs became classics. It all meant that national identity was understated rather than thrusting with grandeur. 'In the 1950s,' explains Anna Valtonen, 'there was a lot of rebuilding after the war. People were moving in huge numbers from the countryside to the cities, so there was a huge interest in the functionality of design, the idea that form follows function. It was all about making kitchens better and easier for housewives.'

As I browse, Eero ponders the stereotype of the shy Finn. 'If you're walking around the lake,' he says, gesturing past his daughter's right shoulder with a muffin from a bountiful plate his wife has just presented, 'you might see someone up ahead coming in your direction. And you both start to worry and look here, there and everywhere, and as you get close to one another it's all very embarrassing, but you would never say hello.

'Now people have moved into the cities. We have very high technology. Nokia used to make rubber boots and then car tyres and then that changed so they started making TVs, then mobile phones. They're always getting better and better. They now have 40 per cent of the mobile phones in the world.'

He expands his thoughts with the same quixotic pizzazz of his work. 'It is the country with the best strawberries in the world, no question. There is no terrorism, it's clean, the weather is good. If I'm driving my car to Germany, the weather starts to change the moment I arrive in Denmark. [This doesn't accord with my own experience of Finnish weather.] It's a good place to live. There is sailing, hotels, shopping centres. It's great to be a Finn. No country is too far away.'

A pause. 'But maybe it's too close to Russia... Mind you, St Petersburg is only 400 kilometres away! There are a lot of very wealthy people there. Maybe our future is in that direction!'

Chapter 8

Hungary

Fortune should be blamed, or rather divine patience admired, for having given such a beautiful country as Hungary not to humans, but to such monstrous men as Hungarians.
Otto of Freising, 12th-century German bishop and chronicler.

It doesn't exactly inspire confidence.

A Volkswagen Golf has been stuck into the façade above the entrance. The car isn't coming through the wall, fender first, as the head-turning gimmick you might expect. Instead, it has been embedded sideways.

The vehicle's connection with dentistry isn't immediately clear. Then I realise the Autòjavitàs garage is merely sharing a premises with 'Kreatív Dental', the most audacious newcomer to the European molar scene. The two operations share the mission to repair and the activity of drilling, but, one hopes, the affinity ends there.

Welcome to the world of Attila the Gum. He is Hungary's most famous dentist.

I'm met by Attila himself (his surname is Knott, but he's comfortable with the nickname). Tall, angular, wearing a white shirt and yellow and black tie, his blond hair is spiked and even, rather like a boxer's, and his face looks somehow like it's been remodelled.

The waiting room, a bright, busy place with a noisy TV and plenty of greenery, has none of the silent, magazine-shuffling dread you associate with dental surgeries. It could be a bowling alley. Around the walls are British, Irish, German, Danish and American flags.

In what we might call the manufacturing arm of Attila's practice, all the prosthodontics – the moulds, casts, bridges, caps, crowns, implants, veneers and other frightening bits and pieces – are being worked on by his staff. One orderly is using a long, thin sucking nozzle to place lilac-coloured gel between the teeth in a mould of someone's lower mouth. The equipment appears sturdy, if not state of the art. There are blowtorches and hissing noises, and you can't help wondering if a tool malfunctions they pop down to the guys in Autòjavitàs to borrow theirs.

Next to an oven, in which moulds and casts are baked, an operative pours over a fresh one like an Egyptologist examining a 4,000-year-old curio. I suspect there are orderlies who love to work here at night. Alone.

All this activity keeps overheads to a minimum, and the savings are passed on to clients. Attila has three dentists, six technicians, an oral surgeon, three dental hygienists and no waiting list. The customers are Irish, British, German, Danish and American, all willing to fly to Hungary to get their teeth done. It's the big expensive stuff they come for – implants, veneers, root canal and bridge work – and it's offered at a fraction of the prices back home.

Attila promotes a beautiful city on the side, and when you factor in the low-cost flights, it's a package too good to miss. A bit of closed curettage periodontal surgery in the morning and a boat cruise up the Danube in the afternoon, or maybe a visit to one of the city's old coffee houses with their 'delicious pastries' (this is actually a recommendation from Kreatív Dental.) The Irish are flooding in, 30 a month. Quite a few like to combine composite fillings with buying a two-bedroom apartment, an altogether thoughtful approach to what EU enlargement is really all about.

'They are loving our quality, combining our low price,' explains Attila in English not quite as polished as his wall of white teeth. 'We don't need more advertisement because the news of good work goes around. We even have to discuss enlargement of our clinic.'

He continues the tour. 'The quality is outstanding here. The equipment is good, very well-trained technicians. The only difference between this quality work and the quality of work in Ireland and Denmark is profit.

These patients are looking for extensive dental treatment. What maybe they can't afford in their own country, we would be their solution here. Crown and bridge works, implants, gum treatment, sometimes they have to come back two, three times because of the dental problem. We pick them up – we have a hotel nearby – and immediately on arrival they come to the clinic to start the dental work. We tell them it's going to be one visit, or two visits. We don't let anyone go back with unfinished work. Someone might have a little problem, a toothache, they can use a local dentist, but again this is very minor, very seldom.'

This morning there is an Irish client, Alec. 'It's too expensive at home,' he says. 'I've an awful lot of things to be done. It will cost me thousands and thousands of pounds at home. I can't afford it. Simple as that.' He looks at me and says, 'What can go wrong? What could possibly go wrong?

'A couple of friends do it – my wife was doing it and she suggested I come over for a couple of new teeth. So I'm just obeying really. I just came over, will drink a few schnapps and hope they're not going to hurt me.'

He pauses. 'If they hurt me, I'm never going back.'

It's consultation time. Attila the Gum introduces Alec to one of his dental team.

'He's your man.'

'Is he going to hurt me?'

'Not yet.'

Alec sits on the operating chair and immediately folds his arms.

'I had an infection three weeks ago,' he says to no one in particular. 'I don't know what can be done at this stage, probably very little.'

'Can you open wider?'

The X-ray of Alec's mouth is lit up above us. From where I'm standing, it looks like Alec has six teeth on the top and nine on the bottom. It's like The Alamo in there.

'You can rinse, please.'

Attila and his dentist examine the X-ray and become engrossed in a dental conversation. In Hungarian.

Over Alec's head (Alec has started to get agitated), Attila explains to me: 'Some people who come here can have pre-judgement, I can tell them, you have 10 cavities, you need 45 crowns …'

'I don't want to know that,' Alec interrupts.

'Not you, not you,' Attila retorts. 'People are different,' he continues in my direction, ignoring Alec. 'If only I could tell them, you need this and this, six thousand euro …'

'That's what I like,' says Alec.

'… not good enough, so here, some people …'

'I just don't want to know,' Alec again.

'… some people have to be convinced …'

'I don't need to see them, I know what they are.'

As Attila is bent on demonstrating the attractions of Kreatív Dental, Alec is getting more and more worked up about what lies ahead; while he's happy about the money he's saving, he's doesn't want to know the details.

Attila inserts a dental camera into Alec's mouth. On a crystal-clear monitor, the camera roams around the obscene, gooey pinkness of Alec's mouth until it sniffs out a solitary molar, eyeball white, with a black cavity.

'If you want here we make dental work, it would be better to extract this one because this tooth is rather elongated,' says Attila's chief dentist.

Alec stares up at the screen, the camera nozzle still in his mouth.

Attila agrees. 'It's in the way, so if you want to get a nice aesthetical solution you have to take out this tooth, because this tooth is standing in our way, and in order to execute a nice quality work …'

'Which one?' (With his mouth full, it sounds like, 'Where are you from?')

'The last one here on this side, lower.'

'What can you do?' The camera is now out of his mouth. 'I mean, you can't put teeth in here?'

'I will show you. Special combination work. You can put teeth everywhere, some of them your own, some of them not your own …'

'I don't care who they belong to.'

'… so in the future you can bite, you can chew, you can smile!'

'I don't want to know what you're going to do,' says Alec. 'Just tell me, I'll do it.'

'I have to show you what type of work you will get.'

'Why? All you say is, you're going to give me teeth.'

'But I have to explain …'

'As long as you don't explain how you're going to do it.'

A further consultation. It appears that whatever they want to do to Alec's mouth involves some kind of dental plate in the bottom, and in the top. The lower one, however, requires at least one extraction. Given the depleted numbers of Alec's teeth, upper and lower, one *less* tooth is, at this stage in his dental career, a big sacrifice.

Attila changes tack. He reaches for the big argument. 'You can bite, but you cannot chew. If you cannot chew, you cannot start the digestion in your mouth. Digestion starts in the mouth first, not in the stomach. If you keep sending food down to the stomach undigested, you will upset the stomach.'

'I've just been to the doctor and he says I'm perfectly fit. I had a blood test.'

'It won't happen tomorrow, but if you don't chew your food properly, you will get stomach problems. You can create stomach cancer for yourself.'

Alec goes silent. Attila goes in for the kill.

'You don't have teeth in the bottom,' he says, looking Alec in the eye. 'Right now you have nothing, nothing! You cannot get implants in the lower, because you don't have any bone there, so that's history. What is next? We would fix your upper dentition aesthetically, clinically, functionally, not your lower. What good it is?'

'It's good to me. That's what I prefer.'

'But you cannot chew!'

'I don't care.'

I've just seen a grown man reduced to a child. And I can't really blame Attila.

'I prefer not to have the bottom done,' says Alec. He's not budging.

And so the consultation ends. With Attila the Gum's gentle admonishments in his ears, off goes Alec into the Budapest traffic, in the direction of some delicious pastries, or perhaps even his first schnapps.

* * *

Between 2002 and 2006, Budapest was overrun by dentally challenged Irish speculators, drooling over those gilded boulevards with imperial-vintage apartments, all hardwood floors and high ceilings. Next to the

Israelis, the Irish were the number one investors. Some bought brand-new apartments off the plans, renting them to young Hungarians without ever setting foot in the place. Others bought old apartments in the city centre early and probably made a considerable profit. But by 2008, as the global financial crisis gripped, those who expected a quick killing were disappointed.

Where do we begin with Hungarian stereotypes? There *is* something intrinsically Hungarian in the way Attila the Gum cornered the dental tourism market. Hungarians, you see, are cunning geniuses. It is an axiom oft repeated that they will enter a revolving door behind you and come out in front.

'They are very clever, inventive people,' says Stewart Durrant, a university lecturer who arrived in Budapest as a young tourist in 1983 and never left. 'They've had relatively big success in Nobel prizes. Any smallholder or industrialist will have some kind of contraption, whether it's to distil *pálinka* [apricot or plum brandy] or for putting an aerial on the roof. They are bright, well-educated people, though, rather closer to the Balkan mentality in temperament than Northern Europeans.'

The education system has enhanced the Hungarians' innate knack of putting things together, whether it is a brandy-distilling machine or an osseointegrated dental implant. Harry Harron is a former pharmacist from Downpatrick, Co. Down, and has been recruiting doctors and dentists from an agency in Budapest, sending them west. 'Every candidate we send gets a job. They're very good, people are bright and well educated. It's a quite intense selection process with strict criteria for language skills. They're really put through their paces.'

But are they hard workers? 'If a Hungarian is working on a deadline, he doesn't deliver results till the last second,' writes Gábor Vaderna, a literary historian, in *The Essential Guide to Being Hungarian*. 'He is a master at always working at just the right pace. If he must, he speeds up; if need be, he slows down.'

If Hungarian pride is ever wounded that the world doesn't appreciate their brilliance, they are quick to point out all those Nobel prizes. They also invented two things that nearly brought the world to its knees: the Rubik's Cube and the hydrogen bomb. Ernő Rubik, a graduate of the Budapest University of Technology and Economics, invented his eponymous cube in 1975, while Edward Teller was the lead scientist at Los Alamos, the secret US nuclear weapons programme in the Nevada Desert. Others, like Nobel laureate Eugene Wigner, designed the machines that produced plutonium for America's atomic bombs; Leó Szilárd worked with Einstein on the neutron chain reaction; while John von Neumann developed mathematical game theory, building computers that could not only store data but also be programmed to perform operations. So without these Hungarians, neither the threat of nuclear holocaust nor the computer would have existed. The travel writer Nicholas T. Parsons writes that since Hungarians are cynical individualists first and team players second, building the bomb was the 'only well-documented instance of expatriate Hungarians apparently pooling their skills' (*How to be a Magyar*).

It didn't stop with science. Hungarians flocked to Hollywood in the 1920s, with Alexander Korda scooping three Oscars for directing *The Thief of Bagdad* (1940) and Mihály Kertész winning another for *Casablanca* (1942). But it was on the sporting field that Hungarian genius found a mass audience. Puskás was the most celebrated Hungarian of all time. In 1953, he was part of the Hungarian team whose U-shaped formation and free-flowing style famously tore apart a bemused England team, beating them 6–3 at Wembley ending their unbeaten home record which had stood since 1901.

So much for the self-stereotype. But what about the view from beyond their borders? It's not an easy question. Our vantage point from the fringes of Europe has led to a fuzziness about 'Eastern' Europe. That term is in itself loaded, because as Hungarians and Czechs will tell you, they are not Eastern European at all, but Central European, and that carries with it a whole other set of ideas, identities and histories, ones Western powers disregard when it suits them.

When Churchill spoke of the Iron Curtain descending across Eastern Europe, as Mark Pittaway notes in *Eastern Europe, 1939–2000*, it lumped all those countries together in the Western mind. 'The western border of the Soviet bloc – the so-called Iron Curtain – came to symbolise, for those on both sides of the divide, Eastern Europe's apparent exclusion from the continental mainstream,' writes Pittaway.

This exclusion was already established during the Munich Crisis of 1939, when Hitler wanted to annexe the Sudetenland in Czechoslovakia.

One of Neville Chamberlain's justifications for appeasing Hitler was that Czechoslovakia was 'a faraway country' and a people 'of whom we know nothing'. Given that Britain still had an empire stretching right across the globe, this must have seemed very rich to the Czechs. The Iron Curtain not only *divided* Europe, but it *relieved* Western Europe of the burden that the 'East' had become over the centuries. 'The Iron Curtain had also cut the West free of the poorest, most disputatious and disputed part of the Continent,' argues Mark Frankland in *The Patriots' Revolution*. 'National conflicts that for generations tempted the peoples of East Europe to seek advantage in every international crisis had been frozen.'

When the divisions were lifted in 1989, the same limited mental geography was at work. All the countries from the former Soviet bloc got lumped in together once again, leading to tabloid hysteria about hordes of 'poor Eastern Europeans' swamping Western Europe. From Hungary's perspective, this was all wrong. Hungary had a cultural lineage which was distinct: not necessarily Western, but certainly not Eastern either. The political establishment in Budapest felt humiliated by the length of time it took for accession to the EU to be completed.

Central Europe has always had shifting meanings. Geographically it was roughly the area between the Alps and the Baltic, while politically it was the zone before which the Ottoman Empire stopped short. More Catholic or Protestant than the Orthodox lands to the east, it was less inclined to adopt the liberal ideas of the French Revolution to the west. It was home to the Habsburg Empire, culturally dominated by the Germans until World War I, but later more closely identified with Czechoslovakia, Poland and Hungary.

When in the 19th century nationalism surged in the west, Central European intellectuals under the Austrian Empire were inspired and started developing their own nationalist ideals. So it was no surprise that in the last decade of the Soviet Empire, it was those very countries which tried to undermine the socialist dictatorships by appealing to each other's – and, on the other side of the Iron Curtain, to their neighbours' – historical Central European roots. It also explains why their economic and social systems were better equipped to merge with the West when the Wall did come down.

If countries like Czechoslovakia and Hungary were faraway places in 1938, how much further away did they feel in 1990?

The effect of the Wall was to freeze-dry our perceptions of what these countries, and the people living in them, were like. They dissolved into a single set of images, of bare shelves, brutalist architecture, smokestacks and a grim-looking populace.

'Before I arrived, to me Hungary was Eastern Europe, a poor, Communist place,' says Mark Downey, a young property consultant from Dublin who's been working in Budapest for the past nine years. 'My friends all told me the women were like shot putters. I had a kind of black and white war movie image in my mind. There are parts of Hungary that are like that, even in Budapest, but by and large I've found it a very vibrant place. After a year in Budapest, I was amazed by the sheer beauty of the city, the busy-ness of the place. There was a full-blown culture.'

When the system collapsed, we discovered these characters from history reappearing out from under the rubble. 'There is the Pole, devout in the defence of national honour; the moody Hungarian, preoccupied with the survival of his culture and his race; the Czech democrat, straightforward yet with a knack for slyness,' writes Mark Frankland. 'How can such figures from the past reappear in countries that half a century ago were mangled in Hitler's war, then swamped by the Soviet flood?'

What we learn from these figures is that they are still gripped by their own history. The celebrated stereotype of the Hungarian is that he is moody, cynical, awaiting the next disaster and ready to blame everyone else for his misfortunes. Any Hungarian will tell you where it all began (895 ad) and where it ended (Paris, 1920).

In 895, a geographical area below modern-day Slovakia known as the Carpathian Basin was invaded by horsemen with a strange language coming from somewhere way out east (the Urals, in fact). Within decades, the Hungarians were taking advantage of wars in Western Europe between Germanic, Norman, Saracen and Frankish tribes. With a population of only 60,000, Hungary was able to muster 20,000 horsemen, light and fiercely equipped. Their exploits chilled the marrow of Europeans everywhere. According to the *Larousse Encyclopaedia of Ancient and Medieval History*, the 'Hungarian terror' swept across Europe into the tribal zones of Swabia, Thuringia, Lorraine and even Burgundy. Hungarians carved their way into Italy as far as Tuscany, and into present-day France as far as

Nîmes. *Larousse* reports: 'Harvests were burnt, cattle slaughtered, houses and churches left in cinders. All men were killed, the children mutilated, the women tied to what was left of the cattle, which was then driven off to the raiders' camp.'

Not surprisingly, early stereotypes took root and were never dislodged. During a football match between Hungary and Germany in Basel, Switzerland, in 1954, a German TV commentator, miffed at the Hungarians winning, spoke of 'an onslaught from the Steppe'.

'The memories of plundering, barbarian Hungarians supposedly eating raw meat and drinking the blood of their defeated enemies,' writes László Marácz, of the University of Amsterdam, 'even serves to explain the etymology of the English and French word *ogre* – "monster, men-eaters, frightening children in fairy tales". English and French linguists and historians explain the etymology of this word by relating it with *Hongre*, the name of the Hungarians in old French.'

In reality the Hungarian raids were largely political: at the time, the Holy Roman Empire lay on Hungary's western borders, and in order to maintain a balance of power, Hungarians aligned themselves with Germanic tribes outside the Empire to keep imperial forces at bay.

But even as the centuries rolled by, Hungarians must have begun to regret their decision to set up camp in the Carpathian Basin. First they were nearly wiped out by the Mongol-Tatars in 1241, then they were progressively squeezed between the Ottoman Empire inching up from Turkey to the south and east, and, a few centuries later, the expanding Viennese Habsburg Empire (more about them later) to the north and west.

Yet it was precisely because of its geographical location that Hungary was an important place, drawing both negative and positive attention from Europe's power centres. For 300 years, until the beginning of the 14th century, Hungary was a Christian bulwark against the Turks. The image of the terrifying horseman was set aside as the Turkish threat increased; instead, according to Pope Sylvester II, they were the 'living rampart and the shield of Christian Europe'. King Stephen of Hungary, who died in 1038, and King Sancho of Spain, founder of the Castilian state, found themselves at the parlous edges of Europe, and both were lauded throughout Christendom for defending civilisation. Hungary also facilitated the path for pilgrims and crusaders on their way to Jerusalem. 'Two sets of Western images and stereotypes can be constructed,' writes László Marácz. 'Namely, the negative variant of Hungarians as inferior, backward, plundering Asiatic, barbarian intruders in Europe, and the positive variant of Hungarians heroically fighting for the defence of Christian Europe and European liberal values.'

Keeping the Turk at bay was all very well, but Hungarians had their own national aspirations. Hungarians today claim 1,000 years of nationhood and royalty, the symbol of which is St Stephen's Crown. While Western Europe was preoccupied with the Hundred Years War and the Black Death (1346–53), the Hungarian royal family were marrying themselves into advantageous positions and expanding the kingdom nicely. After its discovery in Transylvania, Hungarian gold accounted for three-quarters of all the output of European mines, and the Hungarian forint was competing with the best of Europe's currencies. By the end of King Louis the Great's reign in 1382, the Hungarian kingdom stretched from Poland to the Adriatic.

But trouble was stirring. Hungary was at loggerheads both with Venice and Vienna and had persistent problems with its possessions in the Balkans. In 1453, the fall of Constantinople to the Turks stunned Christendom and had Pope Nicholas V baying for war. Sultan Mohammed II brought his forces into Hungary and besieged the city of Nándorfehérvár (present-day Belgrade) with an army 150,000 strong, only to be defeated by allied Christian troops. Despite the victory, the local powers were divided, fighting continually over the Hungarian crown. The Hungarian nobility were garnering more power and wealth to themselves, and there were peasant revolts against serfdom. By 1500, it was becoming clear that Hungary was emerging as an entity apart: distant from Western Europe, and not a part of the Holy Roman Empire; Christian, but separate from the Orthodox Church to the east; more feudal than the rest of Europe, thanks to the increasing ambitions of the nobility, with an over-reliance on agriculture and under-developed cities. Drifting from the mainstream, Hungary suffered a massive defeat to the Turks at Mohács in 1526, followed by a further defeat at Buda in 1541.

Turkish victories, the squabbling of the nobility and the designs of the Habsburgs all resulted in Hungary being cut in three. The nobles elected two different kings, one of whom, Ferdinand, was a Habsburg: after trying for so long, Vienna had finally got its grip on the Hungarian crown and wouldn't be letting go for a long time. The main, central chunk of Hungary fell to the Ottoman Turks, and in the east, Transylvania became an independent principality, though much under the influence of the Turks.

Hungary was a mess. It had been fighting the Turks for nearly 150 years. Ferdinand of Austria, and his rival, John Zápolya, who was supported by a majority of Hungarian nobles and also had developed ties with Istanbul, were soon sparring for the crown. Hungarian nationalists found themselves in a crushing dilemma: they couldn't dream of defeating the Habsburgs without the help of the Turks, and they would never beat the Turks without the support of the Habsburgs.

Meanwhile, as Hungary sank into war, depopulation and division, Europe was engaged in momentous developments: King Henry VIII set up his Church of England, Michelangelo was painting the Sistine Chapel, capitalism was taking root, a middle class was emerging, trade and the arts were flourishing and cities were growing. In Hungary, by contrast, the nobility were grabbing more power and some nine million peasants were condemned to serfdom. The gulf began to grow, and some historians argue that it has yet to be bridged.

When the Reformation came along, most of Hungary followed Luther and Calvin, much to the fury of the Catholic Habsburgs and Germans. In this context, negative stereotypes about the Hungarians increased among German-speaking Catholics in Vienna and elsewhere. Where once they praised the heroism of the Christian Magyars fighting the Turk, they were now excoriated as uncontrollable, unreliable traitors, helping the heathen Turk just to annoy the Germans.

* * *

So much for the state of Hungary in the 16th century. But to fully appreciate the melancholic Hungarian soul and why the country has gone through such a desperately unfortunate history, I drive out of Budapest on the new EU-funded M3, and head north east to the heart of the Carpathian Basin, the great Hungarian plain known as the Puszta.

It's a place of gloriously unpronounceable place names – try Jászárokszállás or Füzesabony. As dusk settles over the stubble fields, I turn off at Mezőtárkány, heading into the Steppe from which Magyar horsemen wreaked such havoc. My destination is Hortobágy (it rhymes with 'badge', since the 'y' is silent), a small village that is the essential locus of Hungarian identity.

The Puszta is a flat wilderness dappled by lakes and rivers, floodplains and grasslands. Tonight, with the sun setting, it is eerily tranquil, but even the wilderness resonates with the pessimism of the Magyars, right down to the frogs: from deep within the shallows, the red-bellied toad blurts out a lonely, melancholic mating call all night long.

The Puszta has been a curse and a blessing. Its sprawling flatness left Hungary vulnerable to invasion, yet its grasslands sustained a form of animal husbandry that kept the population alive when it otherwise would have starved. It allowed tribes from the Caucasus and beyond – Huns, Scythians, Sarmatians – to bring their herding expertise into the European peninsula. It has also, supposedly, shaped the powerful yearnings in the Hungarian mind for freedom and open spaces, and reminds Hungarians of their roots as roaming horse and cattle herders.

After a night at the Club Hotel, I meet János, who will guide me around the Puszta. Our first trip is a carriage ride – shared with German and Russian tourists – out into the grasslands. The pale grasses stretch off into a milky horizon uninterrupted by hill or household. The distinctive pallor is due to the heavy alkaline soils, the low iron count inhibiting strong natural colours.

The great plain before us is dominated by the Tisza River. It rises in Ukraine and eventually joins the Danube in Vojvodina, Serbia. The flow has been forever slow. Twisting and snaking, it renders the plain prone to flooding. In these conditions, livestock eclipsed crops, since people and herds could move quickly to higher ground. While Western Europe concentrated on cereals, Hungary stuck to cattle. 'If the crops failed, there was famine like you had in Ireland,' says János, 'but if crops failed in Hungary the definition of famine was eating meat without bread. In the West, livestock weighed only 100 kilo per animal, but these beasts weigh five times as much.'

It soon becomes clear that you're nothing in the Puszta without a herd. First we encounter Racka sheep with their long, gracefully twirled horns pointing straight up from the head, and their black and reddish-brown fleece coats, rockstar-long. These are exceptionally adaptable animals, largely immune to disease, producing on average 2 kilograms of wool. In a pen nearby, we meet the strangest pigs I've ever seen. Forget all you think you know about smooth-skinned porkies. The Mangalica is tightly bound in matted bristling curls, as thickly endowed as a beard on a Dubliner. They were first sent to Hungary by a Serbian prince in 1833 and flourished in the opened-up grasslands. Today, after a century and a half of cross-breeding, they are prized for their cholesterol-free fat and meat.

As we trundle further into this dreamscape of curly-haired pigs and long-horned sheep, our next encounter is with the king of the Steppe, the grey cow. These are the 500-kilo beasts that saved Hungary even in times of endless warfare. From the 13th century they were the cash-cows of Central Europe; the pastures they fed on were fertilised by floods every spring, yielding the finest meat.

'In 15th-century Europe, the focus was on textiles, industry and trade,' explains János. 'Cities like Vienna, Nuremburg, Venice all had land around them to grow textiles and the plants which provided colouring agents. But they had to feed people – and that was good for the Hungarians. We had millions of animals and so they drove them, perhaps 100,000 at a time, to sell in towns and cities. From the 15th to the 19th centuries it was big business. The cattle were very tough. They could survive a 1,000-kilometre walk. The Turks, Austrians and Germans – even during the worst warfare – always supported the cattle trade. The Hungarians used *Haduks* – armed herdsmen – to protect the cattle. They created roads 40 metres wide for the cattle drivers. By the time the Hungarian cattle drivers arrived in Nuremburg, they were paid by butchers in textiles.'

By 1580, Hungary was a major world producer of live cattle. Huge estate barons grew rich on cattle and wine exports. But the cattle trade had an unusual side effect. When the herdsmen returned from the urban markets of the German lands, they brought back ideas with their new fabrics. During the religious turbulence, cattle herders decided their hardy, unluxurious lifestyle chimed perfectly with Calvinism. From 1552 to 1715, Debrecen – a city just 30 kilometres from our carriage ride – became almost exclusively Calvinist thanks to the ideas imported by the cattle herders, soon becoming the Calvinist Rome, a major centre of Bible printing.

We stop at a row of huts were modern-day horse and cattle herders sleep; they continue to husband animals in ways that have changed little over centuries and are still practised in Mongolia. To the delight of the Austrian and Russian tourists, the herders, with traditional broad-brimmed hats and long, blue, loose-fitting trousers and tunics buttoned to the neck, put their horses through a number of tricks. One set piece is for the herder to render his horse flat on a given signal. It's done in seconds. 'The plains were always easy to invade,' says János ruefully. 'When people invaded, the men simply disappeared. Our ancestors had no other choice, so that's why they learned to get their horses flat on the ground at such speed.'

The Puszta had a deeply engrained social structure with a hierarchy built around the sheep herders, with herd boys (*bojtárs*) on the bottom of the heap and the leaders (*számadó*) enjoying immense status at the top. Horsemen and cattle herders were held in higher esteem; their long embroidered felt cloaks called *cifraszúr* (ornate for Catholic herders, more austere for the Calvinists) were symbols of social standing. During courtship, they would be left in the farmhouse of a girl the herder was wooing, so that if his advances weren't welcome, the cloak was left out on the porch the following morning.

The Puszta also carried its own fading set of myths and belief systems, witches, shamans, outlaws, gypsy bands, wise shepherds and latter-day horse whisperers who could do everything from curing rabies to calling back stray animals. Its influence on Hungarian identity can't be understated, but is waning with each passing decade. The word for a cowherd, for example, is *gulyás*, and that's where the national dish, goulash, gets its name.

During lunch János ponders the melancholic disposition of the Hungarians. 'Were it not for the Hungarians, there would have been a major Slav empire,' he says, to the lugubrious strains of a gypsy violin playing at our table. 'We always had to protect ourselves.'

It's this sense of paranoia about the forces ranged against Hungary, co-mingled with a sense of their own destiny to do great – if unspecified – things, which goes some way to explaining the Hungarian mindset. 'Since time immemorial,' writes Paul Lendvai in *Hungary: The Art of Survival*, 'the spirit of the Magyars has wavered between devotion to their mission as founders of the great kingdom of St Stephen's Crown in the Carpathian Basin and a deep-rooted fear of extermination, surrounded by hostile Romanians, Slavs and Germans.'

Many observers allude to the Hungarian language and the fact that it was geographically out of place. Although influenced by tribes and peoples the Magyars encountered during their epic journey into the Carpathian Basin, Hungarian is basically Finno-Ugric, meaning it originated somewhere around the Urals or even in western Siberia, and 75 per cent of Hungarian speech derives from it. It was only in the 19th century that Hungarians learned that their closest linguistic cousins were the Finns. That was something of a disappointment to Hungarians (no disrespect to the Finns), who dreamed of a connection with the Huns or a Sumero-Babylonian culture. Hungarian and Finnish do have a similar grammatical structure, but they can barely understand each other: a Hungarian TV documentary in the 1990s followed the fortunes of Hungarians who went to Finland to get married. The Hungarians never stopped talking, while the Finns never said a word.

The language is agglutinative, meaning suffixes are juxtaposed with the root word, and much depends on the mode of inflection. Word order is everything. If a question is asked, the reply must have a given word order. If another word order is offered instead, it answers *another* question. One Hungarian writer has described the mother tongue as simultaneously the softest cradle and most solid coffin. It's no wonder they've felt misunderstood.

These days, Hortobágy keeps its heritage alive through a National Park, although it can be said to have been a national treasure since the 1860s. The experience of the Puszta during Communist times was, according to János, pretty disastrous. 'When the Communists took over, they didn't trust anyone who was involved with horses. They were sent to the Puszta simply as labourers, and the skills were lost and the culture destroyed.' Not only that, the new Communist government had the bright idea of using the Puszta to grow rice – white gold, they called it – building ditches to carve out fields. It was a disaster. The scheme produced only about 500 kilos per hectare before it was abandoned. 'They paid no attention to the environmental implications. We've been trying to get money to dismantle the infrastructure ever since,' complains János.

After lunch we meet Erika Molnár, the wife of a horse herdsman. She's been weaving for two years, but before that she worked in administration for a construction company in a neighbouring village. Her husband, Imre Juhasz, has been a herdsman since he was 16 and has worked the plains for 25 years. During frequent thunderstorms, Imre would have to stay outdoors with the animals, pacifying them in their fright to prevent them from bolting. Before the advent of electric fences, he started work at 3 a.m. and worked until 9 a.m., then he would drive the horses to their stables and work a further shift on the plain from 9 p.m. until midnight. His hours have changed, but he'll still sleep in the stable or in one of the huts on the Puszta. The advent of the mobile phone has made life, and their marriage, a lot easier.

'During Communist times, people in rural areas still had work horses which were brought to the Puszta for summer grazing,' says Erika. 'Now it's an expensive hobby. There are fewer private horses and they belong to rich people and entrepreneurs.'

Imre has won the best horse-herder title five times. Even today, it's a popular job despite the smaller herds. 'You get many Sunday cowboys, but most don't really have the skills. You have to be born a herdsman, not just to love it.'

Their four-year-old son, Balint, is already keen. He has his own herdsman costume and was first on horseback at the age of two. 'He knows it's not for playing. He knows it's serious,' says Erika, laughing.

But what does it mean to be Hungarian and to be living in the Puszta? 'For an animal keeper, the new EU regulations get harder and harder. Hungarians like freedom and they don't like paying taxes. Freedom! No limits! No borders! No taxes!' says Erika with a gust of animation. 'It's a natural way to live. The sun rises on one side and sets on the other horizon.'

It's a touching reflection, but I'm wondering just how well preserved Hungary's relationship with the Puszta, in general, and the horse in particular, is in a mechanised, globalised age. At the beginning of the 19th century there were reputedly 5 million horses in Hungary. Horses were sacrificial animals when the Hungarians arrived in the Carpathian Basin, and horseflesh was still eaten until the Middle Ages until banned by a pope. Queen Maria Theresa, the Habsburg monarch, was crazy about horses, and Empress Sisi, the wife of Emperor Franz Josef, visited the small town of Gödöllő east of Budapest just for the horses. In 1877, on the country estate of Count Ernő Blaskovich, the indomitable mare Kincsem ('My Treasure') entered 54 races and won every single one.

But since the ruination of the Communist period, few Hungarians today ever get up on a horse, and there are plenty of urban cynics who are happy to debunk the whole mythology of the Puszta and the nomadic horsemen of the Hungarian Steppe.

Leaving the Puszta for an early flight, I drive through the flat darkness, past herds of grey cattle and Racka sheep. In the turgid waters, the lonely red-bellied toads continue their plaintive seduction. However neither the frogs, nor the Puszta's geographical vulnerability, can fully explain Hungarian pessimism.

For that, we need to return to Hungary's recent history.

* * *

In the two centuries after Hungary was split into three parts, it just about managed to survive between the rock of the Habsburgs and the hard place of the Turks. Despite a scattering of failed insurrections against Vienna, Hungary realised its destiny lay more with the Austrians and Europe than the Ottoman Empire. Peace was reached with Vienna in 1711, just as Austria was enhancing and expanding her empire. In 1740, Maria Theresa became Empress. The following year she took the Hungarian and Bohemian crowns, winning over a majority of Hungarian nobles in the process. As attacks by the Turks dwindled, she introduced badly needed economic and social reforms to Hungary and eased restrictions on the language. The economy grew and so did the ethnic composition of the country, with Serbs, Romanians and Slovaks all flooding in to find work. Towards the end of the 18th century, 45 per cent of the subjects of the Habsburg Empire lived in Hungary, and they weren't all Magyars.

After the relatively enlightened rule of Marie Theresa, the throne passed to Francis II, the last Holy Roman Emperor. He was an uncompromising monarchist, unsympathetic to Hungarian aspirations, opposed to the Enlightenment and determined to face down Napoleon's attempts to overturn the European order with promises of liberty and equality. Napoleon had tried to elicit the support of the Hungarians against Vienna, appealing to their 'ancient and illustrious origins', but to no avail. According to French experts at the time, most Hungarians felt somehow protected by the Austrian Habsburgs and trusted them more than Napoleon or even the Hungarian nobility.

After the defeat and exile of Napoleon, the Congress of Vienna in 1815 redrew the political map of Europe. Royalty pursued the principle of absolutism to put manners on anyone brave enough to attempt egalitarian politics. Once again a national movement took root in Hungary, alongside a parallel golden age of art and literature. In such a climate, revolution would not be long coming and it exploded in 1848.

It swept across Europe, from Naples to Paris to Vienna. It was only a matter of time before it spread to Hungary. The country had a population of 14 million, including a growing and restive middle class demanding greater recognition. They were supported by the swollen ranks of ethnic minorities (Hungarians only made up 41.4 per cent of the population). Liberals and radicals, led by the lawyer Lajos Kossuth, presented a 12-point programme demanding a free press, civil and religious liberty and an end to serfdom. Initially the demands were largely met and a new assembly was installed, and although sovereignty was still the preserve of the Viennese monarchy, Hungary seemed to be on the road to full independence.

But, as so often is the case in that crowded cockpit of European politics, the new deal had let the minorities' genie out of the bottle. Despite a peaceful six months of revolution against Austria and declarations of independence, Vienna played the Croatian card, encouraging loyal (Catholic) Croats to take up arms against Hungary. It was to be a turning point. Despite an insurrection in Vienna by Austrian insurgents which was supported by Kossuth and his Hungarian army, internal disagreements about how far independence should go weakened the Hungarian cause. In 1849, Vienna abolished her previous concessions and declared Hungary permanently bound to Austria. In a fatal blow, the Russian Tsar Nicholas I came to Vienna's assistance: the brief period of independence was crushed by the overwhelming military superiority of Russia and Austria. The Russian intervention left a bitterness that many Hungarians feel to this day; during the uprising against Soviet rule in 1956, the students and workers modelled their demands on the 1848 revolutionaries' 12-point plan. They, too, were crushed by Russian force.

Despite the Tsar's appeal for clemency, some 150 Hungarian nobles, independence leaders and generals were executed by the Austrian Emperor Franz Josef. Lajos Kossuth went into exile.

The Hungarians had worked hard to garner international help for their movement. Although they failed to get any real political support (Britain flatly refused to tinker with the balance of power, bluntly insisting Hungary should remain part of the Austrian Empire), they did win the admiration of Western liberals, inspired by what they saw as the romantic, freedom-loving Hungarians. Once again, stereotypes were reversed, writes László Marácz:

> The expressions *csikosok* 'horseherds', *betyárok* 'outlaws', *huszárok* 'hussars', *cigányok* 'gypsies', *puszta* … became familiar. German writers, like Lenau and Schiller, and composers, like Franz Liszt, helped spread these exotic images of Hungary to the West. The romantic image of 'freedom-loving Hungary' also had a political counterpart, namely, 'liberal Hungary' resisting the centralism of Vienna.

In 1867, in a self-interested concession to Hungarian sensitivities, and on foot of wars lost against Prussia and Italy, the Austrian Emperor Franz Josef created the dual monarchy: henceforth the empire would be known as Austro-Hungarian. Hungarian moderates had lobbied for such a compromise, and they were supported by Empress Sisi. Foreign policy would be decided by Vienna and Hungary would be under the imperial sceptre, but Budapest was given a government, and some space for a sovereign identity within the dual monarchy. The economy grew and infrastructure improved, but the question of the minorities was left unresolved.

Over the next decades, the power struggle in Europe would have profound implications for the Hungarians. They worried about Russian imperial strength, not least because of her intervention in 1849, but also because Hungary was surrounded by Slavic neighbours; they were also suspicious of Bismarck and the unification of Germany in 1871 (until that point, Germany had been an amalgam of 300 kingdoms, statelets and principalities). In this febrile climate, Magyar nationalists were pressurising the Serb, Romanian and Slovak minorities into adopting Hungarian customs and language, a process known as Magyarisation. As World War I loomed, Hungary had to choose between Pan-Germanism and Pan-Slavism. With resignation, they chose the Germans according to the fatalistic axiom, 'If Germany loses, we lose; if she wins, we are lost.'

As events unfolded the Hungarians, once again, backed the wrong horse. Even before the war, all the international goodwill towards the freedom-loving Hungarians of 1848 had been evaporating, especially over Magyarisation. By 1911, some 45.5 per cent of the population were non-Magyar.

'The images of "liberal and constitutional Hungary" were replaced by the images of "Hungarians as brutal oppressors of Hungary's nationalities" and "Hungarians threatening European peace" and "being an obstacle for European progress" on account of Austria-Hungary's alliance with Germany,' writes László Marácz. 'They turned a few decades of Hungarian reliance on German power, which originated from Hungary's vulnerable geopolitical position, into another millennial crime.'

Stereotyping, it seemed, was the order of the day, and leading the fray was the British historian R.W. Seton-Watson. He had once lavished praise on the Hungarians – their brand of Calvinism chimed with his own Scottish Presbyterianism – but after they hitched their wagon to the Germans, the attitude soured. On a trip to Bucharest, he urged the Romanians: 'We together with our French and Russian allies must fight the German danger; but you with the Serbs must put an end to the brutal and artificial domination of the Magyar race over all its neighbours.'

In 1918, Germany was beaten and the Austrian Empire collapsed. There was a clamour by its constituent nationalities – the Czechs, the Slovaks, the Slovenes, Croats and Serbs – for self-determination, and their petitions were received favourably by the victorious Western powers. Hungary's standing during the Paris peace talks was, however, none too high.

'I confess that I regarded, and still regard, that Turanian tribe with acute distaste,' wrote Harold Nicolson, a young British diplomat, at the talks. 'Like their cousins the Turks, they had destroyed much and created nothing. Buda Pest was a false city devoid of any autochthonous reality. For centuries the Magyars had oppressed their subject nationalities. The hour of liberation and of retribution was at hand.'

Indeed it was, and it came to pass during the Treaty of Trianon, in the park of Versailles, on 4 June 1920. At a stroke, Hungary lost a staggering two-thirds of its territory and three-fifths of its population. In all, 3.4 million Hungarians found themselves cut off from the motherland and stranded in newly recast Romania, Czechoslovakia, Italy and the new Yugoslav kingdom of Slovenia, Serbia and Croatia.

The Treaty of Trianon was a shocking humiliation and they feel it to this day. Numerous households still hang the map of pre-1920 Hungary on the wall, and its outline can still be found on bumper stickers. If we want to understand the legendary Hungarian pessimism – or at least its grim cynicism – we should see Trianon as the culmination of centuries of misfortune, bad decisions and foreign treachery, which all left a profound legacy of disappointment. 'Magyar pessimism is rooted in the conviction that history has cheated the nation in the past and is just waiting to do so again,' explains the travel writer Nicholas T. Parsons.

Of course, the reality is that some, if not much, of the misfortune was self-inflicted. As the empire was collapsing, the Hungarian delegations didn't budge an inch on their demands for a federal country with all its territories intact, and were dismissive of the demands of the minorities within her borders. 'The Hungarians stuck firmly to their intransigent position, unwilling to give away an inch of their constitutional prerogatives,' writes Miklós Molnár in *A Concise History of Hungary*.

But the misfortune didn't end there. The shock of Trianon sent the country on a reactionary course under the leadership of Regent Admiral Horthy, the admiral without a ship. Described in the 1920s as a kind of clerico-fascist state, Hungary introduced a raft of anti-Semitic laws (Budapest was seduced by Hitler's promises that they would get back their lost territory if only they supported Nazi Germany). During the war, Hungary see-sawed between both British and German overtures and ended up making the grave mistake of attacking the Soviet Union. Fed up with Admiral Horthy's prevarication and his sluggishness at deporting Jews, Hitler decided to invade in 1944, making the country unique in being at war with just about everybody. Horthy, to his credit, did his best to forestall the mass deportation of Jews, managing to save just over half the 230,000 who had been earmarked for the death camps. In the end, a million Hungarians, including most of the political and military leadership, fled to the West; some 900,000 died and 600,000 were captured by the Russians. The country was left with the dubious legacy of being Hitler's last satellite.

* * *

It's October 2008 and I'm drinking a cappuccino at a café in pleasant afternoon sunshine next to St Stephen's Basilica in Budapest. Crossing the airy and bright square are sharp young businessmen catching the eye of the capital's formidable population of attractive young women. I'm waiting for Ilés Herber, a 28-year-old business management and accounting graduate.

This seems a good vantage point from which to reflect on Hungary's recent history after its bloody awful past. In 1990, Hungary freed itself from Communist dictatorship and within 14 years had joined the European Union. Its integration into the European family seemed effortless, in contrast to its tortured history. At the beginning of 2008, Hungary joined the Schengen free travel area: at a stroke, millions of Hungarians living in neighbouring countries were now free to move back and forth to the motherland from which Trianon had cut them off.

The country had adapted well to Western capitalism. During the latter days of Communist rule, Hungary had enjoyed 'Goulash Socialism', a more flexible approach to the system. There was a measure of private enterprise and comparatively decent living standards. Even before the Wall came down, Hungarians enjoyed an easing of travel restrictions, and when food conditions worsened in the late 1980s, the authorities relaxed the restrictions further. As a result, Hungarians drove to and from Austria in their thousands on shopping sprees, forming, on their return, a bizarre column of Trabants with enormous freezers strapped to their roofs.

Budapest was soon ranked alongside Prague as one of the most exciting old cities to visit for a weekend break (or to get that dental work done). Perhaps the greatest tourist boom has come about, though, not because of dental work but another form of necessary pain: the stag weekend. That's why I'm meeting Ilés Herber. He and three partners set up a stag-weekend company, Budapest Madness. 'I don't earn as much as I could if I sold my life to a multinational,' he says. 'But I'm building something here which has a value. If I decide to stop, I can sell the stag business for a lot of money.'

First a confession: I had just been on such a stag weekend for an American friend. Apart from the usual heavy drinking, the trip involved a soak in the wonderful Széchenyi Baths, an early 20th-century neo-baroque thermal bath complex, followed by a boat trip up the Danube. But this was no ordinary boat trip: part of the programme, in the disco bar below deck, was a strip show by two young Budapest ladies. The delights of the capital's riverside splendour were somewhat lost in the moment.

'Ninety per cent of our clients are English,' says Ilés by way of explanation. 'They go pistol shooting, go-karting, strip club tours, river cruises with lesbian strippers. We also do speed boating, paintballing, sailing and gliding, but the majority of stags go for the old reliables of pistol shooting and strippers. Most of the groups are well behaved, but sometimes we have problems with accommodation.'

Problems?

'They break things. They also are very demanding. They have a contact number, and they think it's 24 hours, so they ring up at three in the morning and say, "We want girls in our hotel room NOW." We don't do this.'

To the chagrin of Budapest's (as yet embryonic) feminist movement, the capital's newest reputation is a stereotype they would rather avoid. It's hard to know who to blame for this – the English stag party hordes or the Hungarians themselves. They're not exactly feminist flag-wavers: Baron Eötvös, the liberal education minister in the 1860s, decreed that 'woman is destined by nature and by her character to home and family life more than to public life'. During the so-called liberation of Bolshevism, women fared little better. The communists saw them as cut-price labour: schools were flooded in the 1960s with girls who would go on to nothing more than low-paid clerical work, while the lucrative jobs went to the men. The reason there are so many concert pianists in Hungary, they say, is that since they need to protect their fingers, they are relieved of washing-up duties.

Budapest is where some 50 per cent of 'mainstream' European pornographic films are made. 'There are three major porn companies based here,' an adult-entertainment source told me. 'There are only a couple of hundred people involved. It doesn't take very much, you know, just a soundman, a cameraman and a couple of actors, and away you go. Amazing, really. You get mothers, fathers, sisters dropping the girls off. They see it as a respectable profession. It's like they were doctors.'

Ilés disagrees, even if he's non-judgemental about such things – it's his business, after all. 'They're not from normal families. It's not a normal thing. I don't know. There are a lot of beautiful girls here. Europeans like Budapest and Hungary – here they can find a lot of good-looking ladies.'

It's true that not a small number of Irish and English expats have found love on the Danube (and not all through stag weekends, I hasten to add). Harry Harron, our friend who runs the recruitment agency in Budapest for doctors and dentists, met his wife, a lawyer, when she was closing a property transaction for a friend. 'I decided to move here, and seven months later I proposed,' says Harry. 'I had to bring a translator along to ask her parents for her hand – it was quite a shocking situation, really. Yet her parents were incredibly warm and gracious. My only form of communication was hugging, kissing and eating their food. But I was always impressed because it was a bit of a risk, them taking in this strange son-in-law.'

Mark Downey, our Irish property contact, agrees. 'Hungarian women make very good wives. They're very homely, like to clean, cook, very family oriented. Very good at understanding what men want. They're very sensually aware. Families will often make jokes about the father having a mistress. You leave the table wondering, is it true? There's a lot of infidelity. They're sexually very open.'

Sexual manners notwithstanding, the experience of most expats seems positive. They find the people friendly and welcoming, and the capital invigorating. 'The Hungarians are very good at making plans and programmes, going on day trips, walks, making a day of something,' says Mark. 'You'll see *Pestiez* [a listings magazine] in pubs and bars in Budapest, and other event guides in every town and village in the country, and you'll see young people looking through these in cafés to arrange their weekends.'

But one Irish businessman had this to say: 'They're very loving and caring with each other at home, but act like wild dogs to each other on the street. Mothers, husbands, daughters – put them behind the wheel of a car and they'll run you over.'

It's true that the private and public spheres seem miles apart. Whether it's down to their cynical individualism, or a hangover from the paranoid atmospherics of Socialism, the conviviality of home life seems to vanish in the public sphere of paying tax and doing business.

'There's still a lot of suspicion,' says Harry Harron. 'People suspect you think they're going to rip you off or deal with them in a tricky way. It slows down the whole business relationship. Nothing is done without a contract – that's not a bad practice, but it slows things down. At home, you move much quicker. It's a bit frustrating at times. People actually think you will be cheated.'

'There's less of a herd mentality,' says Stewart Durrant, our lecturer in business studies at the Central European University. 'They keep themselves – and their dastardly schemes to avoid paying tax – to themselves. There's less gossip over fences about house prices, and there's no interaction between work and social life, so there tends not to be a gossip-driven property boom.'

It may well be that the family gets a disproportionate share of the individual's love and trust. During Communist times, good accommodation was hard to come by, so families had to be close-knit. 'They could be very useful in circumnavigating the Communist system,' writes Nicholas T. Parsons. 'While churches were discredited, families were seen as honourable. A story was told of a Communist official who abused party funds to build villas for his children and then delivered a tearful *apologia* that he had only acted out of parental love.'

The lack of civic trust may also relate to the events of 1956. In that year, Hungarian workers and students rose up in the first ever violent revolution against the Soviet dictatorship, taking on the Russian military machine and dying in their hundreds in the process. The uprising was crushed by Soviet and other Warsaw Pact troops and the leaders executed. The man who took over, János Kádár, had actually supported the revolt, but in an act of breathtaking betrayal agreed to be Moscow's 'yes man' after it was crushed.

'Kádár's crime was that he turned Hungarians against one another,' says Nick Thorpe, the BBC correspondent in Budapest. 'If you're not with us, you're against us. He also bought the intellectuals. People betrayed each other here. It wasn't a hard Communism like in Czechoslovakia or Romania. Here, because of the crushing of the revolution, people went to prison as heroes, but when they came out in 1961 or '62, their health broken, their friends and neighbours would cross to the other side of the street.'

Even for a young Hungarian like Ilés Herber, just 10 when the system collapsed, there is a strong residue of bitterness more deeply felt than any nostalgia the older generation might profess. 'Our family was very religious and they just weren't accepted by the Communists. They had built up a farm with buildings and fields and the Communists just took it over. They just brought a piece of paper and said, all this is ours. The Russians came and used this country. They just stripped the wealth out of it. A lot of old people say it was better, they could get bread for two forints, they always had enough money to eat and get clothes and go to the cinema, but it was just a lie. That's why it failed. Nobody under Communism worked properly. Everyone stole from the factories, but the companies never even missed anything. People had to steal because they had no money. They would steal wheels from a car factory and sell them to someone else.'

But there are good reasons for public cynicism surviving. In September 2006, the prime minister, Ferenc Gyurcsány, told a closed meeting of his Hungarian Socialist Party that the government had been lying about the economy for a year and a half. A tape recording was made public and rioting erupted on the streets. Thousands bayed for his resignation. Most observers agreed that the leaked tape would be a resigning matter in any other country (with the exception of Italy, perhaps), but Gyurcsány brazened it out, even boasting that he was the only politician with the balls to admit he'd been lying. (He did resign in the teeth of the global financial crisis in 2009.)

Communism wasn't toppled in Hungary like it had been in Poland or Czechoslovakia; rather, it simply dissolved itself. In May 1990, the Socialists, the rebranded Communists, had won only 12 per cent of the vote, but by 1994 they were back in power alongside their one-time toughest critics, the former dissident Liberals. There was no naming or shaming of those who had collaborated, except for the leaking of names of those blackmailed into cooperating. 'The agents who ran the system and were acting as policemen have never been named and shamed,' one veteran observer told me. 'They swapped political power for economic power. They drew up legislation to ensure that they could get the farms, the construction projects, the buildings, the land. They knew when to buy and when to sell. People are not coming to terms with who they were. There's very little discussion about it. Everything has been swept under the carpet.'

It's not surprising, then, that Hungarians have become masters of the loophole, the *kis kapu* ('little gateway'), to help them navigate the snapping jaws of the tax system. Modern-day Hungary is bureaucratic and highly taxed. Everyone gets receipts for any kind of work done, since they can set up a company and claim the money against tax. People are known to get a receipt for two postage stamps at the post office if they posted the letters on their way to work.

On the other hand, some foreign entrepreneurs complain that Hungarians will look for the problem before the solution. 'When you get stuck into things, people are extremely engaged and creative,' one told me. 'But generally they like to think there's a difficulty first. People tend to focus on regulations and laws and convince themselves the laws tell you you can't do it, instead of using the regulations as a guide.'

When engaged in the parlous game of analysing stereotypes, the bottom line is that life in post-Communist Hungary is still hard. Salaries outside the capital are very low by Western standards. An OECD report in 2007 found that Hungary was still not getting to grips with bribery and corruption: of 23 recommendations to the government in fighting corruption, only eight had been carried out satisfactorily, while a further 15 were either only partially implemented or not at all. A further report in 2012 complained that the government was still not fully implementing anti-bribery laws.

Ilés Herber, our stag-weekend entrepreneur, has a straightforward explanation for Hungarian pessimism: 'It's because people are poor. They don't have any money and they don't have an idea that life will be better. They work for about one-tenth of what people earn in Western Europe. A teacher earns €500 here, but in Germany she can get €4,000 per month.'

* * *

The Hungarian word for 'fate' – *baslors* – also means 'misfortune'. In the Hungarian mindset, then, there's a fair chance your destiny will be a miserable one. 'To be Hungarian is to be dealt a real blow by life,' writes the critic Péter Pongrácz. 'It is misfortune itself; it is to be an outcast, persecuted, beaten, forced into migration … exist as a minority, live in penury or backwardness; it is to be orphaned, misunderstood in life.'

In a dilapidated equine enclosure next to Budapest's Eastern Railway Station, I've come to meet a middle-aged man who might have an insight into Hungarians and their sense of historical injustice. With thick eyebrows and wearing a sensible green jacket, he is politely applauding a medal ceremony for vaulting, a form of gymnastics on horseback which is big in Germany. Here in Hungary it's a minority sport, an irony the man acknowledges, given the country's long pedigree as a riding nation. 'The Communists drove the riding community back to the Stone Age. Anyone involved with horses was regarded as from the nobility, so they were forced into becoming taxi drivers or road sweepers,' he says. We watch the ceremony for a while; the brightly coloured youngsters come forward on cue to receive their medals, blushing to the strains of Abba's 'The Winner Takes It All'.

'They train for five to 10 hours a day, the good ones,' he continues, gazing fondly at his daughters, Hilda and Sophie, and son, Karl-Konstantin as they collect their medals. 'They get no support from the government. All the sponsorship money comes from US-Hungarians.'

He is well qualified to hold forth on Hungary's place in the world of horse-riding, or indeed the world of anything. His name is Georg, or in the Hungarian spelling, György.

His family name?

Habsburg.

I'm standing next to Archduke and Prince Imperial Georg of Austria, Prince Royal of Hungary and grandson to the last Habsburg emperor,

Charles I, who was effectively deposed when the empire collapsed in 1918. The blond children, with whom he banters in German, are still technically archdukes and archduchesses, and his wife, Eilika, fussing around with the other vaulting moms, is, to be precise, Duchess Eilika Helene Jutta Clementine of Oldenburg.

'Let's go somewhere for lunch,' he says briskly and cheerfully, evidently keen to escape from parenting for a little while. The would-be pretender to the imperial throne – after his brother Karl – is delighted to have just learned that an equestrian event three hours' drive away has been cancelled, and so instead his Audi A4 is taking me to Gundel, an award-winning restaurant next to Budapest Zoo.

A quick reminder of the Habsburg sceptre-print on European history: from its origins in the Swiss canton of Aargau in 1108, the Habsburg dynasty produced scores of counts, kings, consorts, emperors, dukes, princes and archdukes. Simply by marrying well and often (the dynastic motto is 'let others wage wars, but you, happy Austria, shall marry'), they created a global empire.

The dynasty survived the Black Death, the Renaissance, the Reformation, the Enlightenment, revolts and revolutions, and met its demise at the end of the Great War. Its conjugal web produced a handful of Holy Roman Emperors, dozens of German, Spanish, Austrian and Bohemian kings and queens, emperors of Mexico, grand-dukes of Tuscany, queens consort of Portugal and an empress consort of France. There were Margraves of Moravia and Kings of Jerusalem. They ruled and were ruled, possessed and dispossessed, they were murdered by sons, wives, husbands, daughters, enemies, carried off by suicide, regicide and fratricide. Despite a preference for marriage over war, the bloodline fought in – and sometimes started – most of the major European conflicts, winning and losing battles, or negotiating, suing or marrying their way out of trouble.

Frequent intermarriage gave rise to a genetic quirk known as the Habsburg Lip – a pathologic mandibular prognathism, to be precise – where the lower jaw outgrows the upper one. The condition, and not just her imminent appointment, explains Marie Antoinette's demeanour on her way to the guillotine. It also prevented Charles II of Spain from chewing properly.

The family tree, meanwhile, vibrates with names like Joanna the Mad, Philippe the Fair, Guntram the Rich, Otto the Jolly and Rudolphe the Founder. As we enter the restaurant to the beaming smiles – dare I say *curtseys*? – of the staff, it's clear that Georg is buying lunch, so to my mind he'll be called Georg the Decent. 'Try the spinach with goulash,' he says, 'it's really wonderful here.'

By rights, Georg shouldn't really be in Hungary. He was born in Germany in 1964, the son of Otto von Habsburg, who himself was born Archduke Franz Joseph Otto Robert Maria Anton Karl Max Heinrich Sixtus Xaver Felix Renatus Ludwig Gaetan Pius Ignatius of Austria. With the defeat of the Empire, Otto was taken into exile by his father, first to Switzerland and then to the Portuguese island of Madeira. 'Everything was stolen from us,' says Georg. 'We were expelled and our possessions expropriated. Still today in the Austrian constitution there is the Habsburg Law (*Habsburger-Gesetz*) in which all assets were taken. We were forbidden to return and no member of the family was allowed to become president. So I'm precluded from office by birth! Not that we have any big intention of running for president. But if you forbade gypsies from going into politics, the EU would be down on you like a ton of bricks.'

Otto, Georg's father, died on 4 July 2011, at the royally ripe age of 98. In the 1930s he assumed the role of an Austrian patriot, opposing Hitler's annexation and earning himself a death penalty *in absentia*. He spent the war years in Washington, moving back to Europe when the war ended, ending up in a Basque monastery. He was eventually allowed to return to Vienna in 1961 after renouncing all claims to the Austrian throne, later spending two terms as a member of the European Parliament. In 1988, at the age of 76, he was alleged to have punched the Revd Ian Paisley when he held up a banner denouncing John Paul II as the Antichrist during the Pope's visit to the parliament. Paisley later told the Free Presbyterian Church website, 'The Hapsburgs are still lusting for Protestant blood. They are still the same as they were in the days of Luther.'

It was three years after the collapse of the Communist regime that Otto's son Georg returned to Budapest as a 28-year-old. He claims he came to study the language, but he also has substantial business interests. Today, he owns a farm in the village of Sóskút in Pest County, a couple of hours' drive from Budapest, where he lives with Duchess Eilika, the three children, 22 horses and nine ponies. He is president of the Hungarian Red Cross, Hungarian Ambassador at Large and Knight of the Order of the Golden Fleece.

How does he feel about his adoptive country, one his grandparents lorded over?

'Hungary has always been undefendable. Everyone who came here wanted a piece of it: Tatars, Huns, Turks, Russians. But if someone learned the language, they were accepted. It wasn't a question of blood. It's a big melting pot. So I'm respected here.'

Like most Hungarians, Georg shares the pain of Trianon. But he sees EU membership as an extraordinary balm for the wounds. 'Trianon was something horrible for Hungarians. But with the disappearance of borders when we joined the EU, and the Schengen Agreement, it has been an incredible step.'

The Habsburg empire is really a long time ago. We tend to see the modern history of Europe as beginning with the end of World War II, and how that led to the reconciliation that built the EU. But the impact of 800 years of an empire still resonates today through how the Austrians, the Czechs, the Hungarians, the Slovenians and the Germans all subconsciously view each other. The empire's great fear was being overrun by the Turks; today, Austria is, not surprisingly, the member state most implacably opposed to Turkish membership of the EU.

So how, I ask Georg, does it feel to be a Habsburg today?

'When you're in power for 800 years, there are so many different opinions about your family. But by the time you really get to work with history, black and white no longer exist. It's grey. I accept very much the big mistakes my family made. We should have reacted earlier to give Hungary independence. And after the revolution [of 1848–49], we shouldn't have hanged the leaders. That was humiliating people.'

It seems strange to sit here in 2008, in the European capital of stag parties and porn, to listen to a Habsburg voicing regret at his family's decision to hang revolutionaries way back in 1848, with the same tone as if he were regretting the selling off of a beloved piece of land. But Georg seems sincere.

'It's still a national day here. We should have thought more about that.'

But he's not ready to disown the empire. 'It was an incredible development. Think of the cultural diversity of the empire! The infrastructure ... Most people spoke three languages. Think how incredibly rich Vienna was! If you went to the biggest cities of the Austro-Hungarian Empire, there were Slavs, Germans, Hungarians. It was a working United Nations. When you have supranational institutions, you can solve problems between countries. So the monarch could solve problems which might have become wars, but they didn't because the empire was there!'

Just then, a strange thing happens. Something splashes into Georg's double espresso. His free-flowing paean to empire is stopped in its tracks. I look up and see a sparrow sitting on a branch above our table. 'I think a bird just ...' I begin, wondering if I should use profanity before royalty.

Had a bird shat into a Habsburgian goblet of mead, back through the mists of time, such a runic occurrence would surely have prompted an attack on the Turks, a peace treaty with Genoa or a quick crusade. But in our zoo-side restaurant, the sky doesn't darken and the earth is not split asunder.

'Never mind,' sighs Georg, moving the compromised double espresso to one side. 'Let's get the bill.'

Chapter 9

Czech Republic

No country gets everything. The Czech republic has the best beer in the world and the most beautiful women. That's not bad going.
Frank Kuznik, editor, *The Prague Post*

The 13:24 Prague to Nuremburg train lurches out from Praha-Smíchov Station in a graffiti-embroidered suburb of the Czech capital. Weeds colonise the railway tracks and sidings under a sky thick with impending rain. Despite the rather grim vista, I have happy memories of Smíchov. Not the suburb but the beer. Two years after the Velvet Revolution drew the Czechs out of the Soviet embrace, I went on a week of beer drinking with a friend. It was January. Snow was swirling around Prague's cobbled streets, freezing the Baroque architecture into stark melodrama; in the cosy, unadorned cellar pubs, Smíchov was the golden, frothy beer being drained in steady quantities by locals, and the new tourists.

It was before the stampede of stag parties. Through a haze of 25 cent beer and beautiful but unapproachable women, we prided ourselves on our (dubious) pioneering spirit. Ensconced at enormous oak tables, waiters brought us jugs of Smíchov, appearing with fresh supplies the moment the glass appeared empty. Smíchov was the only beer, and goulash the only food, and in our drunken delerium, we probably felt we'd discovered some elemental simplicity the West had abandoned. Years later, on the night before the enlargement of the EU, I excitedly brought some colleagues from Swedish television to U Vejvodu – one of our favourites from that first visit. The pub was unrecognisable: it had been enlarged and souped up, a battery of sports screens glowering over large Euro-American groups of tourists. Gone was the Smíchov and goulash; in their place were oversized laminated menus serving tex mex, pizza and pasta.

Now I'm back to explore Czechs and their love affair with beer. First the facts: each Czech citizen drinks on average 161 litres of beer every year. When you take away the very old, babies and teetotallers, that's a lot of beer per drinker, as Terje B. Englund points out in *The Czechs in a Nutshell.* It certainly is, and it makes them the biggest beer consumers on the planet. 'It's more common than water and it actually gets about as much respect,' says Evan Rail, author of *The Good Beer Guide to the Czech Republic.* 'If they could install a beer tap at home they would.'

It began in 1088 when the Vyšehrad Collegiate Church in Prague assigned a 'tithe of hops' to parishioners, permitting them to brew alcohol. Monks pioneered the tradition over the next centuries, but soon the residents of the new towns being built by German colonisers were extended the right to brew their own. As the practice spread, though, quality suffered; as a result the towns were given proper brewers to teach the locals how it should be done. Thus was born the modern brewery.

Czech beer production steadily increased over the ages, but it was during the great industrial strides of the 19th century that it boomed. The Czech lands were the brewing powerhouse of the Austro-Hungarian Empire. Of the 1,050 breweries scattered throughout the entire empire, 666 were in Bohemia. But it was the arrival of a German, Josef Groll, headhunted from Bavaria to the town of Plzň (in German, Pilsen) in western Bohemia in 1842, that gave production a radical new direction. Things hadn't been going well at the plant: so much had quality declined that angry locals poured 36 barrels of beer out in front of the town hall. Groll's response was to introduce a new brewing method. The results would change the taste and look of beer forever, and put Plzň on the world map.

Until then, brewers had used top fermentation: the yeast went to work at the top of the beer and at higher temperatures. Groll's innovative lower fermentation method meant the yeast was placed at the bottom and worked its way up, creating a frothy head in the process. Fermentation was slower, but more manageable. It was a stunning success. The new beer had a sparkling, golden complexion and the taste of hops moved centre palate. But it was the fuzzy head that gave Plzň an eponymous presence the world over. That's where I'm headed right now.

The train clatters west, wending through thickly wooded countryside, now and again hugging the Vltava River. By 14:50, a plateau of housing blocks hoves into view, then an angular cluster of industrial buildings clutching at a towering red and white smoke stack. The symbols of a Communist past linger defiantly.

The railway station in Plzň is a huge, flaking Sphinx of faded empire. On the higher reaches of the lobby are friezes showing waistcoated factory and farm workers, all forearms and grim faced, with their frowning families and colleagues. There is still a Communist-era feel to the station. A formidable-looking woman behind a glass hatch demands money to use the toilets: a *piosár* costs 5 Czech crowns, or a *kabina* 8 crowns (the price includes individual sheets of toilet paper torn off muscularly by the attendant. I'm later told by more than one local that this is because Czechs will steal anything not nailed down).

The sandstone gates of the Pilsner Urquell Brewery are a short taxi ride away. Today it's owned by the huge South African-American concern SABMiller, one of the six largest brewing groups in the world. Like crocodiles in a pond, the big breweries have been eating each other and everything else in sight. SABMiller now produces Italian beers Peroni and Nastro Azzurro, the Polish favourites Tyskie and Lech, the Romanian beer Ursus, the Hungarian Dreher and the Dutch beer Grolsch.

I'm met by Jiří Mareček, a young Czech who, peering out from under a mop of thick hair, looks like Roger Federer after 10 rounds in the ring. 'Welcome to the World Capital of Beer!' he beams. We're joined by Tereza Zárazová (VIP Services Coordinator, Corporate Affairs). Corporate seduction suitably under way, the tour of the brewery begins.

Plzň is a state-of-the-art campus with the old-world apparatus of beer-making preserved – or fabricated – where appropriate. Like any product whose appeal leans on its historic lineage, a time-honoured authenticity is constantly broadcast. As much a tourist attraction as a production plant, it draws 182,000 visitors annually, including a growing number from Russia and China. But it's also an important production line for SABMiller: every second beer drunk in the Czech Republic – the biggest beer-drinking country in the world – comes from this plant, so it's no surprise SABMiller has been investing heavily. One of two noisy new bottling plants is where 120,000 bottles and cans are washed and filled per hour. The alarming din of upright ranks, shunted and nudged at high speed along the conveyor belts snaking below our walkway, sounds something akin to panic. To Jiří, it sounds like profit. This new hall, with its filtration lines using the latest German technology, ensures, he says, that Pilsner beer will have the same taste abroad as it does in the Czech Republic.

But my hosts are keen to get away from the mass-produced clamour and over to the restored brew house. Here I'm bombarded with a Heaney-esque blend of brewing nomenclature: mash tuns and wort kettles; lauter tuns and mash kettles; pre-mashing and mashing-in. There is copper and steel, 600°C temperatures and natural gas. The entire mashing, grounding, heating and what-have-you process is repeated three times to create the humbly monikered 'unhopped wort', which, in case you didn't know, helps caramelise the dissolved malt matter into malt sugar. In the world of beer-makers, this is key.

After all the mashing and wort and tuns, I need a drink. But they haven't told me about the yeast yet. Or the hops. 'The Žatec,' says Tereza, her cheeks glowing with pride, 'are Saaz semi-early red-bine hops.' Grown in northern Bohemia, these are the alpha males of the hop world. They're added to a wort kettle (via a lauter tun, of course), mixed in with all the earlier mashed stuff and boiled for 90 minutes. What's left is called wort, and when it runs into a cooler, it is free of the Saaz. Over a 12-day period, the added yeast is saturated with sugar, creating (at last) alcohol.

'The thing about this method,' interrupts Jiří, 'is drinkability.' Before I suggest that drinkability is a rather obvious ambition, he explains that it's the biological element that encourages, no less, binge drinking. 'It can make you drink five or six beers because it makes you feel thirsty, so you take another sip!' So now we know: binge drinking is a chemically induced plot by the brewing behemoths. Compensation lawyers across the land, take note.

We head underground into nine kilometres of hand-hewn cellars, where the temperature drops to –1.5°C and the air is as cold and moist as a peat bog on a January dawn. Here one billion hectolitres of beer is matured in 6,000 oak barrels for 30 days, each hermetically sealed with burned sap.

Now it's time. With a solemn nod from Jiří, a cooper produces three glasses and, bent over the tap, fills them from the barrel. We gaze as the liquid climbs up the glass. When it's time to drink I realise I've never drunk beer as fresh as this before. It's cold, amber and very delicious. Jiří, who is exquisitely correct about the drinkability factor, is reflective. 'Beer is psychotherapy for the Czechs. In the US they have shrinks, but here we just have beer. And it's just as good.'

The Czech relationship with beer is at once iconic and matter-of-fact. Walk around a railway station in the morning and you'll see locals drinking beer the way other decent Europeans would drink coffee. You'll see labourers on the cobblestones at the side of the road drinking beer at 8 a.m. with a roll and some cheese. 'The reason they achieve such high levels of consumption,' says our beer expert, Evan Rail, 'is that they are consistent drinkers, but not excessive. They don't binge. They have one bottle at lunch and one bottle at dinner. *Every single day.* And even if the husband and wife share the bottle at the table it still leaves them on track for the 160 litres of beer a year target.'

A survey in August 2007 found that 99 per cent of Czechs consider beer a natural part of the culture. Eighty-five per cent regarded it as one of the country's 'everlasting values', and 68 per cent something they could be proud of. According to Englund in *The Czechs in a Nutshell*, locals treat it like a soft drink. 'A doctor, whom [I] once visited, claimed in *dead earnestness* that fewer than four pints of beer does not count as alcohol.'

The climate, especially in Bohemia, is kind to the grain (in Moravia, they produce wine). In the 19th century, brewers became proper businessmen and beer part of an emerging Czech national identity. In 1850, the Big Five – Prazdroj and Gambrinus in Plzň, Staropramen in Prague, Budvar in České Budějovice and the Velké Popovice brewery in central Bohemia – were all mashing and worting furiously, and by the 1920s, when Czechoslovakia proclaimed the First Republic (a rare democracy surrounded by totalitarianism), beer exports roared ahead.

During the Communist era breweries were nationalised and quality slumped. Even in the dying days of the regime, shoppers would turn the bottles upside down on shelves to check for nasty deposits. But the dictatorship knew how to keep the masses happy: a night of beer at a local *hospoda* (beer house) was enough to make them forget the grim privations of socialism. Czechs will remind you that any attempt to put up the price would have triggered a revolution long before the Velvet one in 1989. Even today, beer prices are significantly cheaper than in the rest of Europe.

The *hospoda* remains a distinctly male dominion. Czechs gather to drink large quantities of beer there, all the while, as Englund points out, 'intensely complaining about your hysterical wife, greedy mistress, imbecilic boss, incompetent government, unlucky football team or whatever. After three or four hours of thorough therapy, your soul will be filled with total relief.'

As a result Czechs have fewer psychiatrists – and more alcoholics – than neighbouring countries. In the *hospoda*, people from all social strata can meet, discussions are both free flowing and migratory, since most people – strangers and friends alike – share large tables. Since the Velvet Revolution, more women have been entering *hospodas*, but old habits die hard: some bars have been known, at least one day a the week, to have the waitresses serve topless.

Even though the number of pubs and restaurants rose by 75 per cent to 35,000 before and after EU accession, the average intake of beer has remained stable. Instead of increasing their consumption, drinkers are getting fussier: pubs have increased ventilation (Czechs are diehard pub smokers), while owners have put more emphasis on interior design and sanitation. 'Consumers are increasingly concerned with the conditions for beer drinking,' says Vaclav Berka, a senior brewmaster at the Plzň plant. 'In comparison with the situation not so long ago, when beer was mostly drunk in low-end pubs with cheap Formica-top tables, the current beer-drinking culture is slowly returning to the style and character of the 19th century.'

The flip side is abuse of the market by big brewers. In Prague, the pubs are dominated by Gambrinus or Staropramen, and there have been investigations into brewing cartels. There are whisper contracts, whereby a major brewery will provide beer mats, décor, lamps and frontages, in return for a guarantee that the pub will only use their beer. As a result, it's hard for tourists to get their hands on the plurality of brands the Czech

Republic now produces. Small independent brew-pubs and regional breweries have actually blossomed despite the domination of the brewing behemoths. At the end of the 1990s there were around 40 small operators, but within a decade that figure had doubled. 'These are producing some very fine beers,' says Rail.

But how passionate Czechs are about what makes good beer remains an open question. If Czechs regard it as intrinsic to their national identity, what, then, if the owners are Belgian or Dutch? What if the ingredients come from China, where much of the world's hop production is based? What happens if there's a bad harvest and the brewery has to buy malt from Bavaria or Poland? If Czech breweries like Pilsner Urquell set up production in Poland or Russia and send only Czech ingredients and a Czech brewmaster, does that still make it Czech beer?

'Czechs are funny people,' says Rail. 'It's very common for them to claim they are very knowledgeable about beer. They think, I'm a Czech, I'm from the country of beer, therefore I know about beer. But they rarely know anything about beer from beyond their borders, and they often don't know about production methods, or ingredients or taste differences.'

The most famous Czech beer is, of course, subject to endless bar-room arguments. Budweiser is the source of one of the most misunderstood brewing disputes. At issue is who should own the right to use the Budweiser name: the Czechs or the Americans. But there are actually *three* pretenders to the Budweiser throne.

Let's start with the best-known Czech variant: Budvar. It was a brewery established in the south-western town of České Budějovice in 1895 as part of a deliberate move by locals to have a brewery run by Czechs, and not German speakers. But it wasn't the first brewery in the town. An older one, Budweiser Bürgerbräu, had been founded in 1795 and was owned and run by German speakers. (Budweiser is simply the German word for a person from Budweis – the German name of the town. České Budějovice is the town's *Czech* name.)

Budweiser Bürgerbräu (ie. the 'German' product) began exporting to the US as early as the 1870s. It was in America in 1876, however, that the St Louis-based brewery, Anheuser-Busch, the third pretender, started using the Budweiser name.

To muddy the waters even further, the brewery run by Czech speakers, established in 1895, and calling itself Budvar, began exporting the beer using the adjective 'Budweiser' on its label. So now there were three companies all claiming the Budweiser name: the original German-speaking one, Anheuser-Busch and now Budvar. The first legal case in 1911 concluded by allowing Anheuser-Busch to use the term *Budweiser*, but only in North America. After World War I, the new republic of Czechoslovakia changed the name of Budweis and Pilsen into the Czech language, and, after World War II, the German speakers were mostly expelled from České Budějovice. But the legal battles haven't finished there: after the fall of the Iron Curtain, both Budvar (still state-owned since it was nationalised by the Communists) and Budweiser Bürgerbräu (still hanging on even though the German speakers have gone) fought to get exclusive rights to use the name Budweiser. Lawsuits have broken out in about 70 countries.

'The original brewery, Budweiser Bürgerbräu, has probably the greatest rights to use the name since it has the geographical and chronological claim since 1795,' concludes Evan Rail. 'Anheuser-Busch has a greater chronological claim than Budvar Budweiser since it was using the name long before, but Budvar Budweiser has a stronger geographical claim. But they are really "frenemies". They've been fighting each other for years, yet since 2007 Anheuser-Busch has the distribution rights for Budvar Budweiser in North America, although they insist that it's labelled Czechvar.' Czechvar is even listed in Anheuser-Busch's product line.

Budvar Budweiser, meanwhile, set up a UK subsidiary in 2002 and has enjoyed a dramatic rise in sales, even sponsoring the Scottish Premier League team Falkirk FC. The irony, though, is that Budvar was originally set up with a Czech nationalist agenda, and yet it has fought Anheuser-Busch all the way just so it could use the *German* word 'Budweiser'.

But globalisation continues to challenge old notions of authenticity. In the 1990s, many old Czech breweries were bought up and shut down. The Dutch brewing giant Heineken now owns one-third of the Czech beer market: Krušovice, Starobrno, Louny, Zlatopramen and Březňák. InBev, the huge Brazilian-Belgian conglomerate, owns Staropramen, Braník and Ostravar. SABMiller owns the Pilsner Urquell Group, which in turn comprises several breweries: Gambrinus (also made in Plzň but in a separate brewery), Kozel and Radegast. Gambrinus is the bestselling beer in the Czech Republic, but the best-loved is Pilsner Urquell. Czechs will drink Gambrinus every day, but over Christmas dinner they'll have Pilsner Urquell.

But the sense of entitlement that beer is accorded is illustrated by a tale from the town of Mladá Boleslav. When the mayor of the town clamped down on beer drinkers who were sullying the image of the parks and public spaces, the drinkers duly produced the Charter of Basic Rights and Liberties as adopted by the Czechoslovak Parliament in 1991. They argued that beer drinking in the park was a human right. The mayor, a true democrat, agreed and backed down.

* * *

But breaking free from the Communist yoke in how you deal with social problems (i.e. drinking) – or medical problems (i.e. drinking) – has posed a dilemma for policy-makers. Prague has its own problems with outdoor drinking, and it's not necessarily beer drinking.

Along a leafy street, and pointedly set apart from the sprawling Bulovka hospital complex overlooking the capital, you will find Clinic 19. Its gable wall as you approach is windowless and freshly plastered, yet its anonymity is initially puzzling: the Czechs are actually fond of doctors and hospitals, making more visits than any country in the world (in 2008 the government tried to force the public to pay 30 kč per visit (around €10) in order to raise badly needed cash, but also to discourage non-essential visits. There was uproar, not just from patients, but from doctors who reasoned that it would be demeaning for them to receive money from patients).

The patients of Clinic 19 are regulars and would enthusiastically agree with the doctors. They are also intimately known to the police. Alcohol is the reason they are here. Alcohol, that is, and window cleaner.

'They buy those cartons of cheap wine – a litre costs around 8 kč [€3.50],' says Dr Vlastimil Chromcak, the director of Clinic 19. 'Then they add a window-cleaning product to strengthen it. That can get the alcohol content up to 30 per cent.'

Dr Chromcak has been in charge for three months. He's actually a paediatrician by trade, but was drafted in to run Prague's main drying-out centre because the previous staff were dismissed following a theft scandal (an undercover TV reporter, posing as a drunk, had filmed the staff stealing cash from the drunks they were supposed to be treating). 'As a paediatric surgeon, I thought I'd seen everything,' says Dr Chromcak, a thickset man in his fifties with deep smudges of fatigue under his eyes, and a voice slurred by exhaustion. 'But when I came here … how wrong I was.'

Czechs may drink more beer than anyone else in the world, but the national pastime is a world away from Clinic 19. The kind of drinking that delivers 'clients' into the dark stairwells and Spartan rooms of the clinic is pathological. They are increasingly young Ukrainian males who've come across the border through Slovakia. As we talk in the shadows, another client is brought in, helped on his feet by two policemen before he slumps onto a tiled seat in a triangular recess in one of the reception rooms.

Dr Chromcak has a look and laughs bitterly. 'We see him every day, or every second day.'

While the building and medical facilities are lent on a grace-and-favour basis by the hospital, responsibility for Prague's drunks falls upon City Hall. But funding is low on the priority list of public expenditure. Technically the issue is regarded as one of public order and self-protection (drunks should be a danger neither to the public nor themselves). But beyond that a long-term strategy seems absent. Police trawl the parks and shadows where alcoholics congregate, round up the usual suspects and bring them to the 15 beds of Clinic 19.

'During the years of Communism we could forcibly treat people against their will. We could get them into counselling and therapy even if they didn't want it. But now, since democracy has arrived, you can't force people to do anything. We offer the clients treatment, but they never take it. Ever. So they dry out here, then usually after 24 hours or so, they're free to go. But they just turn up again a few days later,' says Dr Chromcak.

The therapy applied during Communism involved giving the patient a shot of hard liquor, around 40 per cent proof, then injecting him with a dose of apomorphine to induce vomiting. A negative association would result, and the treatment would continue along those lines. (As Dr Chromcak explains this, I'm wondering whether or not, in my own culture, vomiting up alcohol ever created such a negative association that people actually *stopped* drinking. I'm not so sure.)

Today the options are limited. Even if friends and relatives recommend enforced treatment, the client has a constitutional right to decline it. Yet the level of critical inebriation seems to be getting worse. More and more men are leaving the countryside for the city, with its fatal charms of anonymity and escape. When things don't work out, finding window cleaner is easy. Some clients (the term becomes progressively surreal) come in suffering from alcoholic epilepsy. 'Instead of the brain seeking glucose in order to function properly, eventually the brain requires alcohol. So a form of epilepsy is triggered, and the only way to stop the fit is by a shot of pure alcohol. But we can't do that here so they must find it outside.'

But that isn't difficult. Dr Chromcak describes the luridly comic ritual once the clients are released from Clinic 19. 'Friends and relatives of the staff here have given us second-hand clothes because when the drunks arrive, most of them have soiled themselves. So we shower them down, put them in a room with a medical gown, and the next day they leave. But under law we have to give them back their clothes, which are in a yellow plastic bag. They leave here and go straight to a drinks stand just outside the hospital. There are no chairs there, so it's known around here as The Varicose Vein. They go straight there and get their first shot. Meanwhile the yellow plastic bags, containing their soiled clothes, are dumped behind the bar. Eventually the gardener comes along and has to dispose of them. The drunks then disappear and come back in a day later.'

It's the window cleaner which, though, does serious damage. 'It's really nasty,' says Dr Chromcak, wincing. 'When that stuff is synthesised in the body, the smell is really strong. It just seeps through the entire system. It leads quickly to cirrhosis of the liver. It's very dangerous. Eventually the liver will fail completely.'

The doctor takes me on a tour. Upstairs are rooms for rowdy drunks, but they're more like cells in a psychiatric ward: two beds and a sink and that's it, except that in some of the rooms the beds have leather straps and buckles at ankle and chest level. As we pass one room, arguing breaks out between the orderlies and a drunk in his late thirties. It's not long before the orderlies are strapping the drunk firmly to the bed, face down. Dr

Chromcak shakes his head wearily. 'I didn't think he deserved that,' he sighs, but he does nothing to prevent it. 'Aggressive ones are brought in once in awhile. The regulars are usually quite well behaved.'

At the end of the corridor there is a larger room with two beds. 'This is especially for women.' On the furthest bed, a woman with bleached and bushy hair reclines painfully, turning her head half in our direction. She mumbles something. Dr Chromcak replies gently.

We move on as twilight falls. 'Now,' he says, his face melting into the kind of grin of someone saving the best, or worst, for last, 'I want to show you a special room.'

This special room is in the basement. It has the same austere décor, but here life-support equipment garlands the empty beds. 'This is where we bring patients who are in a serious condition. It's often not the regulars, but people who have, perhaps due to some personal tragedy, really gone overboard with alcohol.' But some of the regulars do end up here. Dr Chromcak describes the practice where they go to Tesco, take a bottle of rum off the shelf, find the spot obscured from the security cameras, drink the entire bottle, and leave it, empty, back on the shelf. 'They walk out on the street, but the heat and alcohol suddenly hit them hard and they collapse.

'They come in here and sometimes we have to connect them to the life-support machine because they might have organ failure,' he continues.

'How many die in here?' I'm almost afraid to ask.

'Two or three,' he replies.

'Two or three per month?'

'Per week.'

'Per *week*?'

'Yes, two or three a week.'

* * *

It's not often you hear much nostalgia for the Communists, but Dr Chromcak's preference for the enforcement methods of old is the product of sheer desperation at the impossibility of weaning hard-core patients off window cleaner. No doubt drying-out clinics the world over will complain about low prioritising by the health service, but perhaps there is something in the Czech reputation for national self-loathing that makes the problem that bit more acute.

Perhaps national self-loathing isn't the right term. It's more like the low opinion Czechs have traditionally had of each other as *individuals*, as opposed to the rather elevated opinion they have of the Czech people as a *nation*. Having met both ends of the Czech drinking spectrum, Jiří Mareček at the Pilsner Urquell Brewery at one end, and world-weary Dr Chromcak at the other, it is time to take a closer look at how the Czechs regard themselves, how they regard their neighbours and how everyone else regards the Czechs.

* * *

I meet the Czech émigré writer Benjamin Kuras, author of *Czechs and Balances*, in the U Dvou Koček pub on Uhelny Trh Square in Prague's Old Town. The capital's cultural history is closing in on all sides. To our left, a building where Mozart once lived, to our right, Charles University, the first in Central Europe, built in 1348. Diagonally opposite is the Estate Theatre, where Mozart directed and premiered the opera *Don Giovanni*, while a street away is Wenceslas Square, synonymous with the Velvet Revolution.

Kuras left Prague a few months after an earlier (failed) revolt: the Prague Spring of 1968. That was when Communist Party General Secretary Alexander Dubček tried to introduce reforms and freedoms in order to give socialism a 'human face'. His movement, which most Czechs supported, was crushed by Soviet tanks and Warsaw Pact troops from Poland, East Germany and Hungary. Kuras moved to London, where he began broadcasting what he describes as anti-Soviet propaganda from the BBC's Central European service.

In his droll, irreverent book, Kuras sees Czechs as an unpredictable bunch who put the perpetual quest for comfort ahead of virtues like heroism and bravery, who pick the wrong leaders, but who ultimately use patience to wait out all the foreigners – Germans, Austrians, Communists – who have sought to rule over them. We begin with the 6th century mythical figure of Lech, the original Czech chieftain, who wandered in from the east and settled on the central Bohemian mountain of Říp. A

Slav, he raised a pastoral, peace-loving, cattle-herding, song-singing tribe that multiplied into the Czech nation. 'The Czechs see themselves – and want to be seen – as tillers, not conquerors. Craftsmen, not warriors. Lovers, not rapists. Lyricists, not dramatists. Stand-up comics, not run-around tragedians,' he writes.

The Czechs soon acquired a chunk of the Moravian empire to the east after it was cut off by Hungarians, and parts of Poland. Along the way there are dynasties, internecine feuds, matricides, fratricides, intrigues and expansions until the arrival, in 920, of good King Wenceslas. He was an uncommonly educated and benign ruler who was, however, murdered by his brother. Wenceslas was later canonised and became one of a number of symbols of Czech statehood and survival, lending his name to the square that became the focal point of the protests in 1989. After his death, Czech lands entered a period of decline as Hungary and Poland expanded. By time the Holy Roman Empire stretched its influence over Bohemia and Moravia, Czech rulers needed the emperor's support to stay in power. The relationship between the two sides was both harmonious and turbulent, but the German influence was steadily advancing. By the 13th century, German colonists were transforming the marshes and forests, bringing in economic advancement and a new legal system. The Germanisation of these areas, which started so long ago, would blow up in Europe's face in 1938.

By the mid-14th century, however, Czech esteem was on the rise. Charles IV was crowned head of the Holy Roman Empire in 1355, so a Czech was now theoretically the secular head of Western Christendom. He ushered in a golden age, revamping Prague, building Gothic churches and restoring the city's old castle. He established Central Europe's first university and built the famous stone bridge which today bears his name and probably a million tourists each year (it's the statue-encrusted centrepiece of the route between the Old Town and Prague Castle). The city became a capital of learning and liberal thought. By the time Charles died in 1379, Prague had become one of the most prestigious cities, and Bohemia one of the most powerful provinces, in all of Europe.

But with his demise came a reversal of fortune: the Black Death swept away up to 15 per cent of the population and Charles's son and successor fell foul of the nobility. Into the vacuum stepped an unlikely figure in a priest's garb, who was to change the face of European politics and become the consummate tragic hero of Czech aspirations. Jan Hus was a preacher from southern Bohemia (his surname means 'goose') who rose through the ranks of the Church to become a preacher in Prague's Old Town. From his pulpit he railed against Church corruption, blaming clerical excesses and the selling of indulgences for the moral decline in which Czechs found themselves. The Hussite message, thundered out long before Martin Luther arrived on the scene, soon caught the popular and royal imagination. The king appointed him rector of Charles University.

But the Pope and the majority of the Catholic clergy were less impressed. German speakers, too, detected a Czech nationalist edge to his fulminations. Buoyed by his success and royal acclaim, though, Hus continued his rhetorical crusade, embarking on a mission to the Church Council in the city of Constance, where he hoped to convert a group of reform-minded clerics to the cause. It was a bad move. He was arrested as a heretic and burned at the stake in July 1415. The story didn't end there, though: Hussites were soon on the rampage, repelling crusades sent against them by the Pope, and proclaiming Hus's four principles, including the separation of Church and state. They mythologised him into a Christ-like figure, executed on false charges after throwing over the tables of the corrupt establishment. To future generations of Czechs he was an iconic hero defending truth to the death. Both the founder of the liberal First Republic between the wars, Tomáš G. Masaryk, and the leader of the Velvet Revolution, Václav Havel, deliberately adopted his slogan, '*Veritas Vincit*' (truth prevails). When the dissident student Jan Palach set fire to himself in public during the Prague Spring, supporters knew his gruesome choice of suicide was no coincidence.

The trouble was, Hus became a champion for just about everyone. Both Benito Mussolini and the Czech Communist Party, of all people, adopted him as a hero. The Communists used the Hussite shield, with the lion of the Bohemian kings adorned by the red star (it suited their ideological loathing of the Germans and the international 'imperialism' of NATO).

'Czechs pride themselves on being secular martyrs,' says Jiři Rak, a writer on Czech myths and lecturer at the Institute of International Studies in Prague. 'Hus has become more of a national figure than a religious one. And it fed into the Czech dilemma. Are we Europeans, or an independent country with everyone against us?'

By the 15th century the Habsburgs took over and German speakers came to dominate. It was not until the 19th century that a Czech national revival began in earnest, and when it did it drew heavily on the Jan Hus myth. Some Czechs even regard his compromise treaty with the Pope, allowing a degree of religious tolerance, as a foretaste of the European Union, recommending as it did the use of treaties to maintain continental peace and order.

The trouble is that peace and order didn't last for too long. Strife between Catholic and Protestant nobles and pretenders in the 16th and 17th centuries violently determined who got their hands on the Czech throne. When a treaty between the Protestant Netherlands and Catholic Spain broke down, the Habsburgs decided to grab what they could and reassert Catholic dominance in Central Europe. The defenestration by Protestant nobles in 1618 of a group of imperial Catholic governors from a window high in Prague Castle was the excuse they needed to teach the Czechs a lesson. At the Battle of White Mountain, a small hill a few kilometres to the west of Prague, Catholic forces beat the 13,000-strong Czech army to a pulp, partly due to the fact that a large number of Czech troops were conforming to the beer-drinking stereotype and were, reportedly, too drunk to fight.

The result rearranged the religious order in Europe and was instrumental in triggering the Thirty Years War; a systematic and brutal re-Catholicisation of Bohemia and Moravia followed. Whole swathes of the Protestant nobility left their homeland. To Czechs, the heroism of Jan Hus was eclipsed by the disastrous Battle of White Mountain.

'Defeatism, lack of self-confidence, low self-esteem … flair for backstabbing and betrayal of one's own friends … the tendency to leave things unfinished and give up hope … desire to cocoon up and blot out unpleasant reality instead of facing it and changing it,' writes Benjamin Kuras in *Czechs and Balances*, 'in short this is the psychological pattern which has the power to turn Czechs into quitters before they can give themselves a chance to be losers.'

Such a national neurosis, it seems, has been confirmed by history: the betrayal of the Czechs by the West over the Munich Agreement in 1938, during which Hitler was handed the German-speaking Sudetenland; the coup that allowed the Communists to take power in 1948; the crushing of the Prague Spring in 1968.

But there is another Czech characteristic whose roots can be traced back to White Mountain. Because large sections of the nobility fled, the gap was filled by the middle and lower classes and the Czechs have congratulated themselves ever since on their special brand of egalitarianism. Some Czech historians see this as a continuing narrative running all the way to Czech Euroscepticism. For example, the national movement in the 19th century was more humanist and less religious than many others pitted against the Austro-Hungarian yoke. During Communist times, the private sector was more ruthlessly expunged than in other Soviet bloc countries; later, too, the Velvet Revolution was led by students and intellectuals, and not by a political elite. Today, as a further reminder of their intolerance of anyone getting above his station, Czechs are the least religious people in Europe.

In fact, White Mountain is regarded by some as the lightening rod for a recalcitrance against whatever the outside world expects of the Czechs. When the country joined the European Union in 2004, and while her prime minister was gathering with his 26 colleagues at Áras an Uachtaráin, the arch Eurosceptic president Václav Klaus called his supporters to the site of the Battle of White Mountain, declaiming that the Czech nation would survive and that her people would never let themselves be betrayed. Klaus has since become the *bête noire* of the EU for his anti-Brussels rhetoric, his claims that global warming is a left-wing plot, and his personal connection with Declan Ganley and the Libertas organisation. Some observers say this has more to do with Klaus's antipathy towards his erstwhile dissident rival Václav Havel than any true reflection of the Czech public's attitude to Europe. 'Surveys repeatedly show that the Czech people are in favour of EU membership,' says Jiří Pehe, from the New York University in Prague.

The sense of egalitarianism is, though, popularly expressed. People prefer the average, and tall poppies are cut to the ground. It's actually illegal to use a noble title like 'prince' before your name. In his book *The Little Czech and the Great Czech Nation,* Ladislav Holy writes that Czechs may have been the embodiment of ordinariness and common sense, but were guilty of envy and pettiness in their dealings with each other. It's said that when a Czech has a goat, his neighbour doesn't want one as well but wants his neighbour's goat to die. Take this from a political magazine in the early 1990s:

> A hero in Bohemia faces many more difficulties than anywhere else because he is confronted – sooner or later – with malicious petty-mindedness and envy… A proud, sincere and truthful person is a thorn in the side of the people of Bohemia, whether he is a politician, an entrepreneur or an artist. Since time immemorial, democracy with us has degenerated into a kind of egalitarianism which is intolerant of authority, rejects responsibility, dissolves everything with doubts and slander.

So when the Czechs stepped over the fallen Iron Curtain in 1989, they were astonished at the wealth of the West, and their envy led to a neurotic self-flagellation. Ladislav Holy wrote in 1996:

> Czechs themselves began to complain about the rudeness of waiters, officials, nurses, shop assistants and anyone else ostensibly employed to serve the public … In Czech political and social life this traditionally manifests itself as extraordinary discord, quarrelsomeness, and intolerance, selfish haggling, and all this even at times when it would be more useful to pull together in the same direction.

At the same time, Czechs, writes Holy, like to preen themselves over their cultural superiority, not as individuals, but as a *nation*. Where else had architecture, classical music and literature harmonised with such sparkling abundance as in Prague? Even this pride met with despair: 'We are wretched, unreliable, immoral, envious, vile, greedy, inept, full of complexes, resentful and full of the residues of totality … We compensate for feeling powerless and untalented with a ridiculously pompous and pretentious messianism.' (*Respekt* Magazine, 1990).

So Czechs are caught between their national glory and their individual shortcomings. 'The little Czech is an ambivalent character,' writes Holy. 'On the one hand he is seen as talented, skilful and ingenious; on the other as shunning high ideals and living his life within the small world of his home, devoting all his efforts to his own and his family's well-being.'

This ambivalence is reflected in a 1992 survey, wherein 76 per cent of the stereotypes Czechs ascribed to themselves were negative: envy (28 per cent), excessive conformism (15 per cent), cunning (15 per cent), egoism (11 per cent) and laziness (8 per cent), not to mention cowardice, quarrelsomeness, hypocrisy, haughtiness and devotion to sensual pleasure. Positive traits included hardworking (17 per cent), skilful (8 per cent) and a sense of humour (8 per cent). Who knows, maybe this explains the massive beer consumption.

But the character of the little Czech has been as much celebrated as loathed. He is immortalised in *The Good Soldier Švejk*, an unfinished satirical novel published in 1923 following the death of its author, Jaroslav Hašek. Švejk is a Czech private in the Austrian imperial army during World War I. Through his adventures, this boozing, cheating, immoral, fibbing anti-hero is either an imbecile or a genius, cleverly undermining the Austrian war effort and ridiculing the army. Švejk has become part of the Czech culture, regularly quoted in newspapers and pubs by beer-drinking aficionados.

'Czech self-stereotypes are often polarised,' the writer Jiří Rak says. 'In the middle of the 19th century Czechs saw themselves as a great nation which had become successful through culture, not conflict. In 1989 there was a turnaround. Everyone was saying Czechs were small minded, provincial, racist, Eurosceptic. It was a very simplified way of looking at oneself. All the positive superlatives of the 19th century were quickly replaced with negative superlatives without really analysing the reality. People were overly critical.'

Another ghost looming large in the complexities of the Czech self-image is the German. Germans were colonising large parts of the Czech lands ever since the 13th century (after the war, some 2.7 million Germans were expelled; 6,500 were murdered and some 20,000 are thought to have died of exhaustion during the forced expulsions).

'The true way to understand Czech stereotypes is to look at our relationship with the Germans,' continues Rak. 'Before 1989 they were all negative, but since 1989 more and more people have begun to talk about the expulsion of the Sudeten Germans, some admitting that on that occasion Czechs were the aggressors. Czechs historically saw themselves as oppressed by the Germans yet able to maintain their identity. It was a Slavic stronghold, resisting German influence and surrounded by German speakers. Germans saw this differently: they saw the Czechs as a Slavic wedge driven into the heart of the German-speaking lands.'

According to the writer Benjamin Kuras, the Czechs *are* losing their sense of envy, working hard and making money like the rest of Europe, *and* getting on better with the Germans.

'People are successful, hardworking entrepreneurs. They're workaholics who have made loads of money. There are now 35,000 Czech golfers out of only 50,000 altogether in Central Europe. We have 82 golf courses. The Czech currency is rising and they've gained a new confidence when they're abroad. There was an inferiority complex up until four or five years ago. Today Czechs have utter contempt for the Austrians. Austria used to be a country they looked up to, now they don't any more. Austrians have always behaved arrogantly towards the Czechs. They treated us like we were barbarians. The Czechs kind of took it, but not any more. They remember that during the Austro-Hungarian Empire the Czech lands contributed 60 per cent of the empire's GDP; we provided the energy, the cars, the manufacturing. Germans are actually behaving better: Austrian tourists or businessmen arrive expecting to be spoken to in German. Germans, on the other hand, realise that they should speak, not Czech, but English. When Volkswagen bought Škoda, they decided to make English, not German, the language of the company. Now Škoda is the most profitable part of the Volkswagen family.'

Kuras argues too that Czech males are learning to outgrow a rather unpleasant Czech stereotype: the wearing of socks and sandals. Perhaps as a combination of Communist drabness and Czech bloody-mindedness, the insistence on wearing socks and sandals has been defended by the Czech male for decades. Sandals are regarded as ordinary shoes that can be worn at any time, under any apparel, suit included, sometimes until Christmas.

'The Czechs have a new style and elegance they didn't have before,' says Kuras. 'Italians are very welcome. They have Czech girlfriends and wives, and they have learned Italian. They've bought a lot of real estate in the Old Town in Prague. As soon as the Iron Curtain came down they moved in right away, getting around the laws forbidding foreigners owning property by setting up Czech companies. They restored the façades and insides of the old buildings beautifully. Italians have never behaved in an insulting or superior way. You couldn't get decent coffee here until five years ago. Now it's the best place in Europe to get coffee.'

But I hear an alternative view from Frank Kuznik, the American editor of *The Prague Post*. 'I was astounded when I arrived here. I expected things to be Westernised. They were, but only on the surface. You'd never see a café like this one, there were no decent restaurants. The mindset was amazing. All the Communists had left, but everyone still had the *mentality*. People fight on trams and in queues. There are turf wars. I feel like telling some guy, hey, the bread will still be there when you get to the counter, you don't have to shove your way in.

'It's still about keeping your head low, not attracting attention, staying out of sight. We do a lot of reviews for plays and concerts, and any time you ring up the production company looking for a photo, the first question is: why? Well, because we're doing a preview. Why? Well, to give you free publicity. It's a real struggle! When you're in promotion or advertising in the West, it's the obvious way of doing business, but here it's still a real difficulty. If you tell them there's no need to do that, that they should adapt, that it's good for business, they'll say, I don't care.'

For Ian Willoughby, an Irish journalist who's lived in Prague for over 10 years, the Czechs are still enjoying the freedom from the collapse of Communism a little too much. 'There are all these ugly shop fronts, tacky, ugly as sin. I'm thinking, who allows this shit? But the answer is that people feel they have the right to put up what they want. They were under the kosh for so long, now they have freedom.

'The Czechs are very liberal. Infidelity is a national sport here. It's really happening everywhere, and really not frowned on. It's just such a regular part of life. Women don't like to be alone. They are willing to be with someone they're not crazy about until they meet the right person. They're not ruthless, but more practical and less romantic about it. Communism compounded it. You couldn't get a place to live or get a flat, you couldn't leave home unless you got married, and then there was nothing to do. People were getting married on average at 21. Ten years later, they're playing away from home because they got married too young. It's not often criticised. Anything goes here.'

The Communist period was traumatic for many Czechs, but their relationship with the era is complex. Czechs talk of a coup that brought the Communist Party to power in 1948, but in the elections two years previously the Communists got 38 per cent of the vote. After the Velvet Revolution, the authorities did take tougher action against those who collaborated with the regime than in some other former Soviet bloc states. In 1991, the lustration law was passed whereby anyone working in public administration had to apply to the new secret services for a certificate to prove they weren't collaborators. Anyone found to be positive was kicked out of the job as a moral, if not literal, punishment for their sins. But only 5 per cent of 400,000 certificates issued were incriminating for the simple reason that if you had collaborated, you wouldn't bother applying.

Yet there *were* many dissidents who were imprisoned, exiled or even executed (180 killed in total). Charter 77, the protest movement led by Václav Havel, was one of the most prominent in the Eastern bloc, and of the 1,900 who signed, most were singled out for repression. But 7,000 signed an *anti*-Charter document, including well-known writers, poets and singers. The reality seemed to be that many adapted and even grew comfortable with the system simply to survive. Even after the Prague Spring, when 50,000 alleged 'liberals' were kicked out of the party, a further 1.8 million were still members. For many foreign observers, and Czechs themselves, this is evidence that, compared to the Poles, who, in a vivid proverbial formulation were prepared to ride against German tanks on horseback, the Czechs preferred a *quiet* life.

'The Czechs' craving for comfort was best understood by the Communist regime,' writes Benjamin Kuras in *Czechs and Balances*. '[It] made life for them dull and idiotic, but compared with the rest of the Communist world, remarkably comfortable. There was hardly a family which had not built itself a second home in the country to escape every weekend – starting at midday on Friday and ending at midday on Monday morning.'

To Frank Kuznik, the legacy remains today. 'Many feel their lives were better under Communism. There were no choices to be made, there was no such thing as a career. Ambition barely exists here: you see it in Prague, but outside the city it drops off pretty quickly. Look at Slovakia: they're about to adopt the euro, but the Czechs keep changing the date and delaying.'

Perhaps it was a natural and very human way to deal with a pretty much unbreakable totalitarian system. The Czechs got on with life through a trade-off: if they kept quiet in return for a half-decent apartment and a Škoda, then the huge, absurd genie of Communism would remain inside the bottle. During the 1970s, in a crushingly dull period of 'normalisation' after the Prague Spring, thousands emigrated. Tennis star Martina Navratilova defected. In the meantime, the neo-Stalinist regime was perfecting another product for export, though one not quite as popular and well received as Ms Navratilova.

* * *

Dr Miroslav Štancl greets me in the lobby of a single-storey Communist-era factory. The cheap marble flooring is fading. Chrome and double glazing have been tacked on as a nod to capitalism, but the shabbiness hasn't quite been glossed over. At a glance, it's difficult to say what exactly goes on in the plant. Staff come and go wearing thick plastic clearance badges. A young couple in the corner on big soft sofa cushions pore over a brochure that might contain their dream home. On the walls are huge black and white prints of the old town of Pardubice about 5 kilometres away. Miroslav apologies for being late, with a boyish giggle. He has a full head of snowy white hair, a squarish face and a twinkle in his dark eyes. Wearing a grey polo shirt with thin vertical green and blue stripes and matching grey slacks, he looks like he's just come off the 18th green after a dreadful round, but, having just sunk a birdie putt, is deserving of a gin and tonic.

A clue to what Miroslav might be involved in can be found in the safety notice next to the receptionist. It reminds visitors that 'working with open fire or heated up materials needs a special permission' and, rather sternly, 'having drunk alcoholic beverages or used drugs you are not allowed to enter'. Should there be an accident, 'get treated yourself in the health centre'. Finally, 'the non keeping of this advices will be solve in the series of the SANCTION.'

It's hard to reconcile these peremptory commands with Miroslav's cheerful demeanour. But we are in the European Union and health and safety standards apply, especially since the company's most infamous brand has struck fear and loathing into Western governments and ordinary people, from Belfast to Lockerbie to Beirut.

For we are in the home of Semtex.

'Come, follow me!' says Miroslav, laughing at his heavily accented English.

We are led out to a parking area flanked by oddly Tudor-style buildings looking like they haven't seen paint since the 1930s. It is a rambling, wooded and weed-strewn campus. Dilapidated workshops here and there lend the appearance of a disused army camp. We're soon led up several flights of stairs to the company library. This is where the Semtex secrets are held, the ingredients and principles that make up its notorious power as the world's best-known plastic explosive.

Explosia was the joint-stock company set up by the Czech government in 1918 to ensure the newly independent republic was capable of defending itself. 'There was a sense that under the Austro-Hungarian Empire, we were protected. Now we were alone,' says Miroslav. 'There was nothing here, just fields. But there were good rail links to Prague and the local people were well educated.' The village outside the town of Pardubice which hosts the plant is called Semtín, hence the name Semtex.

Originally the company only made explosives. When it merged with the chemical company Synthesia it branched into fertilisers, medical supplies and plastics. During World War II, the plant was seized by the Nazis. 'They got some rich loot when they found it,' says Miroslav, almost sadly. Then, in a quaintly conspiratorial tone, he adds, 'It's quite possible they used the explosives to supply the German army!'

Once the Communists took power they set up the East Bohemia Chemical Works on the Explosia campus, in 1954 adding the research arm, of which Miroslav is now in charge. The regime wanted a world-renowned centre for explosives. A new university of chemicals was established nearby so that staff could slot straight into the company upon graduation. At one point Explosia employed 10,000 workers.

From a distance the Kremlin gazed fondly at its new acquisition. Czech and Soviet scientists worked together on joint projects with the Russians repatriating the expertise to the motherland. 'They could direct and dictate,' recalls Miroslav. 'They had the final word.' The dictat was that Czechoslovakia should produce plastic explosives for fellow Warsaw Pact members. Russia was producing its own, although it was based on research done in Semtín. Stanislav Brebera, Miroslav's predecessor, first tried producing a plastic explosive in 1964. Various versions were developed, differing in colour and punch. Then, in 1966, the order came from Prague to develop a special product for the North Vietnamese, one that would rival the American C4 explosive being used for mine clearing and boosting the punch of heavy artillery. Brebera came up with a result: a plastic explosive combining RDX (cyclonite) and PETN (penaerythrite) – in short, the nasty bits – which was similar to C4, but with a significant difference.

'Semtex had an added rubber binder called styrene-butadiene,' explains Miroslav. 'The explosive parameters were the same, but its plasticity was better. It was easier to work with and easier to shape.'

We're now in the realm where the technological anatomy of a subject is so banal that it creates distance from its ultimate reality.

Between 1967 and 1973, some 14 tonnes were shipped to Vietnam, but it was the safe, water-resistant, play-dough texture of Semtex that inspired terrorists over the subsequent three decades. A small amount of the stuff could do enormous damage. Because of its plasticity, it could be shaped to fit into any nook or cranny. Or cassette recorder. It was in such a device that 12 ounces of Semtex were believed to have been moulded by the terrorists who masterminded the Lockerbie bombing in December 1988 which killed 270 people on Pan Am Flight 103 and on the ground, making it Europe's worst-ever terrorist attack.

Stanislav Brebera, now in his eighties and living in Pardubice, was credited with perfecting Semtex, but his life story has two acts. Shortly after he sold his invention to the government for around €700, the country was gripped by the Prague Spring. Brebera supported the liberal reforms, paying the price by losing his top job at the laboratory. He settled into quiet obscurity with his wife on the fourth floor of a housing block in Pardubice. When Synthesia, the company that eventually owned Explosia, was nationalised by the newly independent government in the early '90s, he told the *Christian Science Monitor*: 'It makes me angry that Semtex fell into the wrong hands. Now the world blames my country and me, but I could not stop it. I know now that if you are going to invent, you run the risk that someone will use your creation for something you didn't intend.'

After crushing the popular revolt, Alexander Dubček was replaced by Gustáv Husák who, writes Benjamin Kuras, presided over 'the dullest, drabbest, most idiotic, most loyal and subdued regime in the Soviet bloc... The nation's skills and talents were used to make Czechoslovakia famous for three things: arms sales to every anti-democratic regime on the planet, training of terrorists, and Semtex.'

The Semtex brand went global. Libya imported more than any other country, 690 tons in all, officially to dynamite mountain passes in a road-building programme. In the Explosia research library, Miroslav Štancl is rather coy in explaining this one. 'There was one delivery sent to Libya for building activities,' he says. 'Officially.' He continues along this vein of breathtaking understatement: 'There was speculation that some was later sold to Ireland, where it was, em, abused.'

Miroslav claims that all of the exports of Semtex went through the state company Omnipol. 'There was never any conscious support given to organisations which could abuse explosives – even by a Communist regime.' There is a whiff of wounded innocence about the role of Semtex in Czechoslovakia's foreign policy in the 1970s. I'm sceptical, but Miroslav insists. However, in an interview given to the US National Public Radio in 2002, a former Czech intelligence officer, Olger Chacherney, was quoted as saying: 'This marvellous efficient policy, it was all part of one big Cold War game, with terrorists working for the Communists in a sort of proxy way.'

Semtex is fabled not just because of its flexibility, but also because it's undetectable. But this draws an irritated snort from Miroslav, who sits back on his chair and folds his arms. 'This is a myth which came from the early days when detection systems were not so evolved. The US [makers of C4] used acetone whose vapours are detectable and Semtex didn't use it, so, yes, in the early days it was harder to detect. But detection methods for plastic explosives evolved very quickly. Soon they were being marked with other elements: today you can detect Semtex that hasn't even been marked.'

Miroslav admits that in 1982, the government banned the export of Semtex to any country outside the Warsaw Pact 'partly because of the Irish issue'. Later the new government of Václav Havel was anxious to cleanse the country of its reputation, and it seems that the efforts were in good faith. Experts from Synthesia formed part of the technical committee that drew up the Montreal Convention, a legal instrument allowing security services to detect explosives more easily. From June 1991, Semtex – and all other plastic explosives produced by signatory countries – would contain four marking agents easily detectable by trained dogs, X-ray machines and vapour detectors. Explosia willingly allowed the amount of vapours within Semtex to be increased. Today all exports of Semtex (there are only around 10 tonnes a year) must be strictly licensed by the Ministry of Industry and Trade, although stories of theft still appear. 'Detection methods have really improved,' says Miroslav. 'Now there is a very high sensitivity for the detection of particles. Hand-held detectors can spot explosives and chemicals. The vapour method is easy. You just need to suck in the air that surrounds a shipping container to detect Semtex if, for example, it's being brought in to the US.'

But the rehabilitation of Semtex hasn't stopped there. After the Lockerbie bombing in 1988, Explosia assisted the investigation. According to every conclusion, as reported by the media, the plastic explosives placed in the Toshiba cassette recorder on Pan Am flight 103 was most likely Semtex. The men convicted of the bombing were, after all, members of Libyan intelligence. But even today, in a somewhat touching defence of the company he has worked for all his life, Miroslav Štancl argues that it may *not* have been Semtex.

'There are two substances found together in Semtex 1H: RDX and PETN. They were found together in Lockerbie. But they are also present in detonators. And you might find them together in such circumstances because one was in the plastic explosive, and one was in the detonator. So it could have been *another* explosive.'

Chapter 10

Poland

There are few virtues that the Poles do not possess and few mistakes they have ever avoided.
Winston Churchill

Stanisław Karolkiewicz is with his comrades for the very last time. Ranked pew upon pew, their grey, mottled heads bowed, his comrades grip their berets with both hands. The years have settled their faces into a generalised weariness. Staring up at Stanisław's coffin, they blink behind thick glasses, strain to listen, cough into handkerchiefs. A guard of honour in ceremonial dress and diamond-shaped *rogotywka* caps surrounds the coffin. Today, they are burying another old soldier.

Like many veterans of the Warsaw Uprising, Stanisław survived the Nazis only to be persecuted by the Communists. 'Stanisław was a very strong character,' intones the bishop. 'Even after the uprising, he was imprisoned by the Communists for 10 years. But he kept his dignity. He kept his deep faith in God.'

To capture the quiddity of Polish nationhood, one could do worse than enter the Field Cathedral of the Polish Army in Warsaw's Old Town. The pathos of the uprising, its appalling loss of life, the betrayal of Poland by the Anglo-American allies into Stalin's clutches, the defiance of the Catholic Church towards the Communists – all these elements are thick like incense in the air. There is a monument to the 4,500 Polish officers murdered on Stalin's orders at Katyń in 1940. The huge iron doors are engraved with battle scenes through the ages – Pod Legnicą in

1241, Obrona Jasnej Góry in 1655, Monte Cassino in 1944 – a litany of banners in the wind, horses, death, defeat. Heroic in battle, devoted to the holy Church, forever the victim of history, the stereotype of the Pole is writ large.

To say that the Warsaw Uprising is Poland's Calvary would not be an overestimation. Today street corners are marked with symbols of the rising, while if you visit the UNESCO-protected Old Town you learn that it was levelled by the Nazis, only to be rebuilt in the 1950s. Those unfamiliar with the uprising might recall Roman Polański's film, *The Pianist*, a triple-Oscar winner starring Adrien Brody. But that was about the *Jewish* uprising in the Warsaw ghetto in 1943, and the confusion between the two infuriates many Poles.

On 1 August 1944, Poland had just entered its sixth year of Nazi occupation. It was a reign of terror: hunger and suffering, street executions, national humiliation. The 150,000-strong Polish Home Army, directed by the government-in-exile in London, had been preparing for an uprising since as early as 1941. On the Russian front, the German tide had been turned and the Red Army was advancing west. The Poles could wait for the Soviets to liberate Warsaw, but ran the risk of being condemned as Nazi collaborators. Or they could take matters into their own hands before the Red Army arrived (Stalin's intentions of dominating Eastern Europe were, by then, crystal clear).

For 63 days the outgunned Home Army fought heroically. They captured a few key positions before succumbing to German air attacks and the failure of British and American supply drops (some were shot at by the Soviets, their allies). Throughout, Soviet tanks and troops sat across the Vistula River without intervening. Most Poles suspect Stalin was content to watch the Nazis destroy Warsaw before *he* took over.

Today, the insurgents are a dwindling number. By early 2009, there were 4,000 left, of whom 2,500 were mobile. The average age, including those who acted as teenage scouts, was 81. Edmund Baranowski, white haired and animated, joined the Home Army at 16 while working on a light-bulb production line in the Philips factory. As a member of the company fire brigade (Soviet air raids in August and September 1942 and May 1943 had killed 1,500), he could breach the nightly curfew, making him a useful recruit.

'We began to feel the pressure of the occupation from November 1939,' he recalls. 'I remember when two young women were arrested. One was accused of assaulting a German soldier. The second was a 20-year-old student caught pulling down a propaganda poster. Both women were shot. It was a shocking event. But it was only the foretaste of what was to come.'

Edmund recalls the day the uprising began. 'I went home to say goodbye to my mother. She gave me a picture of the Virgin Mary and made the sign of the cross. She asked me to fetch coal from the cellar for the last time. Then we parted.'

Leo Zbigiew, a thickset man of 84, but who looks 70, recalls the preamble to the uprising. 'When the Wehrmacht arrived, they were just getting organised and nothing really happened. But when the administrators and the police and the SS arrived, the occupation really began. On 26 December 1939, 120 people were executed as part of a reprisal operation, including my friend and his father.'

Leo had been sent to an underground school during the first years of occupation, and had no doubts about joining the Home Army. 'The exceptions were those who didn't join.' In the spring of 1941, Warsaw was a transit point for German troops going to the Eastern Front. Leo reported back any troop or vehicle movements, noting the names of units, the numbers of German troops or anything of interest.

'By 1943, the street executions reached a peak,' Edmund Baranowski continues (his recall of detail, events, the street he was on, even the time of day, is impeccable). 'Posters began to appear saying that the latest killing of a German had resulted in 20 Poles being executed; another 20 would follow if another German soldier died. Three days later, another poster would appear with the list of those executed and the names of those who were about to be executed. There were 2,500 shot dead. In February 1944, the head of the German police, Chief Kutschera, was killed by a group of Home Army soldiers who stopped his car in the street. As the insurgents retreated, many of them were shot. A mass execution followed; 200 people were shot.'

Edmund and Leo were poorly equipped, had no proper uniforms and were constantly short of food. Success was measured in capturing or destroying the odd German tank, or firing from behind a barricade.

For the most part they were on the run from Panzer tanks, or scurrying for cover from artillery shells and dive-bombers. The Germans were using frightening new weapons like the Bellowing Cow that sprayed out incendiary and explosive devices. Streets were being liquidated one after another. Leo recalls the experience of one comrade. 'The fighting was house to house, room to room, staircase to staircase. My friend was creeping through the basement and suddenly he ran headfirst into a German soldier. Both of them screamed in fright and ran away from each other.'

At a very young age, death and heroism for Leo and Edmund were commonplace. 'Even ordinary, quiet people became heroic,' says Edmund. 'They had to become heroes, otherwise they would have died. This generation was pushed to its fate. We lived with death every day. I was absolutely confident I was going to die. There were hundreds lying dead around me.'

As German reaction to the uprising took its toll, insurgents and civilians alike sought refuge in the Old Town. The only safe route was through the sewers. The injured and the dying struggled through the tunnels, sometimes chest deep in effluent. Edmund's unit had been reduced from 16 to 6 by the time he made it to the entrance to the sewers. He describes those he found waiting there.

'They were lying on blankets, on stretchers, on the rubble. There had been amputations – people were missing legs, head injuries, stomach wounds. They begged us to take them with us. We couldn't look into their eyes. One German hand grenade and we would all have been in the same condition. I can see them today, hear their begging voices …'

Edmund raises a clenched fist to his mouth and his frame shakes.

'You can't forget that. We were helpless. We knew what was in store for them. A nurse brought another wounded person – a cousin of one of our unit. He was in a terrible dilemma. He didn't know whether to stay with him or to go with us. A year later, I returned to the spot where they had lain. All I found were just charred bones …'

Carrying two hand grenades, a Mauser rifle and 20 bullets, Edmund and his unit crawled through the sewers, at times only 160 centimetres high. 'We were in an area controlled by the Germans – it was very dangerous, crawling underneath the entry points, because they could throw something inside. It took us seven hours – on the street it would have taken 20 minutes. We emerged on Nowy Świat and Warecka Street. It was a different world. There were nurses, there was a bar, we got drinks. Some officers even had fresh uniforms.'

On 15 September, flying shrapnel left Edmund with a broken jaw, facial injuries and a severed neck artery. A short time later he was captured and sent to a prisoner-of-war camp near Hamburg. On 2 October, the last shot was fired and the Home Army surrendered. Over 15,000 insurgents had been killed or were missing, 17,000 on the German side. Some 200,000 civilians lost their lives. Hitler decreed that the city be razed to dust: in all, 85 per cent of it was destroyed.

* * *

In September 1939, Polish cavalry officers, swords drawn, are reputed to have hurled themselves on horseback against German tanks as they rolled into Poland. This singular image has crystallised the centuries-old myth of the suicidally brave Pole. In fact, the story is not entirely apocryphal. 'In one or two places, isolated squadrons of Polish cavalry found themselves surprised by tanks, and despite their orders to the contrary, did try to fight their way out in the traditional fashion,' writes Norman Davies in *God's Playground: A History of Poland.* 'Short of surrender, that was the only thing cavalrymen could do.' The image is seen as a point of departure between the Czechs and the Poles: the Czechs never rose up (White Mountain in 1620 was the last battle Czechs really fought), but kept their beautiful Prague; the Poles lost Warsaw but kept their pride.

The political reality was that the Poles weren't supposed to defeat the Germans, but to keep the Wehrmacht at bay for two weeks until their allies (Britain and France) came to the rescue. Despite having only 150 tanks to the Wehrmacht's 2,600, the Poles did manage to inflict considerable damage on the German Army. Poland stuck to its side of the bargain; Britain and France never fired a shot in her defence during those first two weeks.

The Second World War, therefore, reaffirmed Poland's historical self-image: a tragic country bullied and butchered by Russia and Germany. For a long time, though, Poland was actually a major European power. The

Polanie ('people of the open fields') were one of several Slavonic tribes who first appeared around the 10th century near present-day Poznań. Over the following 200 years they formed the Piast dynasty and were eventually recognised as part of Christendom by the Vatican, taking crowns here and principalities there. A consolidated Polish kingdom was finally forged under Casimir the Great in the 14th century and the Poles duly spread east. Although German migration into Polish territory was already under way – the Teutonic Knights of Prussia in particular made their presence felt – Poland's expansion east actually won swathes of territory and influence. By 1364 and the Congress of Kraków (hosting five regional kings and dukes), Poland had arrived on the European stage. Kraków was a major city of learning, Latin was the language of the court and Catholicism was the established religion.

Following a royal marriage between a Polish princess and a Lithuanian duke in 1385, Poland and Lithuania entered a powerful union that lasted 187 years. The Commonwealth, as it was first known, stretched from the Baltic to the Crimea. It established kings of Hungary, subdued the Teutonic Knights in Prussia, welcomed in the Renaissance and produced a caste of poets, painters and scientists – including Nicolaus Copernicus (1473–1543), who discovered the earth's motion around the sun.

The Reformation came without too much bloodletting; Poland remained Catholic, but Protestants, Armenians, Orthodox Christians and Jews were all tolerated. From the end of the 16th century until 1795, Poland was the senior partner in the Commonwealth's successor, the Noble Republic (1579–1795), a constitutional, parliamentary monarchy, as close to a democracy as one could get for the time.

Poland, though, had more nobles than anywhere else in Europe. The *szlachta* were a self-important, even exotic group of people (Frederick the Great of Prussia referred to them as the last Cherokees of Europe). They held each other in ornate esteem, but lorded it over a huge underclass of serfs. Their frequent jockeying for increased powers soured the political climate and foreign royalty were often invited in to rule. Then, as a result of the religious wars, Poland's Baltic grain boom went into steep decline in the late 17th century; the Counter-Reformation tainted the outward appearance of religious tolerance; and the creation of the Uniate Church split the Orthodox community in two. Moscow was drawn into Polish affairs and never really left until 1990. When a constitutional crisis prevented the state from raising taxes, the Noble Republic could no longer maintain an army, and invaders duly swooped. Swedes, Cossacks, Turks, Prussians, Muscovites and the Habsburgs all marched in. When the dust settled, three powers emerged which would dominate for the next 150 years: Russia, Austria and Prussia. In 1795 they carved Poland into three pieces. Russia took the eastern part, Prussia the western part and Austria the south. Poland would not be a country again until 1918.

Throughout the 19th century, poets wept for Poland's great misfortune and lionised her warriors of yore. Since the country no longer existed, Romantic writers like Adam Mickiewicz could only dwell in the past or dream of a future. The Poles were now subjects of the Tsar, the Habsburgs or the kings of Prussia. With no political openings to assert their nationhood, tens of thousands volunteered to join foreign armies (others were simply conscripted). General Józef Bem led an army in the Hungarian uprising against the Austrians in 1848, thus solidifying an affinity the two countries still share. On the other hand, two million Polish conscripts fought and died – with little thanks – on the Russian, Austrian and German sides during World War I.

The tradition of Poles fighting overseas continued after independence in 1918. When the Nazis and Soviets carved up the country in 1939, tens of thousands of Polish troops escaped through Romania, Slovakia and Hungary, most reforming as Allied formations that continued fighting. In the Battle of Britain, Polish pilots made up 20 per cent of the RAF's strength (one exclusively Polish squadron knocked out nine Luftwaffe craft for every plane lost, a ratio that was unsurpassed). Polish paratroopers fought at the Battle of Arnheim, and the First Polish Armoured Division played a vital part in the breakout from the Normandy beaches after the D-Day Landings. There were extraordinarily epic tales of forbearance. Tens of thousands of Poles had been banished to Siberia in 1939, but after Hitler invaded Russia Stalin decided to allow General Władyslaw Anders to raise a Polish army from the gulag provided it took on the Germans. The Anders army, 10,000 strong, then embarked on an incredible odyssey through Uzbekistan into British-controlled Persia and on to Palestine. Some Jewish members stayed on to eventually help form the new state of

Israel, but most Poles continued their journey. They fought for the Allies in Tobruk (1943), Monte Cassino (1944) and Bologna (1945).

Their reputation for bravery was enhanced at every turn. On the one hand they needed to impress their Western commanders, while on the other, they had a chance to avenge the Germans in a way they couldn't (yet) do at home. Monte Cassino is long remembered as the bloodiest and most difficult of all the battles between the Allies, as they inched their way up through Italy, and the Germans, who had dug in immovable defences. The town's abbey – just below the German Gustav Line running across Italy – was a critical vantage point. In the end Monte Cassino was the anvil upon which Allied and German troops hammered themselves almost to oblivion in May 1943. To the Poles, it assumed mythic status. It took four Allied assaults to dislodge Axis troops, but it was the bravery of General Anders's Polish II Corps that burned itself into the Polish psyche and earned the Poles breathless Allied respect. 'Soldiers!' General Anders told his troops on the eve of combat. 'The moment for battle has arrived. We have long awaited the moment for revenge and retribution over our hereditary enemy.'

Polish losses were high. In one week of fighting, there were 3,600 casualties, including 860 deaths. 'You don't know how dreadful death can be,' a dying Pole said to his comrades. 'Now I shall have to miss the rest of the battle.' One corporal, staggering into a field hospital with enormous wounds, told the surgeon, 'I shan't let you evacuate me until I've thrown all my grenades.' On the ravaged hillsides, Polish troops low on ammunition were reduced to throwing stones and singing their national anthem at the Germans. On 18 May 1944, Polish troops finally raised a regimental pennant above Monte Cassino's western wall. The abbey was taken. A bugler played the 'Hejnał Mariacki' military call once used to signal the opening of Kraków's gates. The most decisive battle in the Italian campaign was over, and Rome fell to the Allies a few weeks later. Polish valour was affirmed, and the myth took hold in verse.

Czerwone maki na Monte Cassino
Zamiast wody piły polska krew…
(The red flowers of Monte Cassino
Soak up \Polish blood …)

While I was in the library of the Uprising Museum, hearing Edmund and Leo's stories, it became clear just how powerfully these myths had been soldered onto the consciousness. 'Take Somosierra,' Edmund said suddenly. 'Napoleon asked his French troops why they hadn't fought as hard as the Poles. They said the Poles had won because they were drunk. Well, he said, you should be as drunk as Poles next time! This heroism was deeply coded into our systems, even when we were losing hope.'

Somosierra was no clash between Poles and Napoleon in *Poland.* It was an engagement in the Spanish War of Independence against Napoleon in which a Polish light horse brigade – on Napoleon's side – charged against the artillery cannons of the Spanish popular army half a century before the Charge of the Light Brigade. Here Polish bravery actually won the day, even if the losses were appalling, and Napoleon went on to capture Madrid. As Edmund stood on the barricades against the Nazis in Warsaw, it was, he insists, a conscious inspiration.

Poles have forever been up in arms. There were five uprisings against the Russian Empire (1768, 1794, 1830–31, 1863–64, 1905), two against the Austrians (1846) and five against the Germans (1794, 1806, 1846, 1848, 1918–19). All were failures. What the Pole couldn't achieve at the barricades, Romantic poets forged into myth. 'Ordon's Redoubt', by Adam Mickiewicz, recalls the 1830–31 rebellion against Russia, in which Captain Ordon, the defender of Warsaw, blew himself and his fort to pieces as the Russians entered. The poem was recited by Polish fighters in armies the continent over, even if Mickiewicz was later found to have exaggerated the facts. Henryk Sienkiewicz, who went on to win the Nobel Prize for literature, solidified the stereotype in his novel trilogy *With Fire and Sword*, *The Deluge* and *Fire in the Steppe*, set during the Poland-Lithuania Commonwealth. Throughout, the Pole was brave, foolhardy, Catholic, yet with a degree of level-headedness.

This insurrectionary impulse was passed on through generations. Some of the uprisings were almost qualified successes; the 1863 revolt against the Russian Empire saw 80 bloody battles, harsh reprisals and the biggest ever deportation of Poles to Siberia (80,000). Despite the human losses, Polish demands for equal rights and land earned real sympathy across Europe.

This heritage wasn't just the stuff of historical debate. It had real meaning for the Home Army fighters facing the Nazis. 'The uprisings of 1863 and 1944 were needed,' says Leo Zbigniew. 'We knew that both were destined to fail from the beginning. But if it wasn't for 1863, then our identity would have disappeared.'

Not all Poles shared this view. A rival movement in the second half of the 19th century believed in gradually building the nation through education, work, spiritual and cultural renewal, rather than hurling oneself at the enemy. This school of thought continued right up to the Warsaw Uprising. Both sides disagreed on the methods, but shared the same goals.

In fact, the Poles didn't lose every battle they fought. In the Polish-Soviet War of 1919–21, the Red Army, flushed with revolutionary success, set off through Poland to create a bridge into Germany, which they were sure was about to succumb to revolution. By August 1920 the Red Army stood at the gates of Warsaw, but an attack by Marshal Józef Piłsudski from the south split the Soviet advance and the Russians were badly beaten. It was the Red Army's first ever unredeemed defeat (the next was Afghanistan). Simultaneous uprisings against the Germans actually won Poland the cities of Wilno (modern-day Vilnius) and Lwów (today in Ukraine). 'For the people who grew up in the 1920s and 1930s, fighting for the country's freedom could be seen not only as a patriotic duty but also as a tradition that had brought results,' writes Norman Davies in *Rising '44: The Battle for Warsaw.*

But the Warsaw Uprising didn't bring the longed-for result: it ended in horrendous loss of civilian life and the almost complete destruction of the capital. The Nazis weren't defeated (even if they were on the retreat from the Eastern Front) and Stalin carried out his subjugation of Poland anyway, installing a regime that prevailed until 1990. As a result the rising's legacy is bitterly disputed. Should the insurgents have recklessly proceeded, knowing the odds were stacked against them? Why did the Soviets stand idly by (Stalin referred to the insurgents as 'gangsters')? Why did Churchill and Roosevelt – who knew the rising would take place – fail to coordinate support with their Russian allies, leaving the Poles utterly stranded (and later denied the free elections they were promised). 'The Warsaw Rising,' writes Norman Davies, '... demonstrated that great powers may have democracy on the tip of their tongues but not always at the top of their priorities.'

For Leo Zbigniew and Edmund Baranowski, speaking 66 years later, the uprising simply *had* to proceed. Popular fury against the German occupation was at breaking point. 'We never thought to stop our activities just because the Germans were executing so many Poles,' says Edmund. 'To have taken such a step, it would have required only the slightest faith in the occupier, and there was no such faith. There were no groups of Poles who collaborated. They collaborated in Norway and in France, but not in Poland.'

'Back then, the uprising was almost symbolic,' admits Leo. 'It was an act of rebellion against a power that was imposed upon us. For me, it was necessary. We were all Poles and we felt like Poles. There *was* the prospect of victory because Soviet troops were on the other side of the river. Their decision not to help was a political one, but from a military point of view it might have succeeded.'

* * *

At 21:50 on 2 April 2005, I received a call. It was the RTÉ News foreign desk. 'He's gone.'

I ran out of Hotel Amadeus on Mikołajska Street and over to Kraków's Market Square. Karol Józef Wojtyła, Pope John Paul II, had died in his room in the Vatican at 21:37. The world had been watching and waiting, and now the moment had arrived.

Kraków, for centuries the spiritual heart of Poland, had been brooding for weeks. The Pope had been born in Wadowice, just 50 kilometres away, and had been archbishop in Kraków from 1967 until his elevation to pontiff in 1978. He was a colossal ambassador for his people, bestriding as he did the tectonic plates of 20th-century history. The Poles in general, and the Krakovians in particular, would not let him go easily.

In St Mary's Basilica on the Market Square, worshippers were coming to the end of the Stations of the Cross. As they emerged, it was clear the news hadn't yet filtered through so I would be the first to tell them. Some stopped and stared, others broke down in tears. Some fell to their knees, others turned and went straight back into the basilica.

At one minute to ten, I rushed to a live broadcast position on the northern end of Market Square. Things were moving fast. Over my shoulder, to the left of the church, outdoor bars had filled with young people enjoying the unseasonably mild evening. The news reached one of the bars and the customers, unaware of how to react, stood spontaneously en masse and in silence. The bar next door, though, was still unaware, and the customers continued drinking and laughing. It remained thus for a further bizarre two minutes. As I was about to go on air, word was spreading. Anguished, muffled cries echoed across Kraków's main square. Holding my composure to deliver a live insert to the 9 o'clock news in Dublin meant it was one of the toughest broadcasts I have ever had to do.

When it was over I went straight to the Archbishop's Palace on Franciszkanska Street. Already, thousands of people were streaming to the spot just below the main balcony where the Pope used to appear on his visits back to Kraków. Candles were lit, hymns were sung and tears flowed. From afar, Karol Józef Wojtyła had always gently reminded Poles of their own historical national strength. That resource may have atrophied during the century and a half when Poland didn't exist as a country. It may have been all but extinguished during the apocalyptic suffering of the war, and if not, weakened further during the oppressive years of communist rule. But Wojtyła directed them to it during the years of martial law. He had also, with the deftest of political touches, told the totalitarian establishment that their time was up. Now the man they simply knew as *Papa*, their spiritual guide, was gone. As I watched the agony on the faces of the young people who had gathered – not just tears, but great, shuddering cries – I felt like I was looking at a nation that had just been orphaned.

* * *

Poland was always embedded in Europe's Christian tradition, but it wasn't always so monotheistic Catholic. During the Noble Republic, until the three-way partition in 1795, the Catholic Church had held sway, but only just. The elected kings were loyal to Rome, and fresh religious orders from Western Europe ensured the vigour of the Church. But the political changes, the impunity and growing power of the nobles, and the increasing confidence of the other religious groups – Orthodox Christians, Lutherans and Jews – pushed back the hierarchy's influence. When the country was partitioned, the Church was politically in decline (they'd even lost the Jesuits in 1773), but over time the faith of ordinary Poles rallied, especially since their overlords were of a different religion: the Protestant Swedes, the Orthodox Russians and the Lutheran Prussians (the Catholic Austrians were rather better regarded).

In the 19th century, Catholicism became the exclusive badge of Polish identity. The growing bourgeoisie weren't given much thanks for it, though. At a time of anxiety among the monarchies of Europe over calls for emancipation, the Vatican chose to keep relations with the Austrian Habsburgs, the Prussians and the Tsar of Russia sweet at the expense of the Poles (Rome refused to support their uprisings). All the while, radical Polish priests were sent in their thousands to Siberia or were imprisoned by the Prussians. At home, the genuine devotion of rank-and-file clergy to their flock strengthened Poles' identification with the Church. When the National Democratic Movement emerged under Roman Dmowski in the late 19th century, Polish and Catholic became twin sides of the one coin, even if other minorities – Jews, Ukrainians and Germans – made up 40 per cent of the population.

For Romantic poets, it was more than simply a political identification. Adam Mickiewicz saw Poland in messianic terms. The country was a Christ-like figure that would save European nations from slavery and purge itself in the process. Other countries, he wrote, had rejected the original gift of, and belief in, God. The French had embraced honour, the English sea power and commerce, the Spanish political power and the Germans prosperity. These attributes were all blasphemous; only the Poles had clung to freedom, the original gift from God. The kings of Europe were afraid, he wrote, so they decided to kill Poland, to his mind the Christ of nations. 'And they conspired together … and they crucified the Polish Nation and laid it in its grave … But on the third day the soul shall return again to the body, and the Nation shall arise, and free all the peoples of Europe from slavery' (*The Books of the Polish Nation and the Polish Pilgrimage*, 1832).

By the end of World War II, the Polish landscape was altered dramatically. The Jews had been all but wiped out by the Holocaust; the German-speaking parts of Poland had seen their inhabitants, 5 million in all, expelled or killed; the Orthodox Ukrainians had been murdered or deported by Stalin. For the first time in her history Poland found herself ethnically Polish and religiously Catholic. For all its appalling suffering, though, it did not emerge as the Christ-like redeemer of nations: it was now ruled by godless Communists.

Under Stalinist rule the Catholic Church was attacked, priests were arrested and property was confiscated. The regime sought to weaken the Church's appeal by stripping away her popular social functions, creating pseudo-religious and state-run charitable organisations in their place. The repression culminated with the internment, in 1953, of Cardinal Stefan Wyszyński. After Stalin's death though, while the government still intervened in ecclesiastical appointments, the Church was granted some freedoms in return for loyalty to the state. Ironically this pact allowed the hierarchy to centralise its control over all Catholic organisations and, as a result, the Polish Church was in reasonable shape by the 1970s. The Church still maintained two cardinals, 45 seminaries, 73 bishops, over 13,000 churches and 18,000 priests. By the time Karol Wojtyła became Pope John Paul II, the hierarchy had developed an uneasy, if working, relationship with the regime. It could talk tough when it wanted – although too tough would prompt Soviet tanks – and in return it could keep the populace from boiling over in frustration. A working group between both sides met regularly, if quietly. The Church remained, though, the only real sphere of freedom within the system.

The system, therefore, could barely cope with the shock of Karol Wojtyła's election as Pope. On 16 October 1978, the Communist authorities in Warsaw were so stunned they delayed the news for two hours. The effects of a Polish pope were immediate. Hundreds of foreign journalists descended on a country previously shut off from the world. Józefa Hennelowa, the editor of *Tygodnik Powszechny*, a weekly Catholic newspaper closely associated with Karol Wojtyła, recalled: 'We felt we were the epicentre of world interest,' she said. 'The day after he was elected, the paper was uncensored for the first time. We were also suddenly given permission to travel to the Vatican to see the Pope.'

However, such escape was possible only for a select few. A more powerful effect was felt when the Pope made his first visit home in May 1979. 'The first pilgrimage broke all the rules,' recalled Józefa. 'People could suddenly decide where they wanted to go, what they wanted to listen to, in a very spontaneous way. There was an incredible sense of freedom because they were gathering – not because the authorities wanted them to be there – but because they had chosen to be there by themselves.'

The impact was fundamental. 'In the summer of 1979, the Pope said, "Do not be afraid. You don't have the right to be afraid",' recalls Konstanty Gebert, a veteran columnist with *Gazeta Wyborcza* newspaper. 'On that day, Communism disappeared. There were hundreds of thousands of Poles and we realised, we're strong. We're not just a bunch of loonies, we are the people.'

Dissent against the regime was not unprecedented. In 1968, against a backdrop of falling living standards, the closure of a play by the national poet Adam Mickiewicz – on the orders of the Soviet ambassador – prompted open unrest on the streets. The event had followed the support by Polish and Jewish intellectuals for Israel's victory in the Six Day War against Arab regimes (the Arabs were 'supported' by the Russians, so dissident Poles supported the other side). The government's response was overtly anti-Semitic, and 40,000 Polish Jews emigrated to Israel (leaving only about 4,000 altogether). There were further riots by striking miners in 1970, and unrest against the constitutional changes in 1976, which tied Poland even closer to the USSR.

Throughout this period, small opposition groups had appeared. The Pope's visit in 1979, though, allowed these movements to coalesce, so that suddenly the opposition had a *national* character. When, within a year of the visit a series of food price rises triggered a strike at the Gdańsk shipyard, the unrest spread (the local pay offer was not applicable across Poland). The authorities quickly conceded the right to strike and form trade unions in return for recognition of the Party's 'leading role', but it was a fatal mistake. Delegates from new strike committees got together to form a national coordinating committee. They called it Solidarity.

Solidarity did not seek to overthrow the regime. It spoke of 'national reconciliation' involving the Party, the Church and their new movement. The non-confrontational, yet enormously popular, nature of Solidarity left the authorities in a pickle. The USSR was threatening invasion, so action was needed. General Wojciech Jaruzelski, defence minister, was appointed prime minister, and later Party Secretary. When tanks rolled onto the streets on 13 December 1981, they were Polish, not Russian. Martial Law was in effect a military coup by a secret cabal of military and intelligence figures from the Polish and Russian Communist establishments. It was, writes Norman Davies in *Heart of Europe: The Past in Poland's Present*, 'the overthrow of the Soviet-controlled civilian dictatorship by the Soviet-controlled military dictatorship'.

Ten thousand people were arrested and detained. There were deaths and beatings. Solidarity was banned. In the absence of Western intervention, Pope John Paul II provided vital moral support from St Peter's. 'He was receiving Polish delegations, and mentioning Poland during Sunday prayers,' recalls Józefa Hennalowa. 'He made it the major issue of international politics, so it was an umbrella of protection over the Polish Church which could not then be persecuted the way it might have been.'

But it was his second visit to Poland in 1983 which was to prove the most decisive. In the third year of military dictatorship, merely wearing a Solidarity badge could earn you two years in prison. When over a million Poles turned up for a papal mass in Kraków, hundreds managed to smuggle in Solidarity banners and flags in defiance of the authorities. The riot police didn't dare intervene. It was after the mass that General Jaruzelski requested an urgent meeting with the Pope. They met in Wawel Castle, the great Gothic seat of Polish kings. The details of the meeting remain secret, but a close adviser to the Pope, Bishop Tadeusz Pieronek, told me: 'These were very hard, man-to-man talks, very frank, very open. Talks about the future of the country. The Pope spoke to General Jaruzelski in very determined tones about what course the authorities should take.'

It was as tough a line as the Pope could have taken. In 1937, the Vatican may have denounced godless Communism, but under the Polish pontiff a more subtle, even laborious, but ultimately more effective, strategy was adopted. He was careful to avoid straying from the spiritual and the charitable. During visits he was courteous to the regime and attentive to protocol. Lech Wałęsa, the Solidarity leader, was embraced every time, but when he was arrested, the Vatican's response was discreet. By moving ahead with determined speed on ecumenism and building bridges with Judaism, the Pope created an aura around his office, a momentum which dissolved intransigence and left the totalitarian regime of his homeland looking ever more isolated. When the time came, his call for freedom was unmistakeable: celebrating mass before a crowd of 750,000 in Gdańsk in 1987, the Pope used the word 'solidarity' time and time again. The message was clear.

Even though the Solidarity movement had gone underground in 1983, its networks remained intact. In the end, General Jaruzelski's regime ran out of credibility. Society simply turned away from his phoney attempts to make people feel included, disregarding his efforts to bask in the reflected glory of papal visits. With the advent of Mikhail Gorbachev in Moscow, tanks on the streets were no longer an option. Reforms were out because there was no recognised opposition with whom to negotiate (Solidarity was still illegal). So when strikes broke out again in Gdańsk in 1988, the general had no alternative but to invite Lech Wałęsa and Solidarity to roundtable talks. It was the de facto end of the Communist regime. In the elections of 1989, in the second round of voting, every Solidarity candidate except one was elected to the Sejm.

History has accorded an enormous amount of credit to the Pope for the demise of Communism. There's no doubt his careful yet charismatic approach helped to ensure it was achieved without a shot being fired (that then extended to Czechoslovakia, Hungary, East Germany and the Baltic States as well). In Poland he strengthened the resolve of the grassroots, a movement not always in tune with the hierarchy. Following martial law, ordinary priests and parishes were heroic in defending their dignity, and steadfast in erring towards the spiritual and non-violent.

When Pope John Paul II died on 2 April 2005, 16 years after Poland won its full independence for the first time since 1939, many outside observers asked the question: how would the Polish Church, and the Polish people, ever cope without him?

* * *

It didn't take long to find out.

It was 7 January 2007 at St John's Cathedral in Warsaw. The great and the good were gathered for a joyous occasion: the official installation of Bishop Stanisław Wielgus as Archbishop of Warsaw. Present were the Kaczyński twins, Lech and Jarosław, one the president, the other the prime minister of Poland. Two days beforehand, Bishop Wielgus had taken his oath of fidelity in a private ceremony, having been hand-picked by John Paul II's successor, Pope Benedict XVI, on 6 December.

But before the ceremony could get under way, Bishop Wielgus read out a statement which first caused stunned silence, then mayhem. The new archbishop was *resigning* his post just two days after taking his oath. In a shocking confession, he admitted that he'd been an informer for the Służba Bezpieczeństwa (SB), the hated secret police that had persecuted bishops, priests and ordinary Catholics throughout the Communist era.

In a blend of stage management and farce, a statement was read out from the Papal Mission confirming that the Pope had accepted the resignation. It was like turning up to a wedding only to witness a divorce, one caused by the worst kind of infidelity. Some of the audience applauded, some wept. There were angry exchanges between parishioners. Like an Episcopal Grand Old Duke of York, the ex-archbishop filed stone-faced out of the church, leading the same procession of priests he had just led in minutes beforehand. Poland was in a state of shock, the Vatican in a state of acute embarrassment.

It all began with *Gazeta Polska*, a right-wing Catholic news weekly. Shortly after Pope Benedict officially appointed him, the magazine wrote that Bishop Wielgus had been spying for the SB since the late 1960s. On 21 December, the Vatican was forced to announce it had full confidence in him. Wielgus himself issued vehement public denials.

Two urgent investigations were launched, one by the hierarchy, the other by the Polish ombudsman. In a report sent to the Institute of National Remembrance (IPN), an agency set up to examine Poland's recent history, the ombudsman concluded unambiguously – based on secret police files – that between 1973 and 1978, Father Wielgus had spied for the intelligence services. The Church's own investigation confirmed the worst: Bishop Wielgus had been a willing collaborator in defiance of the rules laid down by the Polish Church during Communism.

Bishop Wielgus issued further denials, calling into question the trustworthiness of the documents. He admitted that an SB agent had tried to strong arm him into cooperating before a trip to Munich in 1978, but that he had never signed anything and never harmed anyone. Later he backtracked again, saying he had only provided information relating to his academic work. By January, the evidence against him was stacking up. Before he could jump, the hierarchy pushed.

A few days later, I met Tomasz Sakiewicz, *Gazeta Polska*'s editor. He showed me documents apparently signed by Wielgus and said other proof would be unearthed revealing the scale of his cooperation. 'These tell us,' he said, handing me the papers, 'that he agreed to collect information on people working in West Germany. Here is an instruction what password he should use, how he should sign … It's typical for spy. ... I am very sure he was the most important spy in the Polish Church.'

Did his activities put people in danger?

'The goal was to damage every part of society – if they need to kill someone, they could use this information.'

These were serious allegations. Wielgus was the successor to Stefan Wyszyński, the Archbishop of Warsaw jailed in the 1950s. Warsaw was also the diocese of Fr Jerzy Popiełuszko, the passionate anti-Communist priest and chaplain to the Warsaw steelworks, whose uncompromising sermons against the regime earned him international respect, but also harassment, attempts on his life and finally, on 19 October 1984, kidnapping and death at the hands of the SB (his body was dumped in the River Vistula). For many, Wielgus's collaboration with the very people who murdered a fellow priest was too much to stomach.

But the Wielgus scandal was just one act in a greater drama over Poland's past that had begun to drag the government, the hierarchy, the opposition and even the late Pope into an unseemly brawl over public and private purity.

* * *

Across Eastern Europe, different countries dealt with the past in different ways. Some, like Hungary, felt that the quiet closure ensured a smoother transition to democracy. In others, like East Germany, a tougher line was taken with former Communists and secret police informers. It was called 'lustration'. Borrowed from ancient Greek and Roman purification rituals, lustration was applied in varying degrees, and for various reasons. It sought to block or remove someone from public office because of their Communist background. Naturally, it was open to abuse. Some saw it as justice, others as revenge.

In Poland, the first lustration bill was introduced in 1992 and updated in 1996. For the next 10 years, it was the preserve of the Public Interest Spokesman. However, in 2006, responsibility was passed to the Institute for National Remembrance (IPN), a new statutory body set up with the ambitious, not to say daunting, task of investigating all the crimes committed against the Polish nation since the Nazi invasion of 1939.

In February 2007, I visited an anonymous, low-rise building on Klobudzka Street in Warsaw. It was raining heavily. Following a security check I was led down into the vaults. In long, white-walled storage rooms, crammed into shelves that rolled into each other on runners so they could be locked shut, were 90 kilometres' worth of Communist-era secret police files. Inside each row was information on millions of Poles, from the mundane to the salacious to the politically compromising. The files had once fed the paranoia of the regime and oiled the levers of control, providing the dirt to persecute dissidents or to blackmail citizens into becoming informers. Collectively they were a monument to petty jealousy, vindictiveness, despair and compromise; informing ran right through Polish life from 1945 to 1989.

These days, though, the files were feeding something else. However serious the charges against Archbishop Wielgus, he was, according to critics of the lustration process, the latest victim of a vetting frenzy that was being abused by politicians in the new Poland. Private information gathered by a totalitarian regime a long time ago was being abused, years later, by politicians with an axe to grind, a score to settle or public points to accrue.

Under rules established when Poland became a democracy, some 27,000 people, from MPs to ministers to judges, had been required to say whether or not they had collaborated with the SB. Admitting to the offence didn't necessarily lead to punishment, but failing to come clean could mean a 10-year ban on holding public office. Once you secured a certificate from the IPN that you were 'clean', you could get on with your life.

However, in 2005 the constitutional court decided that information hitherto restricted could be opened up to MPs and researchers. But files began to leak. The details weren't appearing in parliamentary reports, but were splashed over tabloid centre spreads. Suddenly, public figures – who were not actually public servants and therefore hadn't needed to clear their names – were accused of having been informers. They included journalists, TV presenters and singers. And priests.

The political climate in 2007 meant that the crime of collaboration eclipsed ethical questions about privacy. It was largely thanks to the Kaczyński twins, Lech and Jarosław. Their Law and Justice Party (PiS) had swept to power in 2004 on a campaign pledge of purging former Communist figures and their informers from public life. Forming a coalition with the left-wing nationalist Samoobrona (Self-Defence) party, and the ultra-right-wing League of Polish Families, their manifesto was a heady blend of right-wing Catholic orthodoxy and left-wing economics.

There had been genuine public concern over corruption. A significant number of Poles thought that too many former Communists had found lucrative niches in public life. The Kaczyński twins would change all that. Born in Warsaw (their father had taken part in the uprising), the Kaczyńskis had been active Solidarity members in the 1980s, but a very particular form of marginalisation was what had fuelled a resentment now bursting into the open.

It can be traced back to a visit by Pope John Paul II to Warsaw in 1996. As his Popemobile was about to set off, the Pope invited Aleksander Kwaśniewski on board. It was a gesture both diplomatic and strategic: Kwaśniewski had been elected Poland's president the year before, but the trouble was he had been a Communist sports minister in the 1980s.

When they entered roundtable talks with the regime in 1989, Solidarity were not to know that the Berlin Wall would fall nine months later. Polish history taught them, indeed, that freedom could be snatched away at the rumble of a tank. Making a virtue of caution, the movement opted for compromise and drew what became known as the Thick Grey Line under the past, in the hope of consolidating a democratic future. There was no witch hunt of Communists, no public humiliation, no revenge. When the Pope invited Kwaśniewski onto the Popemobile, it was a signal he agreed with the policy.

For those who had suffered during the Communist era and who had strong Catholic faith, like the Kaczyńskis, it was a horrifying moment, a betrayal. While the twins had been sidelined during the birth of the new Poland, ex-Communists had formed parties, got rich and got respectable.

So quietly in the shadows a new strongly Catholic body of opinion-formers was coming of age. When they entered the political market they offered a black and white view of the world. They hadn't tolerated compromise during the regime, and certainly didn't like it under independence. 'They want things to be clear,' Jacek Zakowski, chair of journalism at the Collegium Civitas, told me. 'They don't want a mixture of good and bad, they want the past *bad* and the present *good*. The trouble is that it creates a tension between generations: those raised in Communism knew what life meant. It meant a long chain of compromises, starting in pre-school and lasting an entire life.'

Not so, said the Law and Justice Party. For them, the truth – what was (possibly) contained in those 90 kilometres of files – would purify Poland. 'The truth will liberate us,' Professor Wojciech Roszkowski, a Law and Justice Party MEP, told me in a Warsaw café. 'The truth is important in itself. People have the right to know who was who and what was what in the past.'

So convinced was the party that they strengthened the vetting law. Under new rules, a lot more people – not just MPs, civil servants and judges, but also journalists, officials of state-owned firms, school principals, university academics, diplomats and lawyers – would have to prove that they were beyond reproach, so long as they were born before 1972. In fact, the new law was going to affect 400,000 people.

To supporters of the government, the process should have started years before. Now the public standing of the Church, the media and the state demanded it. To opponents, it was a witch hunt that could be abused for all sorts of reasons. 'In big cities you can find a niche, a place to hide if you are on a list,' said Jacek Zakowski from the Collegium Civitas. 'In small communities, there are lists published by ex-opposition activists, with names and address of those cooperating, secret police officers. This creates really big problems when you are every day exposed to people looking at you and saying, you are a traitor.'

It was a painful moment for Poland. Not only were Poles having to confront the reality that priests and bishops, those heroic defenders of the people, had been collaborating with their oppressors; they were also forced to relive the iniquities of the system, and how it could corrupt otherwise decent people. The more that ordinary people peered into the files, the more the only shade they could see was grey.

Meanwhile, in a twist of appalling historical irony, Lech Kaczyński, who had become president in 2005, was killed alongside his wife Maria and a huge swathe of the Polish establishment in an air disaster, when a Polish Airforce TU-154 crashed while attempting to land in Smolensk in Russia in April 2010. The delegation was due to attend a ceremony marking the 70th anniversity of the Katyn massacre. Conspiracy theories have persisted within the Polish right that the crash was orchestrated by the Russians, although the official Polish investigation concluded that pilot error was the probable cause.

* * *

Janusz Molka is waiting for me in a café near the centre of Warsaw. A heavily built man in his fifties, with a green bomber jacket, a woollen hat and a gummy grin, he might pass for a retired wrestler. He still works out and runs five miles a day. He ate two pizzas and a huge bowl of ice cream in our time talking together. It was the first time I'd shared ice cream with a secret agent.

From 1984 until 1990, Mr Molka did the regime's dirty work. He was an informer, and he recruited informers. His entire existence was devoted to infiltrating, undermining and grinding down the Solidarity movement by whatever means possible. He started out in the third department of the SB, but the quality of his work impressed his superiors. As his status rose, so did his salary. His cover was solid at all times. He worked as a teacher, a member of a mountaineering club or in a publishing house. His handlers even had him 'removed' from his teaching job for 'improper activities' just so he would appear more credible to his Solidarity comrades. Mr Molka gathered intelligence on everybody and everything he came into contact with. He bugged rooms, tapped phones, took photographs. He spied on Lech Kaczyński, now the country's president, who was handling Solidarity's finances in Gdańsk.

But he didn't just spy. 'I was told to try and control the underground movement,' he admits, 'influence decisions, stir dissent, help them to disintegrate.' He had enormous back-up. 'The secret police was rooted in the system. There were cells from the Communist Party in almost every factory and workplace. There were several hundreds of thousands of them. The level of penetration was huge, much better than we could have imagined.

'To recruit informers, I told them, you will lose your job, you'll go to jail, your wife will lose her job and your children will go to an orphanage. We used methods like that. People were giving in to those methods, to blackmail. My duty was to find a weak point – gambling, drinking, financial problems, love affairs – anything to put the victim in a bad light. Many people had families; they couldn't cope with being threatened with jail. Only people who were very strong were able to withstand it. The whole heavy atmosphere was just like a big monster.'

Not surprisingly, those who suffered the worst excesses of the monster were now, in 2007, the least willing to forgive collaborators, no matter how egregiously the monster wore them down. At the Person of the Year Awards run by the newspaper that exposed Archbishop Wielgus, *Gazeta Polska*, I met one such figure. He was, in fact, the winner of the award.

Father Tadeusz Isakowicz-Zaleski, dark haired, pale faced, with a striking black beard, was now the brooding, righteous presence at the heart of the Wielgus crisis. His anger at the collaboration of fellow clergy had been earned the hard way. As a Solidarity chaplain in Kraków in the 1980s, he had been arrested and beaten by the SB. When he made an official complaint to the civilian police, they humiliated him, making him re-enact his torture several times over, filming it for their own amusement. Fr Zaleski's hour had come. He was about to publish a book naming 39 clerics as having spied for the secret police, including four serving bishops.

'I have told all of them,' he declared to me in an interview. 'Some of them gave information about me to the secret police as I carried out my duties. Four wrote to me and admitted collaboration, others reacted very nervously. Some of them called me a devil or a KGB agent. They were shocked. They didn't believe that sooner or later those files would come to the surface.'

According to Fr Zaleski, the Polish hierarchy had as many questions to answer as those individual priests who may have collaborated. To Fr

Zaleski it was a cover-up, a crime comparable to the Church's handling of paedophile priests. One of the reasons, he concedes, was to protect Pope John Paul II in his final years. 'But he would have liked to have known about the situation,' he said, 'because he was for justice. Every priest from Poland had a file on him, so the Pope had a file too. I believe this file is in Moscow.'

The following day in Wawel Castle in Kraków, where that pivotal meeting had taken place between the Pope and General Jaruzelski in 1983, I spoke to Bishop Tadeusz Pieronek, the former secretary general of the Episcopate and one-time close friend and adviser to Karol Wojtyła. He admitted that the Communist system infiltrated all aspects of life, especially the Church. 'It was the natural opposition to Communism,' said the bishop. 'It was the independent stronghold. First they blackmailed priests or church staff. Then priests who needed something, like those constructing a new church, were targeted. Others were just talkers. They simply talked because they had to talk, but they might not have known that everything they said had been scrupulously registered by the secret police.'

Bishop Pieronek was careful not to condemn Fr Zaleski too strongly, and he denied that the Church had tried to cover up the collaboration. But he was furious at the persistent release of the files. 'This wild vetting, day after day, week after week. The names are published, then there's a verdict and a sentence all in one. A person loses their good name, yet they can't access what's in the file. This is unacceptable. The rule of innocent until proven guilty is not working here. This is all against basic Christian values. It doesn't comply with the standards of a civilised society.'

* * *

In the Ochota district of central Warsaw stands the Church of the Divine Providence. To the left of the church, in the faltering afternoon light, a woman prays intently before a statue of the Virgin Mary. Fresh flowers, placed at the Virgin's feet, and a crown of stars lit above her head add colour to the otherwise grey surroundings. Ewa Piechel, a full-time nanny in her sixties, finishes her prayers and approaches with a polite greeting. She then leads me through a side door and down a tenebrous corridor into a broad, brightly lit tabernacle. We are joined by Maria, a retired urban planner, and Barbara, a partly retired chemistry technician. Facing a large Madonna and Child, set on a floral silver escutcheon and flanked by two velvet panels on which hang strings of pearls and other intimate effects (placed there as offerings for prayers answered), the women kneel and begin to pray. In unison, they press through the Chaplet of Divine Mercy.

In a Poland bereft of old certainties and pieties, Maria, Barbara and Ewa find comfort not just in prayer, but in the airwaves: they are members of Rodzina Radia Maryja (the Radio Maryja Family), the religious wing of the world's most controversial Catholic radio station.

To its critics, Radio Maryja is a nasty, demagogic mouthpiece of right-wing Polish nationalism and anti-Semitism; to its supporters, it's a haven of community values in a country disorientated by the headlong plunge into capitalism. 'I was amazed and joyful when I first heard it,' says Ewa. 'It was the first time such a beautiful thing had been created.'

The creator was Father Tadeusz Rydzyk, a Redemptorist priest and former chaplain to Solidarity. Inspired by Christian broadcasting in Germany and in America, he set up the station in December 1991. At the time, Poland was reeling from the upheavals wrought by the collapse of the Soviet Communist system: there had been a sudden transition to democracy (a moral victory for the Catholic Church without doubt), but also sudden and harsh austerity measures, higher prices and the loss of subsidies. They hit older, more rural souls the hardest. With the embrace of wanton materialism and a get-rich-quick business culture, many people felt left behind. Fr Rydzyk saw a niche in the spiritual market.

From his base in Toruń in northern Poland, he expanded Radio Maryja into a spiritual empire whose various elements rang with a defiance of the outside world. There was a TV station, Telewizja Trwam ('I Persist'), a newspaper, *Nasz Dziennik* ('Our Daily'), religious foundations Nasza Przyszłość ('Our Future') and Lux Veritatis ('The Light of Truth'). Radio Maryja itself began broadcasting masses, rosaries, breviaries, a news service, as well as discussion and phone-in programmes (the latter regarded by critics as a forum for anti-Semitism). At its peak in the late 1990s, there were over 2 million listeners, falling to about 1.2 million by 2009. If you drive through Poland, you will see signs indicating the best frequency to use on your radio to receive Radio Maryja (when listeners in Warsaw were unhappy with the signal, they sent 10,000 signatures petitioning for a better frequency).

'Someone from the parish came and spoke to us after mass,' Maria recalls. 'He was so enthusiastic, so passionate and excited about this new radio station that we thought he was disturbed.' She was astounded by what she heard. 'There were readings by the Redemptorists, all about the Bible, all about faith. It was very touching. I'm a big fan of the rosary, and there it was, on the radio, three times a day, morning, noon and evening. I could feel I was praying with other people, not just alone at home. Later there was *The Unfinished Conversation*, a discussion programme where you could phone in. I was so excited I couldn't sleep. In church on Sunday, the sermon is just 15 minutes. But on Radio Maryja, they last much longer.'

Ewa and Maria were both active Catholics during Communism, a devotion that barred them from promotion at work. Barbara only began practising after the Pope's visit in 1979. 'I went with friends to holy mass. Everyone was taking communion, but I wasn't. Then I thought, why not?' Now Barbara prays next to her radio at half six every morning. All three women tune in for the three o'clock prayers (since it coincides with our interview, they insist on the prayer service together before we start). Radio Maryja has become an enormous part of their lives, a source of spiritual comfort and a bulwark against loneliness. They hold prayer meetings, and every fourth Tuesday they discuss spiritual and practical problems. It is also, they claim, their true window to the world. 'It gives the true news,' says Maria firmly. 'When I'm tired of listening to the news and analysis on the public and commercial channels, I tune in to Radio Maryja. It is more accurate. They are more honest about how the financial crisis is going to affect Poland.'

All three women donate money to Radio Maryja every month. They won't say how much, but one says it's around half what she pays to her internet and cable TV provider.

I ask them about the attitude of the official Polish Church. There is silence at first, then Ewa says, 'They don't disturb us. Let's put it this way – some bishops are very devoted to what we're doing, others are not.'

In fact, Radio Maryja's activities have caused deep division within the Polish Church. It faces persistent allegations of promoting anti-Semitic, homophobic and anti-German views. It has involved itself in politics, urging listeners to support pro-Catholic parties. Law and Justice Party (PiS) cabinet ministers regularly appeared on the airwaves in the run-up to the 2007 elections. Bishop Tadeusz Pieronek has described the station as 'sick and dangerous'. He told Reuters, 'Radio Maryja is a real and growing problem. It offers a reduced view on Christianity, and in my view its attachment to a political party is extremely compromising and shameful.'

The Vatican has also expressed concern. In 2006, the papal nuncio wrote to the Episcopate pointing out the 'difficulties caused by some transmissions and the views presented by Radio Maryja'. Despite the tide of complaints, Fr Tadeusz Rydzyk remains the driving force (he declined to be interviewed for this book).

But how strong are the allegations? In February 2008, over a thousand Radio Maryja listeners attended a protest in a Kraków church addressed by two on-air personalities notorious for anti-Semitic views: Professor Jerzy Robert Nowak and Professor Bogusław Wolniewicz. The latter told the gathering, 'Jews are attacking us! We must defend ourselves.' In April 2006, another regular commentator, Stanisław Michalkiewicz, accused 'the men from Judea' of being part of the 'Holocaust industry' that wanted to extract €50 billion through wartime property restitution claims (in fact, experts believe that Jewish claims would represent only 17 per cent of all restitution applications). In July 2007, Fr Rydzyk told students at his media college that the claims would mean the following: '[Jews] will come and will say, give me that coat. Take off those trousers! Give those shoes!' (In June 2008, prosecutors in Toruń dropped a case against Fr Rydzyk, citing lack of evidence.) In January 2000, Ryszard Bender, a historian from the Catholic University of Lublin, speaking on Radio Maryja with a convicted Holocaust denier, Dariusz Ratajczak, claimed Auschwitz was not an extermination camp but merely a 'labour camp' for Jews. During the 2008 funeral of Bronisław Geremek, the intellectual driving force behind Solidarity and later an MEP, Radio Maryja supporters held up a banner saying they were glad God had taken him away. Geremek, who was Jewish, had been killed in a car crash.

I ask Ewa, Barbara and Maria about these claims. Ewa flatly rejects any suggestion that the station is anti-Semitic; only some listeners make anti-Jewish remarks during phone-in programmes. Maria says, 'The priests are taking care of it, making sure that comments are not allowed. Anyone can call.'

Eva nods in agreement. 'Now they have better technology and they're trying to persuade people to stop and they're doing it more effectively. The priests have a special gift to talk to people and some people get excited and nervous and say things that might be objectionable.'

But critics worry about its influence. 'Synagogues aren't being burned down, Jews are not physically being attacked,' says Sergiusz Kowalski, a sociologist and co-author of a book on hate speech. 'But it's painful nonetheless. Many people believe it's just old ladies praying in the churches, but it's not just old ladies. The radio has a permanent public presence. They use euphemistic language, but it is mutually understood. When they say "the dark forces of finance" or "those people – you and I know who they are", then people *do* know who they are referring to. And it's usually the Jews.'

Radio Maryja's antics have cast a harsh light on Poland's attitude to Jews. Until 1989, there was no debate about anti-Semitism, but now it's taking place. 'It's been frank, way beyond my wildest imagination,' says Konstanty Gebert, the *Gazeta Wyborcza* columnist, himself a practising Jew. 'The trouble is that it has shattered the myth of Polish innocence.'

The reason Poland was chosen by Hitler as the base for the industrialised murder of 6 million Jews, says Gebert, is because Poland was where the 'raw materials' lay. Despite the fact that there had been pronounced anti-Semitism in Poland between the wars, it was still amongst the safest places in Europe to be Jewish – until 1938. Ever since the 13th-century Statute of Kalisz, which enshrined wide-ranging rights and legal protections, Poland was one of the most tolerant lands for European Jewry. But in the 19th century, things began to change. As Jews emerged from their ghettoes, their growing economic strength prompted envy and resentment. Meanwhile, the Polish nationalist revival encouraged patriotic leaders – especially those in the new National Democratic Movement – to equate Polish identity exclusively with Catholicism. That required an enemy, and more often than not it was the Jew. There was a pogrom against the Jews in 1881 following the Tsar's assassination, and a boycott of Jewish businesses in 1911–12.

By the 1930s, Poland was, like most other countries in Europe, in the grip of an authoritarian pre-war government and was polarising along ethnic lines – Poles, Germans, Jews and Ukrainians. In small towns and villages, many Orthodox Jews were content to stick to their ghettoes, speaking their own language and following their own customs, while in the cities there was more mixing and sharing of identities. Many Warsaw Uprising fighters were Jewish, and there were numerous examples of Jews being rescued by fellow Poles from the trains bound for Auschwitz and Treblinka (Edmund Baranowski told me they stripped their fire engine of its water pump and hoses in order to hide Jews from the ghetto). But anti-Semitism existed, and Jewish prominence in the professions and in academia in particular bred resentment among the rising Catholic middle classes.

There remains bitter debate about whether Poles collaborated with the Nazis in rounding up Jews. In his book *Neighbors: The Destruction of the Jewish Community in Jedwabne, Poland*, the Polish historian Jan Gross concluded that a massacre of 290 Jews – which included the herding of 250 men, women and children into a barn then set ablaze – had been carried out by Poles, not by occupying Nazis. The book, published in 2001, was met with a hail of controversy, but critically the Institute of National Remembrance (IPN) largely endorsed its findings. A subsequent book, *Fear: Anti-Semitism in Poland after Auschwitz* (2006), claimed that the 250,000 Jews who returned to their homes after the Holocaust faced murder, discrimination and the appropriation of property. The book dealt with the Kielce pogrom, an incident in which 37 Holocaust survivors were beaten to death by a mob in the central Polish town on 4 July 1946. Some accused Gross of using flawed methodology and selective interviews (the book was the subject of the 2008 Radio Maryja demonstration in Kraków mentioned above), but few actually deny the pogrom took place.

Many Jews naturally felt safer in Soviet-occupied Poland rather than under the Nazis. As a result, most supported the new regime, and some rose to prominence. A few became prosecutors (even the torturers) of those Poles accused of collaborating with the Nazis (or even being members of the Home Army), but they constituted a minority of the prosecutors. In the violent post-war political interplay, Jews found themselves increasingly unwelcome. Pogroms, like that in Kielce, forced up to 100,000 to flee into Germany (of all places) in the 1950s.

In the new Poland, a low-level but still unpleasant anti-Semitism is part of the political jockeying as right and left scrap over the vices of blame and the virtues of victimhood. John Paul II's legacy, at least, is seen as helping a public debate to finally take place. 'He clearly said anti-Semitism was a sin – and many people didn't actually realise it,' says Konstanty Gebert. 'Jews were his childhood friends. He had a genuine revulsion at the murder of European Jewry, and he did more to improve relations between the Church and Judaism than anyone else.'

* * *

The stereotype of the Pole as devoted Catholic is still standing, but not quite with the same confidence. Today 95 per cent of the population regards itself as Catholic, ranging from the Radio Maryja listener to the urban sophisticate. 'They're saying, we're part of this culture, of this community which is so strong and powerful that we identify ourselves with it,' says Adam Szostkiewicz, a former Solidarity activist who was interned for six months, and is today a columnist with the current affairs magazine *Polityka*. 'They need it as a cultural institution in life, for births, deaths and marriages. On an everyday level, they don't practise. It's very conservative, or at least very traditional, but it's also one of the most anticlerical countries in Europe. Is it a paradox? Not really. Poles do realise how powerful is the Church's grip on hearts and minds. By being anticlerical, they show they're not happy with it, but they're also acknowledging the status quo.'

Since the death of John Paul II, the Church is open to more scrutiny, as the Wielgus affair has demonstrated. Sex scandals have been few, partly because it's still a major taboo, but also because political betrayal is regarded as worse. 'After freedom,' says Szostkiewicz, 'came all these big questions, which were frozen for 50 years. Twenty years later, the Church is still a very powerful cultural institution, but I'm not sure if Poland is as Catholic as the outside world thinks.'

Immigrant Poles have filled churches in Ireland and in the UK, bringing in particular a surge of new blood into the Irish Church. Vocations are still high: the 307,000 Poles who officially registered in Ireland and the UK from 2004 to 2008 actually brought priests with them. By June 2006, on the eve of Pope Benedict's first visit, Poland had

22.5 seminarians per 100 ordained priests. That compared to only 11.6 in Italy, 9.5 in Spain, 5.6 in France and just 3.6 in Ireland. But even this may now be faltering. In 2007, there was a 10 per cent drop in new vocations, with seminary enrolment down 25 per cent, according to Polish Church figures. In February 2009 a survey by Professor Josef Baniak, from the University of Poznan, found that 53 per cent of the 800 priests surveyed said they would like to have a wife, while 12 per cent admitted that they were already involved in a relationship (the Polish hierarchy rejected the findings as 'full of generalisations').

For the first time since 1795, Poles have enjoyed a sustained period of democracy, stability and prosperity. Poland has a more assertive role in world and European affairs. Throughout the prolonged European economic crisis, Poland is the only country which did not fall into recession (it has, understandably, been in no rush to join the single currency). Following EU enlargement, hundreds of thousands of young Poles fanned out across Europe working in construction, health, hi-tech, catering and pharmaceuticals. In Celtic Tiger Ireland, Poles enjoyed relatively harmonious integration (not withstanding racist attacks in Belfast where enmity was sectarian in nature), with as many as 200,000 thought be employed in Ireland at the height of the boom. The Polish market research agency ARC Rynek i Opinia found that 49 per cent of immigrants expected to stay for as long as possible, maybe up to 10 years, while 18 per cent wanted to stay permanently. High-paying jobs were a big attraction. Despite the numbers who wished to stay, and who were getting mortgages, there was evidence that this was more like *circulation* than immigration. Poles, in other words, were keeping a foot in both countries. Low-cost air travel – seven airlines serving 32 routes – as well as cheap bus travel home sweetened the exile (52 per cent returned two or three times a year), while 20,000 Poles living in Ireland registered to vote in the 2007 Polish elections. A study by the Polish Diaspora Project found that 60 per cent had positive associations with Ireland, while as many as 33 per cent said they were happy in *both* cultures. Poles tended not to like the dirty streets, traffic jams and bad weather, but they did like the Guinness, music and shamrocks. There were 15 Polish-language newspapers or websites, as well as Polish TV and radio programming, while the numbers of Irish people who took

Polish classes or were interested in Polish culture far exceeded those interested in any other culture.

There were problems, of course. Some Poles fell into a poverty trap, whereby highly qualified workers take menial jobs in the hope of picking up better employment later, only to find that when it doesn't materialise, it becomes harder to return home. One study showed that as many as one in five migrant children in schools had little or no English (King-O'Riain and Kropiwiec, *Polish Migrant Workers in Ireland 2006*). Many were arriving without jobs and without good enough English – or cash – to cope with life in Dublin. In September 2005, the Polish edition of *Newsweek* magazine, under the headline '*Inace Nis Vrayu*' ('Not Quite Heaven'), spoke of disillusion, alienation, hunger and even suicide. The Polish embassy said the article was exaggerated, but admitted that they had been trying to impress on Poles that a friendly country didn't necessarily guarantee a happy experience.

The collapse of the Irish economy has taken its toll, with some reports suggesting that 30,000 Poles left Ireland in 2008. The 2011 census showed that there were 122,585 Poles living in Ireland.

* * *

In the years before and after Poland joined the EU, a new stereotype arose: the Polish plumber. In France it was a symbol of all that was frightening about globalisation in general, and EU enlargement in particular: lower-paid workers from the East undercutting French workers. Pascal Lamy, the head of the World Trade Organization (WTO), said that 'plumber-phobia' verged on simple xenophobia, and even the head of the French plumbers union admitted he could be right. France was *short* 6,000 plumbers, and there were only some 150 Polish plumbers employed there, all working on big construction sites. Everywhere they went, though, Poles were getting a reputation (the Irish loved it, the French found it threatening) for being hardworking, trustworthy, versatile and cheap, tailor made for the runaway economic boom (40 per cent of Poles who went to work in Ireland were employed in the construction sector).

'No one ever taught me how to fix plumbing systems. I just looked at it and I knew how to do it. You just need a particular brain. When people tell me something can't be done, I just change into my working clothes and I do it myself and show them it can be done.' This is from Piotr Rzymowski, a self-confessed 'golden hand'. It's the Polish term for someone who can fix or construct just about everything. I meet Piotr in Café Karma in Warsaw. Surrounded by smart young Poles with their MacBooks, he looks somewhat out of place, but at 23 he already has his own construction company. He loves fixing stuff so much that he volunteered to renovate a friend's bathroom simply because, as a new businessman, he missed the labour. Piotr's seven months working in England left him contemptuous of the British work ethic. 'The Brits – they're very limited. They only specialise in one branch. If you're only a painter you don't do anything else. If the regulations say it has to be done in 10 hours, and you finish in eight, then they just sit on their arses for the other two just because the regulations say so. The tempo of work is terrible, the efficiency is terrible. They can't multi-task. They're only focused on one thing, so when they are learning one trade they stick to it. They thought I came from a backward country, but at least the Poles can multi-task.'

This stereotype is a curious one. Piotr reckons it's true, and most foreigners who have ever employed Poles would probably agree. But ask Poles *in Poland* about their national virtues, and you'll get a very different picture.

Poles at home have a low opinion of themselves as a nation. 'There have been numerous studies showing that Poles perceive themselves in a negative manner,' says Michal Bilewicz, a lecturer in sociology at the University of Warsaw. 'We are a nation of individualists. When Polish students were asked to describe the qualities of the Poles, they answered negatively since they don't regard themselves as part of the group. When Dutch students were asked if the Dutch were hardworking, they said yes. The Poles said, ah, no, the Poles are lazy and drink too much. This is because they don't see themselves as part of the same group.'

It can also lead to a curious kind of reverse pride that relates to the earlier stereotype we looked at, that of Polish heroism. Poles cannot separate this heroism from centuries of failure (failed uprisings, etc.), so that when there is something to celebrate, they're not sure how to react. Recently, a small Polish town agonised over how to rename the main square in connection with Monte Cassino. In the end, the square was renamed in honour of 'the *Defenders* of Monte Cassino'. In fact, the *Germans* were the defenders of Monte Cassino and Poles were the *attackers* (and the winners).

There is every reason for Poles to wear the birthmark of victimhood. The country didn't officially exist from 1795 until 1918. During the war *18 per cent* of Poland's population was killed, more than any other country. Worse, after the appalling loss of life, there was no sense that the sacrifice was 'worth it', since the country fell under a new 50-year tyranny. The complex still works on the Polish psyche, says Professor Bogdan Wojciszke from the Institute of Psychology at the Polish Academy of Sciences. 'Poles have always seen themselves as victims, people wronged by others. So those in power were seen as *them* rather than *us*. As a people, they have never identified with the state. In Germany, people happily identify themselves with the state; in Poland, you don't get that feeling.'

It means that there is a default suspicion of anyone who gets into power; anyone, indeed, who succeeds in the world of business. 'In America, where the vast majority of the wealth is in the hands of 1 per cent of the population, a total of 66 per cent of Americans still think the system is fair,' explains Professor Wojciszke. 'In Poland, where the wealth is spread so much more fairly, only 10 per cent believe the system is fair.'

In reality, Poles don't necessarily work much harder than anyone else. Those in the private sector probably work harder than those in the public sector. The ones who have gone abroad are generally, in any case, the more dynamic members of a society. The higher rate of pay they earned in Ireland and the UK was an incentive to work hard and send the money back home (many Poles were quietly building houses at home with the money earned in Ireland). Ironically, the same perceptions were at work in Poland. When all the construction workers and plumbers went to work in Ireland, the building industry in Poland had to draft in thousands of Ukrainian workers. And the perception of Ukrainians by Poles was the same: hardworking, diligent, cheap, etc., etc.

* * *

I leave the Warsaw Uprising Museum with Edmund Baranowski, the 84-year-old veteran, as evening falls.

He reflects on what the uprising means to young Poles. 'How different is our generation to this one! Poland sends troops to Iraq and Afghanistan. They're fully equipped, they have a big advantage over the insurgents. Twenty of them have died. OK, but those soldiers are regarded as being under huge stress, a big trauma. But what is 20 men when you send 10,000? Twenty could be a car crash! We were brought up in different conditions. The contemporary generation never experienced living on the edge of life and death.'

Perhaps there is a profound truth to what Edmund has said, and that somewhere, after 1945, the Poles quietly put aside the stereotype of suicidal bravery. Despite the repressions of the Communist era, there was no uprising, no glorious defeats, no Somosierra. There were outbreaks of unrest, and there was heroism, quiet, dignified, no doubt. For most people, though, life revolved around the sad, petty, endless compromises that allowed them to co-exist with the monster, or just get by.

'After 1945, the Poles were tired of failed uprisings,' says Konstanty Gebert of *Gazeta Wyborcza*. 'The Hungarians rose up against the Communists in 1956, the Poles didn't. Yes, there was a mass strike in Poznań which inspired the Hungarians, the Poles occupied a tank or two, but things actually ended in compromise. During martial law and the eight years which followed, the number of fatalities was 100 – under the military junta in Argentina, they would have killed that number in a slow week. I think that after Warsaw, Poles realised it was better to live on your knees than to die standing.'

For another opinion, I spoke to Andrzej Wajda. He is Poland's greatest living filmmaker, a four times Oscar-nominated director who received an honorary Academy Award in 2000. At 87, he is still directing and hard at work (he has made major films both about Katyń and about the sewers that Edmund struggled through during the uprising), but his personal story qualifies him above all to reflect on Poland's recent history: his father, a cavalry officer, was shot at Katyń as part of Stalin's plan to wipe out Poland's future leaders, officers and intelligentsia (4,500 officers were murdered, but over 20,000 Polish prisoners in total are thought to have been killed). He feels that Solidarity's roundtable talks with the Communist regime in February 1989 are the key to a kind of reformation of the Polish mindset, a decision – tinged with realism – which he places in contrast with the Warsaw Uprising.

'The rising was destined to fail,' he says. 'There was a possibility that it might not have happened at all. There was also the reconstruction of the city: that was a double victory for Stalin. The first was that the rising fell and the Home Army was destroyed, the second was the reconstruction, because Communist Poland had a new propaganda argument. Who destroyed Warsaw? The Polish government in exile. Who rebuilt the city? A government in a friendly alliance with the Soviet Union. So those two defeats were in the minds of those at the roundtable in 1989. When I think about it, it is *beautiful* that Poles eventually found some healthy common sense. They had an *awareness* and they could judge the situation appropriately. They could gain the maximum at a minimum loss. This is the most beautiful thing. It's not true that the Poles – their national character – cannot be reformed.'

Edmund Baranowski thinks, though, that the insurrectionary spirit is intrinsic to being Polish. 'If it happened again today, it would be the same. It's embedded in our genes. I wanted to gain independence with my own blood, not rely on being liberated by anyone else.'

Yet Edmund is still alive (he had a joyful reunion with his mother in 1945).

'What about my comrades dying? I think about it. I'm aware of it. I look at my identity card, and I can see when I was born [he has kept his occupation identity card, complete with German eagle and swastika].

'But I'm 62 years married to Halina, a nurse I met at the barricades. We have lived, and still live, in interesting times.'

Chapter 11
Greece

Farewell, good people who are wrongfully scorned and so unreasonably maligned because you are not well enough known…
Antoine Castellan, French traveller, 1796

Just after lunch on 21 October 2009, Walter Rademacher, a senior official in the EU's statistics agency Eurostat, discovered a letter on his desk. Its contents nearly made him fall off his chair. They were akin to a timer on a nuclear device which had just entered single digits. The letter read: '…we have revised the figures we have given you.'

It had been sent by the Greek Ministry of Finance. The casual admission that the country's budget deficit was higher than previously notified would set in motion a firestorm that would engulf Greece, then Ireland, then Portugal. Within a year the entire eurozone was facing a catastrophic economic collapse, and with it probably the entire European project. The impact on the global economy could only be guessed at.

Mr Rademacher, a 58-year-old family man, and formerly the head of Germany's federal statistics agency, had never in his long career pouring over numbers encountered such shock. 'There are some moments you don't forget in your life,' he recalls. 'For me they have been the fall of the Berlin Wall, 11 September … and now 21 October 2009.'

The numbers he was staring at were frightening. Greece's deficit in 2008 had really been 7.7 per cent, not the 5 per cent contained in the letter sent three weeks earlier. Much worse, the figure for 2009 had been revised upwards to a staggering 12.5 per cent instead of the 3.7 per cent previously notified. This would have immediate political consequences for Greece: a deficit-to-GDP ratio of 12.5 per cent was more than *four* times the limit set down by the Maastricht Treaty. 'I knew this would be a political tsunami,' Mr Rademacher says. 'In a general sense we had our seisemograph on. We knew there was some movement under the ocean. But we had not anticipated this.'

The tsuanmi was not immediately felt. Some headlines referred to the 'shoddy statistics' coming from Athens, but in reality the international media was more worried about Europe's overall economy following the Lehman Brothers collapse. In Brussels the Greek finance minister George Papaconstantinou reassured his colleagues 'that the new government is moving swiftly to restore credibility of statistics'. In fact, there had been problems ever since Greece joined the euro. Between 2001 and 2004, figures had been misreported on no fewer than 11 occasions, with deficit and debt levels constantly being revised upwards. Eurostat issued reprimands on five further occasions right up to 2009.

Eurostat had to immediately get to grips with the mess. It discovered 'inappropriate governance', 'poor cooperation', and an absence of written documents. Questions from Luxembourg to the Greek finance ministry would go unanswered for days, digits got lost here and there, and exasperated officials would be given figures at the last minute *over the phone*.

It appeared that Greece was not simply careless: it was cooking the books. 'There was deliberate misreporting,' Mr Rademacher says. 'That's diplomatic speak for something very serious – lying. This was not the work of frightened bureaucrats in the Greek office of statistics, unable to quite run the sliderule over the figures they were getting from the ministry of finance. There was no firewall between the two Greek institutions. The two levels were working in a close way. This was *deliberate* misrepresentation.'

A breach of trust was one thing, but soon European capitals were getting worried about the hole in Greece's finances that the figures had been disguising. Within six weeks of the letter being sent to Luxembourg, Greece was downgraded by the three main credit ratings agencies. The bond markets took fright. The yields on Greek bonds began to soar.

As 2010 dawned, the crisis was spreading to other peripheral countries. The clamour for financial support became deafening. Initially the German Chancellor Angela Merkel flatly ruled out a rescue, but it was clear that Europe would have to step in, and that Germany would have to pay the most. When Merkel reluctantly agreed, she insisted the IMF would have to be involved, and that would mean painful conditionality. By the time the €110 billion EU-IMF rescue was agreed in May 2010, the seeds of hostility between Greeks and Germans were sown. As Greece's own emergency austerity plans began to cut into living standards, street demonstrations took on an anti-German tone.

The Greek economy was soon in free fall. The conditions attached to the first bail-out drove the country deep into recession; unemployment, emigration, political upheaval and social despair all increased. Suicide rates soared. The centre of Athens became the battleground of violent, sometimes murderous, anger directed at the political establishment, and against Germany. Effigies of Angela Merkel wearing a Hitler moustache appeared in demonstrations, and the theme spread to Greek magazines (*Crash* magazine depicted Merkel and her finance minister Wolfgang Schaüble as concentration camp guards, accusing them of having 'murdered' Europe). One political party, the Independent Greeks, made anti-German sentiment a main policy platform.

Old wounds were reopened. References to Germany's brutal occupation from 1941 to 1944 abounded. The Greek finance ministry drew up a a report on what *Germany* owed *Greece* through war reparations. British newspaper reporters helpfully sought out old World War II resistance fighters in remote mountain villages to ask them what they thought of the German government cutting their pensions. An imagined link between German austerity and its Nazi past took hold and spread to other countries.

Not to be outdone, German MPs, mass-market and mainstream newspapers, talkshow hosts and comedians all launched a campaign of vilification against the Greeks, some of it tongue-in-cheek, some of it deadly serious. Greece was riddled with corrpution. Overpaid, underworked civil servants took long holidays and retired early. Patients regularly bribed doctors. Public-sector jobs were dished out to reward political supporters. Arguments against Greece joining the euro in the first place were reopened. Even Chancellor Merkel, usually careful in her comments, suggested Greeks should retire later and take fewer holidays (Greek unions responded bitterly by claiming, with some justification, that Germans took more holidays than most).

'The stereotype,' wrote Vicky Pryce, the Greek-born economist, in *Greekonomics*, 'of the Greeks began to emerge: Greeks composed a lazy, pampered and corrupt nation where bribery was rife; its citizens were unwilling to pay taxes and received large welfare benefits, were encouraged to take well-paid early retirement and thus enjoyed long siestas and periods in the sun.'

That German taxpayers would be footing the bill fuelled the indignation. In February 2010 the cover of the respected news magazine *Focus* featured the famous Venus de Milo statue, normally armless but now with a restored right arm raising an obscene middle digit. The headline, which triggered a lawsuit, read '*Betrüger in der Euro-Familie*' ('Swindler in the euro family'). But it was the tabloid *Bild-Zeitung* which cornered the market in righteous anger. It remorselessly ridiculed 'bankrupt Greeks', developed an obsession about Greece selling off some of its of islands ('We Give You Cash, You Give Us Corfu!'), and even sent a reporter to hand out *drachma* on the streets of Athens. One headline asked: 'Why are we paying for Greeks to retire in luxury?', while another gasped, 'Just look how well off Greek pensioners are!' On the eve of prime minister George Papandreou's visit to Berlin in March 2010, the paper thundered in an 'open letter' to the Greek leader: 'No one here has to pay thousands of euros in bribes to get a hospital bed. We don't give pensions to generals' daughters who can't find a husband ... Taxi drivers give receipts and farmers don't get billions of euros in EU subsidies for non-existent olive trees.'

In both cases tabloid hysteria was not out of step with political sentiment. An official in Chancellor Merkel's coalition partner declared that Greece *should* sell its islands. Despite attempts by both leaders to tone down the rhetoric, German tourists stayed away in droves (in 2012 bookings were down 30 per cent at a time when Greeks desperately needed visitor revenue).

Where did the truth lie?

The problem for Greece's self-esteem was that the picture of a corrupt state, where tax evasion thrived, where the public sector was bloated and where clientelism flourished, was not far off the mark. Foreign journalists discovered a political culture that beggared belief. Much of it was anecdotal, some was twisted out of context, but much was accurate. The political system had allowed the two rival, dynastic political parties, PASOK on the left and New Democracy on the right, to hand out government jobs to supporters whether or not those jobs were needed or even existed. An internal government report, conveyed to me by an EU ambassador, revealed that a public hospital had 43 gardeners on its books – yet had *no garden*. One transport minister admitted that so few people were using a rail line that it would be cheaper to pay for taxis to take them where they wanted to go (the line was never closed). 'People were pretending to be blind, to be handicapped, to be widowed, just to get benefits,' said one Brussels official familiar with the work of the EU-IMF-ECB troika. 'People just cheated. They cheated because they didn't trust the system.'

Civil service salaries were beefed up by a bizarre system of allowances, payments for things that public sector workers elsewhere were simply expected to do: bonuses for punctuality; for not missing days through sickness; for finishing work that had been requested. In the education ministry there was a €100-per-month *envelope-carrying allowance*. Vicky Pryce, in *Greekonomics*, chronicled some of the reported examples: railway workers receiving €420 per month for washing their hands, bus workers getting €310 for coming to work on time, coastguard workers earning an €840 *propeller bonus*, electricity workers getting an extra €870 per month because they knew how to send a fax.

Everyone and no one was to blame. On my first post-crisis trip to Athens in January 2010, the taxi driver spat curses at the political class all the way along the new EU-funded airport motorway, railing against thieving politicians and corruption – before presenting me with a sheaf of empty receipts in the hope that I would hire him later.

Tax evasion was rife. Greeks seemed neither to trust each other, nor state instituions. A European Commission study found that VAT receipts were 30 per cent less than what they should have been compared to an EU average of just 11 per cent. The shortfall cost the government on average 3.3 per cent of GDP a year, one and a half times the amount that the huge and gruelling austerity programme was expected to deliver in the 2012 draft budget. Foreign companies would negotiate a tax deal with the government rather than abide by a standard set of rules. Personal and business income tax were equally problematic. In 2009, almost 60 per cent of Greek taxpayers reported incomes below the tax-free threshold and so paid no income tax. Almost 90 per cent said they earned below €28,000, while only 1,700 declared incomes of €250,000 or more. Whatever the truth behind the declarations, some 30 per cent of taxpayers were paying 95 per cent of the total personal income tax take. Even company employees and pensioners, who were less likely to hide payments, appeared to be declaring incomes way below their actual levels, with 42 per cent of that category claiming to be earning no more than €10,000 per year in 2009.

In 2011, the then interior minister Giorgios Petalotis, who was trying to make a start on the tax system, told me, 'We discovered in many cases that people had villas, pools, helicopters… and yet didn't pay a single euro in tax.'

By 2010, tax arrears had reached 14.5 per cent of GDP. When offenders *were* sanctioned, they simply appealed to the courts. According to a 2012 study by Georgia Kaplanoglou and Vassilis T. Rapanos in *South European Society and Politics*, cases representing a further 13.5 per cent of GDP – or 150,000 files – were tied up in the legal system. Resolution took between 7 and 10 years. Greeks, according to a Eurobarometer survey, were both top of the league in working undeclared hours and not expecting a fine or prison sentence. When the then finance minister George Papaconstantinou was asked to explain to his fellow eurozone ministers why things had gone so wrong, he told startled colleagues: 'The first thing a government does in an election year is to pull the tax collectors off the streets.'

Whether Greeks liked it or not, the world was seeing Greece as a dysfuntional, over-extended, impoverished and violently divided state. It was paralysed by protesters raging against a government they had elected, against the system from which many must have benefited, and against the international lenders who were the only entitities prepared to lend Greece money. Greece was lurking dangerously close to a debt default. European politicians openly flirted with a Greek exit from the eurozone. 'Greece is something that we are able to deal with and, at the same time, something that we can do without,' said Jean Leonetti, the French Europe minister.

* * *

And yet…

For every clarion call for Greece to leave, there were plenty of voices insisting that Greece must stay. Greece was the birthplace of democracy, of Western civilisation, of European values. The former French president

Valéry Giscard d'Estaing declared: 'Europe without Greece is like a child without a passport.' Critics wondered, 'How could the cradle of civilisation get into this mess?' Greeks wondered, 'How could the rest of Europe treat the cradle of civilisation like this?' In fact Greece *was* a special case for historical reasons, and because by mid-2012 it was clear to everyone – not least Angela Merkel – that a messy Greek default and euro exit could prove catastrophic to the global economy.

But what stereotypes did we hold of the Greeks before 21 October 2009? How did Greeks see themselves, and how far from the grotesque caricature that was gripping Europe were those more benign snapshots?

To the modern European sensibility, shaped by films such as *Shirley Valentine* and *My Big Fat Greek Wedding*, or by island-hoping hedonism, or by the package-holiday histrionics of the dancing waiter, Greeks were loveable, boisterous, crafty, emotional, superstitious and roguish. They had a touch of the Latin lover (in the '60s and '70s northern European females were subject to *kamaki*, a word deriving from spear-fishing which referred to getting hit on by Greek men on Aegean beaches). Who else but a Greek shipping magnate – Aristotle Onassis – could romance Jackie Kennedy on his yacht in the months before her husband's assassination, and then marry her afterwards? The Greek diaspora was millenia-old and had sunk deep roots of likeability and influence on every continent. Zorba the Greek, the rugged, rambunctious hero immortalised in Nikos Kazantzakis' 1946 novel and later by the 1964 triple Academy Award-winning film, personified the life-embracing, shoulder-shrugging élan of the Greek islander. Greeks in celluloid fought and resisted like no others, from *The 300 Spartans*, to the *Guns of Navarone*, to *Captain Corelli's Mandolin*. In rhetoric they were lionised by Churchill for their valour in World War II, 'Hence we will not say that Greeks fight like heroes, but that heroes fight like Greeks.'

Greece was the fulcrum between Europe and the Middle East, a thoroughfare for crusader heading east and Ottoman invader heading west, the font of the Orthodox faith, and the frontline in the Cold War. It has been, in short, a nation hard to ignore. Nor could the 21st-century debt crisis avoid references to the *world's* debt to Greece: art, culture, history, democracy, rhetoric, medicine, geography, mathematics, theatre… there was not a single pillar of human progress for which we did not apparently owe thanks to the ancient Greeks.

* * *

This stunning efflorescence reached its peak between the 8th and 4th centuries bc. Ancient Greeks were blessed by climate and geography. Hours of sunshine made for an outdoor, communal life, indispensible to the gatherings of democracy and drama. Greek dominion over the seas produced a restless race of adventurers who created city-states across both the Mediterranean and Black Seas (Syracuse, Marseille, Naples, Messina, Sevastopol all derive from Greek names). The manner in which Greeks thought about the world around them, the *kosmos*, spawned a radical philosophical tradition that became the foundation of Western thought. The Homeric myths produced a Pantheon of gods – Zeus, Apollo, Artemis, Pallas Athene, Poseidon, Hermes, Dionysus, Pluto, Persephone, *et al.* – who were presented in human form and had human characteristics, thus placing humanity at the centre of Greek thought. 'The gods are constantly present in the *Iliad* and *The Odyssey*,' writes Diarmaid MacCulloch in *A History of Christianity*, 'an intrusive and often disruptive force in human lives: often fickle, petty, partisan, passionate, competitive – in other words, rather like Greeks themselves.'

When the Greek city-states united to defeat the Persian Empire, Greece's golden age rose to its zenith. Defeat of the Persians had implanted the notion – later adopted by the Romans – of an advanced civilisation (the Greeks) surrounded by barbarians. Religion did not limit curiosity about the world, and those questions not answered by the sacred were pursued through poetry, prose and philosophy, a system of knowledge and wisdom by which to order everyday life. Socrates, Plato and Aristotle provided the foundations of how later Europeans – both Christian and Muslim – would organise their thoughts about how the universe worked. Greek fascination with the beauty of the human form both changed Western art and, through the Renaissance, man's relationship with himself and with God. Euripides, Sophocles and Aeschylus, who sought to resolve political and personal folly and tragedy through theatre, set a path for Shakespeare to follow. The city-states sought a system to organise their nascent societies, to expand and to fight wars, one which could be updated without being divinely appointed. The result was democracy, in its earliest form a rule which allowed males over 30 to contribute to decision-making (Cleisthenes the Alcmaeonid started it in 507 bc, but Pericles in the 5th and Demosthenes in the 4th centuries bc are regarded as the pre-eminent Greek democrats).

Athens bequeathed unsurpassed excellence in every field of human endeavour. Five of the seven wonders of the ancient world were masterpieces of Greek architecture. Its influence spread far and wide, forcing itself on every neighbouring civilisation, not least the Romans. Over time, and beyond the Greek golden age, such processes – Hellenisation – inspired the Macedonian general Alexander the Great to spread his own hybrid empire stretching all the way to China. 'The name "Greek" should no longer be thought of as a matter of race,' wrote the orator Isocrates, 'but a matter of intelligence.'

Despite the Hellenic era passing into twilight, the new Byzantine Empire to the east, calved from the declining Roman Empire, became a Greek and Christian Orthodox rival to the emerging Holy Roman (and Catholic) Empire. It had long since become the crossroads of Christian belief (St Paul and the Evangelists all wrote in Greek, their second language). 'One way or another,' writes Norman Davies in *A History of Europe*, 'enough has survived for that one small, East European country to be regularly acclaimed as "the Mother of Europe", the "Source of the West", a vital ingredient, if not the sole fountain-head, of Europe.'

* * *

The Byzantine Empire, with its capital in Constantinople (Byzantium), survived for nearly a thousand years after the Roman Empire collapsed in the 5th century. At its peak it controlled much of the southern and eastern Mediterranean, but its fortunes ebbed and flowed as the new Muslim threat emerged from Arabia. A devastating *Western* crusade in 1204 – when Venetians, Franks and other Europeans sacked Orthodox Constantinople – fragmented the empire between rival Greek and Latin realms. But it was soon eclipsed by a new Turkic force, ominously appearing to the east, which would eventually overthrow the Byzantine Empire and capture its headquarters. When the Ottoman Sultan Mehmed the Conqueror broke through the seige walls of Constantinople on 27 May 1453, it struck terror into Christian Europe, and set in motion the *Tourkokratía*, the 400-year occupation of Greek lands.

Nearly 600 years on, the Ottoman occupation is often the first port of call when explanations are sought for the Greek debt crisis. Indeed, as David Marsh recalls in *The Euro: the Battle for the New Global Currency*, the legacy of occupation was on the minds of eurozone capitals when it waved Greece through due to its 'antique glories, its long and painful history of foreign intrusion ranging from the Ottomans to the Nazis…'

Summarising a prolonged epoch is a treacherous business, but Ottoman rule was by no means absolute nor unremittingly tryannical. The first 200 years actually provided some stability following numerous conflicts with Western powers, but overall the experience was not a happy one. Greek lands were settled by Muslims from Anatolia; Orthodox Christianity was supplanted by Islam as the new state faith; relentless invasions through the Balkans as far as the gates of Vienna led to endless war and repressive taxation, not to mention the massacres of Christians in beseiged cities which refused to surrender.

Greeks were often not just second- but *third*-class citizens. In Thessaloniki Muslims came first, followed – after their expulsion from Spain and arrival in 1500 – by Jews. Greek children were often conscripted (or kidnapped) to form part of the Sultan's hereditary household guard, the Janissaires, while Christian women were considered war booty in the event of a successful siege. Greeks coped by leaving in their droves, or by converting to Islam.

But the official attitude could also be lenient. Sultan Mehmed was well disposed towards the Greek population, admiring their culture and urging them to regard him as their protector, a figurehead more reliable than the Pope. Within months of capturing Constantinople, he oversaw the appointment of a new Patriarch, giving the Orthodox Church the freedom to run their own education system (its teaching role was, however, strictly ecclesiastical). Some Orthodox churches were looted or converted into mosques, but not all. By 1547 there were 65 churches in Istanbul. Sultans, or their Grand Viziers, married Greek and Serbian princesses. The hated conscription of Greek boys nevertheless saw many rise to heights of privilege within the military and bureaucracy. Indeed, many Christians, long since losing faith in the ability of the Byzantine ruling class to protect them, actually welcomed the prospects that the new system offered. Furthermore, the crimes committed by 'Latin' crusaders against the Byzantines lingered in the memory. 'Faced with the apparent choice,' writes Mark Mazower in *Salonica, City of Ghosts*, 'between the reviled Catholics (their sack of Constantinople in 1204 never to be forgotten) and the Muslim Turks, many opted for the latter.'

Nor were the Ottomans the only oppressors around. Athens had fallen into the hands of Catalan mercenaries and later Neapolitan merchants before being claimed by the Sultan. Genoans ran islands such as Chios, while the Venetians ruled Crete for 450 years, as well as Cyprus and parts of the Peloponnese. Over two centuries there were, in fact, 27 uprisings against Venice (in Cyprus, in 1570, Venetians put 500 Greeks to the sword when they suspected them of planning an uprising in advance of a Turkish invasion). One hundred years later Greeks welcomed the Ottoman invaders of Crete as liberators, many later converting to Islam. Cities which surrendered without a fight were treated with moderation, their nobility entitled to keep their estates and privileges.

In the 17th and 18th centuries the Ottomans were fighting battles on many fronts. This was a mixed blessing for the Greeks. Various treaties resulting from military setbacks saw Greek status and earning power rise. Merchants with the right kind of licences could trade (and avoid Ottoman taxes) throughout the empire and beyond. By sea, Greek freebooters, or pirates, drawn from the poor islands and coastlines, plundered cargo throughout the eastern Mediterranean. From 1774 seaborne Greek entrepreneurs were entitled to sail under the Russian flag, eventually controlling trade routes to Venice, Odessa, Alexandria and Marseille.

On terra firma, however, life was harsh. In theory, all land belonged to the Sultan, with the rural poor subjected to various levels of subsistence tenure. Small holdings were hereditary, but there was little or no scope for the peasant to improve his lot. For centuries the economy remained stagnant. Greek Christians – those not taken by the Janissaries – were not subject to military service and so were subject to a poll tax not applied to Muslims. Over time, changes to the system of granting land to military veterans, and the need to raise more taxes to fill the Sultan's war-depleted treasury, led to further hardship and resentment. Instead of sending out tax collectors from the capital to far-flung provinces, the authorities introduced tax farming (a system also used in feudal Europe): the tax farmer would pay the bid price to the treasury then keep for himself all the taxes he had collected. Or, he would sell to subcontractors the right to collect taxes. Either way the system was widely open to abuse. 'Not surprisingly,' writes David Brewer in *Greece, The Hidden Centuries*, 'tax farmers were unscrupulous in wringing the maximum, legally or otherwise, from their victims in order to realise their profit.'

In the 16th to 18th centuries foreign travellers began to arrive in Greece, and were naturally curious about the Sultan's Christian subjects. Some early stereotypes were unkind. Greeks were crafty and cunning – the Trojan horse trick was not easily forgotten – or even drunken. Any traveller of the time versed in St Paul would have known that 'Cretans are always liars, evil brutes, lazy gluttons'. Once the Renaissance awoke the dazzling Ancient Greek civilisation in European minds, a whole new set of images presented themselves. As such it became impossible for the Greeks (as perhaps it is still today) to be assessed on their *own* merits. In 1502, the Neapolitan poet Jacopo Sannazaro wrote *Arcadia*, beginning a long tradition of the Greek rural idyll (in reality it was based on a land that was fairly bleak and impoverished). Foreigners were either disappointed at the wretched state of these descendants of ancient heroes, or attributed fanciful qualities to those Greeks who rose up against the empire. Greeks were 'wholly degenerate from their ancestors in valour, virtue and learning,' snorted the early 17th-century Scottish traveller William Lithgow. Whatever about their ancient qualities, observed Pierre Belon, a French naturalist, 'all the Greek…areas are in such an amazing state of ignorance that there is not a single city in the entire country that has a university and not a trace of pleasure in learning the arts and sciences.'

Other travellers were, however, enchanted by what they found. Richard Chandler, an Englishman, found the Greeks full of *joie de vivre*, athletic, free spirited, spontaneously breaking into music or dancing, and deeply devout. The French traveller Antoine Castellan wrote in 1796: 'Their fundamental character seemed to be a mixture of light-heartedness, weakness, and boastfulness. As easily moved to tears as children, the very next minute they forget the reason for their pity. Excitable as children, they let themselves be carried away to a furious pitch of anger, and quieten down just as easily if they encounter indifference or are overawed by firm treatment… Sensitive to upbraiding and blame, praise pleases them much more than rewards; the slightest success fills them with energy…'

* * *

But it was how Greeks comported themselves in rebellion that had outsiders reaching for superlatives. In 1770, Catherine the Great, long dreaming of a Russian-sponsored Orthodox monarchy arising from the ruins of the Ottoman Empire (she insisted her grandson Constantine be suckled by Greek wet nurses), launched an invasion of Greece that ended in failure. Her commander Count Theodore Orlov blamed the failure (naturally) on the Greeks, accusing them of cowardice, recklessness and of being fixated on plunder. British newspaper reports tended to agree. The *Gentleman's Magazine* reported that when their Russian allies showed up, the Greeks discovered the 'manly bravery of their renowned ancestors', but when the Turks appeared, 'in a moment their courage failed them.' *The Annual Register* opined that that it would have been naïve to think that the Greeks, 'immersed in corruption of two thousand years … should all at once do more than inherit the valour of their ancestors.'

While for some foreign observers Greek servitude was all the more acute since they were descended from heroes, for others those ancient virtues were all too apparent. 'I see the most regular forms,' gushed the French scholar Pierre Augustin Guys, 'black, bright eyes animated with a natural fire, elegant and majestic physiques, a simple and light dress…' (as quoted in David Brewer's *Greece, The Hidden Centuries*).

In the end, external inspiration and internal realities finally drove the Greeks towards independence, although outside financial and diplomatic muscle would be necessary. Greek intellectuals, imbued with the ideals of the Englightenment and the French Revolution, and funded by a growing class of wealthy expats, founded a new independence movement on the ashes of the failed Russian invasion. Growing resentment over increasingly harsh taxation would provide the impetus. Meanwhile, a wave of poets, intellectuals and aristrocrats were steadily making their way to Greece. Temples were excavated and pictorial travel books published. Dreamers wondered if a golden age might return to Athens if the Turks were kicked out. 'They opened the eyes of the cultural world to this birthplace of civilization,' writes Lord Kinross in *The Ottoman Centuries*, 'still inhabited (whatever the more sceptical scholars might say) by the Greeks of old, and awakened in it visions of its renewal.'

In 1821 a coordinated revolt broke out in the Peloponnese and independence was delcared. A constitution was drawn up in 1822, but the Greek propensity for internal division was never far away: a dispute between the mainstream revolutionaries and the Klephts, the mountain brigands-cum-warriors, who had withdrawn into the mountains in the 15th century to avoid Ottoman repression (or simply taxation) and who had been drafted in to do the fighting, drove the country into civil war. By 1825 the Turks had all but recovered their lost ground, but it was to be the greatest European dreamer of the day, Lord Byron, who would help to turn the tide in the Greeks' favour. He arrived in 1823 with a six-figure cheque and an army of 500 rebels bound for Messonlonghi, but when, at the age of just 36, he died of malaria contracted in the local swamps, he became an martyr to the cause, spurring public opinion to press for intervention. In October 1827 a combined force of French, British and Russian ships defeated the Ottoman fleet in the Bay of Navarino. By 1830 the Great Powers recognised Greek independence. It was to be the first country to liberate itself from Ottoman rule.

* * *

Looking at the emnity today between Greeks and Germans, it is unsettling to discover just how instrumental the Germans also were in the rebirth of Greece. Germans were more besotted than any other Europeans by Ancient Greece. Art historian Johann Joachim Winckelmann (1717–1768) wrote ground-breaking books on classical Greece which later became a powerful influence on Goethe and Nietzsche. The Leipzig professor of philosophy Wilhelm Traugott Krug saw in Greece's rebirth the resurrection of Christ. Friedrich Wilhelm Thiersch, professor of ancient philology in Munich, changed his name to *Thyrios* and called for the creation of a German legion to fight against the Turk. On the eve of the Greek revolt, the vast majority of Europe's Philhellenic (or Greek-loving) societies were to be found in Germany. When the fighting started, more Germans volunteered than any other nationality. The reason was simple. 'Many western Europeans,' writes Evangelos Konstantinou in *Graecomania and Philhellenism*, 'viewed the Greeks who were fighting against Ottoman rule as the direct descendants of the ancient Greeks.'

But when independence came knocking, democracy, that gift of those same ancient Greeks, was not on the menu. The revolutionary elite was convinced that Greece needed a strong European monarch. The monarch was to be, of course, German. Step forward 18-year-old Prince Otto of Bavaria who arrived in Greece with a coterie of Bavarian nobles and, naturally, a German bail-out. He won the locals over by adopting the Greek version of his name (*Othon*) and by wearning traditional Hellenic costume. He also provided a degree of unity and stability after years of war, moving the capital to Athens from the north-eastern Peloponnese port city of Nafplio. Not surprisingly, however, a substantial section of the population was none too keen on being ruled by an outsider, and he was soon forced to agree to a new constitution. The problem, as John S. Koliopoulos and Thanos M. Veremis explain in *Greece: the Modern Sequel*, was that the country he inherited was an impoverished, faction-ridden, multi-ethnic backwater. Greece lacked a fully formed working class to man the revolution, or a middle class to run it. There was also an innate suspicion of the West among the pre-independence nobility. Many had enjoyed a profitable niche within the empire and were now opposed to the idea of an independent Greece becoming a Western country.

To this day a source of controversy in Greece, the record of the Orthodox Church in the revolt was mixed. Patriarch Gregory V denounced the rebels and called for their excommunication (despite his stance, he was hanged by the Sultan from the door of the Patriarchal palace in Istanbul on Easter Sunday, 1821). Numerous clergy and bishops, however, took part in the fighting.

Otto was deposed in 1862, living out his days in Bavaria, still deeply in love with his adopted country (on his death in 1867, he was buried in Greek costume). But German influence did not end with Otto's death. Architect Leo von Klenze arrived in Athens and went about removing any works that had been recently added to the Acropolis. Friedrich von Gärtner designed the parliament which overlooks Syntagma Square (familiar as the recent target of protestors chanting anti-German slogans). No fewer than three German architects worked on the restoration of the Temple of Athena Nike. Back in Bavaria, the newly designed Königsplatz in Munich was based on the Acropolis.

* * *

Who were the new Greeks? The Romantic notion that they were all descendants of ancient heroes was fanciful. Multiple visitors – Roman, Slav, Albanian, French, Venetian, Genoan – had traipsed through Greece from early times. The Ottomans brought their own genetic footprint, and through rape, enslavement and inter-marriage, mixed the local DNA further. 'The eventual result of this,' writes Lord Kinross (somewhat enthusiastically) in *The Ottoman Centuries*, 'was the development of an Ottoman race vigorous and rich in the mixture of its blood. Eastern blood – Tatar, Mongol, Circassian, Georgian, Persian, and Arabian – which had already flowed through Turkish veins was now mixed with the blood of the Balkan races and those of Europe beyond…'

Some took this notion too far. Jakob Fallmerayer (1790–1861), a Bavarian scholar, poured scorn on decades of European infatuation with Greece, arguing that modern Greeks were descended, not from ancient heroes, but from Hellenised Slavs and Albanians. 'The race of the Hellenes,' he opined, 'has been wiped out in Europe. Physical beauty, intellectual brilliance, innate harmony and simplicity, art, competition, city, village, the splendour of column and temple – indeed, even the name has disappeared from the surface of the Greek continent…. Not the slightest drop of undiluted Hellenic blood flows in the veins of the Christian population of present-day Greece.'

His arguments were, of course, furiously rejected by the nationalist founders of the new Greece who insisted on an unbroken linguistic and racial line between the new state and its ancient forebears. His dubious notions were to make a final, distressing comeback: classically trained Nazi officers were to study them before the Wehrmacht invaded in 1941, so they felt guilt-free when killing Greek civilians.

But in the 19th century defining a distinct Greek *nation* to which citizens could adhere was a pressing problem. Identity and nationhood were complicated by questions of race, religion and language within the receding Ottoman realm (the same issues would bedevil the Balkans for a further 150 years). There was no escaping Greece's ancient role, a legacy at once inspiring and problematic. Notions of the Greeks being God's chosen race, annointed to civilise those neighbouring lands still yoked to the Turk, inspired nationalist dreams of a greater Greece – a revival of the Byzantine Empire, no less. Through the Great Idea (*Megáli Idéa*), the new country would retrieve lands and populations where Greek was spoken and the Orthodox religion practised. In fact the country's new borders in 1832 contained only 700,000 Greeks, the rest residing in Epirus, Thessaly, Macedonina, Bulgaria, Thrace and in what we now call Turkey (there were still 120,000 Greeks in Istanbul).

In the process those highland outlaws, or Klepths, were to prove decisive. The use of 'irregulars' was sanctioned by the authorities, with brigands being released from prison to join the cause. Thus brigandage was tolerated right into the 20th century and attitudes towards their criminal activity were blurred by admiration for their services to the Greek nation. 'The Klephts and their lineal descendants,' argue Koliopoulos and Veremis, 'were supposed to represent freedom from all attachments and bonds save those of religion and family. They were portrayed not as the hunted outlaws they actually were… but as proud and brave men who could not bear to see themselves and their countrymen groaning under a foreign yoke.'

Could this go some way to explaining a distinct ambivalence towards operating on the fringes, or outside of the law? Koliopoulos and Veremis speculate: 'Abuse of public office for personal ends, though condemned in principle as morally reprehensible, has been pursued with determination and some pride – to the extent that, along with tax evasion, it should be ranked as one of the nation's most consistent pursuits… Like banditry, abuse of public office for personal enrichment has seldom been punished.'

Meanwhile, the economic cost of the country's irredentist ambitions – not to mention the War of Independence – added to its woes in a way only too familiar today. In 1824 a £472,000 loan had been raised through the London Stock Exchange to finance the war, with an additional £1.1 million pounds from other powers in 1825 (speculators skimmed off large amounts before they got to the rebels). Greece defaulted on the loan in 1826 and there were further defaults in 1843 and 1860. After the British loans were paid off in 1878, Greece resumed its heavy borrowing but defaulted once again in 1893. This led to something of a troika forerunner – the International Committee for Greek Debt Management – which monitored Greece's economic policies as well as its tax-collection system. Greece defaulted again on American loans in 1932, an event which kept it out of the markets until a World Bank loan in 1964.

The 20th century brought further upheavals. By the eve of World War I, Greece had won considerable territory. With history apparently on its side (not to mention a British promise of more territory after World War I), Greece made a final but ill-fated bid to realise its Great Idea in the 1922 war with the new Turkish republic. It was a bloody and bitter conflict with accusations of massacres and ethnic cleansing on both sides. In the end it was fought to a stalemate. The war is remembered in Greece as the Asia Minor Catastrophe. The settlement involved the combatants agreeing a huge population exchange. But there were further catastrophes ahead.

* * *

The years that followed provide clues as to how Greece came to rely on the public sector in times of emergency, a reliance which later developed into a dangerous addiction. Between 1923 and the early 1930s, more than a million refugees descended on Greece from Asia Minor as a result of the population swap. Between 1915 and 1925, the number of public-sector employees doubled, with taxes doubling to pay for them. Greece's debt more than trebled. Again, there were outstanding debts to foreign creditors, which hampered access to new loans. In 1932 Greece suspended interest payments and, once again, went into default.

Any hope that promising agricultural exports in the 1930s could set the country on a better path were dashed by the outbreak of World War II. The Nazi occupation would do untold damage to the Greek economy for years to come. As Greece had no major industries to feed into the German war effort, the occupiers settled for straightforward plunder. The cost of the occupation was estimated at 850 billion drachma by 1943. After the war Greece was one of three countries (Austria and Italy were the others) singled out for the first wave of financial help under the Marshall Plan, although fear of the communist menace was by far Washington's biggest motivation. Between 1945 and 1950, Greece received $2.1 billion in aid, more than all the loans contracted between 1821 and 1930 combined. When aid ran out in the 1950s, Greece's response was to involve the state as much as possible. The National Bank of Greece merged with other banks, and other state-run banks were set up to boost growth. Telecommunications and electricity utilities expanded. Tens of thousands of Greeks, meanwhile, emigrated, mostly as 'guest workers' to West Germany.

* * *

But Greece was not a country at peace. A civil war between 1946–49 between communist and rightist forces, in which the latter prevailed, left a highly polarised, paranoid political landscape in which 'legitimate' left-wing or centre-left aspirations were forced into the shadows (or exile) and kept there. The country was still underdeveloped and had a dearth of both data and expertise. One US diplomat noted, 'Greece has eight million politicians but only a handful of economists.'

At the turn of the 1960s one such economist saw himself as being given a messianic duty to change things. His career would prove central to the tumultuous events which gripped Greece over the next two decades, and indeed have a far-reaching impact on Greece's ruinous policies later.

Andreas Papandreou was born into Greece's most famous political dynasty. His father George was the governor of the Aegean island of Chios, and his own son, also George, would, as Greece's prime minister from 2009–2011, become known to the world as the hapless face of the Greek debt crisis. Andreas had been detained and beaten as a left-wing student activist in the 1930s, but much of his young adult life he spent in the United States as a rising economist. He married Margaret, an American citizen, and later befriended J.K. Galbraith who secured a him professorship at the University of Minnesota (he later moved to Berkeley). By the early 1960s he was moving in the liberal circles of John F. Kennedy's New Frontier and had strong contacts in the State Department. Worried about the state of his homeland, he obtained US funding for an

Athens-based think-tank that would co-opt some of the fresh ideas of the Kennedy administration to revitalise the Greek economy.

It would also act as a bridgehead for his own political ambitions. But his first experience of Greek political culture shocked him: 'The dominant guiding force in [the bureacracy's] decisions was their immediate personal or clique interest. A major component of the Greek elite, to put it bluntly, was morally corrupt and tradition bound...' The clientelist nature of the system was also immediately apparent: 'Hundreds of men and women every day would approach me to assure me of their support... but simultaneously to demand the solution of some particular problem that was or should have been a routine matter for the municipal, the regional or the national government. Truck licences, bus licenses, admissions to hospitals and universities, draft deferments – almost anything you could think of were turned over to my staff for action... I had a sinking feeling.'

Papandreou wanted to replace this system with something that would awaken the creativity of the Greek nation. He was also determined to dislodge the right-wing and royalist monolith that had kept a tight grip on the body politic since the Civil War, and had proclaimed a monopoly on Greek nationalism. In November 1963 he secured a parliamentary seat when his father's Centre Union party won a spectacular election victory over the right-wing ERE party. Amid mass street protests against perceived anti-democratic manoeuvrings by the king and a virulently anti-communist faction of army officers – all of whom received sympathetic if covert support from the CIA – Andreas's rising appeal was marked by an increasingly populist edge. Left-wing Greeks who had been brutalised or just felt excluded were brought into the daylight. Their hero offered 'a seamless amalgam of populism and Keynsian economics,' writes Stan Draenos in *Andreas Papandreou: The Making of a Greek Democrat and Political Maverick*. 'In Andreas the politically alienated found their champion.'

Despite his strong American roots, his rhetoric towards the US cooled and he began attracting hostile attention from the United States embassy in Athens. With the young King Constantine II making ever more aggressive inroads into parliamentary politics, Greece became further polarised. On 21 April 1967 the gathering storm clouds that threatened military intervention finally burst. A cabal of right-wing colonels launched a coup, suspended the constitution and installed a repressive dictatorship. At 2.30

a.m. soldiers raided Andreas Papandreou's home. On the roof they found the 14-year-old George huddled in a corner. The boy, who would later became the bail-out prime minister, had a gun held to his head. He was told he would be shot unless he told the raiders where his father was.

* * *

Andreas Papandreou was initially detained but later allowed to leave Greece under pressure from the US administration. When the military regime collapsed in 1974 following an abortive coup attempt in Cyprus, Papandreou returned from exile to found the Panhellenic Socialist Movement (PASOK). It would become a huge, grassroots, populist and left-wing party that would dominate Greek politics until its spectacular collapse in the June 2012 elections.

Much of Greece's current trauma is now attributed to Papandreou's legacy as prime minister, although PASOK naturally claims New Democracy was just as bad. Throughout two terms of office he bestrode the political landscape, regarded as a hero by his followers and a demagogue by his opponents. If, in the early 1960s, he had seen Greece as divided, not between right and left, but between the people and an unyielding establishment, the time had come for him to set that right. He embarked on a massive spending programme to reduce social exclusion and increase the incomes of the poor. He boosted the minimum wage, social-welfare entitlements and pensions, and introduced a national health service. He relaxed the rules on labour law to allow unions to strike (unions then effectively ruled large parts of the state through their control of public utilities). There was funding for parental leave and child care. Third-level education was expanded and the number of students doubled.

But his youthful idealism was abandoned, and he succumbed to the very clientelist, crony-based system that had horrified his early '60s New Frontier vision. Presenting himself as a champion of Greek interests, he threatened to veto Spain and Portugal's accession to the EEC, and to pull Greece out altogether if it didn't get the huge regional subsidies that the newcomers were promised upon accession. In the event Greece ended up receiving more funds than any other country – nearly €6 billion – between 1985–89. But under his watch Greece became synonymous with high-level fraud in the securing and spending of European subsidies. The huge debt-fueled expansion of the civil service, meanwhile, was drawing sharp rebukes from Brussels long before the euro crisis.

Papandreou saw his policies as healing the bitter wounds of the Civil War and restoring the state as an instrument of fairness, rather than a weapon of repression. The income gap *was* reduced, and the demoralising inequalities of post-war Greece were tackled – but at a price: the massive expansion of Greece's national debt and the white-knuckle exploitation of European money. 'He tried to open up the public space to people who were excluded for many decades after the civil war,' says Angelos Athanasopoulos, diplomatic editor of *To Vima* newspaper. 'First he had to infiltrate the state with people of his own mind, to offer a virtual level of prosperity – not based on economic fundamentals, but from money coming from the European community, and channelled through the agriculture sector.'

In its obituary on Andreas Papandreou's death in 1996, *The Economist* concluded: 'For Mr Papandreou, Greek voters were clients… Mr Papandreou was charming, clever and a populist genius. But he held back Greece's economic and political growth. It has to be said that, in the end, he was an anachronistic, unprincipled opportunist.'

* * *

Scanning Greece's troubled history, from the Ottoman occupation to World War II to the military dictatorship, one can only speculate as to how it might have determined the pathologies of which Greeks now stand accused. During the *Toukokratía* Greeks (as well as other subjects) lived on their wits, strove to succeed, or just survive, within a capricious system of repression and advantage. Some rose to the highest ranks of officialdom within the bureaucracy or the Church. Others made fortunes as merchants or in shipping. Others were ground into slavery, poverty, humiliation and exile.

As for modern-day attitudes to tax compliance, it is worth noting that throughout the Ottoman empire taxation was complex and inconsistent, varying according to religion or ethnicity. It was used to encourage conversion to Islam (Christians paid higher taxes), or to *discourage* conversion to Islam (if tax revenues fell). In general, bribery and corruption was a problem from an early date. Troops would seize goods on flimsy evidence, judges would impose harsh or unjustified taxes, forcing villagers to seek help from moneylenders. The Orthodox Church was itself allowed to collect taxes, resulting in clerics bribing higher officials to secure lucrative tax-collecting positions (clerics also fell foul of moneylenders, often passing the costs on to the faithful). The Ottoman hierarchy, meanwhile, from the Sultan to the district governor (Pasha) to the local elite (Beys), dispensed favour and privilege so long as obsequies flowed and palms were greased.

All told, the experience of the Ottoman centuries can only have engendered deeply ambivalent attitudes to authority, to the state, to taxation, to trusting one's fellow citizen, to petitioning those in authority, and generally to getting ahead. Greeks throughout history have felt deeply let down by the West (1204, 1453, 1770, 1825, 1922, 1967) and have not always felt fully enthusiastic about their European destiny. For a long time Greece was barely a normal democracy. In a country long polarised by civil war and radicalised by the repression that followed, the public sector became a weapon of party-political warfare: former communists were barred from the civil service jobs after the war, while until the 1970s union membership required taking an anti-communist oath. The sheer geographical fragmentation of the country, with its hundreds of islands, has never lent itself to a popular allegiance to centralised institutions (wealthy businessmen are known to invest heavily in their island while keeping their savings offshore).

As such, opportunism, perhaps of a kind personified and given official sanction by Andreas Papandreou, has, according to one thoughtful observer, become the *key* vice of the modern Greek. Opportunism, that is, at the expense of cooperation.

'Greeks act more opportunistically than the Swedes or even the French,' says Aristos Doxiadis, an academic, blogger and private-equity professional who has been trying to unravel the vagaries of history and psychology that have landed Greece in its current predicament. He argues that it wasn't so much the impact of the Ottoman system, but the fact that there was no system to replace it. Quoting the contemporary Greek philosopher Stelios Ramfos, Doxiadis contends that, whereas in the West, via the long journey from the Middle Ages, feudalism, the Church, monarchy, the Enlightenment, and to the Industrial Revolution, the European individual understood, or 'internalised', the rules of society and its hierarchies. In other words, the individual subconsciously accepted the need for society to be guided by vertical and horizontal rules.

In Greece, however, after the Ottomans, subsequent hierarchies were resisted. 'It is either a jungle, or a community of corner shops,' he argues. 'We Greeks have subscribed neither to vertical nor to horizontal rules. We are neither obedient nor cooperative. If we have avoided the jungle, it is because we have kept the corner shops.'

Opportunism, he says, while having some redeeming features, leads to corruption, cheating and a chronic lack of trust. Government grants, designed for the common good, end up divided and hived off into personal bank accounts since one recipient of the grant won't trust the other. The same applies to tax evasion and benefit fraud. This defect – for want of a better word – was made worse when government spending ballooned and European subsidies began to flow. It eventually crystalised into what Doxiadis and others have described as a 'rentocracy': state contracts or 'rents' are sought by special-interest groups who then seek payment from the state over the odds. In a rentocracy, favouritism and bribery, rather than merit, are what count. The system saps growth, encourages an expectation of income for doing very little, inflates the bureaucracy with unnecessary public-sector jobs, and nullifies a sense of personal responsibility.

Eventually, private operators will only invest where they feel they can get a higher return from a state contract, rather than invest in an open market. 'Over time this distorts their whole mode of operation: a good salesman is one who can build personal relationships with bureaucrats, a good engineer is one who can draw out a project to make it more expensive,' says Doxiadis. By its very nature, the rentocratic state doesn't demand measurements either for pollution, or hospital care, or police crime figures. To the majority of Greeks the system encourages the expectation of receiving some income from neither work nor capital. 'If they cannot have it,' says Doxiadis, 'they feel wronged.'

So destructive is the rentocracy, argue Michael Mitsopoulos and Theodore Pelagidis in the journal of the US Cato Insitute, that rent-seekers have become like Vikings, 'grab[bing] anything they can while roaming freely through various aspects of social and economic activity… Many small, well-organised groups – ranging from notaries, lawyers, and truckers, to less well-known cases such as loaders and unloaders in ports and public markets as well as trade unionists in publicly owned enterprises – earn significant rents, and therefore have a strong motivation to maintain the status quo and oppose any reforms.'

* * *

But there are other harmful legacies from Ottoman times. The Turks preferred small holders to big land owners, and the new state continued the policy (to this day, most Greeks have a small plot of land somewhere). As a result Greek farmers struggle to compete despite billions in agricultural subsidies. The failure of the new state to set up a land register has also left scope for enormous abuses. Equally, the new state encouraged small businesses. Large corporations, turned off by bureaucracy, corruption, and populist political rhetoric, are thin on the ground. Today 57 per cent of the Greek labour force works in micro-enterprises, those defined as employing no more than nine workers (the figure for Germany is 20 per cent). Greece ranks second among OECD countries (behind Mexico) in having the highest number of self-employed workers. That's laudable in terms of initiative, but problematic when it comes to tax: it's easier to evade tax and disregard labour laws as a small business when receipts can be hidden and workers taken off the books.

Furthermore, families with small businesses tend not to send their offspring to university. Instead sons and daughters will either look for secure, low-paid, public-sector jobs, or will return to the family shop. That means a greater reliance on multiple sources of income and, as a byproduct, greater family flexibility and solidarity. 'If the family shop does well,' says Doxiadis, 'the whole family will work there; if not it will be maintained by one or two members. The system is admirably stable, flexible and long lasting.' But the ambition among Greek teenagers to work in the public sector remains way beyond the European average.

* * *

Greeks have been forced into confronting these realities and there is much soul searching. 'The German arguments are: civil servants are lazy, they leave work earlier than they should, they retire early, etc,' says Angelos Athanasopoulos, the *To Vima* diplomatic editor. 'Our counter-argument is: most of what you say is right, we want to change it. But you don't throw a switch. It takes time, money and a determination to change.'

Certainly there's nothing like the whole world telling you you're lazy before you start to believe it yourself. One man obsessed about this is Peter Economides. He is a South African-born, third-generation Greek who has run ad agencies in South Africa, Hong Kong, Mexico and New York (he was part of the branding team which spectacularly revived the fortunes of Apple in 1997). He has been approached by both the private and public sectors in Greece to help the country improve its international image. It is a tough, confusing sell. 'Crisis, Zorba, Corruption, Acropolis, Ancient Greece, Riots, Mykonos...' he says. 'These are the results in order of profile if you Google Greece.'

'Greeks have a weird tendency,' he tells me the morning after a presentation in Brussels. 'If a Greek *thinks* something, he believes that it's done. Once they've *thought* something, they move on. They're the worst executors in the world.' (This is confirmed by a Brussels observer familiar with the Troika. 'People are hypnotised by the charm of the Greeks,' says the official. 'They promise you you'll become the King of Mambo. They promise to send something, but you'll have to say, ok, we need a deadline, what's your email, give me something concrete!')

They have, continues Economides, a surplus of *both* inferiority *and* superiority complexes. 'They do incredibly well overseas because they work in a structured environment. They are very smart, enterprising people. They work hard abroad but there isn't that same lack of productivity as when they're home, because there the system around them doesn't function.'

He insists no one is to blame except the Greeks themselves, and that it is pointless to blame the structure of the euro, or German and French banks for lending money to Greece. As for the moment in recent history where Greece stood still, he looks no further than our favourite stereotypical Greek: *Zorba.* While he is a crucial emblem for the 'Dionysian' – i.e. free-spirited – values that Greeks should cherish, the problem is that Greeks haven't moved on. 'The film really solidified what this was all about,' he says. 'A lot of visitors who'd already been to

Greece found their experience reflected in that movie. *Shirley Valentine* – it's the same story being told time and time again. Zorba was Dionysus! The Germans, who are far more Apollonian than we are, have a problem today with Dionysus. Because the guy they love – Ioannis, Dmitris, Alexis, whatever his name might be – that they've all met on islands throughout Greece, who might even have overcharged them for coffee, is suddenly a thief and he's lazy.'

Greeks must accept their shortcomings, he says, hope that the system can change, but seize the assets they can exploit. They cannot, he insists, go back to the modus operandi of Andreas Papandreou, of getting by on your wits, of being 'street smart'. 'You can't get by on just outsmarting the other guy in Australia and South Africa,' he says. 'Branding is about psychology, about anthropolgy, about sociology,' he says. When working on the Apple brand his team reached deep into the corporation's DNA to find a way of expressing what made Apple unique. 'Greece,' he says, 'has a richer DNA than any nation on earth. It is the heart, soul and spirit of the Mediterranean. It needs to *own* this, to express this, to inspire and be inspired by this.'

* * *

So what's the answer? Economides doesn't for a moment believe that rebranding Greece will solve its problems (Greece, he laments, has launched 16 ad campaigns since 1990). The culture of corruption, the 'rentocracy', will take generations to eradicate. As for the stereotype that Greeks are lazy, OECD figures show that Greeks work longer (although not necessarily more productive) hours than Germans. This is partly because many have multiple jobs – none of them well-paying – if you include the piece of land, the room that is rented out, and so on; it's also partly the fact that small businesses will extract longer hours from staff rather than hire new workers. In May 2013 the OECD reported that Greeks worked 2,032 hours a year, more than the average of 1,776 hours. The notion that Greeks retire earlier is also largely a myth. In 2008 the average retirement age was 62.2 years; in Germany it was exactly the same.

One enterprising group of volunteers is determined to counter these myths head on. At the height of the crisis and street demonstrations, a group of young volunteers created the Omikron Project. It is based around a series of sharply observed animated films featuring Alex, a kind of likeable young European Everyman who has friends, lives with his family, wants to travel the world, but who must be – the moment we realise he is Greek – a 'lazy, cheating, ungrateful, helpless, corrupt, violent, rude, racist, tax-evading, troublemaking, thieving, vandal…who lives with his mother.' In reality, the film continues, Alex is 'shocked, confused, frustrated, upset', and must rise above this unfair scapegoating for the euro crisis by pointing to the statistics which prove that he works more hours than the European average, gets two days a year *fewer* holidays and will retire three years *later* than the average European, etc. The aim is not just to overturn the offensive caricatures, but also to challenge the rise in what it the organisers call 'crisis pornography'.

'Stereotypes are hardening and no one seems to be doing anything about it,' says coordinator Mehran Khalili. 'But now the stereotypes have morphed into violent Greeks, and poor Greeks, and how much Greeks are suffering. They're confirming the narrative that Greeks somehow deserve it.' The Omikron Project insists it's not sugar-coating Greece's problems. 'The usual charge is that we have to fix the reality first, and then the image later,' says Khalili. 'We think this is highly irresponsible. The image problem has a direct economic effect. No one wants to visit a country if they're told it's endlessly screwed up.' So far the project is, at least, getting noticed. 'Alex' has received a quarter of a million hits on YouTube, mostly from viewers in Greece, but also in the UK, the United States and - most crucially of all - in Germany.

There's no doubt that stereotypes are kept afloat by media coverage. Some media have fallen too readily for the caricature and produced erroneous examples to back it up. In October 2011 the UK *Telegraph* reported that there were more Porsche Cayennes in Greece than taxpayers whose declared income was over €50,000, and that there were more Porches per capita in the city of Larissa than in London or New York. Neither turned out to be true. The number of taxpayers earning €50,000 or more was over 300,000 in 2011, while Porsche revealed that only 1,500 Porsches had been sold in Greece since 2002. In the hyper-connective, hyper-opinionated world of Twitter and Facebook, false notions can be easily spread, yet can take for ever to be erradicated.

'German journalists haven't got over the Greek stereotypes,' says Michalis Pantelouris, a German citizen of Greek parents who grew up in Hamburg and now writes about mutual stereotyping between the Germans and Greeks. 'There are two kinds of stories: one is that there is a corrupt political system, and behind this lies the old stereotype that they don't work very hard and they have this southern, Mediterranean lifestyle. The system resulted in a huge pile of debt, and they can't get out of it because the people are lazy and corrupt. It's easy to explain if you don't dig very deep.'

There are indications, though, that things are changing. Once Angela Merkel, in the summer of 2012, was convinced by advisors that Greece had to stay in the euro, the narrative changed, and the offensive stereotyping by the German media stopped almost overnight. More articles appeared focusing on how much Greeks were suffering, and how far they had travelled. The country lost 20 per cent of its GDP between 2009 and 2012. By the summer of 2013, unemployment stood at 26 per cent, with youth unemployment at 64 per cent, with some 31 per cent of Greeks at risk of poverty, according to 2011 figures. However offensive it is to national pride, many Greeks have turned to soup kitchens for food. Health has been badly hit, too, since people's access to medical care often depended on being employed. Austerity has meant 40 per cent cuts to the health budget; among the repercussions are an increase in HIV rates as needle-exchange programmes have been cut, and the return of malaria in parts of the Peloponnese. Voters have become radicalised, with the extreme right Golden Dawn securing 18 seats in the June 2012 elections.

Greece will probably need further financial support in the years to come. Existing loans from eurozone countries will have to be written off, further alienating European taxpayers. There's no doubt that Greece's international lenders made grave mistakes by applying the tough medecine when they did. The impact of austerity was grossly underestimated and made a bad situation worse. Private-sector debt should have been written down quicker to give the country a chance.

The architects of the euro were clearly either negligent or simply foolish in giving Greece such a benefit of the doubt when it was permitted to join the euro, or in failing to apply the rules more strictly once they were in (in the event Goldman Sachs helped Greece massage the figures to qualify). Walter Rademacher's Eurostat constantly sought more intrusive scrutiny of national budgets because of the dubious statistics coming from Greece, but they were flatly turned down by member states including, you've guessed it, Germany.

Greeks have had to fall back on their resources, be they economic, family or even philosophical. 'Well, we are still here,' a Greek unemployed woman told me in 2011 with weary stocism. Greeks have also revived a spirit of volunteerism. In May 2013, I visited an ad hoc health centre entirely funded through donations and staffed by doctors, nurses, dentists, psychotherapists, paediatricians and ordinary citizens, all operating on a voluntary basis. Forty-five such centres had sprung up across the country. The Omikron Project has itself listed scores of grassroots projects servicing the health, environment, trading, art, housing, education, media and human-rights sectors.

The Greek diaspora has also galvanised its networks and contacts to raise both funds and awareness, and also moral support. In such times Greeks at home and abroad have even, perhaps, sought comfort in stereotypes, in the old notions of what *Greek*-ness meant, prior to the crisis. In a defiant post in August 2013, the US-based Greek news portal *Greekreporter.com* declared: 'We like being Greek: because we have a small, poor country full of big-hearted people... Because we never pay a visit empty handed... Because Socrates, Plato and Aristotle were Greek... Because we invented the theatre... Because we gave birth to democracy... Because when we were building the Parthenon, others were still sleeping in trees.... Because we are not ashamed to burst into tears... Because we dance when we feel blue... Because 97 per cent of the stars are named after Greek words... Because our parents do not forget our existence when we stop being teenagers... Because we face every difficulty with humor... Because our sky is blue, not grey.'

Acknowledgements

Numerous people have helped me navigate the treacherous waters of stereotypes and national character during the eighteen months it took to write this book, among them academics, journalists, writers, ordinary locals and expats. First, though, special thanks to Edwin Higel and Deirdre O'Neill at New Island for helping me get the idea off the ground, and to Eoin Purcell for this edition. I'm also grateful to RTÉ News for giving me the time and space to complete the book, especially Ed Mulhall, former director of news, Michael Good, managing editor, Cathy Milner, foreign editor, and Sean Whelan, my colleague in Brussels and RTÉ's former Europe editor.

For the German chapter I'd like to thank Angela Byrne, Dr James McCabe, Prof Hermann Bausinger, Michael Steininger, Gayle Tufts, Derek Scally, Roland Weibazahl, Michael Mittermeier, Eric T. Hansen, Klaus Kienle, Henning When, Guntram Wolff, Prof Jürgen Wolff, Mark Schieritz, Ulrike Guerot, Lukas Heinser, and Bruce Stokes of the Pew Research Center. In France I owe a debt of gratitude for the hospitality and local knowledge of Peter Cluskey and Adrienne Cullen, likewise to Sean and Caroline Feely, Eugene Maguire and Louise Palinacci. For their expertise, thanks to Polly Platt, Alison Zinder, Jane Lizop, Debra Berg, John Maguire, Charles Hastings, Katherine Garnier, Gary Fallon, François Simon, La Tour D'Argent restaurant, Pierre Fernandez, Sonia Mielke, Maureen Grisot, Elaine Cobbe and Billy Kylie.

For the chapter on Italy, very special thanks to Enrico Terrinoni and Chiara Lucarelli for their help over the years. I'm grateful also to Professor Massimo Canevacci, at Rome's La Sapienza University, Dr Giuseppe Manica, at the Italian Cultural Institute, Brussels, and Mara Tognetti, from Milano Bicocca University. I'd also like to thank Kevin

Buckley, Paul Hanlon, Deirdre Doyle, Ronan Donoghue, Sean Lynch, Orla Ralph, Fiona Johnston and Michael Poole for their practical help or for their entertaining insights on the Italians. For the Spaniards, special thanks to Professors Pedro Schwartz Giron and Charles Powell at San Pablo CEU University, Madrid, Javier Noya from the Real Instituto Elcano, also to Armando Gil in Ronda, Patricia Savelovas for her translations, Antonio Montilla, Tom Burns Marañón, Harold Heckle, Eva Orue and Marta Zuluaga.

In getting to grips with the Greeks I'm indebted to Aristos Doxiadis, Peter Economides, Angelos Athanasopoulos, Xenia Kounalaki, Ireland's ambassador Charles Sheehan, Walter Rademacher at Eurostat, Michalis Pantelouris, Jorgo Chatzimarkakis MEP, Martina Conrads, Mehran Khalili from the Omikron Project and Aikaterini Apostola.

For the chapter on Denmark I'm grateful to Clare MacCarthy, Mette Fugl, Charles Ferrall, Karen Sjørup of Roskilde University, Lone Kühlmann, Anders Agger and Rolien Créton. For the Swedes I owe enormous thanks to the correspondents of the Swedish broadcaster, SVT, namely Christina Johanesson, Rolf Fredriksson and Erika Bjerström. I'm also grateful to Dr David Eberhard at St Göran's Hospital in Stockholm, Tilde de Paula, Colm O'Callaghan, Dr Bent Hougaard, Freidrik Lindstrom, James Savage, Hugh McCarthy, Sean Norton, Thomas Johansson, Terry Greenwood, Claes Tingval, Mattias Svensson, Maria Rankka, Professor Åke Daun, Professor Ulf Jacobsen and Dr Ann Heberlein. For the chapter on Finland I'd like to thank the following: Susanna Turunen of the Finnish broadcaster YLE, Lasse Lehtinen MEP, Eero Aarnio, Antii Liikkanen, Anna Valtonen at Nokia, Renne Klinge and Irina Kyllönen. Special thanks go to Katja Eteläinen at Rovaniemi Tourism and Marketing in Lapland.

For the Hungarians thanks to László Marácz, at the University of Amsterdam, Adam Masat at the Balassi Insitute in Budapest, Nick Thorpe of the BBC, Sabolcs Patai at the Hungarian Tourist Office in Dublin, Paul Olchvary, Georg Habsburg, David Butler, Harry Harron, Mark Downey, Ilés and Anna Herber. In the Czech Republic special thanks to Kristina Alda, Jiří Rak, Frank Kuznik of the *Prague Post*, Benjamin Kuras, Brian Flynn at the Irish Embassy, Ian Willoughby, Evan Rail and everyone at the Pilsner Urquell Brewery in Pilsen. For the Poles thanks to Piotr Kaczynski at the Centre for European Policy Studies, Konstanty Gabert from Gazeta Wyborcza, Michal Bilewicz, Bogdan Wojciszke at the Institute of Psychology, Polish Academy of Science, Andrzej Wajda, Adam Szostkiewicz of Poltyka magazine, Sergiusz Kowalski, Krzysztof Dzięciołowski, Justyna Rutkowska and Piotr Paszkowski.

A special mention goes to the management and research staff at Headline News Facilities, who have been of enormous help, especially Hans Deforce, Andrea Waeyenbergh, Débora Votquenne, Nele Vandeloo, Vanessa Rottiers, Rebekka Deforce and Katrien Gordts, and to the camera crews who have accompanied me through hell and high water in covering European stories for RTÉ: Tom Vantorre, Pol Reygaerts, Bram Verbeke, Bert Degraeve, Evelyne Matthys and Marc Kerremans.

Finally, a special thanks goes to Sean Klein, friend and BBC colleague, whose insights on all things German and whose linguistic skills and encouragement have all been invaluable. Also thanks to Neil Cooke, Ann Dunne, Ronan Anderson and Arbed Saleh for general insights and hospitality. Lastly, a very special thanks to my parents Tim and Nance, and sister Maeve, for all their support over the years.

Bibliography

Atkinson, R., *The Day of Battle: The War in Sicily and Italy 1943–44* (London: Little, Brown, 2007).

Balfour, S. and Quiroga, A., *The Reinvention of Spain: Nation and Identity since Democracy* (Oxford: Oxford University Press, 2007).

Barfoot, C.C. (ed.), *Beyond Pug's Tour: National and Ethnic Stereotyping in Theory and Literary Practice* (Amsterdam: Rodopi, 1997).

Barzini, L., *The Italians* (London: Penguin, 1968).

Beck, U., *German Europe* (Cambridge: Polity, 2013).

Beevor, A. and Cooper, A., *Paris after the Liberation 1944–49* (London: Penguin, 2004).

Beevor, A., *The Battle for Spain: The Spanish Civil War 1936–1938* (London: Phoenix, 2007).

Bori, I. (ed.), *The Complete Guide to Being Hungarian* (Budapest: L'Harmattan, 2005).

Brewer, D., *Greece, The Hidden Centuries: Turkish Rule from the Fall of Constantinople to Greek Independence* (London: I.B. Tauris, 2010).

Brown, A., *Fishing in Utopia: Sweden and the Future that Disappeared* (London: Granta Books, 2008).

Brown, R. and Gaertner, S. (eds), *Blackwell Handbook of Social Psychology: Intergroup Processes* (Oxford: Blackwell Publishing, 2003).

Clarke, S., *A Year in the Merde* (London: Black Swan, 2005).

Davies, N., *Europe: A History* (London: Pimlico, 1997).

Davies, N., *Heart of Europe: The Past in Poland's Present* (Oxford: Oxford University Press, 2001).

Davies, N., *Rising '44: The Battle for Warsaw* (London: Pan Books, 2003).

Davies, N., *God's Playground: A History of Poland, Volume II* (Oxford: Oxford University Press, 2005).

Draenos, S., *Andreas Papandreou: The Making of a Greek Democrat and Political Maverick* (London: I.B Tauris, 2012).

Dyrbye, H., Harris, S. and Golze, T., *The Xenophobe's Guide to the Danes* (London: Oval Books, 2002).

Englund, T.B., *The Czechs in a Nutshell* (Prague: Baset, 2004).

Epton, N., *Love and the French* (London: Cassell, 1959).

Fenby, J., *On the Brink: The Trouble with France* (London: Warner Books, 1999).

Fest, J.C., *Hitler* (London: Penguin/Harcourt Brace Jovanovich, Inc., 1974).

Frankland, M., *The Patriots' Revolution: How East Europe Won Its Freedom* (London: Sinclair Stevenson, 1990).

Ginsborg, P., *Silvio Berlusconi: Television, Power and Patrimony* (London: Verso, 2005).

Hemingway, E., *Death in the Afternoon* (London: Arrow Books, 2004).

Hill, R., *We Europeans* (Brussels: Europublic, 2002).

Hilson, M., *The Nordic Model: Scandinavia since 1945* (London: Reaktion Books, 2008).

Holy, L., *The Little Czech and the Great Czech Nation* (Cambridge: Cambridge University Press, 1996).

Hooper, J., *The New Spaniards* (London: Penguin).
Hvidt, K., *You on Us* (Copenhagen: Royal Danish Ministry of Foreign Affairs, 2002).
Jones, T., *The Dark Heart of Italy* (London: Faber & Faber, 2003).
Judt, T., *Postwar: A History of Europe Since 1945* (London: Penguin, 2005).
Kirby, D., *A Concise History of Finland* (Cambridge: Cambridge University Press, 2006).
Kinross, Lord, *The Ottoman Centuries: The Rise and Fall of the Turkish Empire* (New York: Morrow Quill, 1977).
Koliopoulis, J.S. and Veremis, T.M., *Greece: The Modern Sequel* (London: Hurst, 2004).
Kuras, B., *Czechs and Balances: A Nation's Survival Kit* (Prague: Baronet, 1998).
Lewis, M., *Boomerang: The Biggest Bust* (London: Penguin, 2011).
Lipniacka, E., *The Xenophobe's Guide to the Poles* (London: Oval Books, 2004).
MacCulloch, D., *A History of Christianity* (London: Allen Lane, 2009).
Marsh, D., *The Euro: The Battle for the New Global Currency* (New Haven: Yale University Press 2011).
Mazower, M., *Salonica: City of Ghosts* (London: Harper Perennial, 2005).
Molnár, M., *A Concise History of Hungary* (Cambridge: Cambridge University Press, 2001).
Morris, J., *Spain* (London: Penguin, 1982).
Munkhammar, J., *European Dawn: After the Social Model* (Stockholm: Timbro, 2005).
Nadeau, J.B. and Barlow, J., *Sixty Million Frenchmen Can't Be Wrong* (London: Robson Books, 2004).
Nilson, U., *What Happened to Sweden? While America Became the Only Superpower* (New York: Nordsjernan, 2007).
Orwell, G., *Orwell and the Dispossessed* (London: Penguin, 2001).
Patten, C., *Not Quite the Diplomat: Home Truths About World Affairs* (London: Penguin, 2005).
Paxman, J., *The English: A Portrait of a People* (London: Penguin, 1999).
Pittaway, M., *Eastern Europe 1939–2000* (London: Arnold, 2004).
Platt, P., *Love à la Française* (Skokie, Illinois: MEP Inc., 2008).
Platt, P., *French or Foe?* (London: Distribooks, 2003).
Pryce, V., *Greekonomics: The Euro Crisis and why Politicians Don't Get it* (London: Biteback, 2012).
Ramsden, J., *Don't Mention the War: The British and the Germans since 1890* (London: Abacus, 2006).
Rapaille, C., *Culture Codes* (New York: Broadway Books, 2006).
Reinhardt, C.M. and Rogoff, K.S., *This Time is Different: Eight Centuries of Financial Folly* (Oxford: Princeton University Press, 2009).
Saviano, R., *Gomorrah* (London: Macmillan, 2007).
Sebro, H. and Larsen, J.S. (ed), *Denmark* (Copenhagen: Royal Danish Ministry of Foreign Affairs, 2002).
Severgnini, B., *La Bella Figura: An Insider's Guide to the Italian Mind* (London: Hodder & Stoughton, 2007).
Stern, F., *Five Germanys I Have Known* (New York: Farrar, Straus and Giroux, 2006).
Stille, A., *The Sack of Rome* (New York: Penguin, 2006).
Strathern, P., *The Medici: Godfathers of the Renaissance* (London: Pimlico, 2005).
Tacitus, *The Agricola and the Germania* (London: Penguin, 1986).
Tremlett, G., *Ghosts of Spain* (London: Faber & Faber, 2006).
Zeidenitz, S. and Barkow, B., *The Xenophobe's Guide to the Germans* (London: Oval Books, 2008).
Zeldin, T., *The French* (London: Harvill Press, 1997).